MARK AS STORY

Retrospect and Prospect

Society of Biblical Literature

Resources for Biblical Study

Tom Thatcher, New Testament Editor

Number 65

MARK AS STORY

Retrospect and Prospect

MARK AS STORY

Retrospect and Prospect

Edited by

Kelly R. Iverson

and

Christopher W. Skinner

Society of Biblical Literature
Atlanta

MARK AS STORY
Retrospect and Prospect

Library of Congress Cataloging-in-Publication Data

Mark as story : retrospect and prospect / edited by Kelly R. Iverson and Christopher W.
Skinner.
        p. cm. — (Society of Biblical Literature : resources for biblical study ; no. 65)
    Includes bibliographical references and indexes.
    ISBN 978-1-58983-548-1 (paper binding : alk. paper) -- ISBN 978-1-58983-549-8
(electronic format)
    1. Bible. N.T. Mark—Criticism, interpretation, etc. 2. Bible. N.T. Gospels—Herme-
neutics. 3. Rhoads, David M. Mark as story. 4. Bible. N.T. Mark—Criticism, Narrative. I.
Iverson, Kelly R. II. Skinner, Christopher W. III. Society of Biblical Literature.
    BS2585.52.M34 2011
    226.3'06—dc22   2011008950

19 18 17 16 15 14 13 12 11   5 4 3 2 1
Printed on acid-free, recycled paper conforming to
ANSI/NISO Z39.48-1992 (R1997) and ISO 9706:1994
standards for paper permanence.

For David Rhoads, Donald Michie, and Joanna Dewey …
with appreciation for your many contributions to biblical scholarship …
and our own thinking.

"God made man because he loves stories."
Elie Wiesel

CONTENTS

PART 3: *MARK AS STORY* REFLECTIONS

Preface

This book began as a seemingly innocuous conversation in a Boston hotel during the 2008 meeting of the Society of Biblical Literature. Having just attended a session on the contributions of narrative criticism to New Testament studies, the two of us began discussing formative works that had shaped our own thinking. Pretty soon we found ourselves dreaming out loud about a project that would honor the impact and legacy of *Mark as Story*, the book that formally introduced New Testament studies to the discipline of narrative criticism. Within a few weeks a plan unfolded and to our delight the project began to materialize more rapidly than we had anticipated. Our eventual editor, Tom Thatcher, instantly embraced the idea and received the proposal enthusiastically. From the beginning, Tom proved to be a helpful guide, offering advice where it was needed, while leaving room for our editorial autonomy and creative control. We are grateful for his expertise and genuine concern for the final product.

In the early days of this project we were also delightfully surprised by the responses we received from our would-be contributors. Each invitation to participate was met with excitement. In several instances contributors actually thanked us for undertaking the project. We have commented to one another on numerous occasions how genuinely thankful we are for our all-star cast of contributors. Their skill, conscientious attention to our publication schedule, and passion for the subject matter has not only made this project run smoothly but also has made it an enjoyable adventure. We are especially grateful to those contributors who persevered and remained on board with the project amidst extreme adverse circumstances in their personal lives.

We would also like to thank our families for their love and support. In particular, our wives, Kim and Tara, have made numerous sacrifices that have enabled us to pursue the careers in which we are presently engaged. The imprint of their patience lies under the surface of every page of this volume.

Finally, it goes without saying that this book would not have been possible without David Rhoads, Donald Michie, and Joanna Dewey. Their groundbreaking work was the impetus for this volume, and their eager cooperation has helped bring it to fruition. David, Don, and Joanna, we have both been greatly impacted by your contributions to New Testament scholarship. It has been a privilege for us to honor you and labor alongside you on this book. We dedicate this volume to you with gratitude and admiration.

Kelly and Chris
St. Andrews, Scotland, U.K., and Goldsboro, North Carolina, U.S.A.
January 2011

Abbreviations

AB	Anchor Bible
ABD	*Anchor Bible Dictionary*. Edited by David Noel Freedman. 6 vols. New York: Doubleday, 1992.
AnBib	Analecta biblica
BAR	*Biblical Archaeology Review*
BBR	*Bulletin for Biblical Research*
BDAG	Bauer, W., F. W. Danker, W. F. Arndt, and F. W. Gingrich. *Greek-English Lexicon of the New Testament and Other Early Christian Literature*. 3rd ed. Chicago: University of Chicago Press, 1999.
BETL	Bibliotheca ephemeridum theologicarum lovaniensium
BibInt	*Biblical Interpretation*
BN	*Biblische Notizen*
BNTC	Black's New Testament Commentaries
BTB	*Biblical Theology Bulletin*
BZNW	Beihefte zur Zeitschrift für die neutestamentliche Wissenschaft
CBQ	*Catholic Biblical Quarterly*
CBR	*Currents in Biblical Research*
CGTC	Cambridge Greek Testament Commentary
CurTM	*Currents in Theology and Mission*
GBS	Guides to Biblical Scholarship
HTR	*Harvard Theological Review*
ICC	International Critical Commentary
Int	*Interpretation*
JAAR	*Journal of the American Academy of Religion*
JBL	*Journal of Biblical Literature*
JR	*Journal of Religion*
JSHJ	*Journal for the Study of the Historical Jesus*
JSNT	*Journal for the Study of the New Testament*

JSNTSup	Journal for the Study of the New Testament Supplement Series
JSOT	*Journal for the Study of the Old Testament*
JSOTSup	Journal for the Study of the Old Testament Supplement Series
KEK	Kritisch-exegetischer Kommentar über das Neue Testament (Meyer-Kommentar)
LCL	Loeb Classical Library
LNTS	Library of New Testament Studies
NICNT	New International Commentary on the New Testament
NIDB	*New International Dictionary of the Bible.* Edited by J. D. Douglas and M. C. Tenney. Grand Rapids: Zondervan, 1987.
NovT	*Novum Testamentum*
NRSV	New Revised Standard Version
NTL	New Testament Library
NTS	*New Testament Studies*
PMLA	*Publications of the Modern Language Association*
SBLDS	Society of Biblical Literature Dissertation Series
SBLSBL	Society of Biblical Literature Studies in Biblical Literature
SBLSP	*Society of Biblical Literature Seminar Papers*
SBLSymS	Society of Biblical Literature Symposium Series
SNTSMS	Society for New Testament Studies Monograph Series
SNTSU	*Studien zum Neuen Testament und seiner Umwelt*
SP	Sacra pagina
STRev	*Sewanee Theological Review*
VT	*Vetus Testamentum*
WBC	Word Biblical Commentary
WUNT	Wissenschaftliche Untersuchungen zum Neuen Testament
ZNW	*Zeitschrift für die neutestamentliche Wissenschaft und die Kunde der älteren Kirche*

Telling the Story: The Appearance and Impact of *Mark as Story*

Christopher W. Skinner

All crises begin with the blurring of a paradigm and the consequent loosening of the rules for normal research. As this process develops, the anomaly comes to be more generally recognised as such, more attention is devoted to it by more of the field's eminent authorities. The field begins to look quite different: scientists express explicit discontent, competing articulations of the paradigm proliferate and scholars view a resolution as the subject matter of their discipline. To this end, they first isolate the anomaly more precisely and give it structure. They push the rules of normal science harder than ever to see, in the area of difficulty, just where and how far they can be made to work.[1]

When we see the narrative as containing a closed and self-sufficient world, with its own integrity, its own past and future, its own set of values, its own universe of meaning, we are able to enter the marvelous world of this story.[2]

The 1982 publication of *Mark as Story: An Introduction to the Narrative of a Gospel*,[3] was one of the significant contributions to New Testament studies in the latter half of the twentieth century. *Mark as Story* formally introduced narrative criticism to a world of New Testament scholarship that was dominated by the monolithic historical-critical method.[4] David Rhoads, a New Testa-

---

1. Thomas Kuhn, *The Structure of Scientific Revolutions* (Chicago: University of Chicago Press, 1962), 84.

2. David Rhoads, "Narrative Criticism and the Gospel of Mark," *JAAR* 50 (1982): 414.

3. David Rhoads and Donald Michie, *Mark as Story: An Introduction to the Narrative of a Gospel* (Philadelphia: Fortress, 1982). The second edition appeared as David Rhoads, Joanna Dewey, and Donald Michie, *Mark as Story: An Introduction to the Narrative of a Gospel* (2nd ed.; Minneapolis: Fortress, 1999).

4. This comment is not meant to bracket out the development of narrative hermeneutics from historical criticism. To be sure, narrative criticism came out of and was deeply

ment scholar, and Donald Michie, an English professor, had come together
to apply the insights of literary theory to the Gospel of Mark.[5] The book was
groundbreaking not only for the ideas it advanced but also for its elegant simplicity; it was not a highly theoretical treatise but rather a study in applied
method from two professors collaborating across their respective disciplines.[6]
Though narrative criticism was in its embryonic stages, no one had yet applied
this "new" method to one of the Gospels in its entirety.[7]

By the late 1970s redaction criticism had become the dominant interpretive framework within which Gospel scholars were working.[8] The work of
the early redaction critics had forged a new way forward from the contribu-

---

informed by historical criticism. Even today, in its most complete and intellectually honest
forms, narrative hermeneutics stand on the shoulders of the strongest contributions from
source, form, and redaction criticisms. Mark Allan Powell expresses it well when he writes
that "narrative criticism is certainly not an antihistorical discipline. In fact, a symbiotic
relationship exists between narrative and historical approaches to texts. Although the two
methods cannot be used simultaneously, they can be used side by side in a supplementary
fashion. They might even be viewed as necessary complements, each providing information that is beneficial to the exercise of the other" (*What Is Narrative Criticism?* [GBS; Minneapolis: Augsburg Fortress, 1990], 98).

5. The genesis of this collaboration is recounted in the preface to the first edition of
Mark as Story (xv), though it has been eliminated from the second. While teaching at Carthage College, Rhoads asked Donald Michie, his colleague from the English department,
to show students in his New Testament course how to read the Gospel of Mark as a short
story. Michie's lecture intrigued Rhoads so much that it led to further collaboration and
ultimately to the publication of *Mark as Story*.

6. For their part, Rhoads and Michie believed that the best way to reach scholars was
to write a book they could use with their students. This is one reason for both the simplicity
and the usefulness of *Mark as Story*.

7. In its early stages, narrative criticism was referred to as the "new criticism" and in
some cases the "new literary criticism." This terminology arose out of secular literary critical approaches to English literature where the major emphasis was a close reading of the
text without explicit reference to the extratextual world. For more on this, see Leroy Searle,
"New Criticism," in *The Johns Hopkins Guide to Literary Theory* (2nd ed.; ed. Michael
Groden, Martin Kreiswirth, and Imre Szeman; Baltimore: Johns Hopkins University Press,
2005), 691–98.

8. There is not space here to rehearse the history of redaction criticism and its relative merits and deficiencies vis-à-vis narrative criticism. For a helpful overview of methodological developments from source criticism to modern reader-oriented methods, see
Francis J. Moloney, *The Living Voice of the Gospels* (Peabody, Mass.: Hendrickson, 2007),
309–42. Major contributions to redaction criticism include Willi Marxsen's seminal work,
Der Evangelist Markus: Studien zur Redaktionsgeschichte des Evangeliums (Gottingen: Vandenhoeck & Ruprecht, 1959, translated as *Mark the Evangelist: Studies on the Redaction
History of the Gospel* (Nashville: Abingdon, 1969). This was followed by similar works on
Luke (Hans Conzelmann, *The Theology of St. Luke* [trans. Geoffrey Buswell; New York:

tions of form criticism, but by this time much of the discussion had become focused on reconstructing the world behind the text.[9] Some within Gospels studies grew restless with this approach and came to regard at least a segment of redaction-critical scholarship as a complicated and speculative enterprise with few measurable results. In addition, there was a lack of unanimity among redaction critics as to where the process of study should begin.[10] By contrast, narrative critics assumed a basic and uncomplicated premise: it is preferable to start with what we have rather than what we do not have. Rhoads and Michie began with the text itself, assuming that the final form of Mark should be treated as an autonomous and unified narrative. This simple premise lies at the heart of narrative criticism and has contributed to major changes in the landscape of biblical scholarship.

Not all early readers of *Mark as Story* appreciated the book's simplicity. One early reviewer wrote:

> Rhoads and Michie succeed in summing up the narrative elements in Mark. *Yet their survey cannot be called a significant contribution to the study of Mark or to narrative criticism.* Their presentation of "the story as a whole" prevents them from confronting the questions of Marcan scholarship and results in some simplification and oversimplification.[11]

These comments perhaps tell us more about the reviewer's assumptions than they do about the contributions of the first edition of *Mark as Story*. The reviewer goes on to conclude: "This study does not easily recommend itself to any of the readerships existing inside or outside the scholarly community. NT scholars in need of a solid introduction to narrative criticism ... will have to look elsewhere for satisfaction."[12]

If the previous excerpt told us something about the reviewer's assumptions, this second quotation reveals a great deal more about the assumptions of the academic context(s) into which *Mark as Story* made its entrance. To assert that there was no readily available readership for their book either

---

Harper & Row, 1961]), and Matthew (Gunther Bornkamm, Gerhard Barth, and Heinz Joachim Held, *Tradition and Interpretation in Matthew* [Philadelphia: Westminster, 1963]).

9. For a helpful overview of Markan studies up to the advent of narrative criticism, see Sean P. Kealy, *Mark's Gospel: A History of Its Interpretation* (New York: Paulist, 1982).

10. For a treatment of the merits and deficiencies of Markan redaction criticism, see C. Clifton Black, *The Disciples according to Mark: Markan Redaction in Current Debate* (JSNTSup 27; Sheffield: Sheffield Academic Press, 1989).

11. Susan Marie Praeder, review of David Rhoads and Donald Michie, *Mark as Story: An Introduction to the Narrative of a Gospel*, JBL 103 (1984): 483, emphasis added.

12. Ibid., 484.

within or outside the scholarly community was ultimately to say that Rhoads and Michie had done something new: they had broken ground in a discipline dominated by the search for the world behind the text. In the early 1980s it may have been difficult to predict the impact of a literary approach to the New Testament narratives, but three decades later it is clear that the proverbial mustard seed has grown into one of the great trees in the garden of biblical scholarship. *Mark as Story* surely played an important role in the shift from emphasizing the world behind the text to the story world of the text.[13]

Prior to the publication of *Mark as Story*, there had been signs indicating a shift in interest among biblical scholars, though battles were still being waged over the legitimacy of a literary approach to the biblical narratives. Within Old Testament studies, a segment of scholars working from a literary approach had already begun reading narratives with a focus on the world within the text.[14] This approach slowly began making inroads into New Testament studies, though it would take nearly a decade for New Testament narrative criticism to establish its own voice as a legitimate method alongside source, form, and redaction criticism.

In the United States, important developments that helped bring about a hermeneutical shift were taking place incrementally behind the scenes inside the Society of Biblical Literature's Seminar on Mark between 1974 and 1980.[15] Many of the group's members became leading voices in the shift toward narrative criticism and eventually formed the nucleus of SBL's Literary Aspects Group.[16] During the period in question there was an ongoing struggle between

---

13. It should be noted that other reviews were kinder in their evaluation of the book. See, e.g., positive reviews by Kent Brower in *CBQ* 45 (1983): 701–2, and William G. Doty in *Int* 37 (1983): 301–4.

14. Some early contributions to narrative criticism of the Hebrew Bible include Sean E. McEvenue, *The Narrative Style of the Priestly Writer* (AnBib 50; Rome: Pontifical Biblical Institute, 1971); Jacob Licht, *Storytelling in the Bible* (Jerusalem: Magnes, 1978); Shemaryahu Talmon, "The Presentation of Synchroneity and Simultaneity in Biblical Narrative," in *Scripta Hierosolymitana* (ed. Joseph Heinemann and Shnuel Werses; Jerusalem: Magnes, 1978), 9–26; Michael Fishbane, *Text and Texture: Close Readings of Selected Biblical Texts* (New York: Schocken, 1979); Shimon Bar-Efrat, "Some Observations on the Analysis of Structure in Biblical Narrative," *VT* 30 (1980): 154–73; Robert Alter, *The Art of Biblical Narrative* (New York: Basic, 1981); H. van Dyke Parunak, "Some Axioms for Literary Architecture," *Semitics* 8 (1982): 1–16; idem, "Transitional Techniques in the Bible," *JBL* 102 (1983): 525–48; Peter D. Miscall, *The Workings of Old Testament Narrative* (Philadelphia: Fortress, 1983); Adele Berlin, "Point of View in Biblical Narrative," in *A Sense of Text: The Art of Language in the Study of Biblical Literature* (ed. Stephen A. Geller; Winona Lake, Ind.: Eisenbrauns, 1983) 71–113.

15. Hereafter, the abbreviation SBL is employed for the Society of Biblical Literature.

16. Those who were particularly influential for Rhoads's and Michie's embryonic

Markan redaction critics and those who wanted to study the text as a whole. David Rhoads, a participant in these struggles, had come to favor the latter approach somewhat unexpectedly. In his dissertation he had undertaken a historical study of the Roman-Jewish wars and was convinced that Mark, written around 70 c.e., must fit within that area of historical investigation.[17] But his eventual exasperation with redaction criticism and his recognition that reading the text as a whole was immediately rewarding would together form the basis for his shift toward literary criticism. This shift was also facilitated by several publications.

In the late 1970s Robert Tannehill published two essays aimed at examining Mark from a narrative perspective. The first study appeared in 1977 and focused on the function of Jesus' disciples in Mark's story.[18] In the years immediately preceding Tannehill's essay, the disciples had taken center stage in Markan studies, but the focus had largely been on issues external to the text of Mark.[19] By focusing on the role of the disciples *within* the narrative, Tannehill anticipated a shift in thinking that would ultimately lead to a sustained emphasis on the story world of the text. In 1979, Tannehill published a second

---

thinking on narrative criticism were Thomas Boomershine, Joanna Dewey, Robert Fowler, Werner Kelber, Norman Petersen, Robert Tannehill, and Mary Ann Tolbert. In the early years of the Literary Aspects Group, a great deal of time was devoted to reading secular literary criticism, which led to ongoing refinements in biblical narrative criticism. Eventually the Literary Aspects Group moved away narrative criticism, as devised by Rhoads and Michie, to more reader-oriented readings of the biblical text.

17. A substantially revised version of Rhoads's dissertation was published as *Israel in Revolution: 6–74 C.E. A Political History Based on the Writings of Josephus* (Philadelphia: Fortress, 1976).

18. Robert C. Tannehill, "The Disciples in Mark: The Function of a Narrative Role," *JR* 57 (1977): 386–405.

19. The function of the disciples in Mark had become an important discussion during this period. In 1968, Theodore Weeden published an article entitled "The Heresy That Necessitated Mark's Gospel" (*ZNW* 59 [1968]: 145–58), in which he argued that the disciples were the subject of a polemic aimed at clarifying the christological viewpoint of the Evangelist. Weeden and others working on *theios aner* traditions drew upon the scholarship of Ludwig Bieler (*Theios Aner: Das Bild des "Göttlichen Menschen" in Spätantike und Frühchristentum* [Vienna: Hofels, 1935]), but Weeden was more explicit than anyone to that point in arguing that Mark's polemic against the disciples could help the interpreter understand both the theology and the purpose of Mark's Gospel. Weeden's theory was presented in greater detail in his book *Mark: Traditions in Conflict* (Minneapolis: Fortress, 1971). Weeden's work led to a renewed focus on the role of the disciples vis-à-vis Mark's Christology and spawned a number of attempts to explain the so-called "corrective Christology" of Mark's Gospel.

essay examining the "narrative Christology" of Mark's Gospel.[20] The opening paragraph reads:

> Jesus is the central figure of the Gospel of Mark, and the author is centrally concerned to present (or re-present) Jesus to his readers so that his significance for their lives becomes clear. *He does this in the form of a story. Since this is the case, we need to take seriously the narrative form of Mark in discussing this Gospel's presentation of Jesus Christ.* In other words, we need ways of understanding and appreciating Mark as narrative Christology.[21]

The recognition that Mark uses the story form to explain the significance of Jesus' life and vocation is foundational for the literary study of the Second Gospel as well as the other New Testament narratives.

Other works that were formative for Rhoads's and Michie's early thinking about the story world of the text were Thomas Boomershine's unpublished dissertation (1974),[22] Norman Petersen's "Point of View in Mark's Narrative" (1978),[23] Werner Kelber's *Mark's Story of Jesus* (1979),[24] and Robert Fowler's *Loaves and Fishes* (1981).[25] Each of these studies contributed to the burgeoning growth of literary studies in their application to the New Testament narratives.[26]

---

20. Robert C. Tannehill, "The Gospel of Mark as Narrative Christology," *Semeia* 16 (1979): 57–95.

21. Ibid., 57, emphasis added.

22. Thomas Boomershine, "Mark the Storyteller: A Rhetorical-Critical Investigation of Mark's Passion and Resurrection Narrative" (Ph.D. dissertation, Union Theological Seminary, New York, 1974). Rhoads acknowledges that Boomershine's innovative work was formative for his own thinking about Mark's Gospel and narrative criticism. Though it is not an example of what we have come to think of as classical "narrative criticism," Boomershine's approach to Mark resonated with those who had become weary of redaction criticism and were looking for a new way forward. Boomershine is presently revising his dissertation for publication as a performance-criticism commentary that will provide a detailed study of Mark's passion and resurrection as a story performed for audiences in the post-70 c.e. period.

23. Norman Petersen, "Point of View in Mark's Narrative," *Semeia* 12 (1978): 97–121. Powell (*What Is Narrative Criticism*, 111 n. 26) has referred to Petersen as perhaps the "premier theorist" of early narrative criticism in New Testament studies. See also Petersen's *Literary Criticism for New Testament Critics* (GBS; Philadelphia: Fortress, 1978).

24. Werner Kelber, *Mark's Story of Jesus* (Philadelphia: Fortress, 1979).

25. Robert M. Fowler, *Loaves and Fishes: The Function of the Feeding Stories in the Gospel of Mark* (SBLDS 54; Chico, Calif.: Scholars Press, 1981).

26. In the second edition of *Mark as Story*, Rhoads and Dewey acknowledge Norman Perrin (one-time chair of the Mark group), Thomas Boomershine, Werner Kelber, Norman

In 1982, Rhoads set forth his own assumptions in an essay entitled "Narrative Criticism and the Gospel of Mark."[27] There he argued that the historical-critical methods used by many New Testament scholars had the unfortunate effect of breaking up the text. Scholars used these methods to pursue the questions of modern scholarship, which, in his view, led to a truncated reading of the biblical narratives. Since many of those questions dealt with issues outside the text, this meant that scholars rarely read the Gospels in their entirety.[28] Rhoads and Michie approached the text of Mark as a unified narrative, arguing that it presents a story world into which the reader can and should enter. With the theory taking shape and the assumptions clearly spelled out, all that was left was for scholars to apply these insights in a systematic way to the canonical Gospels. *Mark as Story* was the first book to accomplish this feat, though the other New Testament narratives would be covered in the years immediately following its publication.[29]

READING MARK'S STORY (1982–1999)

The incremental growth of narrative criticism within New Testament studies in the late 1970s and early 1980s led to a full-fledged phenomenon in the late 1980s and throughout the 1990s. Some scholars focused on the methodological and theoretical end of matters,[30] while others began to apply narrative

---

Petersen, and Robert Tannehill for their early contributions to the development of narrative criticism. See *Mark as Story*, 160 n. 4.

27. This essay was originally delivered to the SBL Seminar on Mark in 1980, but it was not formally published until 1982. See n. 2 above for full bibliographic information.

28. He wrote: "Redaction criticism, form criticism, source criticism, and even composition criticism break up the narrative in order to get at the questions they pursue. Distinctions between redaction and tradition, between history and tradition, naturally fragment the text.... By contrast, literary questions about narrative features tend to reveal Mark's Gospel as a whole cloth" ("Narrative Criticism and the Gospel of Mark," 412).

29. See R. Alan Culpepper, *Anatomy of the Fourth Gospel: A Study in Literary Design* (Philadelphia: Fortress, 1983); Robert C. Tannehill, *The Narrative Unity of Luke-Acts: A Literary Interpretation* (2 vols.; Minneapolis: Fortress, 1986–1989); and Jack Dean Kingsbury, *Matthew as Story* (Minneapolis: Augsburg Fortress, 1988).

30. General works on narrative-critical method have appeared with increasing frequency in recent years. A number of works aimed at reading biblical narrative in general (rather than strictly New Testament narratives) have appeared. See, among others, Adele Berlin, *Poetics and Interpretation of Biblical Narrative* (Bible and Literature Series; Sheffield: Almond, 1983); Meir Sternberg, *The Poetics of Biblical Narrative: Ideological Literature and the Drama of Reading* (Indiana Literary Biblical Series; Bloomington: Indiana University Press, 1985); Powell, *What Is Narrative Criticism*; J. P. Fokkelman, *Reading Biblical Narrative: An Introductory Guide* (Louisville: Westminster John Knox, 1991); and D. F. Tolmie,

methods to their exegetical endeavors.[31] Among New Testament scholars, the call to move toward biblical narrative criticism set in motion a process that helped spawn numerous methodological and exegetical trajectories. Once scholars embraced the concept of the story world of the text, methods such as reader-response criticism,[32] feminist criticism,[33] performance criticism,[34] postcolonial criticism,[35] and the numerous approaches that fall under the banner of postmodern criticism[36] had less trouble being recognized as legitimate methods for approaching the text.[37] The battles fought by early narrative

---

Narratology and Biblical Narratives: A Practical Guide (San Francisco: International Scholars Publications, 1999). A helpful work on New Testament narrative criticism is James L. Resseguie, *Narrative Criticism of the New Testament: An Introduction* (Grand Rapids: Baker, 2005). Stephen Moore and Janice Capel Anderson explore narrative method and related reader-oriented methods as they apply to the Gospel of Mark in their important edited work, *Mark and Method: New Approaches in Biblical Studies* (2nd ed.; Minneapolis: Fortress, 2008).

31. E.g., Ernest Best, *Mark: The Gospel as Story* (London: T&T Clark, 1989); and Jack Dean Kingsbury, *Conflict in Mark: Jesus, Disciples, Authorities* (Minneapolis: Fortress, 1989).

32. Robert M. Fowler's *Let the Reader Understand: Reader-Response Criticism and the Gospel of Mark* (Harrisburg, Pa.: Trinity Press International, 2001) is the foundational text for anyone wanting to explore reader-response criticism. See also Fowler's chapter "Reader-Response Criticism: Figuring Mark's Reader," in Moore and Anderson, *Mark and Method*, 59–94.

33. See, e,g., Joanna Dewey, "The Gospel of Mark," in *Searching the Scriptures: A Feminist Commentary* (vol. 2 of *Searching the Scriptures*; ed. Elisabeth Schüssler Fiorenza; New York: Crossroad, 1997), 470–509.

34. See Whitney Shiner, *Proclaiming the Gospel: First Century Performance of Mark* (Harrisburg, Pa.: Trinity Press International, 2003). See also Holly E. Hearon and Philip Ruge Jones, eds., *The Bible in Ancient and Modern Media* (Biblical Performance Criticism; Eugene, Ore.: Cascade, 2009). Rhoads and Dewey are also presently collaborating on a book tentatively titled *Biblical Performance Criticism*. There is a wealth of information related to performance criticism at http://www.biblicalperformancecriticism.org, a site created and maintained by David Rhoads, Peter Perry, and James Maxey.

35. For a work that presents the theory and traces the history of this hermeneutical development, see R. G. Sugirtharajah, *Postcolonial Criticism and Biblical Interpretation* (Oxford: Oxford University Press, 2002). See also the more recent collection of essays in Stephen D. Moore and Fernando F. Segovia, eds., *Postcolonial Biblical Criticism: Interdisciplinary Intersections* (Bible and Postcolonialism; London: T&T Clark, 2005); and Fernando F. Segovia and Mary Ann Tolbert, eds., *Reading from This Place* (2 vols.; Minneapolis: Augsburg Fortress, 1995–2000).

36. For a good overview, see A. K. M. Adam, *What Is Postmodern Biblical Criticism?* (GBS; Minneapolis: Fortress, 1995). See also Edgar V. McKnight, *Postmodern Use of the Bible: The Emergence of Reader-Oriented Criticism* (Nashville: Abingdon, 1988).

37. I do not mean to suggest that the reception of narrative criticism in the academic

critics over the legitimacy of using a literary approach had paved the way for other hermeneutical trends to see the light of day.

In the wake of these developments and his own evolution as a narrative critic, Rhoads soon realized that his original work needed a thorough revision. The second edition, published in 1999, was substantially revised with the assistance of a new contributor, Joanna Dewey.[38] In the late 1970s Rhoads and Dewey had become friends and begun editing one another's work. As a graduate student, Dewey had also been asked to participate in the SBL Seminar on Mark by Norman Perrin.[39] Rhoads and Dewey forged a friendship in this forum, and Dewey subsequently proved to be an important outside contributor to the book's first edition.[40]

In the second edition, Rhoads and Dewey meticulously and methodically reorganized the entire book.[41] They added new discussions, fleshed out some of the first book's undeveloped assumptions, and chronicled developments since 1982—essentially rewriting a great majority of the book. A few of these changes are evident from a simple glance at both books. For instance, in the

---

community has created a situation in which "anything goes" methodologically. Methods of textual study must meet certain criteria to be deemed legitimate by a significant cross-section of biblical scholars. Still, methods such as reader-response, feminist, performance, postcolonial, and postmodern criticisms have had less trouble being recognized as legitimate because narrative critics helped pave the way for their reception in the guild.

38. In the preface to the second edition, the authors note that the book was "substantially rewritten throughout, with no page remaining unchanged" (*Mark as Story*, xi). By this time Joanna Dewey had already established herself as a leading voice in both literary hermeneutics and Markan studies. Between 1976 and the release of the second edition of *Mark as Story*, Dewey published the following related studies: *Disciples of the Way: Mark on Discipleship* (Cincinnati: Women's Division, The United Methodist Church, 1976); *Markan Public Debate: Literary Technique, Concentric Structure and Theology in Mark 2–3:6* (SBLDS 48; Missoula, Mont.: Scholars Press, 1980); "Point of View and the Disciples in Mark," *SBLSP* 21 (1982): 97–106; "Oral Methods of Structuring Narrative in Mark," *Int* 43 (1989): 32–44; "Mark as Interwoven Tapestry: Forecasts and Echoes for a Listening Audience," *CBQ* 53 (1991): 221–36; "Mark as Aural Narrative: Structures as Clues to Understanding," *STRev* 36 (1992): 45–56; "The Gospel of Mark as Oral-Aural Event: Implications for Interpretation," in *The New Literary Criticism and the New Testament* (ed. Edgar V. McKnight and Elizabeth Struthers Malbon; Sheffield: Sheffield Academic Press, 1994), 145–63.

39. While Perrin is known for his work on Markan redaction criticism, toward the end of his life he had become more sympathetic to literary hermeneutics and their implications for reading the New Testament narratives.

40. Dewey's early interest in orality grew out of her desire to restore women to the story world of the text. Thus, her two abiding scholarly interests—narrative studies and feminist issues—came together in this one forum.

41. Donald Michie was unable to participate in the book's revision.

first edition the second chapter was entitled "The Rhetoric" and examined the role of the narrator, point of view, style, narrative patterns, and other literary features. In the second edition the chapter title was changed to "The Narrator," and while much of the chapter remained the same as the first edition, more emphasis was placed on the rhetoric of the narrative as part of the storytelling device of Mark's narrator. Rhoads and Dewey also expanded the first edition's chapter 5 ("The Characters") and divided it into two separate chapters: one that dealt strictly with the role of Jesus in Mark and another that dealt with Mark's other characters. In addition to these changes, the authors also lengthened the book's original concluding chapter and added two appendices and an afterword entitled "Reading as Dialogue: The Ethics of Reading."

One substantive change that is not so obvious at a cursory glance is the newer perspective from which Rhoads and Dewey were now reading the Second Gospel. The first edition had been heavily reliant upon the work of Seymour Chatman and his focus on the process of discovery.[42] In their revision Rhoads and Dewey were influenced more by the writings of Wesley Kort.[43]

Chatman had made a distinction between story and discourse in a way that separated form and content. While Chatman's work had proven insightful for Rhoads's early thinking about narrative criticism, he eventually came to regard this approach as a simplistic and false dichotomy. By contrast, Wesley Kort sought to establish four features of narrative that make up a worldview: narrator, settings, characters, and plot.[44] To these four Rhoads and Dewey added rhetoric. The narrator provides the standards of morality and belief that govern the story. The settings identify the possibilities and limits within which characters act and events take place. Characters reveal the human condition. The plot unveils the dynamics of time as the story moves forward. Rhetoric has to do with the story as a whole—both content and storytelling techniques— that leave an impact on the hearers. In this model the rhetoric becomes the coherent impact of the whole presentation of both story and discourse and

---

42. Seymour Chatman, *Story and Discourse: Narrative Structure in Film and Literature* (Ithaca, N.Y.: Cornell University Press, 1978).

43. See Wesley Kort, *Shriven Selves: Religious Problems in Recent American Fiction* (Philadelphia: Fortress, 1972); idem, *Narrative Elements and Religious Meaning* (Philadelphia: Fortress, 1975); idem, *Moral Fiber: Character and Belief in Recent American Fiction* (Philadelphia: Fortress, 1982); idem, *Modern Fiction and Human Time: A Study in Narrative and Belief* (Gainesville: University of Florida Press, 1986); idem, *Story, Text, and Scripture: Literary Interests in Biblical Narrative* (University Park: Pennsylvania State University Press, 1988).

44. Another strength of Kort's reading of Mark is his tracing of the mounting tension in the Gospel and his attention to the pace at which the narrative unfolds. See especially *Story, Text, and Scripture*.

its impact upon the audience. Rhoads and Dewey found this scheme to be a better fit for their approach to the Gospel of Mark.

In the end, these changes had the practical effect of clarifying the book's various foci and making it even more user-friendly for students and scholars of the New Testament. In its second edition, *Mark as Story* has remained a fixture in undergraduate, graduate, and seminary courses on the Gospel of Mark. Scholars working in Markan studies and narrative criticism continue to cite the book as an authoritative resource. No bibliography of important works on narrative criticism is complete without *Mark as Story*. However, the strongest evidence for the impact of *Mark as Story* in particular and narrative criticism in general is that contemporary scholars routinely employ narrative methods, often without an explicit reference to their methodological choice. Narrative criticism and its attendant assumptions have become an organic part of biblical exegesis in the new millennium, and some (if not much) of this is surely due to the seminal contributions of *Mark as Story*. Contrary to the initial impression of our erstwhile reviewer, *Mark as Story* has proven to be a significant and enduring contribution to both Markan studies and narrative criticism.

MARK AS STORY: RETROSPECT AND PROSPECT

The foregoing survey suggests that the publication of *Mark as Story* marks a turning point in Gospel studies, both for the contribution it made to Markan scholarship and for the methodological insights that it advanced. This book aims to celebrate *Mark as Story* while offering critique, engagement, and exploration of the new hermeneutical vistas that have developed as a result of literary approaches to the text. By investigating various texts and themes in Mark's Gospel, the objective of this book is to reflect upon the rise of narrative criticism and to anticipate future trends in Gospels research. Thus, this volume has the complementary goals of looking backward and forward. The contributors have been brought together to celebrate the achievements of *Mark as Story* and suggest prospects for future research. Those involved in this project, leading voices on the Gospel of Mark and literary methods, have come, with a sense of appreciation for *Mark as Story*, to honor the work of David Rhoads, Donald Michie, and Joanna Dewey. The book is divided into two sections: the first consisting of studies on method and the second consisting of studies on Markan texts and themes from a perspective within narrative criticism or its related methodological trajectories.

Mark Allan Powell begins the first section of the book by questioning whether narrative criticism can be regarded as a hermeneutical method. Powell argues that the *method* of narrative criticism may best be described as text-focused, but the *practice* of narrative criticism is always carried out by persons who hold to either an author-oriented hermeneutic (Warren Carter, Jack Dean Kingsbury, Graham Stanton), a text-oriented hermeneutic (Richard Edwards, James Resseguie), or a reader-oriented hermeneutic (Joanna Dewey, David Rhoads, Mary Ann Tolbert). The result has been the development of three fairly distinct exegetical approaches, all of which are referred to as "narrative criticism." Each employs the same basic reading strategy, albeit with different assumptions and in service of different ends. Despite their differences, all three approaches aim to answer the same question: How should the implied reader respond to the text? Powell points out the assumptions, similarities, and differences in each approach, concluding that narrative criticism has developed into a reading strategy that can be employed by scholars with different hermeneutical interests and goals.

Elizabeth Struthers Malbon has distinguished herself as a leading authority on characters and characterization in the Gospel of Mark.[45] Her essay reflects on substantial changes in scholarly perspectives on both the narrative process and Markan characters since 1982. She notes that narrative criticism, in its development more than in its initial appearance, is best understood as an active appreciation of the narrative process: from an implied author, through a story world of settings, plot, and characters, to an implied audience. She then demonstrates how the changes from the first edition of *Mark as Story* to the second, specifically in the chapters on characters, also illustrate how narrative critics at various times focus on different aspects of the narrative process. Malbon concludes by highlighting a range of scholarly works to illustrate how different views of characters and characterization reflect varying foci of the narrative process.

In his essay, Stephen Moore interacts with the theory of character that emerges from the first edition of *Mark as Story*. Moore begins with the observation that Rhoads and Michie tend to conflate the modern genres of short story and novel to help explain Mark's narrative features, particularly their treatment of Markan characters. In the first edition, Rhoads and Michie rely heavily upon the categories provided by E. M. Forster in his classic *Aspects of the Novel*, in particular the distinction between "round" and "flat" characters.[46] Using categories drawn from Cartesian philosophy and the discipline of animal studies, Moore critiques the theory of character that emerges from the

---

45. See the collected essays on characterization in Elizabeth Struthers Malbon, *In the Company of Jesus: Characters in Mark's Gospel* (Louisville: Westminster John Knox, 2000). See also her more recent study, *Mark's Jesus: Characterization as Narrative Christology* (Waco, Tex.: Baylor University Press, 2009).

46. E. M. Forster, *Aspects of the Novel* (London: Arnold, 1927).

first edition of *Mark as Story*, finding it often to be anachronistic. The modern novel with its signature concept of character has played a crucial ancillary role in the construction of reimagined (nonanimal) human. Moore argues that *Mark as Story* incorporates this same concept of character and thereby becomes the unwitting vehicle of a problematic ideology of human-animal relations. Further, this ideology stands in marked tension with David Rhoads's own ecological work on the New Testament, with the result that Rhoads (on ecology) must be read against Rhoads (with Dewey and Michie on Mark's narrative) in order to construe the topic of character in Mark differently. Moore closes by using his critique as a means of calling us to a more informed and balanced theory of character in Mark and in the other New Testament narratives.

In 2002, Francis J. Moloney published the first full-length exegetical commentary on the Gospel of Mark from an explicitly narrative perspective.[47] In his essay he reflects on the process of writing a narrative commentary on Mark through the grid of the various categories provided by *Mark as Story* (e.g., narrator, setting, character, plot, rhetoric). In particular, Moloney emphasizes how his commentary focuses on two main characters: Jesus and the disciples. While most other characters play an instructive but secondary role in the story, Moloney identifies the relationship between Jesus and the disciples as one key feature driving the plot and bringing the story to its climax at the cross. He notes that during the process of writing the commentary he attempted to resolve the tensions in the narrative by the application of two principles. First, he takes for granted that Mark the storyteller attempted to write an account of the ministry, death, and resurrection of Jesus that coherently communicated what he wanted to say to the original readers. Second, he has attempted to fit everything together into a consistent pattern for his own readers. Thus, even though Mark's story has many elements that are alien to a modern readership, Moloney shows how the Second Gospel possesses unity, structure, and coherence that are instructive for both an original audience (whether real or implied) and a real twenty-first-century audience.

Thomas Boomershine closes out the first section of the book with an essay on audience address in Mark. Boomershine has been a prominent figure in methodological movements toward performance criticism. The recognition that Mark was written to be performed for an audience that was largely uneducated has yielded insights that have taken narrative criticism a step further. Against this backdrop, Boomershine addresses two dimensions of the Second Gospel that are raised by *Mark as Story* but are not resolved: the

---

47. Francis J. Moloney, *The Gospel of Mark* (Peabody, Mass.: Hendrickson, 2002).

analysis of Mark as a story that was addressed to audiences rather than read-ers in the ancient world and the implications of the dynamics of audience address in Mark for our understanding of the audience and purpose of the Gospel in its original historical context. He asserts that performance criti-cism is a logical methodological development and that it is more faithful to the original character of Mark than the narrative-critical assumption of the Markan reader, particularly as that is developed in *Mark as Story*. Against that backdrop, Boomershine discusses the nuances of audience address by demon-strating how Jesus, the central figure of the Gospel, addresses the audience as a series of predominantly Jewish characters. As the story progresses, the listen-ers experience a gradual shift from negative to more positive interactions with Jesus. Boomershine concludes that the reformation of narrative criticism for analyzing ancient stories performed for audiences in the ancient world has the promise of clarifying the meaning and purpose of Mark's story.

R. Alan Culpepper, another pioneer in New Testament narrative criti-cism, begins the second section of the book by examining the notoriously difficult section in Mark 6 that deals with the sending of the Twelve and the death of John the Baptist. Interpreters of Mark have often said that the story of the death of John the Baptist was inserted into the Gospel to provide an interlude for the mission of the disciples and that it has few connections with the rest of the Gospel. Keeping these comments in mind, Culpepper exam-ines the intertextuality of the story as well as the nuances of the way the story is told. He then defines five themes that this complex pericope advances: (1) John's death foreshadows Jesus' death; (2) John's death foreshadows the per-secution Jesus' disciples face; (3) Herod's banquet serves as the antithesis of Jesus' meals; (4) the serving of John's head on a platter anticipates the Last Supper; and (5) the characterization of Herod and his "kingdom" serve as the antithesis of Jesus' announcement of the kingdom of God. Culpepper argues that, while narrative criticism has yet to take seriously the discontinuities in the narrative, it has exposed texture, richness, and depth that earlier histori-cal-critical interpreters have missed.

Morna Hooker's essay examines how the title "Son of God" functions within Mark's story. Hooker argues that "Son of God" links the various parts of Mark's drama together and clearly expresses what Mark believes to be the truth about Jesus. "Son of God" is found in the prologue (1:11), where hear-ers of the Gospel are let into the secret of Jesus' identity, and again in one of the two recognition scenes at the turning point of the drama, when three of the disciples are told the truth about him (9:11). In the denouement, the high priest, representative of the Jewish nation, dismisses Jesus' absurd claim to be Messiah and Son of God (14:62), but the title is then used by the Gentile cen-turion (15:39). She points out that the scenes in the story proper—the cries of the demons and Jesus' parable about the vineyard tenants—remind us from time to time of this truth about Jesus. Peter's acknowledgement that Jesus is the Messiah expresses only part of this truth, but Jesus' words about "the Son of man" continually explain what being the "Son of God" means. For Hooker, Mark skillfully tells the story in a way that demonstrates that it is Jesus' death as king of the Jews that leads Gentiles to acknowledge him as Son of God.

Kelly Iverson offers a fresh consideration of Mark's secrecy motif. The so-called "messianic secret" has been a fixture in Markan conversation for over a century, but despite vigorous dialogue, little consensus has been reached since the publication of William Wrede's *Das Messiasgeheimnis in den Evangelien* in 1901. Iverson argues that, not only is narrative criticism an indispensable tool for shedding light on one of the more long-standing issues in Markan studies, but that the hermeneutical trajectory it sets forth paves the way for a fuller, more complete understanding that transcends the current state of the discussion. Beyond raising issues about the historical Jesus, narrative criticism fosters questions about the messianic secret and the impact of Mark's story that have been widely overlooked. By analyzing Mark's Gospel with a sensitivity to its performance, Iverson explores how the secrecy theme functions as an audience-elevating device that serves a missional purpose within the Second Gospel.

In her essay Holly Hearon argues that narrative criticism has fundamentally changed the way scholars view the biblical text. It has sharpened our attention on the world that exists wholly within the text by focusing on the role of the narrator, plot, setting and character. She notes that in recent years both Joanna Dewey and David Rhoads (among others) have begun to introduce another major shift in how we understand, experience, and interpret the text through the exploration of what Rhoads calls "performance criticism." Where narrative criticism calls attention to the world created within the text, performance criticism explores this same textual world mediated by a performer in the presence of an audience. Drawing upon the work of Whitney Shiner, Philip Ruge-Jones, Margaret Lee, and Brandon Scott, Hearon explores selected dimensions of the text (narrator, setting, conflict, character) that are lifted up in narrative criticism, using Mark 5:21–43 as her focus text. She concludes by proposing methodological shifts that need to occur when engaging the text through performance criticism, with attention to the implications for interpretation.

Robert Fowler's essay concludes the book's second section by analyzing the three sea stories carefully positioned in Mark 4:35–41; 6:45–52; and 8:14–21. The first two of these stories are miracle stories, and in a classroom setting they raise all of the predictable interpretive problems associated with making sense of ancient miracle stories in the postmodern, high-tech world of the twenty-first century. Contemporary students have little experience interpreting two-thousand-year-old miracle stories, and they enter the classroom with little exposure to literary theory. However, they have plenty of experience in watching movies. Fowler's students and, in this case, the readers of his essay are asked to exercise their imaginations to propose countless ingenious ways to film these miracle stories. Invariably, a corporate decision is made that the moviemaker's camera must, sooner or later, place the audience members "in the boat with Jesus." Concerns about the ostensible miraculous nature of these stories fade from our minds as we find ourselves, surprisingly, in the thick of the action on the silver screen. Fowler invites us, as he does his students, to enter the story world of the text by using the secondary context of the electronic age to shed light on the primary context of antiquity.

Fittingly, the book concludes with further reflections from David Rhoads, Donald Michie, and Joanna Dewey. Rhoads, Michie, and Dewey collaborate once again to critically engage the essays in this volume. As they interact with the book's essays, they also discuss where they see the discipline heading and they provide us with a list of prospects for future research.

Part 1
Method and *Mark as Story*

Narrative Criticism: The Emergence of a Prominent Reading Strategy

Mark Allan Powell

When David Rhoads coined the term "narrative criticism" in 1982, he did not mean for that phrase to describe a new *method* for studying the Gospels.[1] His proposal was more modest, namely, that critical study of Mark's Gospel should take seriously the character of that work as a narrative—a literary work that was intended to be understood as a whole, rather than as a collection of pericopes each of which could be analyzed in terms of its probable origins and compositional history. At least initially, narrative criticism was more descriptive of an orientation to Gospel study than it was of a particular exegetical method. The term was employed in distinction from "historical criticism" (an orientation out of which had developed "the historical-critical method").

I am not certain just when narrative criticism came to be regarded as an exegetical method, but for better or worse my book *What Is Narrative Criticism?* (published in 1990) confirmed or solidified its status as such.[2] When I wrote that book, I tried to be descriptive: I picked the most prominent scholars associated with the approach (Rhoads and Michie, R. Alan Culpepper, Jack Dean Kingsbury, and Robert Tannehill),[3] analyzed their work, and tried to

---

1. The term "narrative criticism" first appeared in David Rhoads, "Narrative Criticism and the Gospel of Mark," *JAAR* 50 (1982): 411–26. There he defined narrative criticism as "an approach" that investigates "the formal features of narrative in the texts of the Gospels, features which include aspects of the story-world of the narrative and the rhetorical techniques employed to tell the story" (411–12).

2. Mark Allan Powell, *What Is Narrative Criticism?* (GBS; Minneapolis: Fortress, 1990).

3. David Rhoads and Donald Michie, *Mark as Story: An Introduction to the Narrative of a Gospel* (Philadelphia: Fortress, 1982); later issued in a second edition by David Rhoads, Joanna Dewey, and Donald Michie (2nd ed.; Minneapolis: Fortress, 1999); R. Alan Culpepper, *Anatomy of the Fourth Gospel: A Study in Literary Design* (Philadelphia: Fortress, 1983); Jack Dean Kingsbury, *Matthew as Story* (2nd ed., Philadelphia: Fortress, 1988); Robert C. Tannehill, *The Narrative Unity of Luke-Acts: A Literary Interpretation* (2 vols.;

summarize what they did with texts when they practiced what they called narrative criticism. Obviously, other scholars (including me) who were interested in studying the Gospels "as narratives" might have employed different methodological principles or procedures. But my book described what these four people did, and it reached a relatively large audience. Thus, for many people, narrative criticism essentially came to be defined as "the literary method employed by Culpepper, Kingsbury, Rhoads, and Tannehill in the 1980s."[4]

Of course, these four scholars were themselves drawing upon the works of secular literary critics. In retrospect, they *might* have drawn primarily upon E. D. Hirsch, Mieke Bal, Stanley Fish, Norman Holland, or Jacques Derrida, but they didn't. All four drew primarily upon critics influenced by Russian formalism, French structuralism, and American "New Criticism." The most important of those critics were probably Wayne Booth, Seymour Chatman, and Wolfgang Iser.[5] Further, there was no major, concerted attempt at achieving methodological purity. In retrospect, the biblical scholars seem to have pillaged the works of secular critics, taking what seemed useful and leaving behind anything that did not exhibit obvious potential. The "method" of narrative criticism would emerge as a hodgepodge of observations that had been drawn from the study of secular narratives and deemed relevant for the Gospels. Thus narrative criticism was specifically designed for the interpretation of *biblical* literature: there is no discipline called "narrative criticism" within the field of secular literary studies ("narratology" perhaps comes closest, and it is not always very close).

Minneapolis: Fortress, 1990). The work of other scholars (including Thomas Boomershine, Joanna Dewey, Norman Petersen, and Mary Ann Tolbert) was considered in a less direct way: Rhoads read the manuscript to *What Is Narrative Criticism?* and offered many comments based on contributions those scholars had made to the SBL Seminar on Mark, which had shaped his thinking.

4. I did sneak in some of my own ideas as well, e.g., the distinction between idealistic and realistic empathy on p. 56. At the time, I assumed that if I identified this as my idea, no one would pay attention to it (since I had no credentials as a literary critic); by now, such insecurities have been swallowed up by vanity, and I wish I had taken credit for what was a pretty good contribution to the discipline.

5. See Wayne Booth, *The Rhetoric of Fiction* (2nd ed.; Chicago: University of Chicago Press, 1983); Seymour Chatman, *Story and Discourse: Narrative Structure in Fiction and Film* (Ithaca, N.Y.: Cornell University Press, 1978); Wolfgang Iser, *The Implied Reader: Patterns of Communication in Prose Fiction from Bunyan to Beckett* (Baltimore: Johns Hopkins University Press, 1974); idem, *The Act of Reading: A Theory of Aesthetic Response* (Baltimore: Johns Hopkins University Press, 1978). Also highly influential were works on literary criticism by M. H. Abrams, E. M. Forster, Gérard Genette, W. J. Harvey, Frank Kermode, Gerald Prince, Shlomith Rimmon-Kenan, Robert Scholes, and Boris Uspensky.

The concepts that narrative critics found most relevant for their work tended to favor insights that had originally applied to modern *novels*. In retrospect, this was unnecessary. Secular literary criticism does recognize that there are historically grounded narratives that can be studied from a literary perspective (as compositions that are intended to affect their readers through the conveyance of content that the reader is expected to regard as historically accurate); with regard to English literature, one thinks of Edward Gibbons's *History of the Western World* or Shelby Foote's *The Civil War: A Narrative* or Truman Capote's *In Cold Blood*. But literary criticism of the latter works had little to no impact on the development of narrative criticism: Booth had a special fondness for the works of Jane Austen, Henry James, and James Joyce; Chatman liked Joyce, as well as Joseph Conrad, Gustave Flaubert, and Ernest Hemingway (he also often appealed to films); Iser analyzed Samuel Beckett, John Bunyan, Henry Fielding, Joyce, Sir Walter Scott, and William Thackeray. Thus, for narrative critics, the storylike quality of biblical accounts came to the fore in spite of the obvious historical grounding for these writings' content and influence. This is not to say, however, that any of the narrative critics named above regarded the Gospels *as fiction*. To the contrary, these scholars all recognized that the Gospels do convey reliable information about actual historical events and that they also reflect upon those events theologically in ways that must be understood in terms of the historical contexts of the authors. Accordingly, the earliest narrative critics (and virtually all narrative critics since) understood their discipline as *one* approach to the Gospels, to be practiced alongside others: it is, of course, appropriate to study the Gospels historically or theologically, but it is also possible, appropriate, and worthwhile to study them as narratives in a manner analogous to the study of fiction. That it is *possible* for scholars to do this is no longer debatable (*Mark as Story* established that much). Scholars differ, however, as to why such study is *appropriate* or *worthwhile*, and those differences have precipitated a bit of confusion as to just what narrative criticism is about.

At first, narrative criticism was always called "a text-oriented approach." In secular studies, this phrase had been used to describe formalism, structuralism, and New Criticism, but in biblical studies it was used mainly to distinguish narrative criticism from the "author-oriented approach" of traditional historical study: meaning could be determined by paying attention to the form, structure, and rhetorical dynamics of the work itself, without reference to background information regarding what the author may or may not have intended.[6] But even as the early narrative critics were trying to wean histori-

---

6. Powell, *What Is Narrative Criticism*, 4–6.

cally minded colleagues away from an exclusively author-oriented vision, the secular academy moved decisively away from what it regarded as traditional text-oriented approaches toward "reader-oriented" ones. Considerable interest arose concerning the processes through which readers make sense of texts. Scholars now wanted to analyze the social and literary dynamics that interact when actual human beings produce or create meaning out of texts. Thus, in 1990, I defined narrative criticism as a text-oriented method that could be distinguished from both author- and reader-oriented modes of criticism. At the same time, I averred that "of all the types of literary criticism (practiced in biblical studies), narrative criticism and reader-response are the most similar and they may eventually become indistinguishable."[7] My editor, Dan Via, wrote in the margin of my manuscript, "They should!"

When biblical critics did discover the prominence of reader response in the academy at large, they sought to redress the situation in biblical scholarship but may have overreacted. The concern to be modern produced panic that missed an essential point. In the secular academy, the proliferation of reader-oriented approaches to literature did not consist of simultaneous competing claims to have discovered a "right approach" but rather sprung from a recognition that diverse approaches served different constituencies in various ways. Scholars who were quick to abandon the recently acquired narrative criticism as "outdated" (a *terrible* thing to be in scholarship) did not seem to realize that this method itself might be an example of what so many secular scholars were working so hard to develop within their own guilds: a strategy for understanding a particular type of literature in a particular way for a particular constituency. Meanwhile, scholars who feared that secularization of biblical studies had gone too far adopted their own brand of foolishness, occasionally asserting that meaning derived through narrative criticism was somehow intrinsically or objectively true: meaning lay in the text itself just waiting to be discovered and extracted through dispassionate application of a method, the principles and procedures of which appeared to be beyond critique. The upshot of all this was that, throughout the late 1990s and into the new millennium, different scholars employed narrative criticism for different purposes and sometimes engaged in arguments as to which sort of employment constituted *genuine* narrative criticism.

I now believe that these debates tend to confuse exegesis with hermeneutics. I think that narrative criticism is best described as "a reading strategy," though if someone wants to call it a "method" I have no problem with that. In any case, the principles and procedures of narrative criticism are designed

---

7. Ibid., 21.

to answer one important question: How is the implied reader expected to respond to the text?[8] In practice, however, the critics who use narrative criticism to answer this question invariably operate with either an author-oriented, text-oriented, or reader-oriented hermeneutic. As a result, we have ended up with three fairly distinct approaches to Gospel texts, all of which call themselves narrative criticism and all of which employ the same reading strategy, albeit with different operating assumptions and in service of different ends. I hate to categorize people almost as much as I hate being categorized, but one does get the sense that some scholars practice "author-oriented narrative criticism," some prefer a "text-oriented narrative criticism," and others pursue a "reader-oriented narrative criticism."

What Narrative Criticism Does

The basic goal of narrative criticism is to discern how the implied reader of a narrative would be expected to respond to the text.[9] I do recognize that scholars sometimes differ in what they mean by "the implied reader" (or even on whether that is the term that should be used), but, in practice, the reading strategy called "narrative criticism" usually entails an attempt to discern how some imaginary person construed in a manner deemed appropriate for the text would be expected to respond to that text. If we ask "expected by whom?" the official answer may be "by the implied author," but, in effect, the answer could be "by almost anyone who recognizes a few basic principles regarding how narratives are typically to be understood."

To a certain extent, the concept of an "implied reader" is grounded in common sense and is utilized for economical reasons. Otherwise, discussion about how readers respond to narratives would have to account for an infinite number of factors. Edgar Allan Poe's "The Tell-Tale Heart" is a suspenseful story—unless, perhaps, the reader has seen a movie based on the story and already knows how it is going to turn out. The story "Goldilocks and the Three Bears" has a simple plot that is easy to follow—unless, of course, the reader is reading it in a language that he or she hardly knows and does not recognize many of the words. Such caveats would pile up exponentially, and

---

8. This question obviously implies several others (e.g., What is an implied reader?). I will attend to some of these matters in the next section of this essay.

9. In saying this, I am not proposing that this is what the goal *should* be (though I would agree with that also) but claiming, descriptively, that this is what the goal actually is. I think I could defend the claim in two ways: (1) virtually all biblical scholars who call themselves narrative critics try to do this; and (2) the principles and procedures outlined in virtually all descriptions of the method are designed to accomplish this goal.

one would never be able to take into account every eventuality that might determine how *any* reader could conceivably respond to a story. Therefore, narrative critics employ an economical heuristic device. In effect, they say, let us assume there is a reader who (1) receives the narrative in the manner that they would be expected to receive it,[10] (2) knows everything that the reader of this story would be expected to know—but nothing else,[11] and (3) believes everything the reader of this story is expected to believe—but nothing more.[12] How would such a reader be expected to respond to this narrative?[13] The latter question is much simpler than the impossible-to-answer alternative (How would any reader be expected to respond?). Still, it must be answered in the plural: narrative critics typically end up discerning a range of what would qualify as "expected responses" or ways in which an implied reader might be expected to respond.[14] In practice, then, narrative criticism allows for discernment of what I call "polyvalence within perimeters," the perimeters being set by what would accord with expected responses attributable to the narrative's implied reader.[15] There is polyvalence within these perim-

---

10. For example, the implied reader is expected to read the entire narrative from beginning to end.

11. I maintain that the assumed knowledge that can be attributed to an implied reader encompasses two things: knowledge of the story setting (things revealed within the narrative itself) and knowledge of the discourse setting (matters that would have been common knowledge in the world that produced this story—things that the historical author probably would have assumed "everybody knows"). Thus, the implied reader of Mark's Gospel is expected to remember what was said at one point in the narrative when reading a later portion, and that reader is also expected to know who Moses was, what a centurion does, how much a denarius is worth, and other things that are simply assumed to be common knowledge within the story.

12. The implied reader of Mark is expected to (1) accept the system of beliefs and values of the story world—what is espoused within the narrative itself (e.g., that the world is ruled by a Creator God but is also infested by demons who serve Satan); and (2) accept the system of beliefs and values intrinsic to the discourse setting—things that would have gone unquestioned in the world where this story was produced (e.g., that it would normally be shameful to leave a body unburied to be devoured by animals).

13. Some would maintain that the expected mode of reception for Mark's Gospel is aural, so we should speak of an implied audience rather than an implied reader. I have argued elsewhere that taped presentations of oral performances might have implied audiences, but a *written* text by definition has an implied *reader* (albeit, perhaps, a reader who is expected to perform the text orally). See my *Chasing the Eastern Star* (Louisville: Westminster John Knox, 2001), 85–86, 210 n. 110; cf. 238–40.

14. In my own work I have sometimes employed the term "implied readers" as a way of reminding myself that anticipated responses to a narrative will always be plural.

15. Powell, *Chasing the Eastern Star*, 8, 71. Actually, in that book, I call the phenomenon "polyvalence within parameters." Helpful critics have since corrected my vocabulary:

eters, because divergent and sometimes even contradictory responses might be shown to be attributable to the implied reader as defined above. Still, such polyvalence is limited; outside the perimeters, polyvalence becomes potentially infinite.

The principles and procedures of narrative criticism basically allow critics to classify responses to the text as "expected" or "unexpected" readings. Such classification does not say anything at all about the value or the legitimacy of the reading, though, as we will see, some narrative critics operate with a hermeneutic that assumes valuations not intrinsic to the reading strategy itself. In any case, an *expected reading* would be one that seems to be invited by signals within the text itself (as discernible through narrative criticism). An *unexpected reading* is one that is produced when factors extrinsic to the text cause the reader to resist or ignore the text's signals.

I have illustrated this with an example of four different people reading Mark's passion narrative. They respond emotionally to the narrative: (1) reader one is *inspired* by the story because it presents Jesus as a man of integrity who is willing to die nobly for his convictions; (2) reader two is *traumatized* by the story because it reveals the depth of human depravity on the part of people who denounce, betray, and torture an innocent man; (3) reader three is *comforted* by the story because it portrays Jesus' death as a ransom for many, through which God grants mercy to the undeserving; and (4) reader four is *delighted* by the story because it reports the gruesome execution of a meddlesome busybody who tried to tell everyone else how they should live.[16] Narrative critics would probably classify the first three responses as what I call *expected readings*. Though very different from each other, all three of these readings respond to cues within the text. A reader who is receiving the text in the expected manner, knowing what such a reader is expected to know and believing what such a reader is expected to believe, could be understood to respond in any of these ways. Thus, they illustrate what I call "polyvalence within perimeters." But I would call the fourth response an *unexpected reading*—this person responds to the story in a way that the narrative does not solicit or invite. Such a response would probably be arrived at by a reader who brings something unanticipated to the story (e.g., a value system or attitude toward religion that the implied reader would not be expected to harbor).

---

a *parameter* is a single basis for comparison; *perimeters* are plural boundaries within which something might be found.

16. This illustration and the commentary on it that follows is taken from Powell, *Chasing the Eastern Star*, 60.

Narrative criticism as a method or reading strategy enables us to distinguish expected readings from unexpected ones, but such distinctions can be made without prejudice. In the preceding example, the fourth reading may seem to be not only unexpected but perverse. There is, however, no reason why this would always be the case. Vegans may consider it immoral for a father to kill a fatted calf in celebration of his son's return (see Luke 15:23). The Hadzabe people of Tanzania may think it shameful to entomb a corpse rather than leaving it on the ground to be consumed by animals (see Mark 6:29; 15:46). Most likely, actual readers who held such views would recognize that the New Testament Gospels present story worlds for which different values are operative, but if they did not adjust their perspectives accordingly while reading, they would likely respond to these stories in unexpected ways. Likewise, modern readers whose values are influenced by feminism or capitalism may respond to the Gospels in ways that the implied reader would not. Narrative criticism facilitates awareness of such dynamics without necessarily assuming there is anything wrong with feminism or capitalism (or with veganism or with the Hadzabe attitude toward burial).

When all factors are taken into account, we may end up concluding that no reader of Mark's Gospel (certainly no *modern* reader) will ever respond to the story in the manner expected of its implied reader. What, then, is the point? Ah! Here is where narrative critics diverge.

WHY GOSPEL SCHOLARS USE NARRATIVE CRITICISM

As narrative criticism continued to develop, the initial explorations were confirmed and augmented. Most Gospel scholars who bothered to investigate the discipline were convinced that it was fairly effective at achieving its intended goal: generally speaking, the Gospel narratives could be understood from the perspective of a posited "implied reader," and responses to the stories could be identified as expected or unexpected readings accordingly. The question for scholars was not "Can it be done?" but "Why bother?" What theological or practical difference does it make whether any particular understanding of Mark's Gospel accords with what would hypothetically be arrived at by some imaginary figure who does not actually exist? Some scholars may have dismissed the entire enterprise as pointless, but others found three different reasons for employing this reading strategy.

Author-oriented narrative criticism. A number of historically minded critics discovered that narrative criticism could be used as a tool for discernment of authorial intent. At first, such interest may have seemed surprising because narrative criticism was often touted as exemplary of a paradigm shift *away* from concern for authorial intent (and, indeed, when the discipline was defended the primary apologetic involved justification of exegesis that did not seek to discern the author's intent).[17]

The initial positioning of narrative criticism in opposition to author-oriented exegesis no doubt derived from movements in secular literary criticism where New Criticism (to which narrative criticism owed a great deal) spoke of an "intentional fallacy" and actively discouraged readers from attempting to discern the historical author's intent.[18] The critics involved in that particular movement, however, were often concerned with works by living or recent authors whose explicit statements of intent were thought to limit the work's potential (and the works in question were typically poems, not narratives—a seldom-noted fact). For example, the New Critics maintained that it is not necessary for a reader to know that John Keats was caring for his dying brother when he wrote "Bright Star," a sonnet replete with themes of love and death; indeed, such knowledge can become intrusive, preventing a more direct engagement with the poem.[19] The situation in biblical studies was somewhat different in that no detailed data regarding the Gospel authors' intentions has ever been available; still, narrative critics encouraged an engagement of the text that bracketed out preconceived notions of authorial intent derived from extraneous sources (e.g., descriptions of an Evangelist's intent provided by some early church leader or reconstructions of an Evangelist's intent based on analysis of supposed redactional tendencies).

A significant distinction may be drawn, however, between imposing an extraneous notion of authorial intent upon a narrative and deriving an intrinsic notion of authorial intent from a narrative. In secular literary studies, the concern was to discourage the former, not the latter. As near as I can tell, no one in the New Criticism movement denied that an author's intent *could* be discerned through literary analysis of a work, nor did anyone maintain that an author's intent *should not* be discerned through such analysis. The prospect of doing such a thing simply did not come up, since, if one wanted such information, it was widely available. Thus, biblical critics made a discovery that their secular colleagues had missed or ignored; in essence, they discovered a "bonus application" for a literary method, an application that would appeal to people who were interested in the Bible as something other than literature (e.g., as the testimony of an inspired author whose beliefs, values, and intentions were to be held in high, if not authoritative, esteem).

---

17. Powell, *What Is Narrative Criticism*, 96–98.

18. William K. Wimsatt, "The Intentional Fallacy," in *The Verbal Icon: Studies in the Meaning of Poetry* (Lexington: University Press of Kentucky, 1954), 3–20.

19. S. Berman, "Revolution in Literary Criticism," *Princeton Alumni Weekly* (1984): 10.

The first narrative critics approached this subject judiciously via discussion of the relationship between the imaginary implied reader that narrative criticism might posit for a Gospel and the original "intended readers" for which the Gospel had actually been written. Thus, Rhoads and Michie concluded the first edition of *Mark as Story* by "speculating" what sort of first-century reader "would have responded to the story in much the same way as the implied reader."[20] Culpepper devoted much of his final chapter in *Anatomy of the Fourth Gospel* to consideration of how a literary understanding of the "audience implied by the text" of John's Gospel might inform the ongoing attempt of scholars to reconstruct the character of the first-century Johannine community.[21] Kingsbury proposed that scholars might "use the implied reader of Matthew's story as an index, even if only approximate, of the intended readers"; the information that we infer about Matthew's implied reader from the story can be used to "sketch a picture" of the historical audience for which the book was intended.[22]

Such observations opened a back door to discernment of authorial intent. Basically, the logical case for using narrative criticism to discern the historical intentions of the author of Mark's Gospel could be made as follows:

(1) Narrative critics are able to discern how an imaginary implied reader would be expected to respond to Mark's story; this is the response that the narrative itself solicits or invites.

(2) It is reasonable to assume that the original readers of Mark's Gospel would have been expected to respond in a similar fashion; at the very least, the responses that we may infer for an imaginary implied reader may be taken as an index that approximates the actual response that would have been anticipated for original readers.

(3) Since there is a logical connection between expected responses and inferred intent, the expected response attributable to Mark's implied reader may be taken not only as indicative of the response expected of the Gospel's intended audience but also as definitive of the historical author's actual intent.[23]

---

20. Rhoads and Michie, *Mark as Story*, 140–44. Cf. Rhoads, Dewey, and Michie, *Mark as Story*, 143–45.

21. Culpepper, *Anatomy*, 210–27.

22. Kingsbury, *Matthew as Story* (1986), 120. Cf. idem, *Matthew as Story* (1988), 147.

23. Although I would not generally regard myself as a practitioner of author-oriented narrative criticism, I have published one article that exemplifies the approach. I sought to evaluate J. D. Spong's claim that the historical authors of the New Testament Gospels never intended for the miracle stories they relate to be taken literally, that is, to be understood as accounts of things that had actually happened. As one part of the investigation, I conducted a narrative-critical study of those stories and concluded that the *implied* readers of the Gospels in question were almost certainly expected to believe the miracles actually occurred.

The logic here seems basically sound, though I think the matter may be more complicated than is sometimes recognized. The compositional history of our Gospels sets them apart from narratives that are informed by the intention of a single author from beginning to end. The Evangelist we call Mark probably used material that came from a variety of sources, and some of what we would end up attributing to the viewpoint of the book's implied author might have actually derived from the historical Jesus or from an intermediate author (of one of Mark's sources) rather than from Mark himself. Of course, we might assume that Mark would not have incorporated anything into the book that did not suit his purposes, so whatever the origin of the materials, the book in its final form would convey his intention from start to finish. That may have been the case. Or, perhaps, part of Mark's intention was simply to preserve things that he thought Jesus had said or done, regardless of whether he personally understood or appreciated their import. I do not think that we can know such things for certain.

I do think, however, that the problems associated with using narrative criticism to discern authorial intent are no greater than those associated with using redaction criticism to the same end. The assumption that an Evangelist's primary intentions can be discerned by tracking editorial emendations he is suspected of having made is at least somewhat tenuous logically, and the enterprise becomes even less certain when everything is made to depend upon hypotheses regarding which book used which other book as a source (or, in the case of Mark, hypotheses regarding potential reconstructions of sources that the Evangelist might have possessed and edited). Thus, many redaction critics discovered that narrative criticism offered, at least, a means of checking, supplementing, and/or confirming what they were able to discern through more traditional historical-critical analysis. In the process, quite a few discovered that a method they had initially viewed as antithetical to their conception of the exegetical task actually afforded them an opportunity of accomplishing that task more effectively than before.

One of the most significant scholars to utilize narrative criticism in this regard was Graham Stanton, who may have been the first prominent Euro-

---

Thus, for Spong's contention to be valid, we would have to assume incompetence on the part of (all four) Gospel authors: the historical Evangelists did not intend for the stories to be taken literally but, because they did not know how to write stories very well, they produced narratives that invited literal interpretations on the part of their implied readers. This would not be completely impossible, but I suggested that it is more reasonable to assume that the historical authors intended for their narratives to solicit the responses that they actually do solicit. See Mark Allan Powell, "Authorial Intent and Historical Reporting: Putting Spong's Literalization Thesis to the Test," *JSHJ* 1 (2003): 225–49.

pean scholar to adopt the approach as part of his consistent program.[24] Stanton's goal, however, was to understand Matthew's Gospel within its original
sociohistorical context, and this demanded that the method be practiced
with a modified awareness of the Gospel genre (biography, not novel) and of
appropriate literary conventions (ancient ones, not modern ones).[25] The work
of Warren Carter is more often regarded as exemplary of narrative criticism
than that of Stanton, though Carter also insisted on the caveats articulated
by Stanton: he sought to do narrative criticism of an ancient biography, not
a modern novel.[26] Thus, Carter analyzed the plot, settings, and characters of
Matthew's Gospel as a way of determining how the book would have been
understood by its "authorial audience" (the people who the author had in
mind when composing the work).[27]

In Markan studies, numerous author-oriented critics had used literary-
critical analysis to further their program prior to the emergence of narrative-
criticism. Theodore Weeden, Werner Kelber, Ernest Best, and Vernon Robbins analyzed aspects of Mark's plot, characters, and rhetoric in ways that
were sometimes analogous to what would eventually be termed "narrative
criticism"[28] They did this, however, as a means to understanding the message
that a historical Evangelist had intended to convey to an historical audience.
Likewise, Kingsbury's study of Mark's Christology utilized literary-critical
concepts (point of view, characterization) in an explicit attempt to discern the
historical author's theological intentions.[29] After narrative criticism became
better known or more firmly established, some Markan scholars continued in
the vein of the aforementioned critics, but they now did such work under the
rubric of "narrative criticism" proper. Thus, Jerry Camery-Hoggatt concluded
his study of irony in Mark's Gospel with consideration of the question, "How

---

24. Graham N. Stanton, *A Gospel for a New People: Studies in Matthew* (Edinburgh:
T&T Clark, 1992).

25. Stanton, *Gospel for a New People*, 54–84.

26. Warren Carter, *Matthew: Storyteller, Interpreter, Evangelist* (Peabody, Mass.: Hendrickson, 1996), esp. 35–54.

27. Ibid., 4–5, 279. He derives this concept from Peter J. Rabinowitz, *Before Reading:
Narrative Conventions and the Politics of Interpretation* (Ithaca, N.Y.: Cornell University
Press, 1987), 15–46.

28. Theodore J. Weeden, *Traditions in Conflict* (Philadelphia: Fortress, 1971); Werner
H. Kelber, *Mark's Story of Jesus* (Philadelphia: Fortress, 1979); Ernest Best, *Mark: The Gospel
as Story* (Studies of the New Testament and Its World; Edinburgh: T&T Clark, 1983);
Vernon K. Robbins, *Jesus the Teacher: A Socio-rhetorical Interpretation of Mark* (Philadelphia: Fortress, 1984).

29. Jack Dean Kingsbury, *The Christology of Mark's Gospel* (Philadelphia: Fortress,
1983).

are we to reconstruct the circumstances that gave rise to such concerns?"[30] John Paul Heil's narrative-critical commentary on Mark's Gospel (which he called a "reader-response commentary") explicitly sought to elucidate the text for a reader located "in the first-century Mediterranean regions" of the Roman Empire.[31] Paul Danove concluded his study of the narrative rhetoric of characterization in Mark by detailing implications for "the historical exigency of the composition."[32]

Author-oriented narrative criticism has probably been articulated most clearly and defended most vigorously by Petri Merenlahti and Raimo Hakola. In their article, "Reconceiving Narrative Criticism," they basically call for the discipline to be replaced by a more sophisticated version of 1970s composition analysis: a historical analysis of authorial intent that utilizes some of the principles and procedures practiced by narrative critics, alongside other methods. They claim that such an approach would be more respectful of the Gospel genre:

> In the case of the Gospels, forms of narrative analysis that are more open to questions concerning the ideological and historical background of the texts must be considered preferable, because they pay due attention to the nature of the Gospels as non-fictional narratives. These forms of analysis will welcome any relevant sociological or historical information that helps to understand the complexity of narrative communication in the Gospels.[33]

Merenlahti and Hakola's argument is quite polemical: they seem less interested in establishing that narrative criticism *can* be used in author-oriented exegesis (a point that, by 1999, did not really need establishing) than in maintaining that it cannot or should not be used to further other interests: it is not "natural" to read a Gospel in any way that is nonreferential (i.e., that does not offer historical description).[34] In particular, they are annoyed by the prospect

---

30. Jerry Camery-Hoggatt, *Irony in Mark's Gospel: Text and Subtext* (SNTSMS 72; Cambridge: Cambridge University Press, 1992), 180.

31. John Paul Heil, *The Gospel of Mark as Model for Action: A Reader-Response Commentary* (New York: Paulist, 1992), 4.

32. Paul L. Danove, *The Rhetoric of Characterization of God, Jesus, and Jesus' Disciples in the Gospel of Mark* (JSNTSup 290; London: T&T Clark, 2005), 159–64.

33. Petri Merenlahti and Raimo Hakola, "Reconceiving Narrative Criticism," in *Characterization in the Gospels: Reconceiving Narrative Criticism* (ed. David Rhoads and Kari Syreeni; JSNTSup 184; Sheffield: Sheffield Academic Press, 1999), 48. Other essays in this volume (by a number of Scandinavian scholars) also exemplify the potential for narrative criticism to be used in an author-oriented vein.

34. Ibid., 41–42. As a specific example of "grossly misreading Matthew," they cite my

that non–author-oriented narrative criticism might be meaningful to people of faith who engage the Bible as scripture in terms other than as a testimony to potentially recoverable historical events.[35] The gist of their argument seems to be that all biblical interpreters should operate with the hermeneutic that they employ. Despite this unfortunate cast, however, their work may be regarded positively as illustrative of one major way in which narrative criticism can be and (almost from the start) has been employed.

Before moving on, we should at least pause to appreciate this startlingly ironic moment in the history of biblical interpretation. When the authors of *Mark as Story* first proposed narrative criticism, the primary opposition came from redaction critics who feared that, if the new approach caught on, it would be at the expense of their own discipline. Their fears turned out to be well-founded but for a completely different reason than anyone at the time would have suspected. The emergence of narrative criticism brought about a decline of interest in typical redaction criticism (e.g., emendation analysis) not because scholars lost interest in discerning authorial intent but, rather, because narrative criticism provided them with a more effective means of discerning authorial intent. Basically, narrative criticism turned out to be a better approach for accomplishing the goals of redaction criticism than redaction criticism itself had been.

---

suggestion that it is possible for a reader to understand the conflict between Jesus and the Jewish leaders as generically emblematic of good versus evil rather than as a historically referential account intended to foster anti-Semitism. I would, of course, grant that Matthew composed a narrative that is easily capable of encouraging anti-Jewish attitudes, but I personally doubt that the historical Evangelist's explicit intent was to foster an enduring anti-Semitism in the church. In any case, I do not understand why a preference for reading a text one way has to invalidate other ways of reading it. For my response to Merenlahti and Hakola (and their brief reply to me), see *Chasing the Eastern Star*, 119–20, 200–1 n. 20, 219–20 nn. 186–92, 237.

35. Merenlahti and Hakola, "Reconceiving Narrative Criticism," 44. On this point, they follow Stephen Moore, against me. In a book written for pastors and church leaders, I observed that, since the implied reader is surely assumed to be a person of faith (positively disposed to Jesus and his message), narrative criticism will inevitably reveal how texts are understood from a "faith perspective" (*What Is Narrative Criticism*, 88–89). Then I went on to indicate that this factor might have certain benefits for pastors and other Christian interpreters who want to understand the text from a faith perspective. Moore took this potential as a negative indicator, a reason to warrant the rejection of narrative criticism. See Stephen D. Moore, *Poststructuralism and the New Testament: Derrida and Foucault at the Foot of the Cross* (Minneapolis: Fortress, 1994), 115–16. My position has not changed on this point: I think that people read the Bible for many different reasons, and I do not think that the legitimacy of any method should be questioned simply because people find it useful for purposes that do not interest everyone.

Text-oriented narrative criticism. Some interpreters are interested in using narrative criticism for its own sake, ascribing normative value to the meaning that would be expected of an implied reader and viewing other (unexpected) readings as misunderstandings. Determining how the implied reader would be expected to respond to biblical stories is thus viewed as a complete exegetical process: the response attributable to the implied reader is not valued because it serves as an index for recovering authorial intent (see above) or as a springboard for understanding polyvalence (see below) but because it *is* what the text means. The implied reader's understanding is the intrinsically correct reading of a text; variance from that reading involves degrees of misreading the text, that is, of misunderstanding it.

Richard A. Edwards has operated with such an assumption in his work on Matthew's Gospel.[36] Edwards maintains that it is important to keep narrative criticism distinct from redaction criticism, and he complains that "there are some biblical scholars, who consider themselves narrative critics, who refer to the 'reader' but nevertheless continue to seek the 'author's intention' as their primary analytical task."[37] To preserve methodological purity, he suggests defining the implied reader as "a text-connoted reader," insisting that the implied reader cannot be assumed to know anything that is not actually revealed within the narrative: for example, Matthew's implied reader cannot be assumed to know who "Abraham" is when that name is mentioned in Matt 1:1. Personally, I think that Edwards's approach fails logically. Why would the implied reader know the meaning of *any* of the words that make up the narrative? Why wouldn't the totally uninformed text-connoted reader see all of those words as meaningless squiggles on a piece of paper? Edwards appears to avoid this conundrum by allowing that the text-connoted reader possesses linguistic competence and, so, understands vocabulary, grammar, and syntax, but it seems to me that all of those matters are socially constructed and dependent on information extrinsic to the text. Nevertheless, Edwards has tried harder than anyone to keep narrative criticism entirely "text-centered," and those who have appreciated his published work must have found that radically text-oriented approach to be useful.

Many scholars, however, would maintain that narrative criticism can be text-oriented even if the implied reader is construed more broadly than Edwards wants to allow. The point (for Culpepper, Kingsbury, Rhoads, Dewey, Michie, Tannehill, and others) is not that the implied reader must

---

36. Richard A. Edwards, *Matthew's Narrative Portrait of Disciples: How the Text-Connoted Reader Is Informed* (Harrisburg, Pa.: Trinity Press International, 1997). See also idem, *Matthew's Story of Jesus* (Philadelphia: Fortress, 1985).

37. Edwards, *Matthew's Narrative Portrait*, 6. Cf. ibid., vi., 4–5.

be ignorant of all historically derived information but that the meaning of the text attributable to the (somewhat informed) implied reader transcends historical particularity. Thus, the implied reader's understanding is essentially synonymous with "the meaning of the text," a relatively timeless concept. In making such an assertion, narrative critics have tried, again, to be economical. Early on, one of the purported benefits of narrative criticism was that it removed the pesky need for analogy from the process of biblical interpretation: we no longer need to ask "what the text meant" (an exegetical question) and then ask "what the text means" (a theological question). We can discover "what the text means" through (narrative-critical) exegesis.[38] I believe that most narrative critics have operated, implicitly or explicitly, with some version of this text-oriented hermeneutic. If we focus on Markan studies, I think that this is basically the approach that underlies the first edition of Rhoads and Michie's *Mark as Story*, as well as Kingsbury's *Conflict in Mark*.[39] Both of those books attempt to describe how Mark's implied reader would understand the story (and, to some extent, respond to it). The assumption seems to be that when a modern reader understands the story the way that the implied reader is expected to understand it, then the modern reader has a correct or good understanding of the Gospel. Indeed, possessing such an understanding will be spiritually beneficial: having experienced the story world of Mark's Gospel, contemporary readers "may be able to see and struggle with the real world in new ways and perhaps be better prepared to live more courageous and humane lives."[40]

The text-oriented hermeneutic that often underlies narrative criticism becomes most clear when authors equate faithful response to a Gospel (i.e., by those who view such a narrative as authoritative for their lives) with adopting the understanding of the implied reader or responding to the text in the manner expected of the implied reader. Thus, for Donald Juel, theological appropriation of Mark's Gospel involves "becoming a new Markan community," one that receives the work's arguments and rhetoric the way its implied audience would; Juel finds this promising for Christianity because the situa-

---

38. I critiqued this claim early on: narrative criticism simply redefines the hermeneutical gap without actually removing it. While it may reduce the interpretive chasm between "the meaning then" and "the meaning now," it creates a new one between "the meaning there" (in the story world) and "the meaning here" (in the real world). See Powell, *What Is Narrative Criticism*, 100.

39. Jack Dean Kingsbury, *Conflict in Mark: Jesus, Authorities, Disciples* (Minneapolis: Fortress, 1989).

40. Rhoads and Michie, *Mark as Story*, 142. Cf. Rhoads, Dewey, and Michie, *Mark as Story*, 146.

tion of the implied audience is one that provides more universal resonance than the situation of first-century readers. For example, according to Juel's redactional analysis of Mark, the first readers of the Gospel were probably subject to violent statewide persecution or troubled by the delay of the parousia, neither of which are universal concerns. But the concerns of the implied reader, discernible through narrative criticism, would not be defined with such off-putting specificity; rather, the implied reader is one who risks being tired or indifferent to the demands of faith, one who has lost the ability to be surprised by God. Thus, narrative criticism exposes the (universal) meaning of the text, rather than simply *a* meaning that the text may have had in one particular historical setting.[41]

Likewise, Elizabeth Struthers Malbon concludes her very helpful description of narrative criticism by saying, "if such study can help us align ourselves with the implied reader, our own roles as real readers—and re-readers—of Mark will surely be enriched."[42] Thus, the most desirable response to Mark's Gospel is *alignment* with the implied reader. I take this to mean, at least, that one *understands* Mark's Gospel properly when one's *understanding* is aligned with that of the implied reader; other aspects of alignment (in terms of faith, values, lifestyle) could be implied as well. In any case, for Malbon, the goal or purpose of narrative criticism is to facilitate such alignment, as opposed, for instance, to providing insight useful for reconstructing first-century ideas, thoughts, or events. This also becomes clear in Malbon's impressive work on Mark's Christology. She identifies "Mark's Jesus" as a construct of the Gospel's implied author, recoverable through attention to what the character of Jesus says and does and to what other characters and the Markan narrator say and do in relation to him. In a concluding chapter, she maintains that it is "not epistemologically appropriate simply to assign the point of view of the Markan Jesus to 'the historical Jesus' and the point of view of the narrator to the Markan evangelist."[43] This undercuts any attempt to take the implied reader's understanding of Mark's Jesus as indicative of the intention of the Markan author, but, for Malbon, this does not indicate any failure of narrative-critical method. The goal of narrative criticism is not to shed light on the historical

---

41. Donald H. Juel, *A Master of Surprise: Mark Interpreted* (Minneapolis: Fortress, 1994), 142–46.

42. Elizabeth Struthers Malbon, "Narrative Criticism: How Does the Story Mean?" in *Mark and Method: New Approaches in Biblical Studies* (2nd ed.; ed. Janice Capel Anderson and Stephen D. Moore; Minneapolis: Fortress, 2008), 55. Also in idem, *In the Company of Jesus: Characters in Mark's Gospel* (Louisville: Westminster John Knox, 2000), 40.

43. Elizabeth Struthers Malbon, *Mark's Jesus: Characterization as Narrative Christology* (Waco, Tex.: Baylor University Press, 2009), 254.

Jesus or on the intentions of one of his historical followers (the Evangelist): for narrative criticism, the Gospel stories are not means, but ends.[44]

Reader-oriented narrative criticism. Many interpreters use narrative criticism as a base method to guide them in discerning and understanding disparate and polyvalent responses. By gaining a general idea of how readers are expected to respond to a story, interpreters are able to identify more readily the points at which individuals or communities adopt variant reading strategies, and they are able to probe the processes that determine these.

It has often been said that narrative critics do not care about "real readers," actual flesh-and-blood people who engage texts and interpret them in diverse ways in the real world. The charge is ludicrous: I do not believe I have ever met a narrative critic for whom the "end-game" would not be the engagement of texts by real readers in the real world. As a reading strategy, of course, narrative criticism does attempt to bracket out such real-world responses in order to define the expected response of the implied reader. Thus, it might be correct to say that, *as an exegetical method*, narrative criticism ignores the concerns of real readers; the significant factor, however, is what one does with the data thus acquired. And that factor owes to hermeneutics, not exegesis.

I admit to having been confused over this for a while. Throughout the 1990s I often heard narrative criticism disparaged as antithetical to various schools of ideological criticism that encouraged "resistant reading" as the most faithful response to a text that might solicit responses informed by patriarchalism or anti-Semitism or other unenlightened ethical stances.[45] For quite some time I wondered (occasionally in print) how anti–narrative criticism proponents of resistant reading knew what to resist.[46] Their point did not usually seem to be that a historical author had wanted a few people 1,900 years ago to think in a way that we should now repudiate. Rather, their point usually seemed to be that the Gospel story itself was told in a way that clearly anticipated some sort of (unacceptable) response. Thus, I often suspected these arch-opponents of narrative criticism of being, in fact, narrative critics. They were employing (perhaps intuitively) some sort of reading strategy that allowed them to define the expected response of the work's (implied) reader. It took me a while to realize that the reason these critics despised narrative criticism was that they assumed the latter discipline was *promoting* the understanding of the implied reader as opposed to simply *identifying* it. But I had

---

44. Ibid., 256.

45. On resistant reading, see Judith Fetterly, *The Resisting Reader: A Feminist Approach to American Literature* (Bloomington: Indiana University Press, 1978).

46. Powell, *Chasing the Eastern Star*, 208 n. 94.

never assumed that the use of narrative criticism implied a necessary endorse-ment of the perspective it discerned, and, increasingly, I came to realize that many narrative critics did not operate with that assumption.

Some elements of reader-oriented narrative criticism may be discerned in the early work of Mary Ann Tolbert. In *Sowing the Gospel* (1989), she is more attentive to the reality of polyvalence and the ambiguity of narrative gaps than other narrative critics were at the time.[47] Later, she would demonstrate strong interest in the influence of social location on the reading process: the social location of real readers may affect their perception of what is expected of an implied reader, or it may affect how they evaluate what has been identified as the response expected of an implied reader.[48]

A number of narrative-critical studies have paid attention to how real readers might interact with the expected response of the implied reader.[49] The two books that have explored this concept most intentionally, however, are Robert Fowler's *Let the Reader Understand* and my own *Chasing the Eastern Star*.[50] Both of those books were presented as exercises in reader-response criticism (as their subtitles indicate), but both also employ the principles and procedures of narrative criticism without any attendant assumption that the expected response of the implied reader (to the extent that it is discernible)

---

47. Mary Ann Tolbert, *Sowing the Gospel: Mark's World in Literary-Historical Perspective* (Minneapolis: Fortress, 1989), esp. 7–10 and her discussion of the open ending of Mark (288–99).

48. Fernando F. Segovia and Mary Ann Tolbert, eds., *Social Location and Biblical Interpretation in the United States* and *Social Location and Biblical Interpretation in Global Perspective* (vols. 1 and 2 of *Reading from This Place*; Minneapolis: Fortress, 1995).

49. See, e.g., John A. Darr, *On Character Building: The Reader and the Rhetoric of Characterization in Luke-Acts* (Literary Currents in Biblical Interpretation; Louisville: Westminster John Knox, 1992); James S. Hanson, *The Endangered Promises: Conflict in Mark* (SBLDS 171; Atlanta: Society of Biblical Literature, 2000); David B. Howell, *Matthew's Inclusive Story: A Study in the Narrative Rhetoric of the First Gospel* (JSNTSup 42; Sheffield: JSOT Press, 1990); William S. Kurz, *Reading Luke-Acts: Dynamics of Biblical Narrative* (Louisville: Westminster John Knox, 1993). All of these authors tended to draw more heavily on Wolfgang Iser for their understanding of how to construe "the implied reader," whereas Culpepper, Kingsbury, Rhoads, and Tannehill had drawn more heavily on Wayne Booth's articulation of that concept. A more reader-oriented approach to narrative criticism (again favoring Iser's "implied reader" over that of Booth) also seems to be reflected in James L. Resseguie, *Narrative Criticism of the New Testament: An Introduction* (Grand Rapids: Baker, 2005).

50. Robert M. Fowler, *Let the Reader Understand: Reader-Response Criticism and the Gospel of Mark* (Minneapolis: Augsburg Fortress, 1991). See also his earlier work: *Loaves and Fishes: The Function of the Feeding Stories in the Gospel of Mark* (SBLDS 54; Atlanta: Scholars Press, 1981).

is to be deemed normative in a way that would commend evaluation of reading experiences in general. Of the two works, Fowler's is the more important, preceding my own by a good decade and influencing not only my study but almost every other literary study of Mark's Gospel since.[51] A volume similar to this present one, devoted to the enduring contributions of Fowler's *Let the Reader Understand*, would not be out of place.

At the time *Let the Reader Understand* came out, the book was often regarded as a handbook for a literary alternative to narrative criticism. The "method" of reader-response criticism seemed to overlap with narrative criticism in certain respects but was typically presented as a distinct reading strategy. It is difficult today to see why that would be. If *Let the Reader Understand* had been subtitled *Narrative Criticism and the Gospel of Mark*, no one would have blinked an eye. Likewise, Fowler's chapter on "Reader-Response Criticism" in the book *Mark and Method* follows a chapter by Elizabeth Malbon on "Narrative Criticism," but there is no essential methodological difference between the literary approaches that are presented. Fowler's chapter could have been called "Narrative Criticism, Part Two," and that would not have seemed odd—indeed, I think, it would have been completely appropriate.

To be more specific, Fowler cites a number of moves that distinguish his approach to the Gospels from more text-centered approaches: he emphasizes the *discourse level* or *rhetoric* of the narrative rather than the *story level* of the narrative; he is especially attentive to gaps and ambiguities in the narrative; he tries to discern the intended *effect* on the reader, rather than limiting meaning to the conveyance of a cognitive *message*; and he allows for a plurality of different responses rather than simply defining *the* understanding attributable to an implied reader.[52] But, of course, narrative criticism is interested in all of these things as well. If the earliest narrative-critical studies were inattentive to these concerns, it was simply because such matters belong to a more advanced practice of the discipline. Narrative critics often start out examining the story level of a narrative because that is easiest and most accessible. They focus on what Fowler calls "rhetoric of direction" rather than "rhetoric of indirection" for the same reason. And while it is true that early narrative critics may have sometimes spoken of "how the implied reader understands

---

51. My *Chasing the Eastern Star*, on the other hand, did not sell particularly well, and it is seldom cited. I personally think it is the best book I have ever written, and I would like to blame the modest reception on the publisher for saddling it with a weird title. But then, I wanted to call it *Closer To Fine* or *What a Fool Believes*, either of which might have been worse.

52. Fowler, *Let the Reader Understand*, 2.

the text" (implying a singular, probably cognitive understanding), those who continued to work with the discipline came to realize that it was necessary to define the implied reader's response more broadly (e.g., as a spectrum of potential responses, including emotive and affective ones).[53]

In short, narrative criticism and reader-response criticism as delineated by most practitioners of either approach are almost identical reading strategies (differing sometimes on matters of emphasis). The crucial distinction seems to be the hermeneutical assumptions that sometimes accompany the employment of either strategy. Fowler wanted to discern anticipated responses to Mark's narrative so that readers could interact with those expectations, comparing and contrasting their own experience with the story with what the narrative appears to solicit or invite. There is no sense in Fowler's work that Mark's Gospel is correctly understood when readers conform their understanding to that of the implied reader.[54]

It may seem chauvinistic of me to claim that what Fowler and other biblical critics call reader-response criticism is actually a form of narrative criticism (i.e., "reader-oriented narrative criticism"). I do not want to press the terminology too far, but the point may simply be that there *are* varieties of reader-oriented criticism that have no interest in the concept of an implied reader, and what Fowler calls "reader-response criticism" ought to be distinguished from those approaches. As an umbrella term, *reader-response* includes literary approaches that attempt to read texts from the perspective of any posited reader: a Marxist reader (Marxist criticism), a feminist reader (literary feminist criticism), historical readers (*Wirkungsgeschichte*), and so forth. The variety of reader-response pursued by Fowler and other Gospel scholars is one that (at least initially) attempts to read texts from the perspective of an "implied reader," whose orientation may be defined in terms of certain widely (though not universally) agreed-upon conventions. In biblical studies, this particular variety of reader-response is usually called "narrative criticism."

Thus, one *might* say that reader-response criticism (as practiced by Fowler) is really just one type of narrative criticism. Or one might just as well say that narrative criticism is really just one type of reader response criticism—and

---

53. David Rhoads has said that narrative critics had to learn from reader-response criticism that "rhetoric has to do not only with what the story *means* but also with ... how the narrative affects the readers in the process of reading." See idem, "Narrative Criticism: Practices and Prospects, in *Reading Mark: Engaging the Gospel* (Minneapolis: Augsburg Fortress, 2004), 32.

54. Thus, for example, he is able to commend "resisting reading" as potentially "the most faithful of all" responses to the text. See Robert M. Fowler, "Reader-Response Criticism: Figuring Mark's Reader," in Anderson and Moore, *Mark and Method*, 84.

that is what I do say in *Chasing the Eastern Star*.[55] In that book I attempt to lay out a four-stage process for the study of biblical texts:

(1) Identify actual responses of real readers to the text using what I call *descriptive reader-response criticism*, informed by some appreciation of the text's history of influence (*Wirkungsgeschichte*). I would also include here identification of one's own response to the text.

(2) Discern the expected response of the implied reader by using narrative criticism and compare the responses of actual readers to this. Does one's own response to the text fall within the perimeters of what might be attributed to a reader receiving the text as anticipated? Are there obvious or discernible patterns of divergence from the expected response—for example, have certain people (identified broadly by class, gender, age, religious affiliation, geographical or temporal location, etc.) been more likely to respond in an expected manner than others?

(3) Try to account for disparity between actual responses and those that would be expected of the implied reader. For instance, is such disparity due to readers not knowing things that the implied reader would be expected to know—or is it due to readers knowing things that the implied reader would *not* be expected to know? Or, is the disparity due to readers receiving the text in light of beliefs or values that the implied reader would not be expected to hold?

(4) Evaluate both the expected reading of the text (that which narrative criticism discerns as attributable to the implied reader) and the unexpected readings that may be attributed to actual readers (including, perhaps, one-self). Such evaluation will always be done in light of one's own hermeneutical system (e.g., for me, evangelical Lutheranism), and it is both honest and helpful to acknowledge this.[56]

This scheme is basically a template for the use of narrative criticism. The actual exegetical work that is called for employs the principles and procedures of narrative-critical method. That method, or reading strategy, is designed to define the expected responses of the narrative's implied reader. But since my proposal for textual study carries no incentive for conformity to that response, one might wonder, What's the point? Why bother discerning the expected response of the implied reader if one is not actually going to align oneself with that response, or at least identify that response as a correct or preferred understanding of the text.

I offer two reasons. First, from a practical standpoint, discerning the expected response of the implied reader helps me to identify the factors that

---

55. Powell, *Chasing the Eastern Star*, 63.
56. Ibid., 7–9.

produce divergent readings. If my response is virtually the same as that attributable to the implied reader, then, I might simply assume that the narrative's
rhetoric is working as intended: I respond to the narrative as I do because I
am following the text's signals. One might as well ask, "Why did you think
that movie was funny?" when the obvious answer would be, "Because it was
a comedy!" But when *unexpected* responses arise, I am motivated to find a
rationale. This can be revealing and, sometimes, surprising. I may learn things
about myself or about the history of interpretation.[57] The question, "Why did
you think that movie was funny?" becomes more relevant when posed to
someone who has just seen a film that was *not* intended to be a comedy. The
answer to such a question might reveal something about the film, and it will
almost certainly reveal something about the viewer. Thus, discernment of the
implied reader's expected response helps us to identify matters worthy of further investigation.

Second, I personally regard the New Testament Gospels as authoritative
scripture, so I have theological reasons for wanting to know how readers are
expected to respond to them and for discerning why readers do not respond to
such texts in an unexpected manner. I am aware that some scholars think that
accepting the authority of scripture necessitates responding to the biblical text
the way that we are expected to respond to it. I also admit to "a default preference" for readings that concur with what would be expected of the implied
reader, but I consider the matter more complicated than the foregoing suggestion allows.[58] Sometimes my unexpected response to Mark's narrative may
be due to the fact that I hold to a perspective informed by the whole canon
of scripture, not to mention two millennia of theological reflection upon the
biblical writings. Ultimately, I believe that a theologically informed, canonical
response to Mark's Gospel is preferable to the anticipated response of the Gos-

---

57. For example, in *Chasing the Eastern Star* I examine the popular identification of
the magi in Matt 2 as kings. This is widely acknowledged as an unexpected reading (the
implied reader would not be expected to regard the magi as kings), but what accounts
for it? The usual suggestion is that certain influential historical readers (e.g., Tertullian)
wanted the magi in Matt 2 to fulfill scriptural prophecies about kings (Ps 72:11; Isa 49:7;
60:1–6). My research turned up another, more compelling reason: the magi only came to
be regarded as kings after Augustine treated them as such in eight successive Epiphany
sermons, and he did so for blatantly political and economic reasons: as good kings who
worship Christ (as opposed to evil king Herod, who persecutes him), the magi serve as role
models for Roman emperors, who should follow their example by opening their treasures
and bestowing generous gifts upon those who serve Christ's cause. Supposed fulfillment
of Old Testament prophecy is never mentioned and certainly did not motivate Augustine's
influential equation of the magi with kings.

58. On this, see Powell, *Chasing the Eastern Star*, 179–80.

pel's implied reader. At other times, however, I discover that my response to Mark's narrative diverges from what would be expected of the implied reader because I have been ignorant or because I have been stubborn or selfish—and, then, respect for the narrative's status as scripture does motivate me to conform my response to what would have been expected of me.

A final, stellar example of reader-oriented narrative criticism is presented in the second edition of the book *Mark as Story*. In 1999, Rhoads and Dewey appended an afterword to the book in order to treat a topic that had been ignored seventeen years earlier: "Reading as Dialogue."[59] First, they indicate that any critic's construal of an implied reader's response will be affected by that critic's own particular beliefs, experiences, and commitments. This, of course, is so obvious as to seem pedantic (the sort of thing that should be able to go without saying, but when it *does* go without saying begs objections from the pedantically inclined). But then the authors move on to note that contemporary readers may object to certain elements of Mark's narrative, such as the stereotypical portrayal of Judean leaders as figures who abuse power or the marginalized roles of women characters. Further, Rhoads and Dewey allow that some readers may respond negatively to ways in which the Gospel has been used (they say "misused") by other readers. Still, the authors suggest that the act of reading should be "a genuine dialogue," one in which readers remain open, in spite of reservations, to being transformed by the story.

In short, the 1982 edition of *Mark as Story* was the paradigm for text-oriented narrative criticism, though, as noted above, it granted leeway for the development of what I call author-oriented narrative criticism as well; the 1999 edition of *Mark as Story* retained these features but moved, hermeneutically, toward an embrace of what I call reader-oriented narrative criticism. In its two editions, Rhoads, Dewey, and Michie manage to cover all of the possibilities, exemplifying the use of narrative criticism (a reading strategy) in service of distinct and diverse hermeneutical goals.

CONCLUSION

I believe that narrative criticism is a reading strategy that has been employed by scholars with different hermeneutical interests and goals. There is no exact parallel or analogy for this in secular literary studies, because hermeneutics takes on singular significance when applied to texts regarded as scripture.

---

59. Rhoads, Dewey, and Michie, *Mark as Story*, 147–50. See also David Rhoads, "The Ethics of Reading Mark as Narrative," in *Reading Mark: Engaging the Gospel*, 202–19.

Interpreters who operate with an *author-oriented hermeneutic* tend to use narrative criticism with the belief that expectations attributable to the implied reader probably reflect the historical intentions of the work's actual author. This approach to interpretation is often, though not always, accompanied by a confessional posture that grants authoritative status to authorial intent: acceptance of the Bible as scripture means that people are called to believe whatever message the author intended to convey.

Interpreters who operate with a *text-oriented hermeneutic* tend to use narrative criticism for its own sake, ascribing normative value to a reading that would be expected of an implied reader and declaring other (unexpected) readings to be intrinsically invalid. This perspective usually seems to be informed by a confessional posture that views an "expected response" to scripture as a divinely ordained one. Thus, authoritative status is granted to the exegetically discerned anticipated response of an implied reader rather than to the exegetically defined intention of a historical author: the authoritative or normative meaning of scripture equals what the biblical book means for people who receive it in a manner expected of them rather than what the author of the book intended for it to mean to people.

Finally, interpreters who operate with a *reader-oriented hermeneutic* tend to use narrative criticism as a base method to guide them in discerning and understanding disparate and polyvalent responses. By gaining a general idea of how readers are expected to respond to a story, interpreters are able to identify more readily the points at which individuals or communities adopt variant reading strategies and, so, are able to probe the processes that determine these. Authoritative status might be granted to what is considered to be an expected reading, but it usually is not, since unexpected readings may sometimes derive from imposed perspectives that are deemed biblically and theologically sound.

CHARACTERS IN MARK'S STORY: CHANGING PERSPECTIVES ON THE NARRATIVE PROCESS

Elizabeth Struthers Malbon

As narrative critics, many of us began with some version of Seymour Chatman's diagram of the relationships of the implied author, narrator, narratee, and implied reader within a text or narrative:[1]

real →	implied → author	narrator →	narratee →	implied → reader	real
author					reader

TEXT or NARRATIVE

In fact, one can reflect on the development and diversity of narrative criticism in terms of adaptations of this diagram and/or the focus on different parts of it. Initially, attention focused on the narrative as a whole (the box in the above diagram). Narrative criticism wished to explore the story world of the Gospels rather than reconstruct the historical world of their first-century authors and their communities, as redaction criticism tended to do. Narrative criticism wished to comment on the involvement of the characters with each other in the conflicts of the plot rather than read them as ciphers for opposed groups in the early Christian movement, as Weeden (and sometimes Kelber) seemed to do.[2] The first edition of *Mark as Story* not only

---

1. This diagram, while based on that of Seymour Chatman, *Story and Discourse: Narrative Structure in Fiction and Film* (Ithaca, N.Y.: Cornell University Press, 1978), 151, is presented in the form used in Elizabeth Struthers Malbon, "Narrative Criticism: How Does the Story Mean?" in *Mark and Method: New Approaches in Biblical Studies* (2nd ed.; ed. Janice Capel Anderson and Stephen D. Moore; Minneapolis: Fortress, 2008), 33.

2. Theodore J. Weeden, *Mark: Traditions in Conflict* (Philadelphia: Fortress, 1971). Werner H. Kelber, *The Kingdom in Mark: A New Place and a New Time* (Philadelphia: Fortress, 1974); idem, *Mark's Story of Jesus* (Philadelphia: Fortress, 1979).

represents this focus on the narrative but also served to introduce it to a broader audience.[3]

Later, some New Testament narrative critics, with Markan scholar Robert Fowler in the lead,[4] began to focus more on the implied reader and to become known as reader-response critics, an even stronger movement in secular literary criticism. As Mark Allan Powell points out in the preceding essay in this collection, the difference between narrative criticism (a term only current within biblical scholarship) and reader-response criticism is more one of emphasis than opposition, and the second edition of *Mark as Story* reflects this shift.[5] Later still, some New Testament narrative critics, including David Rhoads, Joanna Dewey, and others exploring orality in both the ancient and contemporary worlds, began to speak of the implied audience rather than the implied reader and, in fact, to speak of real, embodied audiences, both ancient and modern, and even to speak, as performers, *to* real contemporary audiences.[6] Both reader-response criticism and performance criticism focus on the

---

3. David Rhoads and Donald Michie, *Mark as Story: An Introduction to the Narrative of a Gospel* (Philadelphia: Fortress, 1982).

4. Robert M. Fowler, *Loaves and Fishes: The Function of the Feeding Stories in the Gospel of Mark* (SBLDS 54; Chico, Calif.: Society of Biblical Literature, 1981); idem, *Let the Reader Understand: Reader-Response Criticism and the Gospel of Mark* (Minneapolis: Fortress, 1991); idem, "Reader-Response Criticism: Figuring Mark's Reader," in Anderson and Moore, *Mark and Method*, 59–93. See also John A. Darr, *On Character Building: The Reader and the Rhetoric of Characterization in Luke-Acts* (Louisville: Westminster John Knox, 1992); and idem, *Herod the Fox: Audience Criticism and Lukan Characterization* (Sheffield: Sheffield Academic Press, 1998).

5. David Rhoads, Joanna Dewey, and Donald Michie, *Mark as Story: An Introduction to the Narrative of a Gospel* (2nd ed.; Minneapolis: Fortress, 1999).

6. David Rhoads, "Performance Criticism: An Emerging Methodology in Second Testament Studies—Part I," *BTB* 36 (2006): 1–16; idem "Performance Criticism: An Emerging Methodology in Second Testament Studies—Part II," *BTB* 36 (2006): 164–84; Joanna Dewey, "Oral Methods of Structuring Narrative in Mark," *Int* 53 (1989): 32–44; idem, "Mark as Interwoven Tapestry: Forecasts and Echoes for a Listening Audience," *CBQ* 53 (1991): 221–36; idem, "Mark as Aural Narrative: Structures as Clues to Understanding," *STRev* 36 (1992): 45–56; idem, "The Gospel of Mark as an Oral-Aural Event: Implications for Interpretation," in *The New Literary Criticism and the New Testament* (ed. Elizabeth Struthers Malbon and Edgar V. McKnight; JSNTSup 109; Sheffield: Sheffield Academic Press, 1994; Valley Forge, Pa.: Trinity Press International, 1994), 145–63; idem, "The Survival of Mark's Gospel: A Good Story?" *JBL* 123 (2004): 495–507; Thomas E. Boomershine, "Mark, the Storyteller: A Rhetorical-Critical Investigation of Mark's Passion and Resurrection Narrative" (Ph.D. diss., Union Theological Seminary, New York, 1974); Werner H. Kelber, *The Oral and the Written Gospel: The Hermeneutics of Speaking and Writing in the Synoptic Tradition, Mark, Paul, and Q* (Philadelphia: Fortress, 1983); Whitney Shiner, *Follow Me! Disciples in Markan Rhetoric* (SBLDS 145; Atlanta: Scholars Press, 1995); idem, *Proclaiming*

reader/audience aspect of the diagram, with some interpreters sticking more closely to the implied audience (still inside the "narrative" box in the diagram) and others venturing outward to real audiences, either ancient or modern. Nearly all of these New Testament narrative critics, however, right from the beginning, ignored the diagram's distinction between the implied author and the narrator. Such a distinction was generally considered unnecessary or not useful for the Gospels, in either their ancient contexts or their contemporary ones. Some interpreters used "implied author," and some employed "narrator," but the terms used singly became virtually synonymous. In my most recent work, I have come to question the wisdom of this practice.

Narrative criticism, in its development, more than in its initial appearance, is best understood as active appreciation of the narrative *process*, from implied author to implied audience, rather than as simple analysis of a straightforward *product* of a real author passively read by a real reader. This is the significance of the inclusion of four terms *within* the box marked "text or narrative" in the above diagram: all four (implied author, narrator, narratee, implied reader—or implied audience) are considered aspects of the narrative, the narrative process. In my contribution to this volume reflecting on *Mark as Story* retrospectively and prospectively, I consider how these shifts in focus among narrative critics (and those who use many of the same reading strategies without claiming the name) have affected the ways characters and characterization in the Gospels, particularly Mark's Gospel, are explored and explained. First I examine some changes in the way characters are viewed from the first edition of *Mark as Story* (1982) to the second edition (1999), as these changes reflect a shift in focus from "the narrative" as a whole to the reader/audience aspect of the narrative process. Then I present a sampling of ways other narrative critics' views of characters and characterization reflect varying foci of the narrative process.

VIEWING CHARACTERS—FROM THE FIRST
TO THE SECOND EDITION OF *MARK AS STORY*

The first edition of *Mark as Story* (1982) opens with a brief introduction, followed by Rhoads's translation of Mark (ch. 1) and chapters on "The Rhetoric," "The Settings," "The Plot," and "The Characters" (36 pages), and closes with a short conclusion. The chapter on "The Characters" begins: "Characters are

---

the Gospel: First-Century Performance of Mark (Harrisburg, Pa.: Trinity Press International, 2003); Kelly R. Iverson, "Orality and the Gospels: A Survey of Recent Research," *CBR* 8 (2009): 71–106.

a central element of the story world,"[7] a sentence not included in the second edition. The footnote to this opening sentence includes this comment: "Theodore Weeden initiated the study of character in Mark's Gospel in *Mark: Traditions in Conflict*,"[8] also not included in the revision. Thus the 1982 chapter on characters begins by claiming the space of the story world for Markan characters, in opposition to the space of the historical world in which Weeden saw them moving as analogs to early Christian groups in tension.

The second edition of *Mark as Story* (1999) opens with an expanded introduction, followed by Rhoads's translation of Mark (ch. 1) and chapters on "The Narrator," "The Settings," "The Plot," and two chapters on the characters—"The Characters I: Jesus" (18 pages) and "The Characters II: The Authorities, the Disciples, and the People" (21 pages)—followed by a conclusion" subtitled "The Reader," an afterword subtitled "Reading as a Dialogue: The Ethics of Reading," and two appendices presenting aids to the reader: "Appendix 1: Exercises for an Overall Literary Analysis of Mark" and "Appendix 2: Exercises for a Narrative Analysis of Episodes." The increased focus on the reader, at a time when reader-response criticism was growing stronger, is obvious. The first chapter on characters includes a new paragraph in its introduction to clarify the relation of narrative-critical analysis to historical-critical analysis:

> All we know of a given character is what we know from the story. We cannot go beyond what the Markan narrator has told us or implied in order to speculate about the character's actions or motives—either on the basis of the treatment of that character in other Gospels or through efforts to reconstruct the historical character. We are treating these figures only in terms of their characterization in Mark—even when we are using helpful background information from the culture to understand the character better.[9]

Thus in 1999 the relation of Mark's story world, where a claim was staked in 1982, to the social world of the first-century Mediterranean that was the originating historical context of the world behind Mark's Gospel is made explicit. A consistent and timely feature of the second edition of *Mark as Story* is its more explicit reference to background information from the historical social and political culture in interpreting the story—and especially in guiding readers away from misinterpreting the story.

---

7. Rhoads and Michie, *Mark as Story*, 101.
8. Ibid., 154 n. 1.
9. Rhoads, Dewey, and Michie, *Mark as Story*, 98.

The 1982 single chapter on the characters develops under four head-ings—"Jesus," "The Authorities," "The Disciples," and "The Little People"—but it opens with a seven-paragraph introductory statement about characterization that introduces a number of concepts from literary criticism: major and minor characters, "showing" and "telling," reliable and unreliable characters, standards of judgment, comparison and contrast, framing, irony, character traits, and "flat" and "round" characters. The Markan narrator, it is said, "cleverly reveals the characters in such a way that the readers are constantly expanding or shifting their impressions of those [major] characters as the story develops."[10]

The generalizations about characterization that were presented in seven paragraphs in the 1982 edition are expanded to twenty-three paragraphs in the 1999 edition, including the introduction of a heading ("Approaches to Characterization") and six subheadings: "Characters as Types," "Standards of Judgment," "Comparison and Contrast," "Traits of the Characters," "Identification with Characters," and "Summary." All material is reworked carefully (one would be hard pressed to find a single sentence here that remains unchanged). Explanation of "standards of judgment" is expanded noticeably, and new material is added on the social location of characters and ancient type-characters. The role of the reader, which was certainly stated in 1982, is made even more obvious in 1999: "The reader participates actively in the pro-cess of creating the characters in imagination."[11] These changes reflect schol-arly developments in reader-response criticism, social-scientific criticism, and studies of ancient literature.

Under the 1982 heading "Jesus," this main character is explicated in nine subheadings: "Characterization," "Jesus' Authority," "Integrity," "Faith," "Serv-ing and Not Lording over Others," "Renouncing Self, Being Least, and Losing His Life," "Jesus Faces Death," "The Meaning of His Death," and "The Death." The 1999 chapter on Jesus includes additions, subtractions, and revisions of subheadings themselves, resulting in this arrangement: "Characterization," "Agent of the Rule of God," "The Authority of Jesus," "Faith," "Serving and Not Lording over Others," "Renouncing Self, Being Least, and Losing Life for Others," "Jesus Faces Death," "The Execution," "The Meaning of Jesus' Cruci-fixion," and "The Empty Grave." These changes are *not* simply surface editorial changes but careful responses to critical issues in Markan scholarship as nar-rative criticism has developed along with other newer approaches.

---

10. Rhoads and Michie, *Mark as Story*, 103.
11. Rhoads, Dewey, and Michie, *Mark as Story*, 102.

Although the first edition of *Mark as Story* certainly depicted Jesus in relation to God and the rule of God, this aspect becomes even more explicit in the second edition, starting with the addition of several new paragraphs on what it means to identify Jesus as Son of God in Mark[12] and a new subheading: "Agent of the Rule of God."[13] In addition, some significant deletions of earlier material occur. A paragraph with this topic sentence—"The narrator also gradually reveals Jesus to the reader, primarily by means of the literary motif of secrecy"[14]—disappears from the subheading "Characterization" (of Jesus). Paragraphs with these topic sentences—"Jesus is so powerful as to be frightening even to his disciples"[15] and "Jesus' authority from God resembles the royal authority a king exercises over national institutions"[16]—are removed from the subheading on the authority of Jesus. Some of these changes reflect the increased awareness of the critique in New Testament materials of the problematic politics of the Roman Empire that developed in biblical scholarship between 1982 and 1999. The subheadings on "Faith," "Serving and Not Lording over Others," and "Renouncing Self, Being Least, and Losing Life for Others" (to use the 1999 wording), while somewhat shortened and meticulously revised (and those who know Joanna Dewey's feminist work will sense her influence here), are not substantially altered. Significantly added phrases include: "Jesus teaches the disciples … to use their power on behalf of others with less power than themselves—not because it is a personal sacrifice but because it empowers others,"[17] and "In Mark, Jesus is not 'the son of David,' for it is not the 'rule of our father David' that Jesus inaugurates but 'the rule of God'—in which people in family-like relationships are to serve each other and not to lord over anyone."[18]

In the subsection "Jesus Faces Death," more general words such as "victim," "suffering," and "oppression" in the 1982 edition are replaced in the 1999 edition by the more pointed words "rejected," "persecution," and "execution." While both editions state clearly that Jesus' death/execution is *not* "portrayed as his own desire," this statement is followed up differently in the two editions. In 1982 one reads, "Rather, he invites this kind of death because of a conviction that it is necessary; God wills it, and therefore it must

---

12. Ibid., 103–4.
13. Ibid., 105.
14. Rhoads and Michie, *Mark as Story*, 104.
15. Ibid., 105.
16. Ibid., 106.
17. Rhoads, Dewey, and Michie, *Mark as Story*, 107–8.
18. Ibid., 109.

happen so the writings might be fulfilled."[19] In 1999 one reads instead, "Far from passively accepting death, he protests and condemns the attitudes and actions of the authorities, particularly in his riddle to them about the farmers in the vineyard. Nevertheless, he does accept that his execution will be the unavoidable consequence of giving a faithful witness to the rule of God."[20] The 1982 edition of this subsection concludes: "God really does abandon Jesus to his death."[21] But in the 1999 edition the subsection closes: "God does not rescue Jesus from his death."[22] These changes represent a significant movement beyond the more traditionally expressed "theology"—implied narrative theology as interpreted—of the earlier edition.

The subsections on Jesus' death/crucifixion and its meaning are reversed in the two editions, with the 1999 edition presenting the more logical order of "The Execution" followed by "The Meaning of Jesus' Crucifixion." The 1999 edition uses "Judean leaders" where the 1982 edition has "Jewish authorities," and there are other small and thoughtful revisions. A new paragraph at the close of "The Execution" subsection concludes: "Thus the narrator does not depict Jesus' dying a heroic death of 'noble' proportions.... The only triumph Mark depicts in Jesus' death is his human faithfulness to God."[23] Only vestiges remain of the 1982 discussion of "The Meaning of His Death" in the 1999 discussion of "The Meaning of Jesus' Crucifixion." Half the material is new, and the other half is changed, sometimes radically. The 1982 explanation of the saying to give his life "as a ransom for many" reads: "That is, Jesus sees his death as the sacrifice by which God renews the covenant with Israel to include the 'many,' namely, Jews and now gentiles alike who respond positively to the rule of God in Jesus."[24] The 1999 explanation of this phrase reads: "The word 'ransom' was not part of the language of sacrifice but a term that depicted the release of a slave or a hostage. That is, in Mark, Jesus sees his whole life, including his execution, as a means by which people are ransomed or liberated for a life of service in the rule of God."[25] Both editions link Jesus' "body" and "blood" saying at the Passover meal with "covenant," since the Markan text links these words and concepts there. However, in the earlier edition, the covenant saying is linked more closely with the ransom saying: "Jesus sees his death as that ransom, not in the sense of a price to be paid to God but as the

---

19. Rhoads and Michie, *Mark as Story*, 113.
20. Rhoads, Dewey, and Michie, *Mark as Story*, 111.
21. Rhoads and Michie, *Mark as Story*, 113.
22. Rhoads, Dewey, and Michie, *Mark as Story*, 111.
23. Ibid., 112.
24. Rhoads and Michie, *Mark as Story*, 113–4.
25. Rhoads, Dewey, and Michie, *Mark as Story*, 113–4.

sacrifice necessary to seal this covenant for 'the many.'"[26] The later edition explains:

> This [saying at the Passover meal] is not a reference to sacrifice for sin, but to a covenant sacrifice.... Thus the narrator presents Jesus asking, if you will, that his execution seal the covenant of the rule of God with "the many," the new community of Judeans and Gentiles alike who follow Jesus in the way of service and who are willing, if need be, to stand in opposition to the government and risk the consequences.[27]

But prior to this revised discussion of the "ransom" and "covenant" sayings, the 1999 edition adds several paragraphs of new material cautioning the reader explicitly "not to read into Mark theological meanings that later came to be associated with Jesus' death."[28] Certainly these arguments are ones I continue to make with my own students, so I welcome this carefully offered support.[29]

The resurrection was only alluded to in the 1982 edition—perhaps with a nod to Mark's own allusive (and elusive!) ending: "And if there is to be anything after death, it comes through an act of God."[30] A paragraph on "The Empty Grave" in the 1999 edition concludes: "The empty grave is the seal of God's approval. Jesus the Nazarene, who served others, who confronted oppression, and who was executed in the service of the rule of God, *this* is the kind of human God will welcome into the rule of God in the age to come."[31]

After the discussion of Jesus as a character, both editions of *Mark as Story* move to a discussion of the other characters, beginning with "The Authorities." The introductory material on the authorities, under the subheading "Characterization," is shortened in the 1999 edition, mostly by eliminating generalized sentences about character traits that are a level of abstraction away from the actions of the narrative and that are more susceptible to being taken in anti-Jewish or anti-Semitic ways by readers so inclined. This positive change is also strengthened by the use of "Judean" rather than "Jewish" to describe the non-Roman authorities, but especially by new material on "No

---

26. Rhoads and Michie, *Mark as Story*, 114.

27. Rhoads, Dewey, and Michie, *Mark as Story*, 114.

28. Ibid., 113.

29. Cf. Sharyn Dowd and Elizabeth Struthers Malbon, "The Significance of Jesus' Death in Mark: Narrative Context and Authorial Audience," *JBL* 125 (2006): 271–97; repr. in *The Trial and Death of Jesus: Essays on the Passion Narrative in Mark* (ed. Geert Van Oyen and Tom Shepherd; Leuven: Peeters, 2006), 1–31.

30. Rhoads and Michie, *Mark as Story*, 116.

31. Rhoads, Dewey, and Michie, *Mark as Story*, 115.

Authority from God" that makes plain their position under Roman overlord-ship and on "No Love of God or Neighbor" that sticks close to the phrases of the Markan text. The subsection on "Blindness of the Opponents" in the 1982 edition is revised and expanded into two sections in 1999: "Blind and Deaf," which makes plain that "[t]heir expectations about God's activity prevent the authorities from seeing that the rule of God might come outside traditional channels or in unexpected ways";[32] and "Willful Blindness," which helpfully reiterates the ancient view of multiple causes, both human and divine, that was introduced earlier. In addition, the second edition includes at this point brief reference to three exceptions to Mark's general characterization of the authorities as willfully blind, rather than mentioning these three later, along with other minor characters, thus showing that Mark challenges the stereo-typical view he presents.

The first edition subsections on "The Authorities 'Lord over' People" and "The Opponents Save Their Lives" are reordered, revised, and expanded in three subsections in the later edition: "The Authorities Save Themselves," "Fear Is at the Root of Their Actions," and "The Authorities Lord over People." The importance of fear in the actions of the authorities is made more obvious: "For Mark, what lies at the root of the authorities' quest to secure themselves is fear—fear of losing their positions with their Judean and/or Roman patrons, and thus losing face before their peers, as well as losing their power and losing their wealth.... Because they hold power at the expense of others, they possess little security and need to maintain control over them."[33] A final additional subsection concerning the authorities is particularly welcome: "The Reader and the Authorities." Although these ideas are mentioned briefly in the first edition, in the second edition the authors make fuller use of what they have surely learned (from those they have taught) about the myriad ways Mark's narrative has been and can be abused to fuel prejudice. Here they guide their readers into a more sensitive reading:

> Jesus and the authorities each claim to be acting as agents of God. The nar-rator has guided the reader to accept Jesus' claim and reject the authorities' claim—by aligning the narrator's point of view with the point of view of Jesus about the rule of God.... Nevertheless, the portrayals of authority accurately caricature the nature of power. It is not difficult for readers to put themselves in the place of the authorities and to see the self-serving reasons that they behave as they do.[34]

---

32. Ibid., 118.
33. Ibid., 121.
34. Ibid., 122.

Throughout the chapters on characters in the second edition, readers have been encouraged to reflect on different ways of conceiving "power." Not only do Rhoads and Dewey take more explicit care in their revision to consider the implied audience of Mark's story, they exhibit impressive sensitivity to the implied audience of *Mark as Story*. Their work well deserves the accolades it has received from its real audiences.

The next character group to be discussed, in both editions of *Mark as Story*, is the disciples. The second edition adds initial comments about Jesus' other followers—women and minor characters—as well as the social location of the twelve disciples. The disciples have been the focus of much Markan research, both narrative-critical and otherwise. The overview subsection, entitled "Characterization," is revised in 1999 to reflect this debate and the influence of social-scientific categories and expanding knowledge of ancient narratives: "The disciples strive to live on God's terms, leaving all to follow Jesus, clearly able to take risks. At the same time, they live 'on human terms,' preoccupied with their own security, status, and power."[35] "After their initial acceptance of Jesus' call, the disciples move from a lack of understanding to misunderstanding and finally to understanding but with an inability to follow through in action.... Such teaching by negative example is common in ancient narratives."[36] Throughout the revision process, careful attention has been given to subheadings as guides to the reader; the subheading "Loyalty" becomes "Faith, Loyalty, and Authority"; the subheading "Lack of Understanding, Lack of Faith, and Fear" is masterfully revised to become "Lack of Understanding, Fear, and Lack of Faith," with greater clarity on the interrelationship of these three: "Their fear for their well-being prevents them from understanding, and their inability to understand leaves them frightened.... Fear inhibits understanding, and misunderstanding generates fear.... Both fear and lack of understanding are rooted in the lack of trust in the rule of God."[37] The way these interrelationships are expressed in the second edition makes it all the more inviting for the reader to relate to the disciples, just as the discussion of "power" invites the reader to relate to the authorities. These generalizations hold true as well for the revision of the 1982 subsection on "Resistance to Death on the Journey" as the 1999 subsection on "Seeking Glory and Resisting Death on the Journey." Here the reader is told, "In the Markan story world, the desire for control and domination to secure one's self and one's group is tenacious.... [T]he disciples see honor as identity, power as privilege, wealth

---

35. Ibid., 123.
36. Ibid., 124.
37. Ibid., 125.

as blessing, and security as salvation."[38] This explication implicates not only
the personal dimensions of interpreting Mark's story but its political dimensions as well.

The revision process for *Mark as Story* includes contraction as well as
expansion. The first edition subsection "Fear and Misperception in Jerusalem" is presented in two subsections in the second edition, "Fear and Flight in
Jerusalem" and "The Failure of the Disciples," but overall the material is shortened. The language of the subheadings is more stark—flight, not misperception, and failure—as is the language of the commentary: "at this point of fear
and failure, the disciples disappear from the narrative."[39] As the revised material on Jesus added a subsection on "The Empty Grave," so, in reference to the
disciples, a subsection entitled "After the Resurrection" is added, although it
revises some sentences from the previous edition. Here mention is made of
the women at the empty grave who "carry on the character role of the disciples
in the plot," but, "like the disciples, the women fail—in their fear of the power
of God evident in the empty grave."[40] Explicit mention is also made of the
readers (with the flavor of Mark's aside at 13:14): "The fate of the disciples—
like that of the readers—is still open."[41] The final subsection on the disciples
in the second edition is entitled "The Reader and the Disciples" (paralleling a
similar final subsection concerning the authorities), but it is revised from the
first edition subsection entitled "Judgment and Sympathy." Here I discovered
one of the few first-edition sentences whose absence from the second edition
I count as a loss: "The story guides the reader to judge the disciples but not
to reject them."[42] This is, as Rhoads and Dewey recognize, the Markan Jesus'
response to the disciples as well. Both editions do emphasize that "[t]he narrator's characterization of the disciples leads the reader to develop ambivalent
feelings toward them."[43] Yet the second edition of *Mark as Story* is consistently
more oriented to the reader/audience pole of the narrative process than the
first edition.

The final group of characters examined in both editions of *Mark as Story*
consists of the minor characters and the crowd. In the first edition these characters were referred to as "the little people," a not particularly successful term;
in the second edition they are referred to simply as "the people," but frequently
also as the "minor characters." In the revised introductory material, the social

---

38. Ibid., 126.
39. Ibid., 127.
40. Ibid., 128.
41. Ibid.
42. Rhoads and Michie, *Mark as Story*, 129.
43. Ibid., 129; Rhoads, Dewey, and Michie, *Mark as Story*, 128.

and political connotations of "the people" as the common people are lifted up. Although most of the minor characters emerge from the crowds of common people, attention is called to the few who do not: in addition to the three exceptional Judean leaders mentioned in relation to the authorities (Jairus, "the legal expert who is not far from the rule of God," and Joseph of Arimathea), a wealthy woman who anoints Jesus and the Roman centurion. The brief "Characterization" subsection is revised to reflect Markan scholarship on the minor characters as an integrative aspect of the narrative:

> An episode in which a minor character appears is commonly interwoven with those around it by structural patterns and verbal threads. In addition, the narrator often juxtaposes a specific minor character to other characters in adjacent episodes for comparison or contrast. Also, the stories of minor characters sometimes provide important transitions or signal developments in the plot.[44]

The 1982 subsection on "Faith, Being Least, Being a Servant" in 1999 is divided into two, "Faith" and "Losing Life, Being Least, and Serving," both of which show revision, contraction, and expansion. The relationship of faith and healing in clarified: "For Mark, faith does not in itself restore the suppliant, for it is God alone who restores. However, because neither Jesus nor God forces healing, faith becomes essential as a way to release and to receive healing.... By faith, the suppliant is empowered to be a partner in the healing with God."[45] Added to the revision concerned with "Losing Life, Being Least, and Serving" is a reminder of how the minor characters relate to "power": "In general, the minor characters show no concern to be great or to exert power or to acquire wealth, concerns that would inhibit their efforts to meet another's need."[46]

The 1982 subsection on "Foils for the Disciples," is, in 1999, both considerably shortened (with one paragraph being relocated) and generalized to "Comparison and Contrast with Other Characters," including the disciples, the authorities, and Jesus. This move makes room for a new subsection on "Women," with the conclusion that "[t]he women minor characters in particular exemplify the way of discipleship amid the failure and absence of the twelve."[47] The following two subsections have slightly revised subheadings: "Continuing Discipleship" becomes "Ongoing Discipleship," and "Note on the Crowds" becomes "The Crowds." What is at stake in discussing continu-

---

44. Ibid., 130.
45. Ibid., 131.
46. Ibid.
47. Ibid., 133.

ing or ongoing discipleship is the contrast between the minor characters who act according to the "things of God" but in isolated circumstances and the disciples who, under threat of persecution, fail so to act. The second edition adds two concluding sentences that make better sense of this observation: "Everyone within the narrative fails to continue following. That role is left for the reader"[48]—and not too surprisingly this conclusion emphasizes the role of the reader or audience. The discussion of the crowds in the second edition also reiterates the failure theme: "Like the disciples and the minor characters, the crowds too fail in following Jesus."[49] The revised discussion of the minor characters closes, as did the revised discussions of the authorities and the disciples, with a new subsection focused on the reader. And here an observation I first thought was lost from the first edition is relocated and revised:

> Just as Jesus puts forth children and servanthood as models for the disciples and later summons them to notice the self-giving of the poor widow, so the narrator puts forth the minor characters for the readers to notice and to learn from—so that they will be remembered wherever the good news is proclaimed. In fact, it is only by seeing the rule of God in the characters who are "least" that the reader has fully grasped the extent to which the rule of God turns the world upside down.[50]

Both editions of *Mark as Story* follow the discussion of the authorities, disciples, and minor characters (the people) with a brief "Summary" (1982) or "Conclusion" (1999), but their tones are strikingly different, as the second edition consistently moves its focus from the characters within the story world to the readers or audience at its edge. The first edition notes that "the narrative enables the reader to see, through surprising twists and turns, just who the central characters are. Appropriately to Mark's story, the characters are led in the end to a crisis over the issue of death ... and it is in the presence of death that the characters become fully known."[51] Here ends the chapter on characters. The second edition notes that "the narrative enables the readers to see, through surprising twists and turns, just what discipleship entails. Can the reader see the rule of God breaking in through Jesus' words and actions? ... Can the reader be willing to live and die for the good news, trusting God enough to lose one's life for others? For this is what the Gospel of Mark is

---

48. Ibid., 134.
49. Ibid.
50. Ibid., 135.
51. Rhoads and Michie, *Mark as Story*, 135–36.

calling readers to do."[52] And here ends the second of two chapters on characters—not so much on the response of the characters to Jesus' death in the story world but on the response of the reader—implied? ancient? ideal? real? contemporary? One suspects "Yes!" on all counts.[53] In fact, "The Reader" comes to the fore (like the minor characters in the passion narrative) by being named as the subtitle of the revised conclusion, even though both the first and second editions of the book's "conclusion" focus on the reader. But fuller exploration of "the reader" is beyond my present focus on how characters and characterization are viewed.

The narrative criticism of the second edition of *Mark as Story* is a mature narrative criticism, focused on the narrative process from implied reader to implied audience, including the story world of settings, plot, and characters in between. It is a narrative criticism no longer concerned with adolescent issues of identity and separation from parents or relatives, that is, other critical approaches. Rather, it has learned to appreciate the complexity of interpreting the narrative world of a text embedded in an originating historical (and social and political) world and resonating in a contemporary (and social and political) world. It is ironic that I have become a redaction critic of the two editions of this book that has been so important to the development and spread of narrative criticism! But it has been an intriguing experience for me to appreciate in detail, especially with regard to the chapters on characters, how substantial and creative this revision of *Mark as Story* really is, completed by two seasoned scholars who have been in deep conversation with each other—and with numerous other narrative (and other types of) critics—for more years than the span from 1982 to 1999 might suggest. As Janice Capel Anderson notes on the back cover of the second edition, this "makes a good book even better." It also shows the capacity of narrative criticism, as an approach to biblical narratives, to renew itself, to expand and deepen in conversation with a wide variety of approaches, from reader-response criticism to social-scientific criticism, from ancient orality studies to contemporary performance criticism. Narrative criticism seeks to understand and interpret the narrative process, from implied reader to implied audience, and this includes dwelling imaginatively among the characters of the story world.

The increased focus on the role of the reader/audience in the second edition of *Mark as Story* may, of course, be seen in the broader world of New Testament scholarship, perhaps especially from 1982 to 1999. Neither time nor

---

52. Rhoads, Dewey, and Michie, *Mark as Story*, 136.

53. The conclusion to second edition of *Mark as Story* has sections on "The Ideal Reader," "Hypothetical First-Century Audiences," and "Contemporary Readers."

space—to say nothing of the limitations of my own expertise—permits me to survey the scholarly world of narrative criticism from 1982 to the present! My more modest goal is to highlight the way a sampling of works (from other books introducing narrative criticism to articles, anthologies, monographs, and commentaries) have viewed characters and characterization in illustration of the thesis that narrative criticism is best understood as active appreciation of the narrative *process*, from an implied author, through a story world of settings, plot, and characters—all rhetorically presented—to an implied audience, and the corollary that various narrative critics at various times focus on different aspects of that narrative process. The majority of the works I mention below focus on characters in relation to other characters in the Markan narrative, but others focus on characters in relation to readers (or the audience), characters in relation to performers, or characters in relation to the narrator and implied author. The full narrative process, of course, involves all of these aspects.

Characters in Relation to Characters

The first edition of *Mark as Story* was the path setter, but several other books that introduce narrative criticism soon followed. Each book devotes a chapter to characters, combining theoretical discussion with narrative interpretation and focusing on characters in relation to other characters within the story world of the narrative. I find the most useful of these other introductions to be Mark Allan Powell's *What Is Narrative Criticism?*, in the Guides to Biblical Scholarship series, which literally put narrative criticism alongside source, form, and redaction criticism on many scholars' bookshelves.[54] This compact and user-friendly guide offers chapters on "Scripture as Story," "Ways of Reading," "Story and Discourse," "Events," "Characters," "Settings," and "Story as Scripture." Powell's fifth chapter addresses "Characters," with the first half presenting theory—"A Narrative Understanding of Characters"—and the second half a "Case Study: The Religious Leaders in the Synoptic Gospels." As Powell notes, "narrative critics are interested in characterization, that is, the process through which the implied author provides the implied reader with

---

54. Mark Allan Powell, *What Is Narrative Criticism?* (GBS; Minneapolis: Fortress, 1990). See also Stephen H. Smith, *A Lion with Wings: A Narrative-Critical Approach to Mark's Gospel* (Sheffield: Sheffield Academic Press, 1996); Daniel Marguerat and Yvan Bourquin, *How to Read Bible Stories: An Introduction to Narrative Criticism* (trans. John Bowden; London: SCM, 1999); James L. Resseguie, *Narrative Criticism of the New Testament: An Introduction* (Grand Rapids: Baker, 2005).

what is necessary to reconstruct a character from the narrative."[55] The theoretical elements Powell explicates overlap with those of *Mark as Story*—telling and showing (with reference to Uspensky's spatial-temporal, phraseological, psychological, and ideological planes), evaluative point of view, and character traits (including flat or round and static or dynamic characters)—but also include an especially helpful reflection on "Empathy, Sympathy, and Antipathy." Powell distinguishes "realistic empathy" as empathy with characters who are similar to the readers (e.g., the disciples in Matthew's Gospel) from "idealistic sympathy" as empathy with "characters who represent what they would like to be" (e.g., Jesus in Matthew's Gospel).[56] Sympathy and antipathy toward characters are often created by attributing such attitudes to a character with whom the readers have experienced empathy. By their reported words, the religious leaders in the Synoptic Gospels seem polite to Jesus and Jesus seems discourteous to them, but the narrative *shows* their hypocrisy and Jesus' integrity in other ways. The evaluative point of view and the root character trait of the religious leaders are coordinated within each Synoptic Gospel and distinctive among them: in Mark, their evaluation in human terms contributes to their lack of authority; in Matthew, they are blind to revelation from God because they are "evil"; in Luke, they foolishly refuse the offer of repentance and forgiveness because they are self-righteousness. In Mark, the implied reader experiences some antipathy toward the religious leaders as a group but some sympathy for individual exceptions. In Matthew, "antipathy for the leaders is the rule."[57] In Luke, their story is one of "unfulfilled hope and unrealized possibility,"[58] and the implied reader could be expected to share Jesus' sympathy with them. In his conclusion to this chapter on characters, Powell is careful to point out that narrative criticism seeks to avoid the "referential fallacy," for example, evaluating the Gospel portraits of the religious leaders in terms of their historical accuracy, but instead evaluates the poetic or literary effect of their characterization on the implied audience. Powell illustrates how narrative criticism (like redaction criticism but with differing assumptions and conclusions) can contribute to fuller appreciation of the uniqueness of each Gospel.

Like *Mark as Story*, *What Is Narrative Criticism?* deals with characters and characterization by focusing on the categorization and interrelations of characters within the story world of the narrative, understanding the implied author and implied reader (or audience) as aspects of that narrative. Naturally,

---

55. Powell, *What Is Narrative Criticism*, 52.

56. Ibid., 56.

57. Ibid., 64.

58. Ibid., 65.

both books build on a rich array of articles and monographs that offer narrative-critical analyses of individual characters or groups of characters. Such a wealth of articles focuses on characters interacting within the story world that I cannot begin to do justice even in listing them. Thus I will take the easier path—knowing full well the biblical warnings—and mention my own work in this area.

Between 1983 and 1994, I published six articles or essays on Markan characters, exploring the women characters and other "fallible followers"; the disciples, crowds, and readers; the "Jewish leaders" (both of which terms are now recognized as problematic); the poor widow; the disciples; and the minor characters. Originally conceived as chapters of a book, these essays were gathered together and published as *In the Company of Jesus: Characters in Mark's Gospel* in 2000.[59] I had planned to add a chapter on Jesus, but that got out of hand and had to wait until later. The undercurrent in all these essays is that characters exist in relation to other characters (and, of course, in relation to settings and the plot as well). A character cannot be understood alone but only in relationship. As I wrote in the preface, "The richness of Markan characterization is in the interplay, comparisons, and contrasts *between* these characters and in their reaching out to the hearers/readers, both ancient and contemporary."[60] For example, by its complex and composite portrayal of Jesus' fallible followers (women and men, disciples and crowds), Mark's Gospel communicates to the implied audience a twofold message: anyone can be a follower; no one finds it easy. Mark's characterization of Jesus' opponents is also complex: for the most part, the "Jewish leaders" (or Judean authorities) are portrayed flatly as opponents, but there are exceptions; Mark both presents a type and challenges a stereotype. Central to all Markan characters is their response to Jesus; the minor characters extend the response continuum and build a bridge from the characters internal to the narrative to the implied audience at its border. Thus I came to realize through this research and writing that, in Mark's Gospel, minor characters can play major roles; discipleship is more significant than disciples, and characterization is more important than characters.

As the first edition of *Mark as Story* notes, Robert Tannehill's pair of articles on the disciples as characters in Mark were influential in the development of narrative criticism.[61] Markan scholars continue to be intrigued by the dis-

---

59. Elizabeth Struthers Malbon, *In the Company of Jesus: Characters in Mark's Gospel* (Louisville: Westminster John Knox, 2000). Also included is "Narrative Criticism: How Does the Story Mean?"

60. Ibid., x.

61. Robert C. Tannehill, "The Disciples in Mark: The Function of a Narrative Role," *JR*

ciples—and more recently by the connections between the Markan under-standing of discipleship and Markan christology, especially narrative christol-ogy, to use the term introduced by Tannehill. The disciples are only disciples in relation to Jesus, so the interaction of these characters becomes central. Thus, as a sample of monographs dealing with Markan characters in relation to characters, I highlight two fairly recently published dissertations concerned with the disciples in interaction with Jesus. Suzanne Watts Henderson's *Chris-tology and Discipleship in the Gospel of Mark* is "organized around a set of passages that feature the disciples as prominent players in the gospel drama" and based on the observation that "the overarching claim of God's coming kingdom lends striking unity to the gospel's relationship between Christology and discipleship from beginning to end."[62] Her study of discipleship passages in Mark 1–6 concludes with this statement: "[F]aithful discipleship can best be understood not as the correct appraisal of Jesus' Christological identity, but as the disciples' collective participation in Jesus' Christological mission."[63] In Mark's Gospel, it is not saying who Jesus is that makes one a disciple but doing what Jesus does.

To this consideration of the interaction of Jesus and the disciples, Ira Brent Driggers's book *Following God through Mark: Theological Tension in the Second Gospel* adds attention to the often-ignored Markan character God.[64] Driggers illustrates the tension between two ways in which God acts in the story. God acts "in and through Jesus, bringing the long-awaited 'reign of God' into the world," and God also acts "apart from Jesus, speaking from heaven, speaking from Scripture, and … acting directly upon other characters." Drig-gers refers to these two ways as "God's 'invasive' and 'transcendent' modes of action, respectively. Together they constitute the Gospel's primary and under-lying theological tension; and the narrative will consistently reinforce this ten-sion, though often in surprising ways."[65] By a parallel tension, both Jesus' pas-sion and the disciples' failures are doubly explained in Mark—by divine and human causes—with these various tensions ultimately leading the "believing

---

57 (1977): 386–405, repr. in *The Shape of the Gospel: New Testament Essays* (Eugene, Ore.: Cascade, 2007), 135–59; idem, "The Gospel of Mark as Narrative Christology," *Semeia* 16 (1979): 57–95, repr. in *The Shape of the Gospel*, 161–87. Tannehill's original essays are cited in Rhoads and Michie, *Mark as Story*, 154 n. 2.

62. Suzanne Watts Henderson, *Christology and Discipleship in the Gospel of Mark* (SNTSMS 135; Cambridge: Cambridge University Press, 2006), 20, 23.

63. Ibid., 241.

64. Ira Brent Driggers, *Following God through Mark: Theological Tension in the Second Gospel* (Louisville: Westminster John Knox, 2007).

65. Ibid., 2.

audience" to a discipleship of responsibility and an experience of the divine mystery. Both Henderson and Driggers find it essential to consider Markan characters (disciples) in relation to other characters (Jesus and God) in order to understand the Markan narrative.

It may be that biblical commentaries, because of their comprehensive scope, are the last scholarly genre to reflect a "new" critical movement, such as narrative criticism—after articles, monographs, anthologies, and introductory surveys. In his introductory essay to this volume, Christopher Skinner identifies Francis Moloney's *The Gospel of Mark: A Commentary* as "the first full-length exegetical commentary on the Gospel of Mark from an explicitly narrative perspective."[66] As Moloney explicates in his essay in this volume, he is especially attentive to the interaction of Jesus and the disciples in the unfolding Markan plot.

Another recent Markan commentary that attends to the Gospel as narrative is M. Eugene Boring's *Mark: A Commentary*, which adds to the focus on the characters Jesus and the disciples a focus on the character God.[67] While Boring understands Mark's Gospel as "located at the intersection of historical, literary, and theological trajectories,"[68] he opens his introduction with the literary aspects—story, structure, genre—before moving on to sources, date, provenance, and so forth. Narrative-critical categories of plot, characterization, narrator, and readers' response guide the contemporary reader through Mark's literary creation. Boring reads and interprets Mark's Gospel as "a strange story, fraught with reversal and paradox," that is obviously about Jesus, also about the disciples, but really "about God, who only rarely becomes an explicit character, but who is the hidden actor in the whole drama, whose reality spans its whole narrative world from creation to eschaton, and who is not an alternative or competitor to the view that regards Jesus as the principal subject. To tell the story of Jesus is to tell the self-defining story of God."[69]

---

66. Francis J. Moloney, *The Gospel of Mark: A Commentary* (Peabody, Mass.: Hendrickson, 2002).

67. M. Eugene Boring, *Mark: A Commentary* (NTL; Louisville: Westminster John Knox, 2006).

68. Ibid., 24.

69. Ibid., 3. Because my own work on Mark's Gospel is largely in tune with Boring's overall interpretation, I find myself in great agreement with his reading. However, based on my most recent work on Mark's characterization of Jesus as narrative christology, I am uncomfortable with Boring's occasional statements that tend to merge "Jesus" and "God" in Mark's narrative. Boring asserts, "Later Christian theology's quest for a viable theological explanation [of why it was God's will that Jesus die] is based on Mark's own dialectical perspective that 'God' and 'Jesus' are not finally separable persons" (399). Such a statement,

From the methodological introductions by Rhoads, Michie, and Dewey and Powell, to the books by Malbon, Henderson, and Driggers, to the commentaries by Moloney and Boring, we are presented a complex view of characters in relation to characters within Mark's story world. The disciples continue to be of interest, but the disciples not as analogs for some opponents in Mark's historical world but the disciples in relation to other followers, to Jesus, and to God as characters and to the implied audience.

Of course, narrative criticism, including its increasingly complex view of characters and characterization, has its critics as well as its practitioners, and critics help shape the discipline too, as the second edition of *Mark as Story* illustrates so beautifully. Early on, Stephen Moore offered a critique largely from the point of view of deconstruction in *Literary Criticism and the Gospels: The Theoretical Challenge.*[70] Petri Merenlahti presents a critique largely from the point of view of ideological criticism in *Poetics for the Gospels? Rethinking Narrative Criticism.*[71] Later, in an essay entitled "The SS Officer at the Foot of the Cross: A Tragedy in Three Acts," Moore offers a post-Holocaust, postcolonial critique on the way the centurion's statement at the foot of the cross is sometimes interpreted in narrative criticism and reflects on, in the form of a dialogue or play, the potential—and multiple—connections and tensions between Mark's implied audience and real postmodern audiences.[72] As real readers of Mark, Moore and Merenlahti remind us of the range of interpretations that this narrative has and can elicit. The implied reader is actualized in many ways, and a number of Markan scholars since the first edition of *Mark as Story* have focused on implied readers and their actualizations.

I would argue, does not do justice to the multiple levels of Markan narrative christology. See my review in *Int* 62 (2008): 440–42.

70. Stephen D. Moore, *Literary Criticism and the Gospels: The Theoretical Challenge* (New Haven: Yale University Press, 1989).

71. Petri Merenlahti, *Poetics for the Gospels? Rethinking Narrative Criticism* (Edinburgh: T&T Clark, 2002). See also the opening chapter (by Petri Merenlahti and Raimo Hakola) and closing chapter (by David Rhoads) of *Characterization in the Gospels: Reconceiving Narrative Criticism* (ed. David Rhoads and Kari Syreeni; JSNTSup 184; Sheffield: Sheffield Academic Press, 1999).

72. Stephen D. Moore, "The SS Officer at the Foot of the Cross: A Tragedy in Three Acts," in *Between Author and Audience in Mark: Narration, Characterization, Interpretation* (ed. Elizabeth Struthers Malbon; New Testament Monographs 23; Sheffield: Sheffield Phoenix, 2009), 44–61.

CHARACTERS IN RELATION TO READERS OR THE AUDIENCE

As mentioned above, between the first and second editions of *Mark as Story*, narrative criticism was greatly influenced by the development of reader-response criticism with attention to both the implied reader (within the "narrative or text" box in Chatman's diagram) and various real readers, in the ancient world and in the contemporary world (without so much attention to the long centuries between).[73] Reference to some of those interested in the implied reader (Fowler, Darr), the ancient audience (Dewey, Shiner), or the contemporary audience (Rhoads) was made above.[74] One sees reflected here the interests of the active and influential Society of Biblical Literature program unit: The Bible in Ancient and Modern Media (BAMM). In its second edition, *Mark as Story* reflects this shift toward the reader/audience pole of the narrative process, as do numerous essays and monographs, as well as anthologies and commentaries. In all these cases, characters are seen not only in relation to other characters but also—and especially—in relation to the implied audience and often to various real audiences as well. These aspects of the narrative process are only separated artificially.

CHARACTERS IN RELATION TO PERFORMERS

As biblical scholars have come not only to realize but to appreciate that Mark's first-century audiences were hearing and seeing performances of the narrative made to groups, not reading it silently and individually, performance criticism has emerged out of narrative criticism and orality studies. David Rhoads has been a pioneer in reflecting on his own performance of the Markan Gospel as a way of learning about the Markan narrative.[75] Here I wish to highlight an article by another BAMM member, Philip Ruge-Jones, that is part of a dialogue between narrative critics and performance critics, a dialogue in process about how to conceive of the narrator.

---

73. Scholars exploring reception history are interested in real readers' responses to Mark's Gospel throughout the full range of the Common Era, but that subject is beyond the scope of this essay.

74. See notes 4 and 6 above.

75. See note 6 above for Rhoads's overview of performance criticism. See also Holly E. Hearon and Philip Ruge-Jones, eds., *The Bible in Ancient and Modern Media: Story and Performance* (Eugene, Ore.: Cascade, 2009), in honor of Tom Boomershine; the special issue of *CurTM* 37 (2010), on performance criticism, in honor of David Rhoads; and the website "Biblical Performance Criticism: Orality, Memory, Translation, Rhetoric, Discourse," at http://www.biblicalperformancecriticism.org.

In "Omnipresent, Not Omniscient: How Literary Interpretation Confuses the Storyteller's Narrating," Ruge-Jones, on the basis of reflecting on an oral performance of his own, compares the different roles of narrator in performance and in literature.[76] He suggests using two terms, "narrator" for the literary narrator and "storyteller" for the performer, and lists, at the close of his article, characteristics of each. First, on the basis of my work as a narrative critic, I do not agree that all of the characteristics Ruge-Jones ascribes to the literary "narrator" actually apply. For example, I would argue that the Markan narrator from a literary-critical point of view is not omniscient (that role is reserved for God), but Ruge-Jones is correct, of course, to note that *Mark as Story* and much other scholarship do assert the Markan narrator's omniscience. But, secondly, and of more importance here, I disagree with the implication that the "storyteller" *replaces* the literary "narrator" in performance. Instead, the storyteller *frames* the literary narrator (and the implied author, characters, narratee, and implied audience as well) for a new implied and real audience. The "storyteller"—and I think "performer" would be a clearer term, at least with reference to those who present Mark's Gospel orally in the contemporary world—takes on many roles: all the characters and the narrator (as Ruge-Jones so clearly explains, they are embodied by the storyteller) but also the implied author (who assigns these roles and sets up the rhetoric), the narratee (the narrator's direct internal counterpart), and the implied audience (who must interpret the story). My undergraduate students often observe how, in their video performances, both Rhoads and Ruge-Jones take over the interpretive role they as viewers and listeners wish to have! It is possible, but difficult, to resist a live performer, even a recorded live performer—more difficult than resisting an implied author while reading silently. In fact, in taking on all these roles from the narrative, the performer (or "storyteller") becomes not the "narrator" in the narrative (inside the box of Chatman's diagram) but a performer *of* the narrative (including everything in the box: implied author, narrator, narratee, implied audience) at a meta level. In effect, the performer is most analogous to the "real author" because the performance is a new creation; the performance is *not* the Gospel of Mark but a performance of the Gospel of Mark (just as every reading is a reading of the Gospel of Mark). Of course, the performer also has an implied audience (and a real one, too), but that is the implied audience of the specific performance of the Markan narrative, not the implied audience of the so-called literary Markan narrative.

---

76. Philip Ruge-Jones, "Omnipresent, Not Omniscient: How Literary Interpretation Confuses the Storyteller's Narrating," in Malbon, *Between Author and Audience in Mark*, 29–43.

Narrative critics and performance critics are just beginning to think through these various levels.

In this article Ruge-Jones does not consider the literary distinction between the narrator and the implied author because, for the most part, narrative critics of the Gospels have ignored or blurred this distinction themselves. Yet more careful attention to this distinction does prove useful in appreciating aspects of Markan characterization of Jesus and may help narrative critics and performance critics deepen our conversation.

CHARACTERS IN RELATION TO THE NARRATOR AND IMPLIED AUTHOR

The relation of characters to the narrator and of both to the implied reader or audience has long been an interest of mine. In 1993 I co-edited with Adele Berlin *Semeia* 63: *Characterization in Biblical Literature*. We titled part 1 of that volume "Narrators/Characters/Readers."[77] In 2009 I edited another anthology of articles on characterization, with the title *Between Author and Audience in Mark: Narration/Characterization/Interpretation*. Only while working on this paper did I notice the similarity of this subtitle and the title of part 1 of the earlier anthology.

The "narrator" also takes on greater importance in the second edition of *Mark as Story*. Whereas the first chapter after the translation of Mark in the first edition is titled "The Rhetoric," although it opens with a discussion of the narrator, this entire chapter is titled "The Narrator" in the second edition. In addition, in the second edition, these two entities, the reader and the narrator, are presented as the mirror images of each other. The subsection on "Implied Reader" in the concluding chapter of the first edition of *Mark as Story* is replaced by a more elaborated subsection on "The Ideal Reader" in the concluding chapter of the second edition, where it is stated plainly that "[t]he ideal reader is the mirror image of the narrator."[78] On that same page the term "implied ideal reader" is used. So there are actually two changes: equating the ideal reader with the implied reader and paralleling the (implied) ideal reader with the narrator. Such a construction goes against the grain of the diagram that derives from Chatman, presented at the beginning of this essay, where the implied reader is the mirror image of the implied audience, and the narrator is the mirror image of the narratee. Although Rhoads and Dewey are completely in the mainstream in blurring this distinction, my work on the characteriza-

---

77. Elizabeth Struthers Malbon and Adele Berlin, eds., *Semeia* 63 (1993): *Characterization in Biblical Literature.*

78. Rhoads, Dewey, and Michie, *Mark as Story*, 138.

tion of Jesus in Mark's Gospel has made me more cautious of confusing or fusing these categories. I have become more respectful of what keeping to the theoretical model of the narrative process can help us discover about Markan ways of characterization, especially characterization of Jesus.

Although it is generally said that the point of view of the Markan Jesus and the Markan narrator are identical, I have found that they are clearly distinguishable, although not simply opposed. The narrator boldly asserts that Jesus is the Christ, the Son of God (1:1). Jesus is reticent, deflecting honor to God. Perhaps this is why it is so important that the voice (of God) confirm the narrator's point of view (1:11); the Markan Jesus hardly does so! The only two times the narrator mentions God directly it is to attribute the power of the Markan Jesus' teaching and healing to God (1:14; 2:12). Yet the Markan Jesus boldly and insistently proclaims the rule (kingdom) of God, about which the narrator speaks directly just once, and that after Jesus' death (15:43). Furthermore, the Markan Jesus makes assertions about the Son of Humanity, but the narrator is silent. There is thus a tension between the Markan narrator who wants to talk about Jesus and the Markan Jesus who wants to talk about God. In order to conceptualize this distinction between how Jesus is characterized by what the narrator (and other characters as well) say about Jesus and what the character Jesus says himself, I have come to realize how crucial it is to keep in mind that the narrator is not identical with the implied author. The implied author controls the narrator and all the characters. It is the implied author who juxtaposes the presentation of Jesus by the Markan narrator and other characters with the presentation of the Markan Jesus according to his own words and deeds as a character, and it is the Markan implied audience who has to hold the two together. The implied author is the one who allows a character, even the main character, to have a point of view distinct not only from other characters but also from the narrator—and vice versa. In the Gospel of Mark, the tension between the narrator's point of view and Jesus' point of view enables the implied author to present a Jesus whose focus is always on God, even though the narrator keeps focusing on Jesus. One could hardly present the story of Jesus without focusing on Jesus; the narrator is thus not to be blamed. But neither is the implied author to be ignored in creating the gap, the tension, between the points of view of other characters and the narrator and the point of view of the main character, Jesus. This tension between the narrator and Jesus is not a problem to be resolved, not a gap to be filled in, but the mystery that is given by the implied author to the implied audience.[79]

---

79. For the full argument, see Elizabeth Struthers Malbon, *Mark's Jesus: Characterization as Narrative Christology* (Waco, Tex.: Baylor University Press, 2009), from which this

CHARACTERS AND THE NARRATIVE PROCESS

With a focus on characters and characterization, my goal here has been primarily to highlight a sampling of works that, like both editions of *Mark as Story*, present narrative criticism as active appreciation of the narrative *process*, from an implied author, through a story world of settings, plot, and characters—all rhetorically presented—to an implied audience, and, secondarily, to show that various narrative critics at various times focus on different aspects of that narrative process.

The impact of the 1982 edition of *Mark as Story* has been memorable; it was a ground-breaking book in offering the promise of a literary appreciation of a Gospel narrative to a wider audience, including not only students and laity but also biblical scholars who had kept their distance from this "new" approach. But because the narrative criticism it introduced continued to develop alongside other approaches, the book did become dated. Few books deserve a second coming, but *Mark as Story* is surely exceptional. The second edition in 1999 is a creative updating of narrative-critical work that not only embeds fond memories for those of us who argued with and affirmed each other in the Literary Aspects of the Gospels and Acts Group from 1982 to 1999[80] but will continue to serve responsibly to introduce new real readers and real audiences to the challenge and reward of reading and hearing Mark's Gospel as story.

---

paragraph is abstracted, especially from the conclusions to chapters 3 (191) and 5 (243, 257–58). For a detailed and creative exploration of the distinction between the voice of Jesus and the voice of the narrator in Luke, see James M. Dawsey, *The Lukan Voice: Confusion and Irony in the Gospel of Luke* (Macon, Ga.: Mercer University Press, 1986). Although Dawsey does not employ the term "the implied author," he does use the term "author" in this sense: "Obviously the author was an accomplished artist who could control the language of his characters. It is also a credit to his ability as a storyteller that the author allowed his narrator and Jesus to hold different views concerning some elements of the story" (75).

80. Indeed, the official life of this Society of Biblical Literature "group" was marked by the first and second editions of *Mark as Story*.

Why There Are No Humans or Animals in the Gospel of Mark

Stephen D. Moore

We have never been human.
Donna J. Haraway, *When Species Meet*

Mark as Story is aging well.[1] It remains directly relevant for contemporary Markan scholarship—no mean feat after thirty years. What *Mark as Story* was among the first to do—read Mark as plotted narrative—is what large numbers of Markan scholars now routinely do, often in ways so smoothly complementary to redaction criticism that they do not feel the need to nod in the direction of *Mark as Story*. My aim in this essay, however, is not to muse on the comfortable familiarity of *Mark as Story* or the successive stages of its march from the margins to the mainstream of the discipline. My aim is rather to defamiliarize it by expanding the context in which we usually read it. The resulting argument may be adumbrated as follows:

- ▶ *Mark as Story*'s signal strategy is the reading of Mark as *short story*.

- ▶ The modern short story is a by-product of the modern novel, the modern literary genre par excellence.

- ▶ The concept of literary character that comes to expression in the modern novel, and by extension the short story, is the literary corollary of the recentering of European philosophy on the subjective experience of the individual human being, a reorientation inaugurated by Descartes.

---

1. David Rhoads and Donald Michie, *Mark as Story: An Introduction to the Narrative of a Gospel* (Philadelphia: Fortress, 1982; 2nd ed. 1999, with Joanna Dewey). For purposes of this essay, I focus primarily on the first edition as the one that was formative for narrative criticism.

▶ This elevation of human subjectivity was attained by reconceiving human-animal relations in absolutely oppositional terms, a reconception that has been massively determinative of human dealings with the nonhuman world down to the present.

▶ The modern novel with its signature concept of character played a crucial ancillary role in the construction of this reimagined (nonanimal) human.

▶ Through its incorporation of this same concept of character, *Mark as Story* becomes the unwitting vehicle of a problematic ideology of human-animal relations, one that stands in marked tension with David Rhoads's ecological work on the New Testament, so that it now becomes necessary to read with Rhoads against Rhoads et al. in order to construe the topic of character in Mark differently.[2]

Mark as Short Story

Mark as Story might have been titled more precisely *Mark as Short Story*. David Rhoads begins his preface to the first edition as follows: "Five years ago I asked Don Michie, a friend from the Department of English, to show my students of New Testament Introduction how to read one of the gospels as one would read a short story."[3] Rhoads and Michie are explicit that the methods employed in their book are precisely those "developed primarily in the study of modern novels and short stories"[4]—therein lies the book's originality, indeed. In its final endnote, the reader is directed to "a fascinating collection of contemporary short stories on themes which parallel the Gospel of Mark."[5] More specifically, Rhoads and Michie attempt to assimilate Mark to the short-story genre by dispensing with chapter and verse numbers both in the translation of the entire Gospel provided at the beginning of the book

---

2. I am indebted to Scott S. Elliott for drawing my attention to character as a problem in *Mark as Story* and narrative criticism generally; see his "'The Son of Man Goes as It Is Written of Him': The Figuration of Jesus in the Gospel of Mark" (Ph.D. diss., Drew University, 2009), forthcoming as *Reconfiguring Mark's Jesus: Narrative Criticism after Poststructuralism* (Sheffield: Sheffield Phoenix, 2011). I am pursuing a different but related consideration of that problem in this essay. Elliott has recourse to poststructuralist narratology for his analysis, while I have recourse to the theory of the novel and the emerging field of posthuman animality studies.

3. Rhoads and Michie, *Mark as Story*, xv.

4. Ibid., 2.

5. Ibid., 159 n. 10.

and in references to the Gospel throughout the book. In their introduction to the translation they write: "The translation which follows is set out like a short story so that the reader may experience the story as a whole. There are no chapter or verse designations."[6] Coincidentally but conveniently, Mark's length of approximately eleven thousand words puts it comfortably within the length parameters of the modern short story: "anything between five hundred and fifteen thousand words."[7]

Beyond that, what is a short story? Rhoads and Michie offer no definition of the genre, but one of the first works of literary criticism that they cite, M. H. Abrams's classic *A Glossary of Literary Terms*, offers a lengthy one.[8] Abrams's point of departure is the common ground shared by the short story and the novel:

> A short story is a work of prose fiction, and most of the terms for analyzing the component elements, the types, and the various techniques of the *novel* are applicable to the short story as well.... As in the novel, the plot form may be comic, tragic, romantic, or satiric; the story is presented to us from one of many available points of view; and it may be written in the mode of fantasy, realism, or naturalism.[9]

Such an understanding of the short story, however, only takes us so far down the historical stream. Beginning in the late nineteenth century, the short story gradually ceased to be seen as a "condensed novel" and came to be seen instead as capable of certain artistic, frequently subtle effects unattainable by the more unwieldy novel.[10]

Such refinements, however, need not concern us here. Rhoads and Michie consistently conflate the novel and short-story genres. Each chapter of their book begins by naming novels and, occasionally, short stories that use the specific narrative device they are about to investigate in Mark. *Huckleberry Finn, The Catcher in the Rye*, the short stories of Ernest Hemingway, and *War and Peace* are adduced to introduce the different kinds of narrators;[11] Mark's practice of citing scripture is juxtaposed with Seymour's practice in J. D. Salin-

---

6. Ibid., 6.

7. Martin Scofield, *The Cambridge Introduction to the American Short Story* (Cambridge: Cambridge University Press, 2006), 4.

8. M. H. Abrams, *A Glossary of Literary Terms* (5th ed.; New York: Holt, Rinehart & Winston, 1988), 172–74.

9. Ibid., 172, emphasis original.

10. See Adrian Hunter, *The Cambridge Introduction to the Short Story in English* (Cambridge: Cambridge University Press, 2007), 1–4. The expression "condensed novel" is his.

11. Rhoads and Michie, *Mark as Story*, 35–36.

ger's *Franny and Zooey* of listing religious and philosophical quotations on the back of his bedroom door;[12] the chapter on Markan settings begins by reminding us of the significance of the sea in *Moby Dick*, "the path to the town in Eudora Welty's 'A Worn Path,' and the wilderness in Jack London's novels";[13] while the chapter on Markan plot begins by referring us to the role of conflict in such works as William Faulkner's *The Sound and the Fury*, Nathaniel Hawthorne's "Young Goodman Brown," Ernest Hemingway's *The Old Man and the Sea*, Bernard Malamud's *The Assistant*, and Ralph Ellison's *The Invisible Man*.[14] "Mark's gospel was probably written to be heard rather than read," Rhoads and Michie observe. "It would, therefore, be appropriate to refer to the hearers of the drama. We have chosen, however, to deal with the gospel as literature and to discuss its readers."[15] More precisely, and in contrast to other scholars who assimilate Mark to the ancient novel, Rhoads and Michie assimilate Mark to the modern novel, the short story being for them a condensed novel. But what is the modern novel?

INVENTING THE INDIVIDUAL

A vigorous theorization of the novel has long been underway in literary studies. Central to this theorization has been the argument that the novel, as the quintessential modern literary genre, was partly instrumental in the formation of modernity itself, specifically the construction of modern subjectivity.[16] That thesis came to classic expression in Ian Watt's *The Rise of the Novel*, a work whose main lines of argument continue to command widespread assent.[17] Watt's signal move was to propose and elaborate intimate affiliations

---

12. Ibid., 58.

13. Ibid., 63.

14. Ibid., 73.

15. Ibid., 143 n. 1.

16. Cf. Michael McKeon, "Introduction," in *Theory of the Novel: A Historical Approach* (ed. Michael McKeon; Baltimore: Johns Hopkins University Press, 2000), xv.

17. Ian Watt, *The Rise of the Novel: Studies in Defoe, Richardson and Fielding* (London: Chatto & Windus, 1957). Michael McKeon's *The Origins of the English Novel, 1600–1740* (Baltimore: Johns Hopkins University Press, 1987) works largely within the parameters set by Watt. Nancy Armstrong's *Desire and Domestic Fiction: A Political History of the Novel* (Oxford: Oxford University Press, 1987) likewise accepts Watt's thesis that "written representations of the self allowed the modern individual to become an economic and psychological reality" (8) but argues that this "modern individual was first and foremost a woman" (8), as the majority of eighteenth- and nineteenth-century novelists were female. Armstrong's *How Novels Think: The Limits of Individualism from 1719 to 1900* (New York: Columbia University Press, 2005) further develops the position that the formation and

between early modern philosophy's preoccupation with individual subjectivity, epitomized by Descartes's *Cogito ergo sum*, and the early modern novel's preoccupation with individual subjectivity, epitomized by the inner lives of these novels' central characters. For Watt, the early modern novel was the literary innovation that best reflected the individualist reorientation of human subjectivity that was programmatic for Descartes and his philosophical successors. Philosophers and novelists alike now accorded "greater attention to the particular individual than had been common before," resulting in major innovations in prose fiction.[18] The plot now "had to be acted out by particular people in particular circumstances, rather than, as had been common in the past, by general human types against a background primarily determined by the appropriate literary convention."[19]

Watt insists, however, that he is not arguing for crude causal effect. The analogies he adduces do not

> depend in any way on the presumption that the realist tradition in philosophy was a cause of the realism of the novel. That there was some influence is very likely, especially through Locke, whose thought everywhere pervades the eighteenth-century climate of opinion. But if a causal relationship of any importance exists it is probably much less direct: both the philosophical and the literary innovations must be seen as parallel manifestations of larger change—that vast transformation of Western civilization since the Renaissance which has replaced the unified world picture of the Middle Ages with another very different one—one which presents us, essentially, with a developing but unplanned aggregate of particular individuals having particular experiences at particular times and at particular places.[20]

Early modern philosophy itself, then, is an effect of still larger forces. As McKeon phrases it, "[t]he philosophical, the novelistic, and the socioeco-

---

history of the novel is indissociable from the formation and history of the modern individual. The anti-Watt position has been sounded more forcefully by Margaret Anne Doody, *The True Story of the Novel* (New Brunswick, N.J.: Rutgers University Press, 1996), and, most recently, by Steven Moore, *The Novel: An Alternative History. Beginnings to 1600* (New York: Continuum, 2010). Doody and Moore both argue the essential continuity of premodern (even ancient) and modern prose fiction—which, as it happens, is also the enabling assumption of *Mark as Story*.

18. Watt, *The Rise of the Novel*, 18.

19. Ibid., 15. Cf. Mikhail Bakhtin, *The Dialogic Imagination: Four Essays* (ed. Michael Holquist; trans. Caryl Emerson and Michael Holquist; Austin: University of Texas Press, 1981), 110: "the ancient world did not succeed in generating forms and unities that were adequate to the private individual and his life."

20. Watt, *The Rise of the Novel*, 31.

nomic are united during this period in their validation of individual experience, of one or another sort of 'individualism,' which is manifested in the
realm of the social by a number of inseparable phenomena," notably, the con-
solidation of capitalism as economic individualism and the dissemination of a
secularized Protestantism as religious individualism.[21]

TESTING CHARACTER

These considerations prompt a fresh look at the theory of character that
informs *Mark as Story*. Rhoads and Michie draw their theory of character
primarily from E. M. Forster's *Aspects of the Novel*.[22] As we shall see, however,
Forster channels and further refines the modern concept of literary character
excavated by Watt and his successors.

"We may divide characters into flat and round," Forster famously pro-
nounces.[23] Flat characters "[i]n their purest form ... are constructed around a
single idea or quality: when there is more than one factor in them we get the
beginning of the curve towards the round."[24] Forster declines to provide a corresponding definition of "round," preferring to engage in extensive discussion
of numerous novelistic characters as flat or round types.[25] He ends: "As for the
round characters proper, they have already been defined by implication and
no more need be said."[26] But he adds an afterthought: "The test of a round
character is whether it is capable of surprising in a convincing way.... It has
the incalculability of life about it—life within the pages of a book."[27]

Forster's flat/round distinction is fundamental to Rhoads and Michie's
chapter, "The Characters." Mark's Jesus "is a 'round' character," they write,
"not in the sense of having conflicting or changing traits, but because those
traits are many and varied, creating a rich characterization."[28] The authorities,
in contrast, "are 'flat' characters with a few consistent traits, traits which are
in direct contrast to the values of the rule of God."[29] While Jesus is "unpre-

---

21. McKeon, *The Origins of the English Novel*, 2.
22. E. M. Forster, *Aspects of the Novel* (London: Arnold, 1927), a series of engaging
lectures that Forster, himself a accomplished novelist, delivered at Trinity College, Cambridge, in the spring of 1927.
23. Ibid., 67.
24. Ibid.
25. Ibid., 67–78.
26. Ibid., 78.
27. Ibid.
28. Rhoads and Michie, *Mark as Story*, 104.
29. Ibid., 117.

dictable" and has "a mysterious quality about [him]"[30]—thus passing Forster's test of a round character—"[t]he behavior of the opponents is consistent and predictable."[31] Like Jesus, however, "[t]he disciples are 'round' characters," although on different grounds: "they have conflicting traits."[32] The minor characters, finally, such as the leper, Jairus, the Syrophoenician woman, the poor widow, or Joseph of Arimathea, "are 'flat' characters with several consistent traits which they share in common."[33]

Following their initial introduction of the round/flat distinction, Rhoads and Michie explicitly declare Mark's differences from the modern novel—but then proceed to assimilate Mark implicitly to the modern novel.[34] "In modern novels, characters are often dynamic, changing and developing with a consonant transformation of personal traits. In Mark's story, the characters reflect some but not a great deal of change and development."[35] Nevertheless, "[e]vents and conflicts bring out the traits and *true selves* of the [Markan] characters. As the plot develops and moves to a climax, the major characters are shown fully for *who they are* in the face of death."[36] And who they are, implicitly, are "real people": "we recall Hamlet and Huck Finn as we recall real people, not just as elements in a plot. Thus, we can analyze not only what characters 'do,' but also who they 'are,' treating them as autonomous beings and assessing them as we assess real people."[37] Similarly, "the reader reconstructs what kind of 'persons' [Mark's] characters are in the same way that we evaluate people."[38]

---

30. Ibid., 107; cf. 104.

31. Ibid., 118.

32. Ibid., 123.

33. Ibid., 130.

34. Ibid., 102–3.

35. Ibid., 103. Further on ancient characterization, see Mary Ann Tolbert, *Sowing the Gospel: Mark's World in Literary-Historical Perspective* (Minneapolis: Fortress, 1989), 76–78; Fred W. Burnett, "Characterization and the Reader Construction of Characters in the Gospels," *Semeia* 63 (1993): 1–28 *passim*; Elizabeth Struthers Malbon, *In the Company of Jesus: Characters in Mark's Gospel* (Louisville: Westminster John Knox, 2000), 160–61; Whitney Shiner, *Proclaiming the Gospel: First-Century Performance of Mark* (Harrisburg, Pa.: Trinity Press International, 2003), 90–92.

36. Rhoads and Michie, *Mark as Story*, 103, emphasis added. Even the minor characters are made "*personal* and memorable to the reader" and "achieve their *full identity* in acts of service" (133, emphasis added).

37. Ibid., 101.

38. Ibid., 102. Compare Forster in *Aspects of the Novel*, who titles his two chapters on character(s) not "The Characters," as one might expect, given his other chapter titles ("The Story," "The Plot," etc.), but rather "People" and "People (*Continued*)."

Work such as that of Ian Watt, Nancy Armstrong, or Michael McKeon, however,[39] raises fundamental questions as to whether any of the characters that we encounter in premodern narrative can be assimilated to "real people" or "true selves" in the modern mold.[40] McKeon summarizes his own argument as follows (and in terms that would feel comfortably familiar to many biblical scholars):

> Before the modern period, the category of "personal identity" itself lacks the substance it has for us because people tend to conceive of themselves less as individual persons who join together to make social wholes than as components of social wholes that are already given. Character is primarily a fact of kinship, family, clan, tribe, lineage. Components of character that don't appear to us strictly a function of kinship are, in traditional cultures, either implied by kin group (like "race," or "political" or "religious" affiliation) or deeply embedded (like physical appearance or sex) within that determinant social matrix.[41]

"Personal identity" is what we moderns demand in our literary characters, not least when the character is Jesus. This demand helps to explain why *Mark as Story* has been assimilated into the mainstream of the discipline,[42]

---

39. See n. 17 above.

40. Petri Merenlahti also examines this problem in detail, although not with reference to the origins of the modern novel. See his "Characters in the Making: Individuality and Ideology in the Gospels," in *Characterization in the Gospels: Reconceiving Narrative Criticism* (ed. David Rhoads and Kari Syreeni; JSNTSup 184; Sheffield: Sheffield Academic, 1999), 49–72. Elliott's critique of the narrative-critical construal of character is more sweeping. He outlines his agenda as follows: "dislodging the notions of 'unity' and 'coherence' (i.e., with respect to both the narrative and its individual components, such as characters), jettisoning categorizations of characters as 'flat' and 'round,' dispensing with any projection of interiority, and unsettling the dichotomy of story and discourse" ("The Son of Man Goes," xiii).

41. McKeon, *The Origins of the English Novel*, xxv–xxvi. Merenlahti notes that the biblical form critics were "quite emphatic" that the Evangelists "exclude[d] any particular interest in the individual and the personal" ("Characters in the Making," 52). Richard A. Horsley contests the assumption that Mark can be assimilated to a modern Western model of individual Christian discipleship; see his *Hearing the Whole Story: The Politics of Plot in Mark's Gospel* (Louisville: Westminster John Knox, 2001), esp. 82–86.

42. As a striking illustration of such assimilation, consider John R. Donahue and Daniel J. Harrington, *The Gospel of Mark* (SP 2; Collegeville, Minn.: Liturgical Press, 2002), a commentary by two seasoned New Testament scholars, neither of whom would describe himself primarily as a narrative critic or literary critic, but who view the narrative criticism exemplified by *Mark as Story* as an extremely useful addition to their methodological repertoire (see esp. 20–22).

notwithstanding the fact that *Mark as Story's* methodology is often anachronistic ("Here's a narrative device common in modern novels and short stories;
now let's see how it operates in Mark"), and anachronism is the great bugbear
of critical biblical scholarship. Even when narrative criticism subsequent to
Mark as Story quietly drops the explicit appeal to modern novels or short
stories,[43] the implicit appeal to a concept of personal identity in the treatment
of Gospel characters remains.[44] Forster's influential term "round character"
is, in effect, reserved for literary characters who exhibit personal identity.
The modern ideology of personal identity that informs Rhoads and Michie's
analysis of Markan characters, most of all the character of Jesus, comes to
succinct expression in Forster's insistence that "[i]t is only round people who
are fit to perform tragically for any length of time and can move us to any
feelings except humour and appropriateness."[45] Above all, it is only a round
Jesus who is fit to perform the lead role in the narratives deemed foundational
for modern Christian identity. The precise ways in which Rhoads and Michie
equip the Markan Jesus to rise to that role are detailed below. But first a final
important element needs to be added to our interpretive lens.

INVENTING THE HUMAN

The Cartesian elevation of individual subjectivity was obtained by reconceiving the relations between human and nonhuman animals in terms that were
absolutely oppositional and hierarchical. But the term "animal(s)" is perhaps
not the best one in this context. Prior to the Cartesian revolution in philosophy, there were no "animals" in the modern sense. There were "creatures,"
"beasts," and "living things," an arrangement reflected in, and reinforced by,
the early vernacular Bibles. As Laurie Shannon notes, "*animal* never appears
in the benchmark English of the Great Bible (1539), the Geneva Bible (1560),

---

43. R. Alan Culpepper's *Anatomy of the Fourth Gospel: A Study in Literary Design*
(Philadelphia: Fortress, 1983), the other iconic text of narrative criticism, is already more
guarded than *Mark as Story* in its appeal to the modern novel, although Culpepper, too,
maximizes the formal continuities between ancient and modern literary narrative (see
esp. 8–9). Mark W. G. Stibbe, however, while identifying as a narrative critic, takes even
Culpepper severely to task for his "anachronistic" reliance on critical methods developed
from the study of the modern novel (*John as Storyteller: Narrative Criticism and the Fourth
Gospel* [Cambridge: Cambridge University Press, 1992], 10–11, 22).

44. An appeal not limited to narrative criticism. Elliott notes: "modern, Western con-
ceptualizations of the self pervade New Testament studies, and fundamentally unite seemingly disparate approaches, especially with respect to characters" ("The Son of Man Goes,"
10).

45. Forster, *Aspects of the Novel*, 73.

or the King James Version (1611)."[46] Moreover, the continuum evoked by a term such as "creature" also included angels and demons, so that premodern humans were part of a complex, multilayered cosmology. Missing was "the fundamentally modern sense of the animal or animals as humanity's persistent, solitary opposite."[47] Descartes was the creator of the animal in the peculiarly modern sense of the term. What Descartes did was cull the human creature, now conceived as the only creature "equipped with a rational soul, from the entire spectrum of creatures," all others being consigned to "the mechanistic limits of purely instinctual behavior."[48] This radical reconception of the nonhuman animal was subsequently termed the *bête-machine* ("beast-machine") doctrine for its equation of animals with clocks and other machines with automatic moving parts.[49]

Shannon's article was one of fourteen on human-animal relations that appeared in the March 2009 issue of *Publications of the Modern Language Association*, the flagship journal of the Modern Language Association. "Why Animals Now?" is the title of the first article in the collection.[50] The answer is twofold, it would seem. These articles are but one product of an emerging subfield that parades under different names—"animal studies," "animality studies," "posthuman animality studies"—and intersects with the larger field of ecocriticism in literary studies, being in part a recent inflection of that ever

46. Laurie Shannon, "The Eight Animals in Shakespeare; or, Before the Human," *PMLA* 124 (2009): 476. Her title refers to the fact that the term "animal" occurs only eight times in Shakespeare's oeuvre, while the terms "beast" and "creature" occur hundreds of times. "As the *OED* confirms, *animal* hardly appears in English before the end of the sixteenth century" (474).

47. Ibid. Donna Haraway pointedly uses the term "critters" for both human and nonhuman animals. She writes: "Critters are always relationally entangled rather than taxonomically neat" (*When Species Meet* [Posthumanities; Minneapolis: University of Minnesota Press, 2007], 330 n. 33).

48. Shannon, "The Eight Animals in Shakespeare," 476. Descartes was, however, intervening in a debate on animal rationality that extended back to the pre-Socratic Greek philosophers. For a summary of the ancient debate and the contributions of Aristotle in particular, see Janet E. Spittler, *Animals in the Apocryphal Acts of the Apostles: The Wild Kingdom of Early Christian Literature* (WUNT 2/247; Tübingen: Mohr Siebeck, 2008), 15–26.

49. For the doctrine, see René Descartes, *A Discourse on the Method* (trans. Ian Maclean; Oxford World's Classics; Oxford: Oxford University Press, 2006 [French orig. 1637]), 35–49; idem, *Philosophical Essays and Correspondence* (ed. Roger Ariew; trans. Roger Ariew et al.; Indianapolis: Hackett, 2000), 275–76, 292–96 (two letters from 1646 and 1649, respectively).

50. Marianne DeKoven, "Guest Column: Why Animals Now?" *PMLA* 124 (2009): 361–69.

more important field. The second answer is more specific. Human-animal relations have become a locus of intense intellectual energy in the humanities because certain major theorists and philosophers have been writing on them. The most influential of these writings has been Jacques Derrida's "The Animal That Therefore I Am" and the posthumously published book of the same name.[51] Derrida's title is a riposte to Descartes's "I think, therefore I am"—"a summons issued to Descartes," as he himself puts it.[52]

In "Animal Studies and the Deconstruction of Character," a further article in the *PMLA* animal-studies issue, Bruce Boehrer reflects on the relations between Cartesian human/animal dualism and the concept of character that defines the modern novel. He argues that Cartesian subjectivity can itself be regarded as "a new notion of character: not an Aristotelian taxonomy of shared attributes, but rather a sense of personal identity as singular," an identity founded on the privileging of interiority over exteriority.[53] Essentially, it is this same notion of character that is refined and celebrated in the modern novel. Implicit in this literary concept of character, therefore, is the Cartesian concept of human-animal disjunction (and this is where Boehrer pushes beyond Watt, to whom he had nodded earlier in his article). Descartes's *Discourse on the Method* is

> almost equally famous for two distinct philosophical postulates: the cogito and the *bête-machine*. These principles emerge hand in hoof from Descartes's meditations, in symbiotic and mutually reinforcing relation: the former crafts

---

51. Jacques Derrida, "The Animal That Therefore I Am (More to Follow)," trans. David Wills, *Critical Inquiry* 28 (2002): 369–418; idem, *The Animal That Therefore I Am* (ed. Marie-Louise Mallet; trans. David Wills; New York: Fordham University Press, 2008). See also vol. 1 of his *The Beast and the Sovereign* (trans. Geoffrey Bennington; Seminars of Jacques Derrida 1; Chicago: University of Chicago Press, 2009). The work of Donna Haraway has also been highly influential; see her *Primate Visions: Gender, Race, and Nature in the World of Modern Science* (New York: Routledge, 1990); idem, *The Companion Species Manifesto: Dogs, People, and Significant Otherness* (Chicago: Prickly Paradigm, 2003); idem, *When Species Meet*. For an excellent introduction to animal studies, see Cary Wolfe, "Human, All Too Human: 'Animal Studies' and the Humanities," *PMLA* 124 (2009): 564–75, and for an even bigger picture, his *What Is Posthumanism?* (Posthumanities; Minneapolis: University of Minnesota Press, 2009). Independent of this trajectory but valuable for any study of animals in New Testament texts is Ingvild Saelid Gilhus, *Animals, Gods and Humans: Changing Attitudes to Animals in Greek, Roman and Early Christian Ideas* (New York: Routledge, 2006), esp. 161–82. See also Robert M. Grant, *Early Christians and Animals* (New York: Routledge, 1999); Spittler, *Animals in the Apocryphal Acts of the Apostles*.

52. Derrida, *The Animal That Therefore I Am*, 75.

53. Bruce Boehrer, "Animal Studies and the Deconstruction of Character," *PMLA* 124 (2009): 546.

a notion of humanity composed of inwardness and speculation, while the
latter denies such qualities to the nonhuman.... In the process, Descartes's
principles also paved the way for new literary techniques of representing the
human, techniques that in turn proved essential in consolidating the species
distinction on which they themselves were based.[54]

The concept of literary character that permeates the modern novel, and
by extension the short story, is the same concept that informs *Mark as Story*'s
treatment of character, as we saw earlier. Yet I have no desire to tar *Mark as
Story* gleefully with the brush that Boehrer uses on the modern novel. One
reason I admire David Rhoads both as a person and a scholar is that he has
long been committed to producing ethically accountable and socially engaged
scholarship.[55] More specifically in relation to the problems we have been
considering, he was producing ecologically responsible scholarship as early
as 1997.[56] Yet, as Boehrer observes, "if a given philosophical category (the
human) proves defective, it follows that the category's major literary manifestation (character) should share in its inadequacies."[57] A more critical appraisal
of *Mark as Story*'s chapter "The Characters" is therefore in order.

ROUND IS TO FLAT AS HUMAN IS TO ANIMAL

Once again, E. M. Forster's *Aspects of the Novel* provides the most illuminating frame for *Mark as Story*'s portrayal of character, for at least one animal has
strayed into Forster's book and sits at the center of one of its most revealing
scenes. Following an extended discussion of "flat" characters in an assortment
of modern novels, Forster declares:

> So now let us desert these two-dimensional people, and by way of transition
> to the round, let us go to [Jane Austen's] *Mansfield Park*, and look at Lady
> Bertram, sitting on her sofa with pug.[58] Pug is flat, like most animals in fic-
> tion. He is once represented as straying into a rose-bed in a cardboard kind

54. Ibid.

55. See, e.g., certain of the essays in his *Reading Mark, Engaging the Gospel* (Minneapolis: Fortress, 2004) and his edited volume, *From Every People and Nation: The Book of
Revelation in Intercultural Perspective* (Minneapolis: Fortress, 2005).

56. See David Rhoads, "Reading the New Testament in an Environmental Age," *CurTM*
24 (1997): 259–66, which subsequently grew into his "Who Will Speak for the Sparrow?
Eco-Justice Criticism of the New Testament," in *Literary Encounters with the Reign of God*
(ed. Sharon H. Ringe and H. C. Paul Kim; New York: T&T Clark, 2004), 64–86.

57. Boehrer, "Animal Studies and the Deconstruction of Character," 543.

58. Forster is following Austen's own practice of using lowercase for "pug" even when

of way, but that is all, and during most of the book his mistress seems to be cut out of the same simple material as her dog,[59]

although she is "capable of extending into a round [character] when the action require[s] it."[60] Not so poor Pug, her canine companion, who is ever doomed to be flat as cardboard, even when having adventures in the rose bed. In this telling scene, the animal becomes the model and measure of the flat character. Forster's view of what this and every other animal as literary character lacks is thoroughly Cartesian. What Descartes asserted about animals, in effect, is that they do not experience thought, in the human sense of the term. They lack interiority and as such are mere automatons, clockwork creatures. What Forster asserts of literary animals is that they lack "psychology,"[61] and without psychology, interiority, the capacity for individual thought and hence for individuality itself, literary animals are limited to being "four-legged tables moving" or "painted scraps of paper that fly."[62] Forster's enormously influential theory of literary character thus reduces to a rather simple homology: round is to flat as human is to animal.

How does this homology play out in Rhoads and Michie's round/flat reading of Markan characters? As the roundest character in Mark, Jesus is also the model and measure of the human in Mark. Other characters attain to roundness—complexity, interiority, unpredictability, full humanity—on the basis of their respective closeness to or distance from Jesus.[63] As the characters who, however problematically, are closest to Jesus, the disciples partake of his roundness.[64] As the characters who are furthest from Jesus, the group Rhoads and Michie term "the authorities" are also the flattest characters—characters possessed only of "consistent" and "predictable" traits.[65] Relative to Jesus, they are automatons: Rhoads and Michie tell us as much. Relative to Jesus, they are animals: Rhoads and Michie imply as much. For instance, the authorities are incapable of a fully human relationship to death: "They do

---

it functions as a proper name, although she sometimes switches to uppercase in such instances.

59. Forster, *Aspects of the Novel*, 73.

60. Ibid., 134.

61. Ibid., 43. The assertion occurs in another intriguing passage that would also merit close consideration in a different context.

62. Ibid.

63. Cf. Culpepper, *Anatomy of the Fourth Gospel*, 104: "In John's narrative world the individuality of all the characters except Jesus is determined by their encounter with Jesus."

64. Rhoads and Michie, *Mark as Story*, 123.

65. Ibid., 117.

not realize that death is in any way redemptive."[66] Compare Derrida on Heidegger, encapsulating the latter's hyper-Cartesian notion of the animal: "the animal … is held to be incapable of an authentic relation to death."[67] As for the minor characters, they extend toward the round at times, like Lady Bertram, but most often, on Rhoads and Michie's reading, they seem "to be cut out of the same simple material as her dog," as Forster unkindly says of her.[68] Rhoads and Michie consistently use infantilizing language for the minor characters; they are not fully developed, it is implied, either as characters or as human beings. Rhoads and Michie idiosyncratically interpret Mark 9:42, "If any of you put a stumbling block before one of these little ones [*tōn mikrōn toutōn*, τῶν μικρῶν τούτων] who believe in me," as extending to all the minor characters in Mark.[69] Their section on these characters is titled "The Little People."[70] In keeping with this label, the minor characters are said to possess "a childlike, often persistent, faith" and "childlike humility."[71] In their aptitude for loyal service, however, they resemble worker animals more than children; they have "a capacity for sacrificial service"[72] and "achieve their full identity in acts of service."[73] Rhoads and Michie's analysis of any of the three character groups that they single out—the disciples, the authorities, the "little people"—would reward detailed investigation in relation to the round/flat, human/animal hierarchies, but it is their treatment of the character Jesus that merits particular attention.

Jesus is the roundest character in Mark, on Rhoads and Michie's reading, implicitly because he is the character who most fully possesses the complex interiority that Cartesian modernity preconditions us to construe as the definitive trait of human subjectivity. Rhoads and Michie state at the outset of their thirteen-page analysis of Jesus' character: "What Jesus *says* discloses his understanding of himself and his purposes."[74] A modern novel would typically excavate—or, rather, create—that interior understanding by means of extended "inside views" into the protagonist's inmost thought pro-

---

66. Ibid., 122.

67. Derrida, *The Animal That Therefore I Am*, 129; cf. idem, *The Beast and the Sovereign*, 307–8, 322.

68. Forster, *Aspects of the Novel*, 73.

69. Rhoads and Michie, *Mark as Story*, 130.

70. This designation drops away in the second edition, the section being retitled "The People" (Rhoads, Dewey, and Michie, *Mark as Story*, 129).

71. Rhoads and Michie, *Mark as Story*, 130. The term "minor," of course, can itself mean "child," one who has not reached full legal age.

72. Ibid.

73. Ibid., 133.

74. Ibid., 103, emphasis original.

cesses. As Mark, in common with premodern literary narrative in general, only provides relatively "shallow" inside views and even those infrequently, it is left to Rhoads and Michie themselves to open up—or, more accurately, to construct—this rich inner domain. This they accomplish skillfully, mainly through the application to Jesus of adjectives suggestive of a deep inner life. Few of these descriptors would raise eyebrows among critical scholars of Mark; many of them typically occur in the plot-paraphrases common in contemporary critical commentaries on Mark. But one would be hard pressed to find parallels for most of these descriptors in ancient or medieval commentaries on Mark or the other Gospels. They are descriptors that subtly assimilate the Markan Jesus to the character conventions of the modern novel and short story.

Rhoads and Michie's Jesus displays "integrity in living up to his values and commitments."[75] He is "enigmatic," "mysterious," and "unpredictable."[76] "Even among those who favor him, no category of their thinking is adequate to explain Jesus."[77] This does not prevent Rhoads and Michie themselves from repeatedly opening windows on Jesus' psyche. For example, "[e]verything he does and says seems to issue from a conviction that through him 'the rule of God has come near.'"[78] He "is single-minded in his efforts."[79] He "does not expect to gain personally from healing."[80] And so on. Rhoads and Michie's Jesus is most deeply human, however, when confronted with his own limitations. "Sometimes he has perceptive insights about the thoughts or intentions of other characters, although generally the narrator depicts him as not knowing what other characters are thinking or what they will do."[81] "Jesus knows or discovers [the] limits" of his own authority; "he discovers that he has no authority to impose himself on others."[82] "Jesus struggles with these limitations at many points because they leave him frustrated and vulnerable."[83]

Rhoads and Michie's Jesus is an organically evolving character. "Jesus' whole character, in a sense, evolves from [the] formative experience [of his baptism]."[84] "The narrator shows Jesus' character developing" and "gradually

---

75. Ibid.; cf. ibid., 104, 108.
76. Ibid., 103–4; cf. 107.
77. Ibid., 107.
78. Ibid., 105.
79. Ibid.
80. Ibid., 110.
81. Ibid., 106.
82. Ibid., 107.
83. Ibid.
84. Ibid., 105.

reveals Jesus to the reader."[85] In consequence, the reader must "expand and shift [his or her] understanding of Jesus."[86] As much as anything else, *Mark as Story* is the story of Jesus' attainment of full interiority. "At the opening of the story, Jesus—a man of action—powerfully impinges on the world around him. At the end of the story, the focus shifts to what befalls him, to what Jesus endures."[87] In and through his personal crisis, "the full meaning of Jesus' identity" is disclosed to the reader.[88] "[E]ven though Jesus chooses to die in obedience to God, he experiences in death itself abandonment, doubt, and the uncertainty of what the ultimate meaning in all this is."[89] Like the hero of an existentialist novel, Jesus chooses in anguish and acts in despair in a bid to wrest individual meaning from the potential meaninglessness of death.

All of this is perfectly innocuous, at least on the surface. It is simply the mode of reading character in the Gospels that all of us, to a greater or lesser degree, have internalized, whether narrative critic or not. The sinister side of this way of construing character is deeply buried but is beginning to be exhumed, as we have seen. The central modern philosophical category, the human, has been shown to be defective[90] because it is based on a conceptual subjection of the animal, the material corollary of which has been an actual subjugation, even annihilation, of the animal on an unprecedented scale— "a war against the animal," as Derrida phrases it, a "war to the death" that threatens to "end in a world without animals, without any animal worthy of the name living for something other than to become a means for [the human]," whether as source of meat, source of dairy products, source of clothing, domestic pet, hunter's trophy, zoo animal, or experimental life form.[91] The philosophical category of the human has as its principal literary manifestation the version of character peculiar to the modern novel. Since the latter has played a major role in reifying and perpetuating the category, another approach to literary character is needed, one that does not conceive of the human as antithetical to the animal. This Cartesian antithesis has effected both a philosophical and physical erasure of the animal. As Laurie Shannon notes,

---

85. Ibid., 104.
86. Ibid., 105.
87. Ibid., 115; cf. 112.
88. Ibid., 105.
89. Ibid., 116. This sentence does not survive into the second edition; see Rhoads, Dewey, and Michie, *Mark as Story*, 112.
90. Cf. Boehrer, "Animal Studies and the Deconstruction of Character," 543.
91. Derrida, *The Animal That Therefore I Am*, 101–2; cf. idem, *The Beast and the Sovereign*, 302–3.

The disappearance of the more protean *creatures* into the abstract nominal-izations of *animal, the animal,* and *animals* parallels livestock's banishment to a clandestine, dystopian world of industrial food production, where the unspeakable conditions of life depend on invisibility. It mirrors, too, the increasing confinement of wildlife in preserves as wild spaces disappear with alarming speed.[92]

In consequence, a more "creaturely" concept of character is needed.

CHARACTERS AND OTHER CREATURES IN MARK

How might the humanity of the character Jesus in Mark be reinterpreted so as to keep his animality—or, better, his creatureliness—fully and permanently in view? One might begin with that most perplexing of Markan titles for Jesus, "the son of man" (*ho huios tou anthrōpou,* ὁ υἱὸς τοῦ ἀνθρώπου). At first blush, the title might seem to suggest nothing more than an unproblematized (albeit masculinized) humanity, and that, indeed, is how Rhoads and Michie read it: "Jesus used 'son of man' not only to avoid indictment but also to affirm that from beginning to end he is a 'man' who makes no personal claims and who depends on God for his authority and glory."[93] God is Jesus' constitutive other in this formulation. In this regard, although Rhoads and Michie do not say so, their understanding of the "son of man" designation in Mark is con-tinuous with its usage in Ezekiel, in which the prophet is addressed as "son of man" (*ben 'ādām,* בן אדם) some ninety-three times by the deity, and in a fashion that seems designed to put him repeatedly in his place. But while the book of Ezekiel has regularly done duty as "background" for this enigmatic Markan expression, it is not the main scriptural text that has been so adduced. Adela Yarbro Collins gives voice to the most common scholarly construal of the expression when she writes: "Jesus is being presented here as the exalted Son of Man of Daniel 7 in a radically new reception of that text."[94] My initial move, then, in sketching the possible contours of a different approach to the character of Jesus in Mark will be one singularly at odds with narrative-critical strategy—a return to one of the main texts "behind" Mark.

---

92. Shannon, "The Eight Animals in Shakespeare," 477. For the relationship of the creature and the animal, see the discussion under "Inventing the Human" above.

93. Rhoads and Michie, *Mark as Story,* 112.

94. Adela Yarbro Collins, *Mark: A Commentary* (Hermeneia; Minneapolis: Fortress, 2007), 186. So also Joel Marcus, *Mark 1–8: A New Translation with Introduction and Com-mentary* (AB 27; New York: Doubleday, 2000), 223, to cite the other recent major commen-tary on Mark: "Mark, then, has drawn on Daniel 7 and perhaps on other OT traditions."

The relevance of Dan 7 for our purposes is that the nonhuman animal is the constitutive other of the "son of man" (*bar 'ĕnāš*, בר אנש) within that text.[95] Indeed, the animal, or, rather, the animals, are the very reason for the formulation "one like a son of man/one like a human being."[96] Daniel's vision initially is of "four great beasts," the first like a lion with eagles' wings, the second like a bear, the third like a leopard with four wings and four heads, and the fourth a "terrifying and dreadful and exceedingly strong" beast with "great iron teeth" and multiple horns (7:3–8).[97] The throne-room scene ensues, and the judgment of the beasts is described, after which Daniel sees "one like a human being coming with the clouds of heaven" (7:13). "[T]here is an evident contrast between the beasts of the sea and the human figure who comes with the clouds," John J. Collins notes, echoing the scholarly consensus,[98] but he goes on to argue compellingly that the *bar 'ĕnāš* (בר אנש) of Dan 7 is an angelic figure, since human figures seen in the remaining visions of the book regularly turn out to be angels (see 8:15–16; 9:21; 10:5–6; 12:5–7; cf. 3:25).[99]

What Dan 7 presents us with, then, is a cosmology that both anticipates and complicates the Cartesian human/animal dichotomy. On the one hand, Dan 7 articulates an analogous dualism. The expression "one like a human being" in this context means "one who is not a beast," bestiality or animality in Dan 7 being the master metaphor for a humanity out of alignment with the divine order, as emerges from 7:16–27, the interpretation of the vision. On the other hand, the human in Dan 7 is anything but a deep interior repository of essentialized humanity constituted in absolute contradistinction to the animal. Instead, the human is a flickering, interstitial element in Dan 7, a hyphen between the animal, the angelic, and the divine.[100] It is impossible to say where the animal ends and the human begins in Dan 7. In a surreal, proto-Darwinian twist, the lion, which already is also an eagle, has its wings "plucked off" and is "made to stand on two feet like a human being, and a human mind [is] given to it" (7:4), while the "little horn" on the fourth beast has "eyes like human eyes" and "a mouth speaking arrogantly" (7:8). Human-animal hybridity is rampant in this vision.

---

95. Dan 7 falls within the Aramaic section of the book.

96. "There is near universal consensus that the phrase 'one like a son of man' means simply 'one like a human being'" (John J. Collins, *Daniel: A Commentary on the Book of Daniel* [Hermeneia; Minneapolis: Fortress, 1993], 304).

97. NRSV here and in what follows.

98. Collins, *Daniel*, 305.

99. Ibid., 305–6.

100. Cf. Derrida, *The Beast and the Sovereign*, 13, on the divine throne-room scene in Revelation.

The passage from Daniel to Mark is, of course, a complex one. Nevertheless, the unstable positioning of the "one like a human being" in Dan 7 suggests at the very least that the *huios tou anthrōpou* (ὁ υἱὸς τοῦ ἀνθρώπου) title in Mark might be construed as more than an unproblematic affirmation that, as Rhoads and Michie phrase it, "from beginning to end [Jesus] is a 'man.' "[101] Rather than take the Markan Jesus' repeated assertions that he is "the son of humanity"—that is, "the human being"—at face value, one might read them instead as signaling a certain crisis in the category of the human. Against the Danielic backdrop, one explicitly evoked in certain of the eschatological *huios tou anthrōpou* (ὁ υἱὸς τοῦ ἀνθρώπου) passages in Mark (13:26; 14:62; cf. 8:38), the title might be said to parse out fully only in relation to the nonhuman animals from which it acquires its meaning; for what does it mean to say that the Markan Jesus is "the human being"—or "the human animal," as we might say today—if not that he is *not* a nonhuman animal or beast? The beasts driven out from Dan 7 in the process of its incorporation into Mark have not strayed very far, it seems. They lurk in the vicinity of Mark's "son of humanity" title.

What are the implications of this complication for Mark's central character? The beast may be seen not just as the *constitutive* other of this character who awkwardly yet insistently names himself "the human being," but also as the character's *threatening* other. The beast would be that which is always threatening to engulf him—and not only when "the human being" predicts atrocious abuses to his person (8:31; 9:31; 10:33–34; cf. 10:45; 14:21) that, potentially at least, will cause him to slide off the lower end of the honor/ shame gradient into abject animality, but even when "the human being" is least human and most godlike, as in the passages that ascribe godlike powers to him while still on earth (2:10, 28) or the passage that has him enthroned outright at the right hand of God in heaven (14:62; cf. 8:38; 13:26). In Mark, "the human being" occupies a precarious, shifting, unstable space between god and beast, divinity and animality, sacrificer and sacrificed (cf. 10:45).

David Rhoads's brief but incisive ecojustice reading of Mark bears out my ascription of human/nonhuman tensions to this Gospel. "When we look at the whole of Mark," Rhoads writes, "a consistent picture emerges: nature is potentially threatening."[102] Rhoads reads the words "and he was with the wild beasts [*meta tōn thēriōn*, μετὰ τῶν θηρίων]" in the temptation narrative (1:13) as "an aperture" into this picture of nature in Mark.[103] "Wild beasts

---

101. Rhoads and Michie, *Mark as Story*, 112.
102. Rhoads, "Who Will Speak for the Sparrow?" 75.
103. Ibid., 74. Rhoads is interacting here with Richard Bauckham's "Jesus and the Wild Animals (Mark 1:13): A Christological Image for an Ecological Age," in *Jesus of Nazareth: Lord and Christ. Essays on the Historical Jesus and New Testament Christology* (ed. Joel B.

are examples of nondomesticated creation, which poses a threat to humans."[104] Presumably, it is the threat of physical danger that Rhoads has in mind here. I have been suggesting that the animal also poses an ontological threat to the human in Mark, and that threat simmers in places other than the *huios tou anthrōpou* (ὁ υἱὸς τοῦ ἀνθρώπου) title. Many of the same elements that we noted in Dan 7 are especially present in the Gerasene demoniac episode. Rhoads's list of "[e]gregious examples of disparaging attitudes toward nature in the New Testament" begins with "the drowning of two thousand pigs in the Sea of Galilee (Mark 5:1–20)."[105] I would simply add that the category of the animal is especially fraught in this episode. The creatures that are annihilated here are natural/supernatural hybrids. Bestiality and the demonic combine inextricably in them ("And the unclean spirits … entered the swine," 5:13). They represent, indeed, the literal demonization of the animal in Mark—not even the wild animal in this instance, but the domestic animal. Moreover, even before the demons have merged with the swine, they have named themselves in a way that blurs any clear distinction between them and the human empire of the day ("My name is Legion; for we are many," 5:9).[106] The human is a hyphen between the demonic and the animal in the swine, just as the human is a hyphen between the divine and the animal in the exorcist, Jesus, as we saw earlier. Whether the exorcist, the narrator, or both are responsible for the fate of the swine, the latter's spectacular destruction ("and the herd, numbering about two thousand, rushed down the steep bank … and were drowned in the sea," 5:13) eloquently bespeaks the category crisis in which the human is embroiled in this narrative. The other-than-human and the more-

---

Green and Max Turner; Grand Rapids: Eerdmans, 1994), 3–21. Further ecological work on Mark includes Keith D. Dyer, "When Is the End Not the End? The Fate of Earth in Biblical Eschatology (Mark 13)," in *The Earth Story in the New Testament* (ed. Norman C. Habel and Vicky Balabanski; The Earth Bible 5; Cleveland: Pilgrim, 2002), 44–56; William Loader, "Good News—for the Earth? Reflections on Mark 1.1–15," in Habel and Balabanski, *The Earth Story in the New Testament*, 28–43; Susan Miller, "The Descent of Darkness over the Land: Listening to the Voice of Earth in Mark 15:33," in *Exploring Ecological Hermeneutics* (ed. Norman C. Habel and Peter Trudinger; SBLSymS 46; Atlanta: Society of Biblical Literature, 2008), 123–30; and Elaine Wainwright, "Healing Ointment/Healing Bodies: Gift and Identification in an Ecofeminist Reading of Mark 14:3–9," in Habel and Trudinger, *Exploring Ecological Hermeneutics*, 131–40.

104. Rhoads, "Who Will Speak for the Sparrow?" 75.

105. Ibid., 67.

106. In recent decades, numerous scholars have read "Legion" as a reference to Rome. For a summary of and reflection on the debate, see Stephen D. Moore, *Empire and Apocalypse: Postcolonialism and the New Testament* (The Bible in the Modern World 12; Sheffield: Sheffield Phoenix, 2006), 24–32.

than-human embodied in the demon-possessed pigs are the objects of violent expulsion as the human attempts to establish itself.

The final scene that begs inclusion in any consideration of the nonhuman animal in Mark brings us to the relations between femininity and animality in this Gospel. "The linkage between animals and women," writes Marianne DeKoven, "is historically and culturally pervasive.… Women and animals go together."[107] They certainly go together in Mark; one of the principal scenes in the Gospel to feature a female character employs a woman/animal equation. "Let the children be fed first, for it is not fair to take the children's food and throw it to the dogs," is Jesus' infamous reply to the Syrophoenician woman who begs him to heal her daughter (7:27). The Syrophoenician woman is a flat character, in Rhoads and Michie's schema—but so are all the women characters in Mark, on their reading, which points either to a problem with Mark or a problem with the reading (to the extent that the two can be distinguished).[108] As a flat character, the Syrophoenician woman is implicitly aligned with Forster's Lady Bertram, who, as we recall, "seems to be cut out of the same simple material as her dog."[109] But the Syrophoenician woman is a dog that talks back.[110] She is, indeed, the only "flat" female character who talks back to the "round" male protagonist in Mark, and to that extent she may be thought of as speaking on behalf of all of the allegedly flat, supposedly simple, apparently animal-like characters in this Gospel.

Rhoads and Michie write of the Syrophoenician woman:

> The little people … measure up to the standards of judgment which Jesus introduces later in the story: renouncing oneself, losing one's life, being least, and being servant. The Syrophoenician woman is a good example. Although Jesus refers to her, a gentile, as a little dog, she willingly lowers herself to the status of a dog in order that the demon might be exorcised from her daughter: "Lord, even the *little dogs down under* the table eat the *little* children's *crumbs*." She is willing to diminish herself, renounce herself, be least, in order to serve her daughter.[111]

---

107. DeKoven, "Why Animals Now?" 366. Cf. Haraway, *The Companion Species Manifesto*, 3: "I want my readers to know why I consider dog writing to be a branch of feminist theory, or the other way around"—a statement with particular resonance for the Markan passage we are about to discuss.

108. See Rhoads and Michie, *Mark as Story*, 129–36 *passim*.

109. Forster, *Aspects of the Novel*, 73.

110. "And Say the Animal Responded?" is the title of the third chapter of Derrida's *The Animal That Therefore I Am*, a chapter that attempts "to break with the Cartesian tradition of the animal-machine without language and without response" (119).

111. Rhoads and Michie, *Mark as Story*, 131, emphasis original.

To fault Rhoads and Michie for collaborating in the Markan Jesus' infantiliza-
tion and animalization of the female would be facile. The year, after all, is
1982, and barn-sized targets of this sort litter the landscape of New Testament
scholarship.[112] But a different response to Jesus' exchange with the Syropheonician woman is needed today, and that response ideally ought to take the
measure not just of the male-female relations in the episode but of the human-
animal relations in it as well, recognizing that the two sets of relations are
complexly coimplicated. In critical reflection on this pericope and on Mark
in general, gender egalitarianism now needs to be complemented and complicated by what Rosi Braidotti has termed the "bioegalitarian turn."[113] Later in
the same article, Braidotti makes a statement that seems to mimic in a posthumanist register the Syrophoenician woman's willingness "to lower herself
to the status of a dog."[114] Braidotti writes: "Becoming animal, minoritarian, or
world speaks to my feminist self, partly because my sex, historically speaking,
never made it into full humanity, so my allegiance to that category is at best
negotiable and never to be taken for granted."[115] But the category itself is now
increasingly shown to be a constructed one, as we saw earlier, and so itself in
need of renegotiation.

To the extent that we are all now needing to become animal again—or,
more precisely, to realize that we have never been anything but—it is the
Syropheonician woman, however "flat," and not her interlocutor, however
"round," who emerges as the more enlightened partner in their exchange. We
are accustomed to hearing that Jesus learns a soteriological lesson from that
exchange; as Rhoads and Michie, for instance, phrase it, "the Syrophoenician
woman overcomes Jesus' unwillingness to heal gentiles."[116] But it now appears
that she has an ecosystemic message as well to teach this self-proclaimed
"human being" who has declared her and her ethnic kin to be nonhuman
animals. An adequate deciphering of that message will have to await another
essay. This deciphering (or reciphering) will be a challenging exercise, both
because the animalization of women and subordinated racial/ethnic subjects

---

112. The wording softens in the second edition; see Rhoads, Dewey, and Michie, *Mark
as Story*, 131: "The Syrophoenician woman exemplifies being least. She cleverly accepts
Jesus' reference to her as a dog in order to get her daughter exorcised." More particularly,
Rhoads returns to the episode in "Jesus and the Syrophoenician Woman" in his *Reading
Mark, Engaging the Gospel*, 63–94, and in a way informed by feminist scholarship (see esp.
90–92).

113. Rosi Braidotti, "Animals, Anomalies, and Inorganic Others," *PMLA* 124 (2009):
526.

114. Rhoads and Michie's expression; see the block quotation above.

115. Braidotti, "Animals, Anomalies, and Inorganic Others," 531.

116. Rhoads and Michie, *Mark as Story*, 131.

has engendered an exceptionally complex and fraught debate[117] and because dogs and other nonhuman animals "are not here just to think with,"[118] a factor that any bioegalitarian engagement with the pericope would also need to take fully into account. Suffice it for now to say that a narrative-critical approach to Markan characterization that would be attuned to human-nonhuman relations and ecojustice issues generally might do no better than to start with this densely knotted episode and work out from it. The round/flat character distinction that has played such a significant role in New Testament narrative criticism,[119] but which is ultimately rooted in Cartesian assumptions now shown to be deeply problematic, would likely not survive the exercise. We would begin to read Mark narratively in ways that no longer map it unreflectively onto the modern novel or short story—but not only because of our inbred disciplinary aversion to anachronism. "Humans" and "animals" alike would vanish from the text to be replaced by creatures that are less and more than either category.

"To be human is to be a biological creature," writes Rhoads, "to be counted among the animals as Homo sapiens, a higher primate, a mammal."[120] How should such a creature approach the Gospel of Mark in an ecocidal age? Out of a posthuman paradigm, I have been suggesting, recognizing that Mark is a prehuman text—which is also to recognize that the concepts of the human and the animal that we have inherited from the Enlightenment are now best seen as but the products of an interim period—albeit the formative period for almost every facet of our culture, critical biblical scholarship included— "bookended by a pre- and posthumanism that think the human/animal distinction quite otherwise."[121]

---

117. For a partial summary of the debate, see Neel Ahuja, "Postcolonial Critique in a Multispecies World," *PMLA* 124 (2009), esp. 557–59.

118. Haraway, *The Companion Species Manifesto*, 5. Gilhus notes how "[i]n the animal world of the Gospels, centre stage is dominated by metaphorical sheep and miraculous fish" (*Animals, Gods and Humans*, 181). Animals tend to function as "symbolic capital" in these texts, with a corresponding "lack of focus on real animals" (181).

119. See, e.g., Culpepper, *Anatomy of the Fourth Gospel*, 102–3; Mark Allan Powell, *What Is Narrative Criticism?* (GBS; Minneapolis: Fortress, 1990), 55, 61–64, 104; James L. Resseguie, *Narrative Criticism of the New Testament: An Introduction* (Grand Rapids: Baker, 2005), 123–26; Elizabeth Struthers Malbon, "Narrative Criticism: How Does the Story Mean?" in *Mark and Method: New Approaches in Biblical Studies* (2nd ed.; ed. Janice Capel Anderson and Stephen D. Moore; Minneapolis: Fortress, 2008), 35. Many more examples could be listed.

120. Rhoads, "Who Will Speak for the Sparrow?" 83.

121. Wolfe, "Human, All Too Human," 564.

Writing a Narrative Commentary
on the Gospel of Mark

Francis J. Moloney, S.D.B.

Interpreters of my generation were not brought up in a scholarly world where professional interest in narrative theory was significant. Each of us was no doubt influenced by different factors to adopt such an approach to the Gospels. One that most influenced me was the first edition of *Mark as Story*.[1] After years of teaching and thinking about the Gospel of Mark, always impressed by its power, this book showed admirably how close attention to the literary features of narrator, setting, plot, characters, and the reader(s) that can be traced within a narrative could lead to a fresh understanding of the Gospel of Mark as a deliberately contrived "whole utterance," a passionate and unified story that runs from 1:1 to 16:8. There may be places where the passion is somewhat hidden, but a new world in the interpretation of "Mark as story" opened up.

As we mark the nearly thirty years that have passed since *Mark as Story* was published, it may be of value to share the principles that guided my attempts to start from the insights of that publication eventually to produce something that, in my opinion, was more demanding: a narrative commentary on the Gospel of Mark. David Rhoads, Joanna Dewey, and Donald Michie were able to focus upon crucial features of narrative theory and show how they could be effectively applied to the Markan narrative. This enabled chapters and sections of their fine book to identify the role of the narrator, describe the setting(s) of

---

1. David Rhoads, Joanna Dewey, and Donald Michie, *Mark as Story: An Introduction to the Narrative of a Gospel* (2nd ed.; Minneapolis: Fortress, 1999). The first edition, without the collaboration of Joanna Dewey, was published in 1982. The other works that "turned my head" were R. Alan Culpepper, *Anatomy of the Fourth Gospel: A Study in Literary Design* (Philadelphia: Fortress, 1983); Seymour Chatman, *Story and Discourse: Narrative Structure in Film and Literature* (Ithaca, N.Y.: Cornell University Press, 1978); Gérard Genette, *Narrative Discourse: An Essay in Method* (trans. Jane A. Lewin; Ithaca, N.Y.: Cornell University Press, 1980); and Shlomith Rimmon-Kenan, *Narrative Fiction: Contemporary Poetics* (New Accents; London: Methuen, 1983).

the Gospel story, trace the plot and ways the characters interact within that plot to catch the imagination of the readers of the story—those for whom it was written, and all subsequent readers.

A full-scale narrative commentary must allow the story of the Gospel to dictate its own terms. Many factors, including *Mark as Story*, had led me to the conviction that the Gospel of Mark had to be read as a carefully articulated and unified story. Mark 1:1–16:8 was not originally written, read, or listened to as a series of loosely connected pericopes. Many commentaries, and certainly all liturgical use of the text, present the Gospel in this way. As I set out on my mission of writing a narrative commentary on Mark, allowing my interpretation to be determined by the literary and theological unity of the story, I came to accept that the element in the narrative that had to be traced and eventually used as the "backbone" for my commentary was the *unfolding of a unified plot*, from 1:1 to 16:8. Working verse by verse, and turning over the pages of the story, doing my best to be an (undoubtedly poor) implied reader, I found that the narrator, the setting(s), the characters, and the involvement of the reader emerged from their function within, and subordinated to, the plot.[2]

TRACING THE HAND OF THE STORYTELLER

It has often been said that a successful story has a good beginning, to catch the initial attention of the reader, a good central section to maintain that interest, and a good conclusion, to render satisfying the reading experience of the whole utterance.[3] The Gospel of Mark stands up well to this test.[4]

THE BEGINNING

The story begins with a solemn statement that what follows is "good news" (*euangelion*, εὐαγγέλιον) and an announcement little short of a confession of

---

2. I was necessarily a poor "implied reader," as I am a "real reader," and I already knew the story well. I had to try to block that out so that each verse and turn of the page brought its own surprises. An implied reader emerges *from the text* and is only aware of what has been said and done *to that point* in the reading experience. But in a good story the implied reader and the real reader are very close by the time the book comes to its close. For me, Mark is a very good story. See Francis J. Moloney, *The Gospel of Mark: A Commentary* (Peabody, Mass.: Hendrickson, 2002).

3. Well articulated by Aristotle, *Poet.* 7.3–7 (Greek text and English translation available in Aristotle, *Poetics* [Halliwell, LCL], 54–57).

4. Attribution of the Gospel to "Mark" respects the tradition. We do not know who "the real author" was. For the discussion, see C. Clifton Black, *Mark: Images of an Apostolic Interpreter* (Studies on Personalities of the New Testament; Minneapolis: Fortress, 2001).

faith, that Jesus of Nazareth, whose story is about to be told, is the Christ, the much-awaited Jewish Messiah, and the Son of God (Mark 1:1). This announcement of the "good news" is followed by a gradual introduction of Jesus into the story. Initially he is absent, but he is witnessed to by means of God's prophetic word that declares that he is "the Lord" (1:2–3), by John the Baptist, who points away from himself to a "mightier one" who comes to baptize with the Holy Spirit (1:4–8). At this stage, Jesus appears on the scene, but he does not say or do anything. He is baptized by John the Baptist, and as he rises from the waters of the Jordan the heavens split apart, the Spirit descends upon him like a dove. A voice from heaven, the voice of God, proclaims: "You are my beloved Son; with you I am well pleased" (1:9–11). Only in the final two verses of what can justifiably be called a "prologue" to the Gospel of Mark, does Jesus move into action. He is driven by the Spirit into the desert, is tempted by Satan, and is apparently victorious, as he is "with the wild beasts; and the angels ministered to him," restoring the idyllic situation of the first Adam (1:12–13; see Gen 2:19–20; 8:6–12; Isa 11:6–8). The only people privy to all the information provided by 1:1–13 are the readers and listeners. Not even the Baptist has read or heard verses 1–3. The readers and listeners to what follows enter the story well-armed with information about Jesus: Messiah, Son of God, Lord, mightier one, filled with and driven by the Holy Spirit, the beloved Son in whom God is well pleased, the one in whom God's original design for creation is restored.

THE CENTER-PIECE

There are many twists and turns in the story as it runs from 1:14 to 8:26. But in 8:27–30 another moment of truth arrives. Characters in the story (including the disciples) have been guessing about Jesus. Who can he be (see, e.g., 1:27, 45; 2:12; 3:22; 4:41; 5:20; 6:2–3, 48–50; 7:37)? The readers/listeners know who Jesus is because they have read or heard the prologue (1:1–13), but none of the other characters in the drama have done so. At Caesarea Philippi, Jesus asks his disciples who people say he is. They respond: John the Baptist, Elijah, or one of the prophets (8:27–28). The readers/listeners know this is wrong. It does not match the truths about Jesus' person stated in 1:1–13. Jesus then asks his disciples who they think he is. Peter, representing the disciples, confesses that Jesus is the Christ (8:29). This is part of the mystery of Jesus (see 1:1), but not the whole story (cf. 1:11). For this reason, "He charged them to say nothing about him" (8:30). This command to silence, after Peter has at least partially answered Jesus' question, is surprising. If this is not the whole answer to the mystery of Jesus, then more is to come, and a new direction is taken by the story with the first of Jesus' passion predictions in 8:31. There Jesus speaks of himself, for the first time, as the Son of Man who must suffer and die, yet rise from the dead on the third day.

The Ending

From 8:31 until 15:47 Jesus lives out his destiny as the Son of Man who willingly accepts God's design for him to suffer an ignominious death (see especially 14:36). Along the way he attempts to draw his disciples into this mystery, but they cannot or will not understand. They find it impossible to accept that "the Son of Man also came not to be served but to serve, and to give his life as a ransom for many" (10:45). Each time Jesus spoke of the Son of Man's future suffering and death, he also announced that he would rise after three days (8:31; 9:31; 10:34). The readers/listeners have followed the story through Jesus' failure to hold the allegiance of the disciples, his bringing Jerusalem and its leaders to a standstill, his words on the end of Jerusalem and the world (11:1–13:37), his lonely and ignominious death at the hands of the Romans (14:1–15:47). The disciples have betrayed him (14:1–2, 10–11), fled in fear (14:50), and denied him (14:66–72), while some women look on from afar (15:40–41, 47). The readers/listeners are ready for the story's dénouement. Not surprisingly, 16:1–8 provides spectacular proof that Jesus' story did not end with his death but that he has been raised (16:6). The women who had been at the cross and at the burial see the empty tomb and hear the Easter proclamation from the young man at the tomb (16:1–6). But in an intriguing end to the story, they are told by the young man dressed in a white robe to inform the disciples and Peter that he is going before them into Galilee, as Jesus had told them (16:7; cf. 14:28). "And they went out and fled from the tomb; for trembling and astonishment had come upon them; and they said nothing to anyone, for they were afraid" (16:8). Thus ends the Gospel of Mark![5] At first glance, and even beyond a first glance, this hardly seems to serve as a satisfactory dénouement. Jesus' unconditional obedience to his Father (see 14:36) has been satisfactorily resolved, as God has raised him from the dead after three days, as Jesus had promised (8:31; 9:31; 10:32–34).

But there is much that is left unresolved: What of the disciples and the women? As we will see, the answer to these questions is not found *within*

---

5. The early scribes added more satisfactory endings. They are found in most Bibles, but they are scribal additions to a Gospel that the second-century scribes found unsatisfactory, as have many since. Scholars discuss whether or not the Gospel ended at 16:8 or whether there was a lost ending. On this discussion, insisting that 16:8 is the intended end of the Gospel, see Moloney, *Mark*, 339–54, and notes 4–11. More recently, see the important study of Kelly R. Iverson, "A Further Word on Final Γάρ," *CBQ* 68 (2006): 79–94.

the narrative but in the lives of those who read and listen to the story. Like the prologue (1:1–13), 16:1–8 addresses readers and listeners. As such, it can be regarded as an epilogue, and this partially explains the strangeness of the ending at 16:8.

TEXTUAL MARKERS

The informative prologue (1:1–13), the surprising center-piece (8:27–30), and the even more startling conclusion (16:1–8) provide the bedrock of the plot, our first indications of a narrative that is a deliberate literary and theological design of a gifted storyteller. Not all interpreters and commentators would read these three turning points in the way suggested, but in this I was broadly following what could be regarded as "majority opinion."[6] But what of the rest of the story (1:14–8:26 and 8:31–15:47)? It should not be surprising that a storyteller who is so careful in the construction of the beginning, the center-piece, and the conclusion to his Gospel will leave further hints of his literary design. There are a number of features within the Gospel of Mark where the storyteller shows his hand by means of what I have called "textual markers." Textual markers are places in the story where the hand of the author is most in evidence. They offer the reader clear hints that the storyteller is "up to something."[7]

The most obvious textual marker in any narrative is a summary, where the narrator pauses to open a new section in the story, to draw a conclusion, or to pass a critical comment upon events just reported. There are many summaries in Mark (see, e.g., 1:14–15, 39, 45b; 4:33–34; 6:6b, 53–56; 9:30–31; 10:1, 13). Another textual marker is repetition. For example, there are two bread miracles in Mark 6:31–44 and 8:1–9. The passion predictions are found three times: in 8:31; 9:31; and 10:32–34. There are two accounts of the cure of a blind man in 8:22–26 (the man at Bethsaida) and 10:46–52 (blind Bartimaeus). Another feature of Mark's story is his practice of what has been called "intercalation." This term indicates a literary pattern where the narrator begins a story but breaks it halfway through to insert another story. Once the central account is closed, the storyteller concludes the original story. The

---

6. My description of 16:1–8 as an "epilogue," in some way matching the "prologue" of 1:1–13, is original. On this, see below. For an outstanding recent commentary on the Gospel of Mark that represents this "majority opinion," see Joel Marcus, *Mark 1–16* (2 vols.; AB 27–27A; New York: Doubleday, 2000–2009). On 16:1–8 as an "epilogue," see Marcus, *Mark 1–16*, 1:62–64; 2:1079–87.

7. Rhoads, Dewey, and Michie (*Mark as Story*, 39–62) identify what I have called "textual markers" as evidence of the presence of an omniscient narrator.

most famous "intercalations" in Mark are the account of the healing of Jairus's daughter, in the middle of which Jesus heals the woman with a flow of blood (Mark 5:21–43), and the cursing of the fig tree, in the middle of which Jesus brings an end to the financial and cultic activities of the Jerusalem temple (11:12–25). But there are several other examples of this Markan practice (see 3:20–35 [Jesus' family]; 6:6b–30 [disciples on mission]; 14:1–11 [Judas's betrayal], 53–72 [Peter's denials]).[8]

Other textual markers are found when the narrator shifts the action from one place to another (a change in the geography of the story), from one period of time to another (a change in the time frame of the story), or from one set of characters to another (a change in the author's focus upon characters). The Gospel of Mark has many such indications (e.g., 1:35; 2:1, 23; 3:7; 4:35; 7:24, 31).[9] My attempt to write a commentary that takes into account the narrative purpose of the storyteller must focus upon these obvious signs of an original "author at work." Mark certainly used traditions that were earlier than him and came to him in various forms. For the purposes of his story of Jesus' life, teaching, death, and resurrection, he set them down in a certain order, some of which may have already been in place in the earlier tradition and some of which were original to Mark. In the end, the story emerges as the narrator tells it, and the best way to appreciate this is to devote attention to those places where the Markan literary activity is most in evidence.[10]

A word of warning: no single textual marker in itself indicates an important change of direction in the plot. It is generally a combination of several. An important example that plays a crucial role in uncovering Mark's literary design across 1:14–8:26 is the use of the summaries in 1:14–15; 3:7–12; and 6:6a. I provided a long list of "summaries" above that only went as far as 10:13; that is but a limited sample. There are many summaries in Mark's Gospel, but only 1:14–15; 3:7–12; and 6:6a are *immediately* followed by material dealing with the disciples. Only here in the Gospel is this combination of features found: a summary statement, immediately followed by a passage that deals

---

8. This is a conservative list. Others are regularly suggested. See Tom Shepherd, "The Narrative Function of Markan Intercalation," *NTS* (1995): 522–40. I have argued elsewhere, and this argument will be briefly resumed below, that the whole of 14:1–15:47 can be read as an extended use of intercalation. See Moloney, *Mark*, 276–79.

9. On these, and other, "settings," see Rhoads, Dewey, and Michie, *Mark as Story*, 63–72.

10. Readers well-versed in Gospel criticism will be aware that this principle is very important for what has been called redaction criticism. It is equally important for a form of narrative criticism that is the natural product of redaction criticism. I believe that, in narrative-critical terms, the real author (Mark?), the implied author, and the narrator are of one and the same mind.

with the disciples (the vocation of the first disciples [1:16–20], the establishment of the Twelve [3:13–19], and the mission of the Twelve [6:7–30]).

The Plot of the Gospel of Mark

Literary critics have many approaches to the plot of a narrative, but—for our
purposes—the following general description is useful: "The plot in a dramatic
or narrative work is the structure of its actions, as these are rendered and
ordered toward achieving particular emotional and artistic effects."[11] The plot
of the Gospel of Mark has been devised not only to have emotional and artistic effects (and it certainly does that), but also to convey a message about Jesus,
the Christ, the Son of God (see 1:1), and the various characters who interact
with Jesus during the course of the story, especially the disciples.[12] Within
the limits that this essay imposes, allow me to indicate the way plot has determined my understanding the Markan message about Jesus, his disciples, and
other characters in the story.

As we have seen, "the beginning" of the story is announced in 1:1, and it
runs from 1:1 to 1:13, forming a prologue to the Gospel.[13] Jesus' first appearance on the scene, proclaiming the good news of the impinging presence of

---

11. M. H. Abrams, *A Glossary of Literary Terms* (5th ed.; New York: Holt, Rinehart
& Winston, 1985), 139. For a more focused description of Mark's plot as a portrait of the
conflicts that result from the arrival of the rule of God, see Rhoads, Dewey, and Michie,
Mark as Story, 73–97. See also Brendan Byrne, *A Costly Freedom: A Theological Reading of
Mark's Gospel* (Collegeville, Minn.: Liturgical Press, 2008). I regard this focus as somewhat
limited.

12. The interaction between Jesus and the characters is, as I hope to indicate below,
the essential dynamic that keeps the story moving. On these "other characters," see Rhoads,
Dewey, and Michie, *Mark as Story*, 98–115 (Jesus), 116–35 (the authorities, the disciples,
and the people). There are many monographs on these characters. For a survey of the
many studies of the disciples, see C. Clifton Black, *The Disciples according to Mark: Markan
Redaction in Current Debate* (JSNTSup 27; Sheffield: Sheffield Academic Press, 1989). See
also the valuable studies of Susan Miller, *Women in Mark's Gospel* (JSNTSup 266; London:
T&T Clark, 2004); Kelly R. Iverson, *Gentiles in the Gospel of Mark* (LNTS 339; London:
T&T Clark, 2007), and especially Elizabeth S. Malbon, *In the Company of Jesus: Characters
in Mark's Gospel* (Louisville: Westminster John Knox, 2000).

13. The practice of opening ancient "stories" with a prologue was widespread. Mark is
not the only Gospel with a prologue. John's prologue (1:1–18) is famous, but equally effective prologues are found in Matthew (1:1–4:16) and Luke (1:1–4:13). Readers and listeners
become privileged "insiders" to the mystery of what God has done in and through Jesus
Christ. The characters "in the story" have not read or heard the prologue, and they must
respond on the basis of their encounter with Jesus' person, words, and deeds. The reader/
listener follows their response from her or his privileged position.

God as king (1:14–15), is the first of a string of summary statements, followed by material dealing with disciples (1:16–20; 3:7–19; 6:6a–30) that appears to determine the literary design of 1:14–8:26. The midpoint is highlighted by Peter's confession and Jesus' command to silence (8:27–30). These events close the first half of the Gospel and are followed by the first passion prediction (8:31), as Jesus sets off on his journey to Jerusalem. The second half of the Gospel has begun. As Jesus journeys to Jerusalem, he twice cures blind men (8:22–26; 10:46–52). On arrival in Jerusalem, he closes down the temple, reduces the leaders of Israel to silence, and speaks of the end of Jerusalem and of the world (11:1–13:37). The carefully argued account of Jesus' passion follows (14:1–15:47). The end of the story reports the morning after the Sabbath, as women go to anoint the body of the crucified Jesus and discover an empty tomb, hear the Easter message, and flee in fear (16:1–8). Textual markers indicate the following overall shape of the narration.

1.   The Gospel begins: the prologue (1:1–13).

2.   Jesus opens his ministry in Galilee (1:14–15) and continues there until the next major turning point (1:16–8:26).

3.   Jesus asks his disciples who they think he is and warns them against a possible partial understanding of his messianic status (8:27–30).

4.   Jesus announces his journey to Jerusalem and the forthcoming death and resurrection of the Son of Man for the first time (8:31). Between two miracles in which blind men are cured (8:22–26 [the blind man at Bethsaida] and 10:46–52 [blind Bartimaeus]), Jesus journeys to Jerusalem and instructs his disciples as he continues to speak of his oncoming death and resurrection (8:22–10:52).

5.   On arrival in Jerusalem (11:1–11), Jesus brings Israel's cult to an end, reduces the leaders of Israel to silence, and speaks of the end of Jerusalem and the end of the world, instructing his disciples to "watch" (11:12–13:37).

6.   After a final evening (Passover) meal with his disciples, Jesus is betrayed by Judas, arrested, denied by Peter, tried by the Jewish authorities and by the Roman authorities, crucified, and buried, as women watch from a distance (14:1–15:47).

7. Women discover an empty tomb, hear the Markan Easter proc-
    lamation, but flee in fear. They fail to report to the disciples and
    Peter that Jesus is going ahead of them into Galilee, as he had
    told them (16:1–8; cf. 14:28).

The careful ordering of a succession of events, outlined above, marks a
new beginning in the history of Christian literature. To the best of our knowledge, Mark's Gospel was the first attempt on the part of early Christians to
communicate what God had done for humankind through the life, teaching,
death, and resurrection of Jesus *in a narrative form*.[14] We must remember that
the first readers and hearers of the story now found in the Gospel of Mark
already knew the basic facts about Jesus' life. According to the first verses of
the Gospel of Luke, they had been "delivered to us by those who from the
beginning were eyewitnesses and ministers of the word" (Luke 1:2). But Mark
did not simply wish to put down in writing what they already knew. If the
power of the narrative is any indication, this story passionately proclaims
something about God, the Christ, and the followers of Jesus. Whatever the
first readers knew of the life story of Jesus of Nazareth was subverted by the
Markan story. The account of Jesus' presence in Galilee, his single journey to
Jerusalem to be rejected, tried, and crucified, the resurrection, and the surprising silence of the women at the empty tomb, *told in this way*, was not
familiar. The *radical newness* of the Markan story must be kept in mind.[15] It
is an original way of telling the life of Jesus. A narrative commentary must be
determined by that originality.

MARK 1:14–8:30

The overall plot of the Gospel has been traced—to this point—by focusing on
the obvious beginning, midpoint, and end of the story, sketching in the rest of
the plot with the help of the major textual markers. If careful storytelling high-

---

14. The expression "gospel" (Old English *God-Spel*) means "good news." It translates
the Greek εὐαγγέλιον (*euangelion*). The term had been used in pre-Christian times to speak
of major events in the lives of a nation or a ruling dynasty, etc. Prior to Mark's Gospel, it had
also been used extensively by Paul to summarize his message of the saving event of Jesus'
death and resurrection. However, in Mark 1:1 "gospel" is used to speak of the beginnings
of a "story." That use of the word "Gospel" is now part of Christian language, and Mark
invented it.

15. See the important essay by Eduard Schweizer, "Mark's Theological Achievement,"
in *The Interpretation of Mark* (ed. William Telford; Investigations in Religion and Theology
7; Philadelphia: Fortress, 1985), 42–63.

lights these key moments places in the story, it is only to be expected that the bulk of the story also reflects careful plotting. Indeed, continuing to focus our attention upon the textual markers, we will find that 1:14–8:30 and 8:31–15:47 have also been designed to "achieve particular artistic and emotional effects." You will have noticed that I include 8:27–30 in my description of the first half of the Gospel, even though I have also singled it out as the center-point of the Gospel. As we proceed further, you will also find that I include 8:22–26 in the first section of the second half of the story. We encounter here an important feature of all good narratives. We tend to create divisions between one part of the story and the next, but good stories do not work like that. As one part of the Gospel of Mark draws to closure in 8:27–30, another section is already being foreshadowed in 8:22–30.[16]

After the prologue (1:1–13), where the reader/listener is soundly informed about the person, the mission, and even the destiny of Jesus, the first half of the Gospel (1:14–8:30) establishes relationships, as well as raising questions concerning the person of Jesus among characters in the story who are ignorant of 1:1–13. From the very first moment of the Gospel, Jesus calls all who hear to "repent and believe in the gospel" (1:14–15). As he bursts upon the scene, he immediately calls the first disciples to "follow" him (1:16–20). Mark certainly tells a passionate story about Jesus, the Christ, Son of God (1:1), but he is equally passionate about the challenge to "follow" a suffering Son of Man to Jerusalem and beyond. This theme will dominate the second half of the story (8:31–15:47), but it is not absent from 1:14–8:30. The responses of the Twelve, the followers of Jesus, the crowds, the Jewish leaders, the Romans, the Gentiles, and the several "minor characters" all instruct the reader on how one should or should not respond to what God has done in and through Jesus, the Christ, the Son of God.[17]

On three occasions across 1:14–8:30 the narrator slows down the fast-moving story to summarize Jesus' ministry at that stage. These summaries of Jesus' activities cannot be easily tied to a fixed setting. They offer, in a more general fashion, illustrations of that activity (see 1:14–15; 3:7–12; 6:6b). The Gospel of Mark contains other similar summaries of Jesus' ministry (see, e.g., 1:39, 45b; 4:33–34; 6:53–56; 9:30–31; 10:1, 13). What is unique about the gen-

---

16. Indeed, the second half of the narrative is clearly foreshadowed by the discussion between Jesus and the disciples in the boat in 8:14–21, including his accusation that they are blind (see 8:18). For extensive consideration of this phenomenon in the Gospel of Mark, see Joanna Dewey, "Mark as Interwoven Tapestry: Forecasts and Echoes for a Listening Audience," *CBQ* 53 (1991): 225–36; Elizabeth Struthers Malbon, "Echoes and Foreshadowings in Mark 4–8: Reading and ReReading," *JBL* 112 (1993): 211–30.

17. See above, note 11.

eral descriptions of Jesus' ministry in 1:14–15; 3:7–12; and 6:6b, however, is that each of these summaries is followed by material that deals with disciples and discipleship (1:16–20; 3:13–19; 6:7–30). The summaries, and the associated report of Jesus' association with his disciples, are followed by a series of episodes during which three different audiences respond to the words and deeds of Jesus. At the end of each episode, a decision is made about Jesus. Two of the decisions are negative (3:6 [the Pharisees and the Herodians]; 6:1–6a [people from "his own country"]), and the third is a misunderstanding (8:29 [Peter, responding on behalf of the disciples]).

The three summaries lead directly into passages that deal with disciples and conclude with a response to Jesus indicating Mark's careful plotting of 1:14–8:30. The three sections unfold as follows.

(1) *Jesus and the leaders of Israel* (1:14–3:6). In 1:14–15 we read a summary of the ministry of Jesus: "Now after John was arrested, Jesus came to Galilee, proclaiming the good news of God, and saying, 'The time is fulfilled and the kingdom of God has come near, repent and believe in the good news.'" This summary is followed by the account of the vocation of the first disciples (1:16–20). Initially, Jesus' presence in the midst of the demonic, the sick, and the impure sweeps all evil away (1:21–45), but opposition mounts. In five episodes Jesus' authority continues to manifest itself, but rejection of this authority mounts, leading to a decision that he must be eliminated. The five episodes are elegantly assembled and told.[18] Jesus forgives the sin of the paralytic, and "some of the scribes question his authority *in their hearts*," but the miracle affirms his authority (2:13–17). Jesus shares his table with tax collectors and sinners, and the "scribes of the Pharisees" complain to the disciples (2:13–17). When others are fasting, "people" ask Jesus why he does not fast. He tells them they will fast when the bridegroom is *taken away* from them (2:18–22). As Jesus and his disciples eat grain they have plucked along the way, "the Pharisees" question Jesus on the right observance of the law (2:23–38). Again on a Sabbath, Jesus cures the man with a withered hand as his opponents watch, in order to condemn him. He reduces them to silence and grieves over their *hardness of heart* (3:1–6). A decision is made: "The Pharisees went out and immediately conspired with the Herodians against him, how to destroy him" (3:6).[19]

---

18. See Moloney, *Mark*, 60–71 and references there, especially to the work of Joanna Dewey.

19. Care must be taken with the use of the expressions associated with Israel and Judaism. For Mark, the first part of his story of Jesus' ministry in Galilee is entirely focused upon a Jewish region and the Jewish leadership. The geographical locations and the characters involved in the story will be broadened in 5:1–20 and also in later episodes (see 7:24–8:10).

(2) *Jesus and his new family* (3:7–6:6a). In 3:7–12 we find a lengthy general statement about Jesus' Galilean ministry. It concludes with the summary: "He had cured many so that all who had diseases pressed upon him to touch him. Whenever the unclean spirits saw him, they fell down before him and shouted, 'You are the Son of God!' But he sternly ordered them not to make him known" (3:10–12). This summary leads into the account of Jesus' institution of the Twelve (3:13–19). But his ministry meets opposition from his family and from Israel (3:20–30). He establishes new principles for belonging to his family (3:31–35) and teaches his new family, the disciples to whom the mystery of the kingdom is revealed, through parables that insist upon the relentless growth of the kingdom, despite opposition and difficulty (4:1–34). The disciples then follow him through a stunning series of miracles that steadily show Jesus' authority over nature (the calming of the storm), the demonic (the Gerasene demoniac), human sickness (the woman with the flow of blood), and death itself (the daughter of Jairus) (4:35–5:43). As Jesus returns to his hometown, his own people ask the correct question: "Where does this man get all this? What is the wisdom given to him? What mighty works are wrought by his hands?" (6:2). Readers and listeners, who have read and heard the prologue (1:1–13), know the answer to that question, but the people from his home village do not. They reject him: "'Is not this the carpenter, the son of Mary and brother of James and Joses and Judas and Simon, and are not his sisters here with us?' And they took offense at him" (6:3). Jesus was "amazed at their unbelief" (6:6a).

(3) *Jesus and his disciples* (6:6b–8:30). Following Jesus' rejection in his hometown, we find a brief general summary about his ministry in Galilee: "Then he went about among the villages teaching" (6:6b). Jesus sends out the Twelve on a mission that parallels his own (6:6b–13). While they are on their successful mission, Mark reports the death of John the Baptist, a forerunner to the death of Jesus and an indication of the cost of discipleship (6:14–29). It will cost no less than everything. But the disciples return to tell Jesus all the wonderful things that they have said and done (6:30). They have not understood the true source of their missionary success, their "being with" Jesus (cf. 3:14).[20] The remainder of this section is marked by the repetition of the multiplication of the loaves and fishes (6:31–44; 8:1–10). It features the issues of food and purity, of Jesus' universal presence to both Jew and Gentile, and the necessary involvement of the disciples in Jesus' mission to nourish all who

---

Their attitude to Jesus is the issue in the Markan story. This intensifies in 11:1–15:47. See further, Rhoads, Dewey, and Michie, *Mark as Story*, 116–22.

20. See Francis J. Moloney, "Mark 6:6b–30: Mission, the Baptist, and Failure," *CBQ* 63 (2001): 663–79.

come to him in need (6:37: "You give them something to eat"). The narrative is marked by increasing hostility between Jesus and the Jews, especially in his conflict with the Pharisees over what is pure and impure (7:1–23). The lack of understanding among the disciples also increases. Jesus leaves Israel and cures the Syrophoenician woman (7:24–30) and a deaf and dumb man from the Decapolis (7:31–37). Rejected by his own, he cures (7:24–37) and feeds (8:1–9) Gentiles. Despite their hesitations, his disciples, his new family, also become more deeply involved with his ministry (see 6:7–13, 30–44; 8:1–9). After further discussions with the disciples, who fail to recognize Jesus and what he has done in the two bread miracles (8:11–21), a blind man stumbles to sight (8:22–26). He moves from blindness to partial sight to full sight. This staged movement from "blindness" to "sight" is repeated in another key, as the first half of the Gospel closes and the second opens. Jesus broaches the question that has been lurking behind the narrative since 1:14: "Who do people say that I am?" (8:27). The response shows that "the people" are blind to the true identity of Jesus. But when Jesus asks his disciples, "Who do you say that I am" (8:28), Peter responds: "You are the Christ" (8:29). The reader/listener, informed by the storyteller at 1:1, has known from the outset that Jesus is the Christ. The question "who is Jesus?" has been answered. There is a sense in which Peter is correct, but there is a danger that this confession reflects only "partial sight," matching the partial sight of "men who look like trees, walking" (8:24). Jesus' words to the disciples ("them") sounds a warning bell and opens the door to the second part of the Gospel: "He charged them to tell no one about him" (8:30).

Jesus' commanding his disciples to silence in 8:30 closes the first half of the story and points toward the second half, which opens with the first prediction of his future death and resurrection in Jerusalem (8:31). It is only in Jesus' self-revelation as the Son of Man who must suffer and rise again that the fullness of sight emerges. The remainder of the Gospel will reflect the relentless attempts of Jesus to instruct his disciples, matched by the struggle of the disciples to move away from their partial sight, their expectation that Jesus will be the expected all-conquering Davidic Messiah. It will end in failure (cf. 14:50–52) and promise (cf. 14:28; 16:7).

MARK 8:22–15:47

Textual markers across 8:22–15:47 indicate a plot that has three major moments. The first half of the Gospel raised the question of the identity of Jesus, and that was partially answered in 8:27–30. The second half of the Gospel tells of a suffering and finally vindicated Son of Man, Messiah, and Son of God whom the Jewish leaders and the people reject and whom the disciples cannot or will not understand. It unfolds in three unified sections. As we have already mentioned, 8:22–30 does not simply bring the first half of the Gospel to a close. These passages, on blindness and the identity of Jesus, also open the second half of the story.[21] Obvious changes of place, characters, and situations occur across this second half of the story.

(1) *Jesus and the disciples' journey to Jerusalem* (8:2–10:52). This section of the story is circumscribed by two cures of blind men: 8:22–26 (the blind man at Bethsaida) and 10:46–52 (blind Bartimaeus.) Between these miracles, one of which has a blind man stumbling to sight (8:22–26) and the other a blind man leaping to his feet at Jesus' call and following him down "the way" (10:46–52), Jesus journeys to Jerusalem and predicts his future suffering, death, and resurrection three times (8:31; 9:31; 10:32–35). *Immediately* after each passion prediction, the disciples fail to accept and understand the destiny of the man they are following and, implicitly, their own destiny as his disciples. Peter fails (8:32–33), all the disciples fail (9:32–34), the sons of Zebedee, and then the other ten disciples fail (10:36–40, 41–44). Jesus never abandons his fragile followers. After each failure, he instructs them on the need to take up the cross (8:34–9:1), on service and receptivity (9:35–50), on the need to abandon hopes for human authority and power (10:36–44). Jesus teaches his disciples by means of other words and events: the transfiguration, the lesson of the boy they could not heal (9:1–29), the practice of discipleship in marriage, and in the correct understanding and use of possessions (10:1–31). He closes his instruction of the disciples on the way to Jerusalem with words that describe Jesus' own role: "For the Son of Man also came not to be served but to serve, and to give his life as a ransom for many" (10:45). Bartimaeus shows that it is possible. He abandons what little he has and follows Jesus down the way (10:46–52).

(2) *Endings in Jerusalem* (11:1–13:37). A radical change of setting indicates the beginning of the next stage of the plot. In a way that questions all expected messianic expectations, Jesus enters Jerusalem (11:1–11). Framed by the cursing of the fig tree, he *brings to an end* all temple practices and replaces them with faith, prayer, and forgiveness (11:12–25). Still in the temple, he encounters and *brings to an end* Israel's religious authority. He condemns their lack of care for the Lord's vineyard and systematically reduces to silence the Pharisees, the Sadduccees, and the scribes (11:27–12:40). In their place, he points to the widow who has nothing but, like Bartimaeus, gave her very life

---

21. On this, see the excellent work of one of my students, Gregg S. Morrison, "The Turning Point in the Gospel of Mark: A Study in Markan Christology" (Ph.D. diss., The Catholic University of America, 2008).

(12:41–44). Finally, he tells of *the end* of Jerusalem (13:1–23) and *the end* of the world (13:24–37). Despite all of these "endings," the rejected stone will become the cornerstone of a new temple (12:10). The disciples and their followers will suffer much, but none of this marks the end of the new temple built on the rejected cornerstone (cf. 12:10–11; 14:57–58; 15:29–38). "The gospel must first be preached to all nations" (13:10). But the end will come, when the angels will gather the elect from the four corners of the earth to present them to the Son of Man (13:27). In the meantime, as Jesus must suffer through the evening, at midnight and at cock-crow, the disciples are to be attentive servants, at their post watching, as they do not know when the master of the household will come: in the evening, at midnight, or at cock-crow (13:32–37).

(3) *The passion and death of Jesus* (14:1–15:47). The second half of the story ends with a description of the passion, death, and burial of Jesus that is distinguished by obvious textual markers: an extended use of intercalation. In 14:1–72 one finds eleven distinct pericopes, moving between the darkness of failure and the light of Jesus. At its center, in the sixth scene, Jesus celebrates his final meal—which will be the first of many meals—with his disciples.[22] The passage is arranged as follows:

[A] 14:1–2: The plot of the Jewish leaders
  [B] 14:3–9: The anointing *of Jesus*
[A] 14:10–11: Judas, *one of the Twelve*, joins the plot of 14:1–2
  [B] 14:12–16: *Jesus* sees to the preparation for a Passover meal
[A] 14:17–21: Jesus predicts the betrayal *of Judas, one of the Twelve*
  [B] 14:22–25: Jesus **shares the meal, giving bread and wine to** the disciples
[A] 14:26–31: Jesus predicts the future denials *of Peter* and the flight *of all the disciples*
  [B] 14:32–42: The prayer *of Jesus* in Gethsemane
[A] 14:43–52: Judas, *one of the Twelve*, along with representatives of the Jewish leaders arrest Jesus, and *all the disciples* flee
  [B] 14:53–65: The self-revelation *of Jesus* at the Jewish hearing
[A] 14:66–72: *Peter* denies Jesus three times

The eleven brief scenes in this arrangement shift systematically from portrayals or predictions of disciples' failures to a presentation of the person of Jesus. Poignantly, and importantly for the Markan understanding of Jesus and his

---

22. See Francis J. Moloney, "Literary Strategies in the Markan Passion Narrative (Mark 14,1–15,47)," *SNTSU* 28 (2003): 5–25.

disciples, at the very center, in the sixth scene (14:21–25), the failing disciples and Jesus share a meal. The Markan theme of Jesus' never-failing presence, breaking his body and shedding his blood for a new covenant with his fragile, failing disciples, is succinctly articulated by means of this literary structure. The same literary pattern is found in 15:1–47. Here there are nine pericopes, and the fifth, central, passage is the point toward which the Gospel has been moving since 2:10: Jesus' crucifixion.[23]

> [A] 15:1–5: The self-revelation *of Jesus* as the Roman hearing begins
>   [B] 15:6–11: The question of Barabbas
> [A] 15:12–15: Pilate ironically proclaims *Jesus* innocent and king as the Roman hearing closes
>   [B] 15:16–20a: The Roman soldiers ironically proclaim the truth as they mock Jesus
> [C] **15:20b–25: The crucifixion *of Jesus***
>   [B] 15:26–32: Passers-by and the Jewish leaders ironically proclaim the truth as they mock Jesus
> [A] 15:33–39: The death *of Jesus*, proclaimed Son of God
>   [B] 15:40–41: The women at the cross
> [A] 15:42–47: The burial *of Jesus*

The disciples have abandoned Jesus, who has died alone and in agony and despair (15:34, 37). The women watch, and a Gentile—seeing the way Jesus died—has confessed that he was the Son of God (15:39; cf. 1:11; 9:7). The reader/listener knows that the death of Jesus is not the end of the story. On the basis of what he or she has learned in 1:1–13, Jesus' promises that he would rise on the third day (8:31; 9:31; 10:34), that he would drink the new cup with his disciples in the kingdom (14:25), and that he would go before them into Galilee (14:28), must be fulfilled. The word of Jesus will not be uttered in vain.

THE EPILOGUE: MARK 16:1–8

In a context of wonder (16:1–5), the young man dressed in a white robe announces to the women who had been at the cross and burial that the crucified and buried Jesus "has been raised" (16:6). The women are told of the promise that Jesus would go before his disciples into Galilee (16:7). What he said he would do (14:28), he is now doing (16:7). But the women fail to speak

---

23. See Francis J. Moloney, "The Centrality of the Cross: Literary and Theological Reflections on Mark 15:20b–25," *Pacifica* 21 (2008): 245–56.

to anyone because they, like the disciples before them, flee in fear (16:6–8; cf. 14:50).

Everything in this epilogue points beyond the limitations of the Markan story to the existence of a believing Christian community. The prologue to the Gospel (1:1–13) informed the reader that Jesus was the Christ (1:1), the Lord (1:3), the mightier one (1:7), one who would baptize with the Holy Spirit (1:8), the beloved Son of God (1:11), restoring God's original creative design (1:12–13). The original Markan community accepted this confession of faith and attempted to live as authentic disciples of Jesus, taking up their cross, receptive servants of all, in imitation of Jesus (see 8:31–10:44), who came to serve and not be served and to lay down his life (10:45). Yet in human terms, the disciples, both men and women (14:50–52; 16:8), fail to follow Jesus through the cross to resurrection. In the same human terms, even Jesus failed, crying out in anguish from the cross (15:34, 37). But Jesus' apparent failure is his victory. On the cross he is King, Messiah and Son of God (15:26, 31–32, 39), and God has entered the story by raising his Son from the dead: "He has been raised" (16:6b, ēgerthē, ἠγέρθη). He is no longer in the place where they laid him (16:6c).

The author believes and wishes to communicate that the exalted christological claims of the prologue (1:1–13) have been vindicated by the story of the suffering and crucified Jesus, especially by means of the Easter proclamation of the epilogue (16:1–8). The affirmation of God's project by means of the prologue (1:1–13) and the epilogue (16:1–8) also points to God's vindication of failed disciples. The original readers of the Gospel of Mark, aware of their fragility, were encouraged by a story that told of the inability of the original disciples, men and women, to overcome their fear and follow Jesus through the cross to resurrection (14:50; 16:8). But the reader/listener is aware that, as God has transformed the failure of Jesus by the resurrection (16:6), his promise to the failing disciples of a meeting in Galilee (14:28; 16:7) has also eventuated. God, and not human beings, generated the new temple, built upon the rejected cornerstone (12:10–11; 14:57–58; 15:29, 38). The existence of the Gospel and its original intended readership are proof of that fact.

The accomplishment of Jesus' promises is not found *in the text*. The existence of the Markan community and its story of Jesus indicate that it is taking place *among the readers of the text*, in the experience of the original readers (and hearers) of the Gospel of Mark. But that is not the end of the process. The proclamation of the Gospel of Mark in fragile Christian communities, experiencing their own versions of fear and flight, for almost two thousand years, suggests that the accomplishment of the promise of 14:28 and 16:7 continues in the Christian experience of the subsequent readers (and hearers) of the Gospel. What Jesus promised (14:28; 16:7) happened for the Markan community and continues to happen among generations of fragile followers of Jesus. As Christian disciples continue to fail and flee in fear, they are told that God's action in and through the risen Jesus overcomes all such failure.[24] Jesus is going before them into Galilee. There they will see him. The epilogue, the conclusion to Mark's Gospel, is not a message of failure but a resounding affirmation of God's design to overcome all imaginable human failure (16:1–8) in and through the action of God's beloved Son (1:1–13). Words addressed to the struggling disciples at the transfiguration are addressed to all who take up this Gospel: "Listen to him" (see 9:7).

CONCLUSION

By means of this well-constructed plot, the narrator takes readers who are already familiar with the story through a new telling that transforms its well-known ending. Mark faced a problem stated some twenty years before the Gospel appeared: "For Jews demand signs and Greeks seek wisdom, but we preach Christ crucified, a stumbling block to Jews and folly to Gentiles, but to those who are called, both Jews and Greeks, Christ the power of God and the wisdom of God. For the foolishness of God is wiser than human wisdom, and the weakness of God is stronger than any human strength" (1 Cor 1:22–25). Mark attempts to solve the scandal of the cross by means of a story that begins as "the good news" that Jesus is the Christ, the Son of God (1:1, 11), and ends with a scream from a cross and an agonizing death, an empty tomb, and an Easter message that is not delivered (15:33–16:8). A story of the Christ and the Son of God that ends in this fashion is a narrative repetition of the Pauline message: "the foolishness of God is wiser than human wisdom, and the weakness of God is stronger than any human strength" (1 Cor 1:25).

This essay has attempted to indicate the elements *in the Markan narrative* that determined the writing of a narrative commentary on the Gospel. However, lest my reader comes to think that this process is now obvious, allow me to conclude with a word of warning. It must not be thought that, having discovered the plot and the way the characters interact through the unfolding of that plot, the journey is over. There are places in the Gospel of Mark where a reader finds the logic of the movement from one episode to the next hard to follow. We have become used to stories that flow smoothly and tend to judge them according to the author's ability to lead the reader gently from one

24. For similar suggestions, see Thomas Boomershine, "Mark 16:8 and the Apostolic Commission," *JBL* 100 (1981): 234–39; Robert C. Tannehill, "The Gospel of Mark as Narrative Christology," *Semeia* 16 (1980): 82–84; Rhoads, Dewey, and Michie, *Mark as Story*, 142–43.

episode to the next. Such an easy passage is not always the case in the Gospel of Mark. One good example of this is found in 9:42–48, where a series of sayings of Jesus that may have originally been independent have been placed side by side on the basis of the repetition of the same words in the sayings ("cause to sin" [see 9:42, 43, 45, 44] and "salt" [9:49, 50]). But the link between each saying is hard to trace, and one must strain one's imagination to follow the logic of 9:42–48. These moments of obscurity in the narrative indicate the respect that the early writers in the Christian church had for the traditions that came to them. Mark was certainly a creative writer, but he respected words and events from the life of Jesus that he received. As the first attempt to tell the life of Jesus that proclaimed that Jesus was the Christ, the Son of God, Mark's story must not be judged by the criteria we use to judge an enjoyable novel.

I resolved the tensions in the narrative by the application of two principles. In the first instance, I took it for granted that Mark the storyteller attempted to write an account of the ministry, death, and resurrection of Jesus that coherently communicated what he wanted to say to the original readers. The fact that we are historically, culturally, and even religiously distant from those original readers means that we must allow ourselves to be challenged by the strangeness of this ancient text.[25] A danger for all narrative critics is that, among the various "setting(s)" they trace in a Gospel, insufficient attention is given to *the original historical and cultural setting* that produced the text. The rich results of 150 years of historical-critical scholarship must not be abandoned.

Second, I strove "even if unconsciously, to fit everything together in a consistent pattern."[26] My striving may be judged as an imposition of my literary and theological biases. That is an inevitable, and indeed acceptable, part of the reading, listening, and interpreting process. It is true that we shape the meaning of what we read in the light of our own experiences and understanding. But the text has also shaped me. This is particularly the case when Christians read or listen to the Gospel. It is respect and admiration for a text that has been read again and again by many Christian individuals and within the life of the Christian church for almost two thousand years that inspires my striving to understand the message of the Gospel of Mark. "Every element in the story is there for a reason, which we will discover only by combing back and

---

25. On the readers of the Markan story, see Rhoads, Dewey, and Michie, *Mark as Story*, 137–46.

26. W. Iser, *The Implied Reader: Patterns of Communication in Prose Fiction from Bunyan to Beckett* (Baltimore: Johns Hopkins University Press, 1978), 283.

forth through the text until it yields its own narrative coherence."[27] To "give up" on a section of the narrative—or even on the Gospel as a whole—because it does not speak to me according to my expectations is to forget that, while we always bring ourselves to our reading, we must also allow this important text to speak to us *in its own terms*.

In 1921 perhaps the most significant New Testament scholar of the twentieth century, Rudolf Bultmann, assessed the Markan narrative as follows: "In Mark we can still see clearly, and most easily in comparison with Luke, that the most ancient tradition consisted of individual sections, and the connection together is secondary.... Mark is not sufficiently master of his material to be able to venture on a systematic construction himself."[28] Almost a century later, our current understanding of *Mark as Story*, a narrative whole of considerable power and passion, has led me to claim that the exact opposite is the case.

---

27. Ched Myers, *Binding the Strong Man: A Political Reading of Mark's Story of Jesus* (Maryknoll, N.Y.: Orbis, 1986), 109.

28. Rudolf Bultmann, *History of the Synoptic Tradition* (trans. John Marsh; Oxford: Basil Blackwell, 1968 [orig. German: 1921]), 338, 350.

Audience Address and Purpose in the Performance of Mark

Thomas E. Boomershine

The publication of *Mark as Story* in 1982 was a major step in the development of a new paradigm for the study and interpretation of the Gospels in ancient and modern media. The systematic application of what the authors call "narrative criticism" began the process of the reconception of Mark in the context of the media culture of antiquity. This new vision was given impetus by the adaptation of the methods of literary criticism that were developed for the study of the modern novel.[1] By close attention to the intrinsic features of Mark as a narrative, a new body of scholarship has drawn a rich picture of Mark that has begun the process of removing the shadow that Hans Frei aptly named the "eclipse" of biblical narrative.[2]

This intersection of ancient and modern media culture is only the latest stage of this development in biblical study. "Historical criticism" in its classical form was the product of an earlier intersection between the Bible and what Wellek and Warren termed extrinsic methods of literary criticism. Historical criticism created a picture of the meaning of a literary work by identifying the complex of extrinsic forces—for example, cultural and political movements, biography of the author, and, most important, the history of the sources and traditions—that led to the final work.[3] The study of Mark (as well as the Gospels and the Bible) as texts produced by editors of earlier documents and designed to be read in silence by readers draws a picture of Mark that makes

---

1. For the classic example of an "intrinsic" methodology for the study of the novel, see Wayne Booth, *The Rhetoric of Fiction* (Chicago: University of Chicago Press, 1961); also Seymour Chatman, *Story and Discourse: Narrative Structure in Fiction and Film* (Ithaca, N.Y.: Cornell University Press, 1978).

2. Hans Frei, *The Eclipse of Biblical Narrative* (New Haven: Yale University Press, 1974).

3. Rene Wellek and Austin Warren, *Theory of Literature* (New York: Harcourt, Brace, 1942).

sense to readers of history and theology who have lived in the media cultures of the eighteenth–twentieth centuries.

The foundational contribution of *Mark as Story* is that it approaches Mark in a manner that is appropriate to the form of the Gospel, namely, narrative. Rather than interpreting Mark as a source of referential information in the categories of the literatures of "history" and "theology," this work initiated the study of Mark as a narrative. By paying attention to the dynamics of the interaction of the narrator, the characters and the plot of Mark's narrative in its final form, the book succeeded in drawing a complex and nuanced description of the story world of Mark as experienced by readers. In the first edition, the authors acknowledge that their approach may be more appropriate to the way modern readers experience the Gospel than to the way Mark was experienced in the ancient context: "Mark's gospel was probably written to be heard rather than read. It would, therefore, be appropriate to refer to the hearers of the drama. We have chosen, however, to deal with the gospel as literature and to discuss its readers."[4] The second edition is more attentive to the original medium of the Gospel:

> We have chosen here to focus on the literary reading of Mark rather than on an oral hearing, because most modern people will read the Gospel rather than hear it, and because our purpose is to suggest ways of reading. Nevertheless, our interpretations, particularly in regard to the role of the narrator, the character of the disciples, and the understanding of plot, have been influenced by our work on oral narrative.[5]

Both editions, however, were deliberately directed at modern readers who would "read" rather than hear Mark, namely, college and seminary students, even though the authors were aware of, and even employed, insights arrived at by taking into account the original oral medium. And the book has been highly successful in enabling a generation of students to experience Mark in a mode that is more accessible than traditional historical criticism has provided.

Furthermore, interpreting Mark as addressed to readers is in continuity with the assumptions of most scholarly investigations of Mark. The present conclusions about the historical audiences of Mark have been developed within what can be called the textual paradigm. This paradigm is a hermeneutical circle of assumptions about the medium of Mark. In this paradigm it

---

4. David Rhoads and Donald Michie, *Mark as Story: An Introduction to the Narrative of a Gospel* (Philadelphia: Fortress, 1982), 143 n. 1.

5. David Rhoads, Joanna Dewey, and Donald Michie, *Mark as Story: An Introduction to the Narrative of a Gospel* (2nd ed.; Minneapolis: Fortress, 1999), xii.

has been assumed that Mark was a text read by an audience of readers.[6] This assumption is often explicitly named, as, for example, in Joel Marcus's recent superb commentary, where he frequently refers to Mark's reader.[7]

This assumption has been most graphically developed in reader-response criticism. The most critically informed development of this approach to Mark is Robert Fowler's comprehensive survey and detailed application to the exegesis of Mark's text, appropriately titled *Let the Reader Understand*. As he summarizes at one point, "Mark's Gospel is designed to guide, direct, and illuminate the reader vigorously and authoritatively, but at the same time challenge, puzzle, and humble its reader."[8] The focus of Fowler's analysis is making explicit in great detail the facets of "the reading experience." For example, in his exegesis of the crucifixion scene, he identifies the narrator's use of opacity, irony, paradox, metaphor, and ambiguity as dimensions of Mark's indirect moves in engaging his readers in the experience of the crucifixion.

The "reading experience" implies a picture of the reception of Mark as that of a single person sitting alone reading the manuscript, generally in silence as in modern reading but perhaps aloud. This picture sometimes includes the possibility that the reader may read the manuscript aloud to a small group of listeners.

The dominant concept of Mark's audience and the manuscript's purpose for the audience is a natural inference within this framework. The most frequent conclusion of Markan scholars is that the audience of Mark consists of readers who are members of first-century Christian communities that already believe in Jesus. This makes sense when the controlling presupposition is that Mark is a text read by readers. It is highly unlikely that persons outside the believing communities of Christians in the first century would go to the trouble and expense of purchasing a manuscript of Mark and reading it. The readers of a Markan manuscript would most naturally be persons who are committed members of a community of believers. The Gospel may have been written for an individual community of which the author was a member.

---

6. See, for example, Ernest Best, "Mark's Readers: A Profile," in *The Four Gospels 1992: Festschrift Frans Neirynck* (ed. Frans van Segbroeck, Christopher M. Tuckett, Gilbert Van Belle, and Jozef Verheyden; 2 vols.; BETL 100; Leuven: Leuven University Press, 1992), 2:839–58.

7. Joel Marcus, *Mark 1–8* (AB 27; New York: Doubleday, 2000), 468: "The woman's hope that her daughter will be healed, and the reader's, seem to be dashed by Jesus' response." However, Marcus also locates the genre of Mark as part of a liturgical drama in which the Gospel was read as part of the liturgy in Mark's Christian community (67–69).

8. Robert Fowler, *Let the Reader Understand: Reader-Response Criticism and the Gospel of Mark* (Minneapolis: Fortress, 1991), 220.

Joel Marcus argues strongly that this is the historical probability.[9] Richard Bauckham and Mary Ann Tolbert have imagined Mark as being written for broad distribution to Christian communities throughout the Greco-Roman world,[10] but they share the assumption that Mark was written for an audience of readers.

The purpose of the Gospel when interpreted in this context is primarily to reinforce in various ways the beliefs and identity of the reader as a follower of Jesus. Thus, Adela Yarbro Collins summarizes Mark's purposes: "One was to reassert the messiahship of Jesus and to redefine it over against the messianic pretenders during the Jewish war that began in 66 C.E. Another was to interpret actual or expected persecution (or both) as discipleship in imitation of Christ."[11] Both of these purposes are congruent with the function of Mark's manuscript when read by a believing reader.

Another dimension of this paradigm is the congruence between the medium of contemporary Markan scholarship and its audiences and the original medium and purpose of Mark. Just as contemporary scholars and the audiences they address in commentaries and monographs read the text in silence, so also it is assumed that Mark addressed an audience of persons who read the text in silence. The function of Markan scholarship is to call detailed attention to what a reader sees in the text. The historical validity of this methodology is based on the assumption that this was how Mark's text was originally experienced. That is, scholarship is paying close attention to the reading experience of the original readers of Mark and within those parameters to alert modern readers to dimensions of the meanings of the text.

An integral part of this medium of Markan scholarship is "criticism." Scholars are trained as critics who read Mark from a psychological distance. That distance is an integral dimension of reading a text with one's eyes in silence. Indeed, the name of the dominant methodology for the study of Mark is "historical *criticism*." Among the range of meanings of this methodology, it means the *critical* reading of biblical texts in their original historical context. The media dimension of this methodology is silent reading with an attitude of critical detachment.[12] Silent reading is what a scholar does in the study. Silent

---

9. Marcus, *Mark 1–8*, 25–28.

10. Richard Bauckham, "For Whom Were Gospels Written?" in *The Gospels for All Christians: Rethinking the Gospel Audiences* (ed. Richard Bauckham; Grand Rapids: Eerdmans, 1997), 9–48; see also Mary Ann Tolbert, *Sowing the Gospel: Mark's World in Literary-Historical Perspective* (Philadelphia: Fortress, 1989), 304.

11. Adela Yarbro Collins, *Mark* (Hermeneia; Minneapolis: Fortress, 2007), 102.

12. Fowler writes well about the centrality of his commitment to criticism at the end of his book. He is reflecting on the ways in which Matthew, Luke, John, and Tatian have

"critical" reading is the dominant experience of Mark in the media world of contemporary biblical scholarship.

It is not coincidental that various dimensions of the "critical" readings of Mark have been found to be central to the meaning and purpose of Mark in its original historical context. Wrede's exploration of the messianic secret is based on an exposition of the theological questions that were raised for Mark's readers by Jesus' persistent injunctions to silence about his identity.[13] An entire school of Markan interpretation has been based on the conclusion that Mark is inviting his readers to be critical of the disciples and their various failures in understanding and action.[14] In his major work on the relationship of Mark to the oral and literate cultures of antiquity, Werner Kelber extended Mark's critical purpose to the criticism of the entire oral Gospel tradition represented in Mark by Peter and the apostles.[15] That is, modern "critical" readers of Mark have found that there were "critical" readers of Mark in the ancient world as well. Criticism may be an inevitable dimension of silent reading.

PERFORMANCE CRITICISM AND THE ORIGINAL AUDIENCES OF MARK

A new framework of Markan scholarship in particular and biblical scholarship in general is emerging at a new intersection between ancient and modern media cultures. The results of recent research by both classical and biblical scholars paint a different picture of the media cultures of the ancient world

---

each in different ways retold Mark's story and made Mark forever a precursor. Even though he would like to experience Mark without these revisions, he recognizes that if he were to retell Mark's story, he would probably also revise it and turn Mark into a precursor. "Yet my own vocation is not storyteller but critic. If I were a storyteller, I would like to write a Gospel that places Mark's successors in such a light that the shadows they have cast upon Mark for centuries would be dispelled and the highlights they have shone upon Mark would be muted. I would like to construct a grid for reading Matthew that blocks out Matthew and allows only Mark's Gospel to be seen as it was before Matthew came along. Nevertheless, such a reading experience is a pipe dream—no such magical reading grid will ever be produced—so I shall continue to trust the powers of criticism to serve reading" (*Let the Reader Understand*, 206).

13. William Wrede, *The Messianic Secret* (trans. J. C. G. Greig; Cambridge: James Clarke, 1971); trans. of *Das Messiasgeheimnis in den Evangelien: Zugleich ein Beitrag zum Verständnis des Markusevangeliums* (Göttingen: Vandenhoeck & Ruprecht, 1901).

14. This identification of Mark as a critic of the disciples had its initial book-length exposition in Theodore J. Weeden, *Mark: Traditions in Conflict* (Philadelphia: Fortress, 1971).

15. Werner Kelber, *The Oral and the Written Gospel: The Hermeneutics of Speaking and Writing in the Synoptic Tradition, Mark, Paul and Q* (Philadelphia: Fortress, 1983; repr., Bloomington: Indiana University Press, 1997).

than has been assumed by this textual paradigm of Mark and his readers. Only a cursory summary of the results of this research is possible here. (1) Literacy was minimal. Current estimates are that the rates of literacy in urban areas in the first century were somewhere between 5 and 10 percent of the population, with significantly lower rates in rural areas. Thus, the overwhelming major- ity of people could not read.[16] (2) Manuscripts had to be copied by hand, were relatively rare by modern standards, and were relatively expensive. Only rich individuals and communities were able to acquire manuscripts of ancient writings in the first century.[17] (3) Manuscripts were normally "published" by public performance for audiences. Audiences could range from a few people to a large group.[18] (4) A biblical manuscript was a recording of sound that the author assumed would be reproduced as sound by those who performed it. The audiences heard the manuscript rather than reading it with their eyes. (5) Manuscripts were usually memorized and performed from memory rather than read from a text. This made possible a high degree of interaction between the performer and the audience.[19] (6) Performances of stories were highly emotional and physically demonstrative. Highly expressive gestures were a crucial dimension of performance.[20] (7) Performances of ancient stories were often long and could last anywhere from an hour to all night, as was the case with some performances of Homer.

The mass production of books, mass literacy, and silent reading were much later developments in the history of literacy and book production. The assumption that these practices were widespread in the first century is an

---

16. See William Harris, *Ancient Literacy* (Cambridge: Harvard University Press, 1989).

17. Harry Y. Gamble, *Books and Readers in the Early Church: A History of Early Chris-tian Texts* (New Haven: Yale University Press, 1995); idem, "Literacy and Book Culture," in *Dictionary of New Testament Background* (ed. Craig A. Evans and Stanley E. Porter; Down- ers Grove, Ill.: InterVarsity Press, 2000), 644–48.

18. See Moses Hadas (*Ancilla to Classical Reading* [New York: Columbia University Press, 1954], 50–77) for a series of citations from ancient literature showing that perfor- mance of written works was the primary mode of publication. Even historical works were "published" by oral recitation, as is evident in Lucian's opening of his book *Herodotus,* in which he tells the story of Herodotus taking the opportunity of the Olympic Games to read his work: "He seized the moment when the gathering was at its fullest, and every city had sent the flower of its citizens; then he appeared in the temple hall, bent not on sightseeing but on bidding for an Olympic victory of his own; he recited his Histories and bewitched his hearers" (60).

19. Whitney Shiner, *Proclaiming the Gospel: First-Century Performance of Mark* (Har- risburg, Pa.: Trinity Press International, 2003), 103–26.

20. Ibid., 77–98.

anachronism. The media world of the first century was very different from the media world of the eighteenth–twenty-first centuries.

When the Gospel of Mark is interpreted in the context of the media world of the first century c.e., the medium of Mark has to be reconceived. The most comprehensive study of Mark in the context of the media world of the first century is Whitney Shiner's groundbreaking work, *Proclaiming the Gospel: First-Century Performance of Mark*.[21] Shiner bases his conclusions about Mark's original medium on a comprehensive examination of ancient rhetorical writings that describe often in great detail the character of first-century rhetorical culture. In Shiner's reconstruction of the first-century media culture, the Gospel of Mark was usually performed for audiences. The original medium of Mark was the sounds of the story and the gestures of the storytellers who performed it. Storytellers normally learned Mark's story by heart and performed the story. Usually, the whole Gospel was told at one time, which took approximately two hours.

This understanding of Mark is congruent with Eusebius's description of Mark's use of the manuscript he had written. Immediately following his citation of the Papias tradition that Mark had written his Gospel by recording Peter's proclamation in writing at the request of the Christian community in Rome, he states the following about what Mark did with his manuscript: "And they say that this Mark was the first that was sent to Egypt, and that he proclaimed the Gospel which he had written, and first established churches in Alexandria."[22]

Regardless of the uncertainty of its historical accuracy, this account reflects the assumption of an author some three centuries later that the account he had received—as "they say"—was historically credible, namely, that Mark was sent to Egypt, where he "performed" the Gospel for audiences in Alexandria and established churches there. That is, Eusebius's description is congruent with the conclusion that Mark's story was *proclaimed orally*. Seen in this context, the primary purpose of the manuscript was to facilitate and resource these proclamations/performances of the story. It is also implicit in Eusebius's description that some of those who heard Mark's proclamation were converted and became the basis for the establishment of churches. In view of the further probability that Mark was highly popular and was developed by Matthew and Luke, it is also probable that Mark was not performed for only one local community such as Alexandria, as reported by Eusebius, or

---

21. Ibid.,171–79.
22. Eusebius, *Hist. eccl.* 3.16.1. The reference to "they" probably refers to Papias and the Elder who are quoted in the preceding paragraph.

Antioch or Rome, but was performed in many cities and towns throughout the Greco-Roman world. If we want to reconstruct the meaning of Mark for its original audiences, therefore, we need to evaluate the data of the text as essentially a script for storytelling performances of Mark's story.

This in turn raises a methodological issue that has not been resolved since the first introduction to what was then called "rhetorical criticism" of the study of Mark.[23] How can we as modern readers study ancient narratives in a manner that is appropriate to their original media culture? Specifically, how can we *hear* in contrast to *read* Mark's stories?

David Rhoads has taken the next step in the development of an approach to this problem in his essays on "performance criticism."[24] This work has, in turn, grown out of his own performances of Mark. Performance criticism is based on the conclusion that the accurate perception and interpretation of biblical literature in its original historical context requires that we conceive and experience the books of the Bible in performance. When applied to Mark, performance criticism is redrawing the picture of Mark from a narrative read by readers to a story performed for audiences.

In light of the recognition that the medium of biblical scholarship must be appropriate to the original medium of the Bible, the ancient character of Mark as performance literature suggests that the methodologies of Markan scholarship must shift from silent reading to oral performance as a primary medium of research, pedagogy, and proclamation. If we as Markan scholars want to understand the meaning of Mark's Gospel in its original context, we may need, as far as possible, to ground our research in performing and hearing Mark rather than reading it. Therefore, as an integral part of this initial exploration of audience address in Mark, this essay will include a new intersection of ancient and modern media in a series of video performances of sections of Mark that are available at http://www.gotell.org/pages/markaudience .html. The Internet and video recordings now make it possible to integrate performances of ancient compositions with contemporary scholarly analyses of those compositions. The references to those recordings are indicated in the

---

23. David Rhoads and Don Michie have graciously acknowledged the contribution of my earlier dissertation to their work. See Rhoads and Michie, *Mark as Story*, 143 n. 1. See Thomas E. Boomershine, "Mark the Storyteller: A Rhetorical-Critical Investigation of Mark's Passion and Resurrection Narrative" (Ph.D. diss., Union Theological Seminary, New York, 1974). An integral part of that dissertation was an audio-tape of the passion narrative in Greek and in English.

24. David Rhoads, "Performance Criticism: An Emerging Methodology in Second Temple Studies—Part I," *BTB* 36 (2006): 118–33; idem, "Performance Criticism: An Emerging Methodology in Second Temple Studies—Part II," *BTB* 36 (2006): 164–84.

essay by an asterisk (*). It is highly recommended that readers of this essay go online and watch the videos of the stories in the sequence indicated by the numbering in the essay.

There are a variety of issues in relation to this study of Mark in its original context that are significantly impacted by the shift in methodology described above. The issue with which the present essay is concerned is the question of the makeup of the audience for whom Mark originally intended his story. The reigning consensus that has resulted from approaching Mark as a text read by readers is that the audience must have been Christians. This is usually qualified to say that they are *Gentile* Christians. The study of audience address from the perspective of Mark as a story performed for a listening, not a reading, audience points strongly to a different conclusion.

DATA OF MARKAN AUDIENCE ADDRESS

In the original performances of Mark, there were three major components: the performer or storyteller; the story that the storyteller told with its characters, particularly Jesus; and the audiences. In the course of the performance, the storytellers were first and foremost themselves speaking as themselves to the audience, that is, speaking as who they were in their daily life and not as this or that character in the secondary world of the story. This contrasts with ancient theater, in which each actor "became" a particular character in the drama. The most important task of a storyteller, in contrast to an actor, is to establish a positive relationship with the audience. The central feature of that relationship is credibility and trust, the credibility of the storyteller and the audience's confidence that the storyteller will tell them a good story. Thus, at the beginning of the story, Mark, the storyteller, introduced the subject of the story as a direct address to the audience: "the beginning of the good news of Jesus Christ."

In the performance of stories, storytellers have a complex role. In contrast to drama, in which a single actor presents the words and actions of one particular character, storytellers embody all of the characters of the story. In Mark, the major character is Jesus. At many points in the story, the storyteller addresses the audience *as Jesus*. This involves a move from being oneself to presenting and embodying Jesus. It was probably signaled by a change of voice, accent, attitude, or tone as well as gestures. In Mark's story, John the Baptist introduces Jesus and the story of Jesus' baptism, while the testing in the wilderness is the first description of Jesus' actions. But the first presentation of Jesus as a character is his address to the audience as the people of Galilee: "The time is fulfilled. The kingdom of God is at hand. Change your minds and believe in this good news" (1:15).*[1] In the telling of the story, the storyteller becomes Jesus and presents him as a different character than the storyteller.

This change in character happens throughout the story in the many speeches of Jesus. But while the major character that the storyteller presents is Jesus, the storyteller also presents many other characters. In what we now call chapters 1 and 2, for example, the storyteller embodies the demon-possessed man in the synagogue, Simon, the begging leper, the skeptical scribes in the house, the critical scribes of the Pharisees, the disciples of John and the Pharisees, and the accusing Pharisees.

The audience also has a complex role. Since the only people present in a storytelling performance are the storyteller and the audience, the impact of the story depends to a significant degree on the engagement and responses of the audience. Every storyteller experiences this. There are good audiences who respond freely, laugh a lot, and interact with the story enthusiastically and sympathetically. There are bad, unresponsive audiences who are indifferent, hostile, or critical and who do not laugh or even smile. For a bad audience, a storyteller will often shorten the story in order to get it over as soon as possible.

A central dimension of the interaction of audiences with storytellers is created by a storyteller's address to the audience.[25] Most of the time, storytellers present the events of the story to the audience as themselves. In the telling of Mark, they may dramatize some of the short interactions between characters such as the conversation between Jesus and the leper. But most of the story is direct address by the storytellers to the audience as themselves. However, when the storyteller "becomes" a character, often Jesus, and addresses another character in the story, such as the scribes sitting in the crowded house into which the paralytic is lowered, the audience is in turn invited to "become" that other character listening to and interacting with Jesus for the duration of that address by Jesus. The storyteller as Jesus addresses the audience as the scribes who were grumbling to themselves: "Why do you question like this in your hearts? What is easier to say to the paralytic, 'Your sins are forgiven' or to say to him, 'Get up, take up your pallet and walk'? But that you may know that the Son of Man has authority on earth to forgive sins...." Then the storyteller steps back out of the character of Jesus into his role as narrator, briefly addressing the audience as his own listeners, "he said to the paralytic," and then again assuming the role of Jesus the storyteller kneels down and speaks to the paralytic.*[2] This shift in the listeners from being themselves to identification with the characters addressed by Jesus increases in its experiential

---

25. Most of the available video performances of Mark, including those of David Rhoads, are conceived as dramatic productions in which the audience is not addressed directly but is invited to watch the imagined interactions of the characters of the story on the other side of "the fourth wall" of the theater. Storytelling is a different performance art than drama.

impact in correlation with the length of the speech. The longer Jesus addresses the audience as a particular character, the more deeply the audience identifies with and "becomes" that character. Furthermore, just as storytellers change their presentational identity to embody the various characters of the story, the audience experiences changes in their identity by being addressed as a range of different characters in the story.

If this happened in the ancient performances of Mark's story, as is highly probable, we can identify the character of the audience for whom Mark may have performed his story. We will approach this question through an analysis of audience address in the Gospel. We begin this analysis by gathering and presenting some data. Where does Mark, usually as Jesus but a few times as narrator or as other characters in his story, address various characters, and who are the characters he addresses? This essay will limit the analysis of Markan audience address to speeches of two or more sentences, each of which constitutes a "period" in the Greek text."[26] The following chart identifies the instances in Mark's story where Mark as a storyteller addresses the audience as particular characters (usually Jesus) in the story for two or more periods. The chart lists the story in which the speech occurs and the location and length of the speech, the character who is the speaker, and the character by whom the audience is addressed.

AUDIENCE ADDRESS IN MARK

Story and Address to the Audience	Speaker Embodied by the Storyteller	Audience Addressed as …
John's baptism (1:7–8)	John the Baptist	people of Judea, etc.
proclamation of the kingdom (1:15)	Jesus	people of Galilee
healing of paralytic (2:8–10)	Jesus	scribes
eating with tax collectors (2:17)	Jesus	scribes of the Pharisees
question about fasting (2:19–22)	Jesus	disciples of John and the Pharisees

26. See Margaret Ellen Lee and Bernard Brandon Scott, *Sound Mapping the New Testament* (Salem, Ore.: Polebridge, 2009), 108–11.

shucking grain on Sabbath (2:25–28)	Jesus	Pharisees
man with withered hand (3:4–5)	Jesus	people in the synagogue
Jesus and Beelzebul (3:23–29)	Jesus	scribes from Jerusalem
Jesus and his mother and brothers (3:33–35)	Jesus	the group sitting around Jesus
parable of the sower (4:3–9)	Jesus	the crowd
purpose of parables, the meaning of the sower parable, and parables of the kingdom (4:11–32)	Jesus	those around Jesus with the Twelve
mission of the Twelve (6:10–11)	Jesus	the Twelve
tradition of the elders: cleanliness laws (7:3–4)	Mark	audience
tradition of the elders (7:6–13)	Jesus	Pharisees and scribes
tradition of the elders (7:14–15)	Jesus	the crowd
tradition of the elders (7:18–22)	Jesus	disciples
demand for a sign (8:12)	Jesus	Pharisees
leaven of the Pharisees and bread discourse (8:15–21)	Jesus	disciples

messianic confession, passion prophecy and discipleship (8:34–9:1)	Jesus	crowd with the disciples
transfiguration (9:12–13)	Jesus	Peter, James, and John
second passion prophecy (9:31)	Jesus	disciples
Who is the greatest? (9:35–37)	Jesus	disciples
the other exorcist (9:39–50)	Jesus	disciples
teaching about divorce (10:5–9)	Jesus	Pharisees
teaching about divorce (10:11–12)	Jesus	disciples
blessing the children (10:14–15)	Jesus	disciples
rich man (10:18–21)	Jesus	the rich man
rich man (10:23–27)	Jesus	disciples
rich man (10:29–31)	Jesus	Peter
third passion prophecy (10:33–34)	Jesus	disciples
James and John's request for position (10:42–45)	Jesus	disciples
the cleansing of the temple (11:17)	Jesus	the chief priests and crowd in the temple
the fig tree (11:22–26)	Jesus	disciples
parable of the vineyard (12:1–11)	Jesus	the chief priests, scribes, and elders

the resurrection controversy (12:24–27)	Jesus	Sadducees
Messiah David's son? (12:35–37)	Jesus	crowd in the temple
denouncing of the scribes (12:38–40)	Jesus	crowd in the temple
the widow's gift (12:43–44)	Jesus	disciples
apocalyptic discourse (13:4–37)	Jesus	Peter, James, John, and Andrew
anointing by woman (14:6–9)	Jesus	those who rebuked the woman
preparations for Passover (14:13–15)	Jesus	two disciples
betrayal prophecy (14:18–21)	Jesus	the Twelve
the Last Supper (14:22–25)	Jesus	the Twelve
prophecy of desertion and denial (14:27–30)	Jesus	the Twelve and Peter
Gethsemane (14:37–38, 41–42)	Jesus	Peter and Peter, James, and John
the arrest (14:48–49)	Jesus	the crowd from the priests, scribes, and elders
the trial before the Council (14:63–64)	high priest	the Council
the trial before Pilate (15:9, 12–14)	Pilate	the crowd
the resurrection (16:6–7)	young man	Mary Magdalene, Mary, and Salome

The category of "speaker" in the chart above reveals the basic structure of audience address. In speeches of two or more periods, the storyteller addresses the audience as Jesus most of the time (forty-five of fifty). The other characters who address the audience are John the Baptist, Mark as narrator, the high priest, Pilate, and the young man at the tomb. The category of "audience addressed as" reveals another fact that is surprising in the context of the Gentile Christian audiences envisioned by many Markan scholars. The most striking fact about the addresses to the audience is that the audience is almost always addressed as various groups of Jews.

The only exception to the address of the audience as Jews occurs in the story of Jesus' dispute with the Pharisees over the purity laws. The storyteller's explanation of the cleanliness laws (7:3–5) is addressed to the audience as persons who do not know these Jewish customs, that is, as non-Jews. This is a sign that the composer of the Gospel recognizes and wants to include non-Jews in the audiences of the story. That is, the audiences that are projected as the potential audiences for the performances of the Gospel are primarily, but not exclusively, Jewish.

This is a paradigmatic example of the difference made by the medium in which Mark is experienced. When the Gospel is read in silence, this comment appears to be an inside address to the reader. Scholars have often inferred from this comment that the audience of Mark is Gentiles. When the Gospel is heard as addressed to audiences, however, this comment is not directed to a reader but is directed to any in the audience who may not be familiar with Jewish customs. The comment indicates only that Mark as the composer of this story projects that there may be Gentiles in its potential audiences. This comment is a storytelling gesture of audience inclusion. The storyteller introduces it after a considerable amount of time during which he has been inviting his listeners to experience being a series of various Jewish characters who are addressed by Jesus. The purpose is to keep on board any Gentiles who might find it difficult to maintain involvement with the story without this essential information.

Another revealing dimension of audience address in Mark is the way in which the audience is invited to move from being addressed as those who are Jesus' opponents to those who are Jesus' disciples. In this structure of audience address, the storyteller as Jesus moves from addressing the audience as (1) Jesus' opponents who are in conflict with him to addressing them as (2) those around Jesus, often the disciples or the Twelve. This pattern is first established in the opening section of the Gospel. After the initial brief addresses by the storyteller as John the Baptist to the audience as the people of Judea (1:7–8), and then by Jesus to the audience as the people of Galilee (1:15), the audience is addressed for an extended time as the various groups with whom Jesus is in conflictual dialogue: the scribes (2:8–10), the scribes of the Pharisees (2:17), the disciples of John and the Pharisees (2:19–22), the Pharisees (2:25–28), the people in the synagogue who are, by inference, Pharisees (3:4–5), and, climactically, the scribes from Jerusalem (3:23–29). That is, the audience is predominantly addressed in the early parts of the story as various groups of Jews who are in conflict with Jesus.

Furthermore, there is a distinct escalation in the tone and content of the conflict. Jesus' address to the audience as the scribes in the paralytic story is moderate in tone. The address in each of the stories that follows is increasingly intense in tone and content. The longest and most conflictual address in this series is the address to the audience as the scribes who have come down from Jerusalem. They accuse Jesus of being possessed by Beelzebul and of casting out demons by the prince of demons. The climax of Jesus' speech is his description of their accusation as blasphemy against the Holy Spirit that will never be forgiven.

This series of stories ends with the most intimate address to the audience to this point in the Gospel, the story of Jesus' mother and brothers (3:31–35). The storyteller as Jesus addresses the audience as those seated around Jesus: "Who are my mother and my brothers?" Looking around at those who were seated around him, he says, "Here are my mother and my brothers. Whoever does the will of God is my brother and sister and mother."*3 In the performance of the story, the storyteller addresses this saying to all those in the audience with a gesture of wide-open arms of inclusion. This is implicitly an invitation to the audience to move from identifying with those who are in conflict with Jesus to being one of those in Jesus' intimate circle of friends. This address to the audience as Jesus' followers is then continued throughout Jesus' parabolic address (4:1–32).

The next instance of this pattern in Mark's story is the dialogue about the purity laws. This story begins with the storyteller's description to the audience of the Pharisees' critique of Jesus for allowing his disciples to eat with unwashed hands (7:1–5). This introduction is followed by Jesus' highly confrontational address to the audience as the Pharisees and scribes. This speech begins with Jesus' citation of Isaiah as prophesying their hypocrisy and ends with the accusation that in many ways they abrogate the law of God by the handing on of their tradition (7:6–13). Then the audience is briefly addressed as the crowd (7:14–15). The climax of the dialogue is an extensive address to the audience as his disciples. This speech is introduced by the relocation of the address from a public to a private place: "When he had left the crowd and entered the house…" (7:17). In the telling of the story, this introduction was probably accompanied by some gesture, perhaps a simple movement to the side and sitting down. It is also an indication of a lowering of the volume of the speech. The storyteller as Jesus moves from heated public argumentation through explanation to a sympathetic crowd to private explanation to the audience as the disciples.*4 These storytelling moves in sound and gesture create intimacy between the character of Jesus and the audience.

There are two smaller instances of this pattern in audience address prior to the stories of Jesus in Jerusalem. The first is the story of the Pharisees demanding a sign, followed by Jesus' speech to the disciples about the leaven of the Pharisees and the bread in the boat (8:11–13, 14–21). The audience is addressed as the Pharisees who were testing him, expressed in their desire for a sign. The tone of the storyteller's voice as Jesus is best described as exasperation mixed with anger. The discussion is abruptly ended with the description of Jesus getting back into the boat. The trip back to the other side of the lake is the context in which the storyteller as Jesus discusses the significance of the loaves, with the audience addressed as the disciples (8:14–21).*5 While Jesus continues to express exasperation with the disciples, the tone is more the exasperation of a teacher whose students just do not get it. There is a real possibility that the storyteller smiled and even laughed in the delivery of this speech of Jesus. The dynamic of these two stories is an invitation to the audience to experience Jesus as moving from public prophet to private teacher, a move from being addressed as an ongoing adversary to a disciple who nonetheless remains confused about the meaning of the seven and twelve baskets.[27]

The second instance of this pattern in audience address is the divorce controversy. Once again, the Pharisees engage Jesus in another test, this time about divorce law. The public discussion is addressed to the audience as the Pharisees (10:5–9). In contrast to the earlier stories of legal dispute, there is no sign here that the words of Jesus were delivered with a tone of anger or frustration. This rabbinic ruling about divorce law appears to have been delivered in a straightforward and authoritative manner, in spite of the fact that their question is introduced as still another testing of Jesus. Once again the scene shifts to the more intimate setting of the house. The storyteller as Jesus addresses the audience as the disciples for a short explanation of his legal opinion.*6 This move from public pronouncement to private discussion about the law has the same rabbinic dynamic as the earlier story about the purity laws.

The most extensive and highly developed instance of this pattern of audience address is the stories of Jesus in Jerusalem. The longest address to the

---

27. Even Joel Marcus admits to his own ongoing puzzlement in his delightful expression of hope for the future of his own understanding of Mark after sixteen years of labor on the commentary: "I look forward to meeting the author someday and finally discovering what the numbers in 8:19–21 are all about, among other mysteries" (*Mark 8–16* [AB 27A; New Haven: Yale University Press, 2009], xii).

audience as Jesus' opponents in the Gospel is the parable of the vineyard and the wicked tenants (12:1–11). It is addressed to the audience as the chief priests, scribes, and elders. This highly confrontational parable is followed by the controversy about the resurrection in which the audience is addressed as Sadducees. Jesus' pronouncement in this story ends with a dismissal of the Sadducees: "You are quite wrong." After the relatively cordial story of Jesus' discussion with the scribe, the audience is addressed as the crowd in the temple. The storyteller presents Jesus addressing the audience as a large and sympathetic crowd. He first speaks with them about the scribes' teaching that the Messiah must be the son of David, then levels a climactic denunciation against the scribes. The next move toward more intimate and confidential address to the audience is the story of the widow's gift, where the audience is addressed as the disciples.

The climax of the stories of Jesus in Jerusalem prior to the passion narrative is the most extensive and intimate conversation in the entire Gospel. The so-called apocalyptic discourse (13:4–37) is addressed to the audience as the four disciples who are sitting with Jesus on the Mount of Olives overlooking the temple. In this long address, the storyteller invites the audience into a relationship of intimacy and belief in Jesus.*7 This intimacy and reinforcement of belief is directly related to Jesus' prophecies about the Jewish-Roman war that have probably been fulfilled in the audience's recent experience of the war and the destruction of the temple.[28]

This invitation to an intimate relationship with the character of Jesus is the culmination of the storyteller's appeals to the audience throughout the story. Repeatedly in narrative sequence after narrative sequence, Mark as the teller of the tale invites the audience to move from a relationship of opposition and confrontation with Jesus to a relationship of belief and discipleship. In this structuring of audience address, Mark first engages his audience as adversaries of Jesus. The listeners are invited to enter into a series of testing confrontations with Jesus revolving primarily around the interpretation of the law. The listeners are then invited to engage with Jesus as the members of a sympathetic crowd. This climactic setting in the narrative sequences described above resonated with the real-world setting of a storytelling performance in which a crowd of people gathered around a storyteller. The culmination of this implicit appeal to the members of the audience is a storytelling invitation to enter into and identify themselves with Jesus' disciples listening to Jesus in small, private

---

28. See Joel Marcus, "The Jewish War and the *Sitz im Leben* of Mark," *JBL* 111 (1992): 441–62. The social and political context of Mark that Marcus outlines in this article is congruent with the picture of Mark in performance.

settings, usually in a house. This setting of the story is consistent with a frequent setting for the telling of Mark's story in private homes to relatively small
groups of people who would gather for an evening of storytelling.

Further evidence that this pattern of audience address was intentional is
the progressive structure of engagement with the dynamic of being addressed
as a disciple. The first significant address to the audience as persons close to
Jesus occurs, as we have seen above, in the story of Jesus and his mother and
brothers (3:31–35). There the character with whom the audience is invited to
identify is named "the crowd sitting around him" (*ekathēto peri auton ochlos*,
ἐκάθητο περὶ αὐτὸν ὄχλος), literally "the sitting-around-him crowd." In the first
teaching discourse that immediately follows this story (4:1), there is an elaborate description of the super-large crowd (*ochlos pleistos*, ὄχλος πλεῖστος) that
gathered along the shore of the sea. The storyteller as Jesus then addresses the
audience as that large crowd, with Jesus probably seated and speaking in a
loud voice with a slow tempo, as one would find it necessary in speaking to a
crowd. After the parable, the storyteller shifts the setting to an unnamed place
(4:10) where Jesus is alone, and the character addressed in the long discourse
that follows is "those who were around him with the Twelve" (*hoi peri auton
syn tois dōdeka*, οἱ περὶ αὐτὸν σὺν τοῖς δώδεκα). This name is a step closer to
being addressed as a disciple, but this character is "those who were around
him *with* the Twelve" rather than "the Twelve" by themselves. The probable
purpose of this rather strange name is the construction of a dynamic structure
that invites the audience to draw closer to Jesus in small, incremental steps.

Furthermore, the content of Jesus' speech in this discourse (4:10–32) is
a series of implicit invitations to the audience to experience being "insiders"
in the Jesus group and to reflect on the quality of their engagement with the
story. The first episode of Jesus' speech about the mystery of the kingdom of
God is an explicit address to the audience about the gift offered to them as
followers of Jesus. Furthermore, the identification of "the mystery," like the
motif of the messianic secret, is a classic storytelling lure to an audience to
stick around and hear the rest of the story. The contrast between those who
are "inside" and those who are "outside" identifies a choice that the audience
must make about whether to remain "outsiders" or to become "insiders." Both
the interpretation of the parable of the sower (4:13–20) as a parable about
different ways of "hearing" and the saying about "hearing" (the saying can
mean both "pay attention to *what* you hear" and "pay attention to *how* you
hear" [as in Matt 7:14; Luke 12:49]) address the quality of the audience's present engagement with the story.[29] This series of teaching stories (4:1–32) is the

---

29. On the use of *tis* in reference to extent or degree ("how"), see BDAG, 1007, s.v. τίς.

longest and most intensive interaction up to this point in the story between the main character, Jesus, and the audience, who are addressed first as "the great crowd" and then as "those around the Twelve."

The first speech addressed to the audience as "the Twelve" does not occur until the story of the mission of the Twelve (6:10–11). Jesus' speech has an interesting structure. The storyteller reports the first half of Jesus' instructions to the Twelve in indirect discourse (6:7–9). Only after this introduction does the storyteller as Jesus address the audience directly as "the Twelve." This is the final incremental step in the storytelling process of inviting the audience to accept being addressed as disciples.

Prior to the messianic confession and discipleship discourse, the audience is addressed once more as "the disciples" in the concluding speech about the purity laws (7:18–22). The major discipleship discourse that follows Peter's realization (8:27–29), however, is addressed to the audience as "the crowd with the disciples" (8:34). Once again, the storyteller steps back from having Jesus address the audience as "the disciples" or "the Twelve" and addresses them as "the crowd with the disciples." Like the earlier address to the audience as "those who were around him with the Twelve," this name for Jesus' addressee is initially puzzling because it is difficult as a description of the actual scene. How did Jesus gather a crowd in between his confrontation with Peter and his pronouncements about discipleship? The function of this comment, however, is probably less to describe what happened at Caesarea Philippi than to describe the gestures and gathering of the audience by the storyteller.

This is the turning point in the addresses to the audience as Jesus' disciples. After the discipleship discourse, the audience is addressed as the disciples most of the time (chs. 9–10) in the story of the journey up to Jerusalem. Only the teaching about divorce and the conversation with the rich man are exceptions, and both of those introduce discussions with the audience as the disciples. These stories firmly establish the relationship between the storyteller as Jesus and the audience as disciples prior to the events in Jerusalem that end with the longest and most intimate conversation with the four disciples seated on the Mount of Olives.

Thus, the addresses to the audience as disciples are structured to move the audience *from* a distanced relationship with the character of Jesus *to* an identification of themselves as Jesus' disciples. This dynamic in the relationship between the storyteller and the audience is experienced far more clearly in oral performance for a listening audience than when it is read alone in silence. In oral performance the storyteller can generate waves of emotional interaction upon which she or he seeks to carry the audience toward the desired outcome of an intimate relationship with Jesus that readers in the context of a wholly different rhetorical tradition do not experience.

Another sign of the importance of audience address for the composition of the Gospels is the structure of the other three Gospels. While similar patterns of audience address, namely, interspersed addresses to the audience as opponents and disciples throughout the prepassion story, are present in Matthew and Luke, John has a highly distinctive structure of audience address that engages audiences in a clearly marked, progressive relationship with Jesus over the entire story prior to the passion narrative.[30] In the first four chapters of the Gospel, the storyteller as Jesus addresses the audience as a series of Jewish groups who are both interested in him and even believe in him: the audience as themselves in the prologue, then in subsequent narratives first as the disciples, particularly Nathanael, then as the Jews in the temple, Nicodemus, the disciples of John, and the Samaritan woman.

In John 5 there is a major shift in audience address. Beginning with Jesus' response to the Jews persecuting him after the Sabbath healing of the man at the pool of Bethzatha, the storyteller as Jesus consistently addresses the audience as various groups of Jews (e.g., the Pharisees, the Jews who want to kill or stone him or who believe in him, the crowd, and simply the Jews) who for eight chapters (5–12) alternate between extreme opposition and belief in Jesus. This continues through the entry into Jerusalem, with the only exception being the brief address to the audience as his disciples at the end of the so-called "bread of life" discourse (6:60–70). These long addresses to the audience as Jews torn between opposition and belief have their climax in a series of four addresses, the first by the storyteller as Jesus to the audience as Philip and Andrew (12:23–28), then as the crowd (12:29–36), then by "John" to the audience as themselves (12:37–43), and finally as Jesus to the audience as themselves (12:44–50).

The third section of audience address in John is Jesus' last words to the eleven disciples in the aftermath of the washing of the disciples' feet and the departure of Judas (13–17). This is the longest and most intimate discourse of Jesus in the entire Gospel tradition. Thus, in John the same pattern of audience address that is present in smaller sections of Mark provides the structure for the whole of John's story prior to the passion narrative.

The sign that the composer of John consciously constructs this pattern of audience address is that there are only two relatively short addresses to the audience as the disciples from the story of the man at the pool of Bethzatha to the triumphal entry (6:60–70; 12:23–28). In fact, there are only two additional

---

30. For a fuller discussion of the structure of audience address in John, see Thomas E. Boomershine, "The Medium and Message of John: Audience Address and Audience Identity in the Fourth Gospel," in *The Fourth Gospel in First-Century Media Culture* (ed. Anthony Le Donne and Tom Thatcher; London: T&T Clark, 2011).

addresses to the audience as the disciples in the initial section of John's story (chs. 1–4): Jesus' response to Nathanael's "over the top" confession (1:50–53) and his response to the disciples wanting him to eat something after his conversation with the Samaritan woman (4:34–38). This is in marked contrast to the three synoptic Gospels, in which there are addresses to the audience as the disciples throughout the stories prior to the passion narrative.

This pattern of audience address in John is similar to Mark and may have been a distinctive adaptation of Mark's story. Mark establishes initial engagement with Jesus in the addresses to the audience by John the Baptist and Jesus himself (1:7–8, 15), moves to an extended series of addresses to the audience as various Jewish groups in conflict with Jesus (2:8–10, 17, 19–22, 25–28; 3:4–5, 23–29), and ends with an extended address to the audience as those close to Jesus (3:33–35; 4:11–32). But while Mark repeats this pattern several times, it is always within a shorter storytelling compass, the longest being four chapters (1–4; 11–13). In John, this pattern is extended with minor variations over the entire story prior to the passion narrative (1–17). These patterns of audience address in the story world of the Gospels of Mark and John are evidence that this was a structural dimension of the Gospel storytelling tradition.

The addresses to the audience in Mark's passion story are further confirmation of this compositional structuring in the Gospel of Mark. As can be seen from the chart above, in the passion narrative prior to the arrest, the storyteller as Jesus addresses the audience as various groups of the disciples. With the exception of the Passover preparation instructions to the two disciples and the highly intimate speech interpreting the meaning of the bread and wine at the meal, Jesus' speeches address the responses of the disciples to the events of the passion. Jesus' counterrebuke of those who rebuked the woman who anointed him is implicitly linked with Judas's offer to betray him. Once again, this is more evident when the story is performed than when it is read in silence, because of the emotional level of Jesus' rebuke of those who denounce the woman.*[8] The prophecies of betrayal (14:18–21) and desertion/denial (14:27–30) engage the audience in identification with the disciples' disbelief and resistance to the prophecies that are more or less immediately fulfilled.

The climax of Jesus' addresses to the audience prior to the arrest is Gethsemane. This is the quietest, the most intimate, and the most emotionally intense interaction of the storyteller as Jesus with the audience as disciples in the entire story. The threefold repetition of Jesus' plea that they stay awake may have had a direct connection with the audience's struggle to stay awake after an evening of some nearly two hours of storytelling. The audience is invited to identify fully with Peter, James, and John as they hear the disappointment in their teacher's voice. In each of these instances the audience is invited to recognize the disciples' responses of betrayal, flight and denial as wrong responses with which they can fully identify.

The storyteller's addresses to the audience as Jesus, the high priest, and Pilate are the climax of the plot of Jesus' opponents. In each of these addresses, the audience is directly addressed as "you." Thus, after the arrest, the story-teller as Jesus asks the audience as the crowd from the authorities, "Have *you* come out as against an insurrectionist [*lēstēs*, λῃστής]...?" (14:48–49). After Jesus' confession, the storyteller as the high priest asks the audience as the council, "*You* have heard his blasphemy. How does it appear to *you*?" (14:63–64). Finally, the storyteller as Pilate addresses the audience as the crowd: "Do *you* want me to release for *you* the king of the Jews?" (15:9), and "What, then, shall I do with the one *you* call king of the Jews?" (15:12).* These speeches all share the same performance dynamic of requiring the audience to answer these questions internally. It is also significant that the questions at the arrest and the Pilate trial address issues directly related to the audience's experience of the insurrection that led to the Roman-Jewish war. Jesus' question to the crowd arresting him as an insurrectionist (*lēstēs*, λῃστής) and the crowd's choice at the Pilate trial between Barabbas, an insurrectionist (*stasiastēs*, στασιαστής), and Jesus frame these direct questions to the audience in the same terms that Josephus uses frequently to describe the various groups that led the revolution.[31] These questions are formed to resonate with the experience of *Jewish* audiences who lived in the aftermath of the destruction of Jerusalem and the temple. The storyteller's implicit appeal to the audiences of the story is to identify the arrest and crucifixion of Jesus as mistakes that are associated with the disasters of the war.

The final address in Mark's story by the storyteller (as a character) is the address of "the young man" dressed in white to the audience as Mary Magdalene, Mary, and Salome (16:6–7). This speech is the climax of the entire two-hour story. The speech is quiet, slow, and intimate. The audience's identification with the women has been established in the stories of their presence at Jesus' crucifixion and burial (15:40–41, 47). As a result, the audience experiences the young man's words as addressed to them. The climactic imperative addressed to the audience is the command to "go, tell..." (16:7). The women's response of flight and saying nothing to anyone completes the cycle of wrong responses by the characters with whom the audience has been invited to iden-

---

31. The terms that Mark uses to describe Barabbas would have had the implications of revolutionary activity for Mark's audiences in the aftermath of the Roman-Jewish war. This is evident from Josephus's usage of these same terms to refer to the insurgents. For documentation and an excellent discussion of this dimension of Mark's language in the arrest and trial stories, see Marcus, *Mark 8–16*, 1029.

tify. In each instance, the impact of this story experience is to be implicated in these wrong responses and implicitly invited to reflect on this response and to do its opposite: staying awake, staying with Jesus in times of persecution, openly confessing being a disciple, choosing Jesus as Messiah rather than the insurrectionists, and telling the story. This final address to the audience is consistent with the performance function of the addresses to the audience throughout the story. These addresses involve the audience in direct interaction with the characters and events of the story.

THE CHARACTERISTICS OF MARK'S AUDIENCES

The instances and patterns of the Markan storyteller's addresses to the audiences of the story as various characters are a source of direct information about the characteristics of Mark's audiences.

1. The audiences are almost always addressed as various groups of Jews. The sequence of Jewish groups can be seen on the chart and can be summarized here: the people of Judea and Galilee, the scribes and scribes of the Pharisees, the disciples of John the Baptist and the Pharisees, the Pharisees at several points in the story, the scribes from Jerusalem, the crowd at several points in the story, including the Pilate trial, the group sitting around Jesus, those around Jesus with the Twelve, the people in the Nazareth synagogue, the Twelve and the disciples many times, the crowd with the disciples, Peter/Andrew/James/John, the chief priests/scribes/elders, the Sadducees, the crowd in the temple, the Sanhedrin, and Mary Magdalene/Mary/Salome. By far the most frequent character embodied by the storyteller in these addresses to the audience is Jesus. No other character has more than one major address to the audience. Thus, the primary dynamic of address to the audience as characters in the story is the storyteller as Jesus speaking to the audience as a wide-ranging spectrum of Jewish groups.

2. Non-Jews are addressed as a minor but integral part of Mark's audiences. At one point in the story (7:3–5), Gentiles are addressed directly by the storyteller and are thereby included in the projected audiences of the Gospel.

3. The translations of Hebrew and Aramaic terms by the storyteller are an indication that the audiences are addressed as Greek-speaking Jews and Gentiles who may not know Hebrew or Aramaic.

4. Mark's audiences are addressed as Jewish persons who are invited to move from identifying with groups who are opposed to Jesus to identifying with Jesus' disciples. This pattern is present in progressive sections of the Gospel (2–4; 7:1–22; 8:11–21; 10:1–12; 12–13) and in the majority of stories before and after the messianic confession. Before the messianic confession, the audience is frequently addressed as groups who are opposed to Jesus.

After Peter's moment of recognition, the audience is predominantly addressed as disciples.

5. The audiences are addressed as persons who are implicitly asked to move gradually from being identified as part of crowds interested in listening to Jesus to being identified as Jesus' disciples. This movement in audience address from being addressed as "those outside" to "those inside" is carefully nuanced in incremental steps. These include addresses to the audience in relatively long discourses by Jesus as, for example, "those around Jesus with the Twelve" and "the crowd with the disciples." The addresses to the audience as those "inside" are sometimes located in a story space where Jesus is alone or inside a house. This storytelling location is also a sign that these talks are quieter, smaller in gesture, and more intimate than the public discourses.

This data has implications for our reconstructions of the actual historical audiences of Mark's Gospel. The data of audience address in Mark's Gospel indicates that the story was structured for predominantly Jewish audiences who did not believe that Jesus is the Messiah. Mark's purpose is evident in the structure of audience address in the story. The story is structured to move the audiences from identifying themselves as Jesus' critics to identifying themselves as Jesus' disciples. Furthermore, those who are interested in Jesus, as are most of those who would have begun listening to Mark's story, are invited by the storyteller to move from a relationship of interest on the periphery of the story to a place "inside" the community of those who have an intimate relationship with Jesus.

There is nothing in this data that would indicate that Mark's story was directed to those outside the nascent Christian communities to the exclusion of those who were already members of believing communities. However, believers are *addressed as* Jews who are either critics of Jesus or are only interested in his teaching from a distance. That is, the structure of audience address does not support the assumption that Mark was composed for performances to audiences that were either an individual believing community, as Joel Marcus envisions, or the network of *Christian* communities in the Greco-Roman world, as Richard Bauckham has proposed. The story may have been told in *believing* communities, but those believers are addressed as persons who are either outside or on the periphery of discipleship communities. The audiences are addressed as disciples, but only after a long period of storytelling invitations to move from a position of identification with critics or with a supportive crowd on the outer perimeters of the communities of disciples. Thus, there are several allusions in Jesus' apocalyptic discourse to the experience of communities of Jesus' followers. But that only happens after a long process of audience inclusion in which the audience is invited by the dynamics of audience address to move from a position of opposition to the interested periphery to the inner circle of the Twelve and then the four and three disciples closest to Jesus.

The Gospel of Mark has a radically different structure of audience address than the letters of Paul that are addressed to small communities of believers. Mark is addressed to the great community of Jews throughout the Greco-Roman world, all of whom were seeking for a way forward in the aftermath of the war. A major theme implicit in the structure of audience address is an appeal to the audience to reject the way of insurrection and to believe in a messiah who taught and practiced healing and feeding of both Jews and Gentiles. A dimension of Jesus' teaching was a critique of the purity laws that were a barrier to Jews having virtually any relationship with Gentiles. However, while Gentiles are the object of Jesus' actions in several stories, the audience is addressed as Gentiles only once in the story. The Gospel of Mark is addressed to Jews and Gentiles in a manner that assumes they are fully cognizant of the realities of hostility between Jews and Gentiles. This relationship is, however, addressed from a Jewish perspective. The Gentiles are those on the other side of the sea (5:1–20), those who are appropriately called "dogs" (7:27), those who will mock, spit on, and kill the Messiah (10:34), and those who practice leadership by domination rather than service (10:42). Gentiles are, therefore, invited to be part of the audiences of the Gospel, but only as they are willing to enter into the Jewish world of Mark's story. As one might expect in the aftermath of the war, the Gospel of Mark addresses audiences in which the relationships between Jews and Gentiles are even more highly polarized than in the letters of Paul.

The analysis of the dynamics of audience address requires that Markan scholarship reexamine the conclusion that the Gospel of Mark was anti-Jewish. The central fact that requires this reexamination is that the audiences of the story were, with one exception, addressed as Jews. Furthermore, for the first hour of the story the storyteller presents Jesus addressing the audiences as Jews who are critics of Jesus. This is a structure of audience interaction that is characteristic of *intra-Jewish* conflict rather than *anti-Jewish* conflict. In its original context, the Gospel of Mark is no more anti-Jewish than the book of Jeremiah or the book of Exodus. In both of these books, the audience is addressed as members of Israelite communities by storytellers who embody characters such as Moses and Jeremiah, who themselves are in steady conflict with the people of Israel. The literature of Israel is full of violent intra-Jewish conflict in which various authors appeal to Jews to reject the policies and actions of other Jewish groups.

What is distinctive about Mark's story in the context of the literature of Israel is the inclusion of Gentiles in the projected audiences of the story. Gentile members of Mark's audiences were invited to join audiences of Jews and to experience the story of Jesus as an integral part of the wider Jewish community. The storytellers of Mark's Gospel did not address their audience as Gentiles for whom Jews are "the others," as would be required if the story's purpose was anti-Jewish. The audiences of Mark are addressed as Jews for whom Gentiles are "the others." The structure of audience address in Mark requires that we imagine a social and political context in which non-Jews were invited to join Jews in listening to a Jewish story of which they were an integral part, both in the story itself and in their participation in the audiences for whom the story is performed. This is congruent with the social and political context of the Jewish community in the immediate aftermath of the war outlined by Joel Marcus.[32] But the data of audience address indicate that the audiences of Mark were not addressed as communities in which either Gentiles or members of believing communities were the majority. The audiences of Mark were addressed as Jews and Gentiles who were invited by the story to move from a position of opposition to Jesus to a position of identifying with Jesus' disciples. The audiences of Mark are, therefore, primarily addressed as Jews who do not believe that Jesus is the Messiah. The historical probability is that this was the dominant character of the audiences for which the Gospel was performed. The primary purpose of the story was to move its listeners from opposition to Jesus to belief in Jesus as the Messiah, the Son of God.

In conclusion, the process of the investigation of Mark as a narrative initiated in public discussion by the publication of *Mark as Story* has been a complex process that is already evolving in new directions. Performance criticism is a logical and historically appropriate methodological development that is more congruent with the original character of Mark than narrative criticism, with its assumption of Markan readers as developed in *Mark as Story*. The recognition that Mark was not a book read by readers but was a composition performed by oral performers, initially storytellers, is of primary importance for the interpretation of Mark in its original historical context. Oral performance encourages identification with characters and the experience of being addressed by a character in the story that is easily jettisoned when other strategies of reception, such as silent reading of a mute text, replace those of the oral storyteller. Silent reading in particular allows the reader to remain an observer on the outside of the events being narrated, especially when the events involve characters with whom the reader does not readily identify. Mark as a storyteller, on the other hand, utilizes a panoply of resources for engaging the audience in a dynamic identification with the characters of the story. Mark's story creates an imaginative world that connected with the real world of both

---

32. See n. 29 above.

Jewish and Gentile first-century audiences. We have described the moves of audience address in which the same central speaker, Jesus, addresses the audience as a series of characters. These characters are predominantly Jewish, and the listeners' experience in the course of the story moves from critical to more positive engagements with Jesus. Hearing and performing Mark provides new data that will change our perceptions of Mark's audiences and the meaning of Mark's story for those audiences.

PART 2
MARK AS STORY APPLIED

MARK 6:17–29 IN ITS NARRATIVE CONTEXT: KINGDOMS IN CONFLICT

R. Alan Culpepper

My friendship with David Rhoads began when we were both graduate students at Duke talking about our dissertations over coffee. Later we ran up long-distance phone bills talking about narrative criticism of the Gospels when there were not many others with whom we could talk, so it is a privilege to celebrate that conversation, our friendship, and the profound impact of David's work.

The sea-change introduced by David Rhoads, Don Michie, and Joanna Dewey was the notion that the Gospel of Mark is a coherent narrative and that every part of it has a role in its plot, thematic development, and scheme of characterization. Prior to the advent of narrative criticism, which started in Markan scholarship, Gospel scholarship focused on recovering the sources of the Gospels, the stages of their composition, their community setting, and the theology of the Evangelists.[1] In the first pages of *Mark as Story*, Rhoads and Michie declare: "The purpose of this book is to aid in recovering the experience of the Gospel of Mark as unified narrative," and further, "the study of narrative emphasizes the unity of the final text."[2] Narrative criticism focused on the Gospel as a narrative text while affirming the continuing importance of other issues and approaches to interpreting the Gospel.

One of the most perceptive critics of narrative criticism has been Stephen Moore, who chronicled the movement of literary theory in New Testament criticism from redaction criticism to narrative criticism, to reader-response

---

1. Stephen D. Moore, *Literary Criticism and the Gospels: The Theoretical Challenge* (New Haven: Yale University Press, 1989), 7.

2. David Rhoads and Donald Michie, *Mark as Story: An Introduction to the Narrative of a Gospel* (Philadelphia: Fortress, 1982), 2–3. See also David Rhoads, Joanna Dewey, and Donald Michie, *Mark as Story: An Introduction to the Narrative of a Gospel* (2nd ed.; Minneapolis: Fortress, 1999).

criticism, and on to poststructuralism and deconstruction. Where he deals with narrative criticism, his critique is first that, "in appropriating narrative theory, narrative critics regularly defuse it. An accusation often leveled at American literary critics is that they domesticate French theory when they import it."[3] As an example of this domestication, Moore cites Genette's unsettling work on Proust. Genette demonstrates that Proust's narrative, which appears to represent "a world and a character's experience of it," is actually "fraught with repeated violations, both flagrant and subtle, of the conventions of representation to which it ostensibly subscribes."[4] In contrast, "the view of the gospel text which narrative critics (Rhoads, Tannehill, Petersen, Culpepper, Kingsbury, et al.) have urged is ultimately a comforting one. It reassures us that in the wake of a long history of fragmentation, exposure, of internal contradictions and the like, it is now once again possible using the methods of literary criticism to see that the gospel narratives do after all possess wholeness and internal consistency."[5]

MARK 6:14–29 AS A TEST CASE FOR CONTINUITY

Against the background of the attention of narrative criticism to the coherence of the Gospel narrative and Moore's critique of the predilection of narrative critics to find unity in the Gospel, the case of the narrative of the death of John the Baptist offers fertile ground for further study because it has often been observed that it is something of an anomaly in the Gospel and fits only loosely in its context. The story is recalled almost as an afterthought to explain Herod's response to the reports of Jesus' activities. It is a coherent and discrete unit that does not require the Gospel narrative, and its style or tone is noticeably different: "Mark's account of the death of John is an anecdote unlike anything else in this Gospel."[6] Eduard Schweizer noted that "it is the only story in Mark which is not directly a story about Jesus, and it is written in a cultured style which shows that it must have been established in written form before Mark."[7] Indeed, Bussmann, cited by Hoehner, contended that it was inserted

---

3. Stephen D. Moore, *Poststructuralism and the New Testament: Derrida and Foucault at the Foot of the Cross* (Minneapolis: Fortress, 1994), 54.

4. Ibid., 53.

5. Ibid. This paragraph is reproduced from my essay, "Vingt ans d'analyse narrative des évangiles: Nouvelles perspectives et problèmes en suspens," *La Bible en récits* (ed. Daniel Marguerat; Geneva: Labor et Fides, 2003), 73–93.

6. John Painter, *Mark's Gospel: Worlds in Conflict* (London: Routledge, 1997), 102.

7. Eduard Schweizer, *The Good News according to Mark* (Atlanta: John Knox, 1970), 132.

into Mark by a later editor, and Lohmeyer believed Mark took it from a written source and inserted it in his Gospel without altering it.[8]

Formally, the story is a "completing analepsis" that fills a gap by reporting an event that had taken place earlier in the story but had not been related to the reader.[9] It functions "as an interlude or a parenthesis in Mark's narrative"[10] that "fills the interval between the sending out of the Twelve and their return to Jesus."[11] Morna Hooker's comment represents the view of many:

> Between the account of the sending out of the Twelve and that of their return, Mark inserts an account of Herod's reaction to the rumours about Jesus, together with the story of his beheading of John the Baptist. There seems no logical connection between the two themes, but the somewhat artificial insertion provides an interlude for the disciples to complete their mission.[12]

Josephus reports the death of John at the hands of Herod in *Ant.* 18.116–119, but it will not serve our purposes here to compare the ways in which each reports John's death.[13] Ross Kraemer concludes that "the reports in Josephus and the Gospels [are] separate narratives that cannot and should not be amalgamated."[14] Matthew closely follows Mark, but with significant differences. Luke repeats only the first part of the story (Mark 6:14–16) in Luke 9:7–9, and John omits it entirely.

Even before the development of narrative criticism, however, critics and commentaries were already noting subtle connections with the plot and themes of the rest of the Gospel. Cranfield observed that,

---

8. Harold W. Hoehner, *Herod Antipas: A Contemporary of Jesus Christ* (Grand Rapids: Zondervan, 1972), 113; Ernst Lohmeyer, *Das Evangelium des Markus* (KEK; Göttingen: Vandenhoeck & Ruprecht, 1953), 117–18.

9. Gérard Genette, *Narrative Discourse: An Essay in Method* (trans. Jane E. Lewin; Ithaca, N.Y.: Cornell University Press, 1980), 40; R. Alan Culpepper, *Anatomy of the Fourth Gospel: A Study in Literary Design* (Philadelphia: Fortress, 1983), 58–60.

10. Robert A. Guelich, *Mark 1–8:26* (WBC 34A; Dallas: Word, 1989), 328.

11. C. E. B. Cranfield, *The Gospel according to St. Mark* (CGTC; Cambridge: Cambridge University Press, 1959), 208; Paul J. Achtemeier, "Toward the Isolation of Pre-Markan Miracle Catenae," *JBL* 89 (1970): 270.

12. Morna D. Hooker, *The Gospel according to St. Mark* (BNTC; London: Black, 1991), 158.

13. See Camille Focant, "La tête du prophète sur un plat, ou, L'anti-repas d'alliance (Mc 6.14–29)," *NTS* 47 (2001): 336–40; Paul V. Harrison, "Competing Accounts of the Baptist's Demise: Josephus versus the Gospels," *Faith and Mission* 24 (2007): 26–42.

14. Ross S. Kraemer, "Implicating Herodias and Her Daughter in the Death of John the Baptist: A (Christian) Theological Strategy?" *JBL* 125 (2006): 340.

Though not directly concerned with Jesus, it is yet relevant to the history of Jesus, the passion of the Forerunner being a pointer to the subsequent passion of the Messiah (cf. ii.19f.). The parallels between vi.17–29 and xv.1–47 are interesting: e.g. Herod's fear of John as ἀνὴρ δίκαιος καὶ ἅγιος (v. 20) and Pilate's attitude to Jesus (xv.5, 14); Herodias' implacable hatred of John and the Jewish leaders' implacable hatred of Jesus; Herod's and Pilate's yielding to pressure; the details of the burials of John and Jesus.[15]

Guelich also saw thematic continuities between the story of John's beheading and the rest of the Gospel:

Viewed within the framework of Mark's Gospel, 6:14–29 provides a key scene. Herod identifies Jesus with John.... Therefore, the cruel fate of the Baptist becomes a harbinger of Jesus' ultimate rejection.... Therefore, 6:14–29 is parenthetical only in terms of the sending out and return of the Twelve. Thematically, Mark has selected and introduced a story closely interwoven with the flow of Jesus' story.[16]

The question of the functions of Mark 6:14–29 and its relationship to its context calls for further attention. Is it an "artificial insertion" with no logical connection to its context? How does it function as "a harbinger of Jesus' ultimate rejection," and are there still other thematic continuities between it and the larger narrative?

GENRE AND INTERTEXTUALITY: THE STORY OF THE TRUE PROPHET, THE WICKED QUEEN, AND THE DUPED KING

The story sparkles with themes drawn from familiar stories. Wicked kings persecute and kill the righteous:

Wicked King	Righteous Victim	Text
Pharaoh	the Israelites	Exod 1:15–22; 5:1–23
Joash	Zechariah	2 Chr 24:20–22
Nebuchadnezzar	Shadrach, Meshach, and Abednego	Dan 3:12–30

---

15. Cranfield, *St. Mark*, 208–9.
16. Robert A. Guelich, *Mark 1–8:26* (WBC 34A; Dallas: Word Books, 1989), 328–29.

Darius	Daniel	Dan 6:10–28
Antiochus Epiphanes	pious Jews	1 Macc 1:41–50; 2:15–28
Antiochus Epiphanes	Eleazar	2 Macc 6:18–31
Antiochus Epiphanes	the seven brothers	2 Macc 7
Herod the Great	the innocents in Bethlehem	Matt 2:16–18

Abraham Smith has traced the genre of tyrant versus philosopher and found that "Mark repeatedly drew on stock features about a tyrant to portray Herod Antipas."[17] These stock features include: "(1) the tyrant's paranoia; (2) the tyrant's possession of a bodyguard; (3) the tyrant's display of excess, and (4) the tyrant's encounter with a philosopher."[18] Manipulative women were also associated with tyrants: "Aspasia (the wife of Pericles), Cleopatra (the lover of Mark Antony), and Olympias (the wife of Philip II of Macedon and mother of Alexander the Great)."[19]

The report of Herodias's intent to kill John sets up further levels of intrigue: the plot dynamic of how she will get Herod to act contrary to his intent to protect John and echoes of Jezebel's persecution of the prophet Elijah. René Girard astutely observed that "no sooner is the woman married than she loses all direct influence over her husband. She cannot obtain from him even the head of an insignificant little prophet like John the Baptist."[20]

Mark constructs connections between John the Baptist and Elijah earlier in the narrative, so the reader is prepared to note the connections between this story and the story of Elijah, Ahab, and Jezebel. When John is introduced, he is wrapped in the characterization of a prophet (1:2–8). Like Elijah, he comes before "the great and terrible day of the Lord" (Mal 4:5). John's diet of locusts (Lev 11:21–22) and wild honey (1 Kgs 14:33; 2 Kgs 18:32) identifies him as a "wilderness man." His dress is that of a prophet. King Ahaziah recognized Elijah when his messengers reported that they had met "a hairy man, with a

---

17. Abraham Smith, "Tyranny Exposed: Mark's Typological Characterization of Herod Antipas (Mark 6:14–29)," *BibInt* 14 (2006): 262.

18. Ibid., 271.

19. Ibid., 275.

20. René Girard, "Scandal and the Dance: Salome in the Gospel of Mark," *New Literary History* 15 (1984): 312.

leather belt around his waist" (2 Kgs 1:8), and Zechariah warns that on the day of the Lord the prophets will be ashamed: "they will not put on a hairy mantle in order to deceive" (13:4). Appropriately, John is conventionally depicted as "a hairy man" in Christian art. Mark tells us in the introduction that some speculated that "it is Elijah" (6:15). When we hear that John preaches against the sins of the "king" and that Herodias "has it in for him" (6:19), the reader is ominously reminded of Jezebel's vow to kill the prophet (1 Kgs 19:2; cf. 18:3–4).

Mark later confirms the connections that are only suggested in the story of John's death, when Jesus declares, "But I tell you Elijah has come, and they did to him whatever they pleased, as it is written about him" (9:13). In a detailed comparison of Jezebel and Herodias, Hoffeditz and Yates observe three major parallels between the two: both "incite their husbands to do evil," the portrayals of the two contain "overtones of sexual promiscuity and misconduct," and "both figures engage in a life and death struggle with a messenger of God who confronts their sinful ways."[21]

Duran finds that Esther and Herodias "become respectively positive and negative examples of the manipulative power of women's sex, the power to instigate killing."[22] Both find their opportune moment at a banquet, and both turn a pleased king's promise to their own ends. Herod's promise to give whatever the girl asks, up to half his kingdom, is reminiscent of King Artaxerxes' repeated promise to Esther the queen (Esth 5:3, 6–7; 7:2–3). Esther prepares a banquet for the king and voices her petition, saying, "if it pleases the king" (see the note that the girl's dance "pleased" Herod in 6:22). In the end, the Jews are saved, and the wicked Haman is executed. The intertextuality serves to heighten the reader's negative response to Herodias: "The reader who knows and loves Esther and Judith hates Herodias, the more so for the resemblance to them."[23]

After reviewing the role of queens in Israelite history and literature, Linda Schearing summarizes her findings:

> Of all the Israelite and Judean queens named in the book of Kings, only four are given more than cursory mention: Bathsheba, Maacah, Jezebel, and Athaliah. Of these four, all but Bathsheba are portrayed in negative terms. Their characterization employs identifiable negative elements and casts them into a character "type"—that of the "wicked queen/queen mother."

---

21. David M. Hoffeditz and Gary E. Yates, "*Femme Fatale* Redux: Intertextual Connection to the Elijah/Jezebel Narratives in Mark 6:14–29," *BBR* 15 (2005): 200.

22. Nicole Duran, "Having Men for Dinner: Deadly Banquets and Biblical Women," *BTB* 35 (2005): 117.

23. Ibid., 123.

This type casting of queens warns the reader of the dangers of women in power.[24]

Contrasting the roles of the "wicked queen/queen mother" and the "foreign woman," Schearing further notes that, "whereas the foreign woman relies on seductive wiles to achieve her ends, the wicked queen's power resides in her position: she commands rather than charms others into obedience."[25] Herodias cannot command Herod, so she reverts to seductive wiles through her surrogate.

Persian and Jewish histories contain several well-known stories of queens who were involved in intrigue or who brought ruin on the king. Herodotus tells a story with similar elements. King Xerxes fell in love first with his brother's (Masistes's) wife and then with her daughter, Artaÿnte. Xerxes' wife Amestris gave him a specially woven, beautiful cloak, which he paraded in front of Artaÿnte. Because he was delighted with Artaÿnte, he bade her ask whatever she wanted. When she asked for the cloak, he offered her cities, gold, and an army instead, but she insisted and wore the cloak in triumph. Amestris blamed Masistes's wife, the girl's mother, and plotted to kill her. She "waited for the moment," which came at the king's birthday feast, then asked the king for Masistes's wife. Being bound by law to grant the request, and much against his will, he consented. Amestris sent the king's bodyguard to savagely mutilate Masistes's wife. Masistes fled to raise a revolt in Bactria, but the king caught him and killed him (Herodotus, *Hist.* 9.109–113).

Another story of the female trickster is found in Plutarch's biography of Artaxerxes II of Persia (d. 359 B.C.E.). Parysatis, Artaxerxes' mother, plotted the death of Masabates, one of the king's faithful eunuchs. After challenging the king to a game of dice, she lost deliberately, paid the wager, then challenged the king to a second game, with a eunuch at stake. When she won the second game, she asked for Masabates and immediately flayed him alive (Plutarch, *Art.* 17).

Herod the Great had killed Marianne when he suspected her of involvement in a plot to overthrow him (Josephus, *Ant.* 15.222–239). Herodias herself, jealous that her brother Agrippa I had been given the title "king," later prompted Antipas to go to Rome to ask Emperor Gaius for the same title. Instead, both Herod Antipas and Herodias were banished to Gaul (Josephus, *Ant.* 18.252–253) or Spain (Josephus, *J.W.* 2.183), and Gaius awarded Herodias's possessions to her brother Agrippa (Josephus, *J.W.* 18.254). Queens were

---

24. Linda S. Schearing, "Queen," *ABD* 5:586.
25. Ibid.

so often involved in such intrigue that they were by nature suspect in Rome.[26] Criticism reached such fervor that Titus had to order Berenice to leave Rome (Suetonius, *Tit.* 7).

The theme of the king who cannot control his own family is a familiar refrain in Greek tragedy and later in Shakespeare (*Macbeth, King Lear*). The story of the beheading of John the Baptist has also found its way into paintings (Lorenzo Monaco, Fra Lippo Lippi, Titian, Caravaggio, Rembrandt), plays (Flaubert, Mallarmé, Wilde, Yeats), operas (Richard Strauss), and films.[27] Megan Becker-Lekrone traces the growth and influence of the intertextuality that has embellished the Salome myth, including the detail that it was Oscar Wilde who named the dance in Mark 6 the "famous" dance of the seven veils.[28]

In other stories female killers put to death wicked kings. Jael drives a tent stake through the head of Sisera (Judg 5:24). Judith beheads Holofernes (following a banquet), puts his head in her food bag, then hangs it on the parapet of the city wall (Jdt 13:6–10; 14:1). As a variation on a theme, Mark's account of John's death follows the pattern of Judith's song of triumph over Holofernes:

> She anointed her face with perfume;
> she fastened her hair with a tiara
> and put on a linen gown to beguile him.
> Her sandal ravished his eyes,
> her beauty captivated his mind,
> and the sword severed his neck! (Jdt 16:6–9)

Herodias is, if anything, even craftier than Judith because she uses her daughter (or Herod's daughter!) to beguile the king and call for him to behead the prophet, while she remains in the background until the triumphal moment arrives, when her daughter presents her John's head on a platter. These connections are unique to Mark, however, because only Mark reports that Herodias wanted to kill John.

In contemporary gender criticism, Janice Capel Anderson argues that interpretations of the daughter and her dance, whether innocent or erotic, are "male constructions of female gender."[29] Jennifer Glancy seeks "to unveil

---

26. D. C. Braund, "Berenice in Rome," *Historia* 33 (1984): 120–23.

27. For a survey of the cinematic versions, see Alice Bach, "Calling the Shots: Directing Salome's Dance of Death," *Semeia* 74 (1996): 103–26.

28. Megan Becker-Leckrone, "Salome: The Fetishization of a Textual Corpus," *New Literary History* 26 (1995): 254.

29. Janice Capel Anderson, "Feminist Criticism: The Dancing Daughter," in *Mark and Method: New Approaches in Biblical Studies* (ed. Janice Capel Anderson and Stephen D. Moore; Minneapolis: Fortress, 1992), 126.

assumptions about gender, especially masculinity, that shape Mark 6:17–29,"[30] and Mikeal Parsons contends that, "read through the lens of gender analysis, John's beheading is a horrible example of the extent to which an oppressive gender system collaborates to remove those persons who rise up in protest against it."[31]

THE STORY: A WEAVE OF PLAIN SENSE, EMBELLISHMENTS,
ASIDES, CONNECTIONS, AND IMPLICATIONS

The Nestle-Aland Greek New Testament divides Mark 6:14–29 into three paragraphs. Verses 14–16 report and explain Herod's identification of Jesus as John, "who had been raised." For the reader, Herod's announcement, "whom I beheaded," is dramatic new information. The logic of Herod's identification of Jesus is that (1) "the powers" are at work in him—witness the reports in verse 13 and earlier accounts of Jesus' miracles. (2) These powers are at work in him because he has been raised from the dead. This premise is suggestive because the reader has not been told that John performed miracles during his preaching ministry, whereas miracles were a distinguishing element of Jesus' ministry, and the Christian reader knows that Jesus was (later) raised from the dead. Herod is correct in his understanding that Jesus exercised wondrous powers, but he did not know the origin of those powers (1:1, 11). He was also correct in surmising that there was a relationship between Jesus and John, but he did not know the true nature of that relationship. Strictly, Herod's logic might suggest that Jesus' powers did not become active until after John's death (see Mark 1:14–15). Moreover, Herod's association of Jesus with John confirms the forerunner theme that is established in Mark (1:2–3, 7–11) but presumably would not have been known to Herod. (3) John had been killed; Jesus' powers are evidence that he had been raised from the dead. Therefore, (4) Jesus was John who had been raised from the dead. The logic does not hold up, but the thematic emphasis is made nevertheless. Further, the pattern Mark develops of preaching and being arrested—which is established by John, followed by Jesus, and implied as the fate of the disciples (1:14–15; 13:9–11)—is now extended two steps: being killed by the authorities and then being raised from the dead. On the other hand, the story may

---

30. Jennifer A. Glancy, "Unveiling Masculinity: The Construction of Gender in Mark 6:17–29," *BibInt* 2 (1994): 34–50.

31. Mikeal C. Parsons, "Re-membering John the Baptist," in *Redeeming Men: Religion and Masculinities* (ed. Stephen B. Boyd, W. Merle Longwood, and Mark W. Muesse; Louisville: Westminster John Knox, 1996), 98.

also serve as a Christian apologetic that Jesus cannot be John the Baptist resurrected.[32]

The exposition continues in the second paragraph, verses 17–20. Four points are worth noting. First, the reader has been told that John was "handed over," a term Mark uses to suggest the arrest of the faithful through the betrayal of the unfaithful (1:14; 3:19; 9:31; 13, 9, 11, etc.), but the reader did not know that John was arrested by Herod (v. 17). Second, Herod accepts full responsibility for John's death ("whom I beheaded"; v. 16), which is technically correct, but the ensuing story explains how Herod was tricked into executing John. Third, Herod is called "king." Technically, his title was "tetrarch" or "ruler of a fourth part" (of Herod the Great's kingdom). Ironically, Josephus records that the emperor deposed Herod Antipas and banished him to Gaul when, at Herodias's prompting, Herod requested the title "king" (Josephus, *Ant.* 8.240–255; *J. W.* 2.183). By designating Herod as "king," however, Mark accomplished two things that will become important later in the story. Making Herod a king strengthens the typecasting of Herodias as a wicked queen, playing the part of Jezebel. More important, it sets up the contrast between Jesus as king and Herod as a representative of earthly kings. The term *basileus* (βασιλεύς) occurs twelve times in Mark, in a very significant pattern: five times in this story (6:14–29) in reference to Herod Antipas, once in 13:9 in the prophecy of the arrest of the disciples, and six times in the passion narrative (15:2–32) in reference to Jesus as "king of the Jews/Israel." The term therefore establishes the antithesis in Mark between Jesus and Herod, with Herod functioning as a representative of the political powers opposed to Jesus and the kingdom of God. Fourth, Herodias is introduced with the scandalous identification, "the wife of Philip, his brother, because he [Herod Antipas] had married her." The characterization establishes Herod and Herodias as representatives of (wicked) pagan royalty, echoing the report that David took Bathsheba, "the wife of Uriah" (Matt 1:6; 2 Sam 11:3; 12:10).

The narrative exposition that provides the background for the beheading of John is carried by four narrative asides beginning with *gar* ("for"): "for Jesus' name had become known" (6:14); "for Herod himself had sent men who arrested John…." (6:17); "for John had been telling Herod, 'It is not lawful for you to have your brother's wife'" (6:18); "for Herod feared John, knowing that he was a righteous and holy man, and he protected him" 6:20). The second, third, and fourth of these narrative asides occur in the second paragraph (6:17–20), which explains why Herod arrested John. Robert Fowler notes that this is the most concentrated collection of "for" clauses in Mark: "a dense web

---

32. Kraemer, "Implicating Herodias and Her Daughter," 341.

of commentary by the narrator."[33] The sense is somewhat ambiguous because it might mean that Herod arrested John because John was condemning him for marrying Herodias (6:18), but at least implicit is the sense that Herodias prompted Herod to arrest John (6:19) because of what he was saying about them. The background of Herod's marriage to Herodias is provided by Josephus (*Ant.* 18.116–119), but neither Josephus nor the other Gospels set up the opposition between Herod and Herodias, with Herodias wanting to kill John and Herod protecting him (cf. Matt 14:5). Mark has established that each character's response to "the word" is a key to interpreting their role (4:13–20). The rocky soil receives the seed "with great joy" (4:16); the seed that falls among the thorns is choked by "the cares of the age" and "other desires" (4:19).[34] Herod hears John gladly (cf. 12:37) but is perplexed by what he hears.[35] Herodias, playing the role of temptress through her daughter, will quickly snatch away the seed (4:15).

In the third paragraph, verses 21–29, the story moves from summary to scene, background to action. The "opportune day" (*hēmeras eukairou*, ἡμέρας εὐχαίρου, 6:21), Herod's birthday celebration, provides the context for Herodias to carry out her plans. Later Judas Iscariot will also seek an opportune time (*eukairōs*, εὐχαίρως, 14:11). Banquets, and birthday celebrations especially, were viewed by the righteous as evidence of waste and wickedness. Pharaoh celebrated his birthday with a feast for all his servants and restored the chief cupbearer and hanged the chief baker (Gen 40:20–23). Esther prepared a banquet for Artaxerxes and Haman (Esth 5:8; 6:14–7:1). At Belshazzar's banquet in Dan 5, the king learns that his days and the days of his kingdom are numbered, and that night he is killed. The Herodian princes celebrated not only their birthday but also the anniversary of their accession (Josephus, *Ant.* 19.321), sometimes with monthly celebrations (2 Macc 6:7), and early interpreters shared the condemnation of birthday celebrations.[36] The Venerable Bede commented: "We hear at the same time of three evil deeds done: the inauspicious celebration of a birthday, the lewd dancing of a girl, and the rash

33. Robert M. Fowler, *Let the Reader Understand: Reader-Response Criticism and the Gospel of Mark* (Minneapolis: Fortress, 1991), 93.

34. Mary Ann Tolbert, *Sowing the Gospel: Mark's World in Literary-Historical Perspective* (Minneapolis: Fortress, 1989), 158.

35. Roger L. Omanson, *A Textual Guide to the Greek New Testament* (Stuttgart: Deutsche Bibelgesellschaft, 2006), 71–72.

36. Emil Schürer, *The History of the Jewish People in the Age of Jesus Christ* (ed. Geza Vermes, Martin Goodman, and Fergus Millar; rev. ed.; 3 vols.; Edinburgh: T&T Clark, 1973), 1:347 n. 26.

oath of a king."[37] Origen reported that he found "in no Scripture that a birth-day was kept by a righteous man" (*Comm. Matt.* 10.22), and Jerome believed that only wicked persons celebrated birthdays with great banquets (Jerome, *Opp.* 7.101).[38] By direct characterization of both Herod and Herodias and by the implicit characterization of the setting (a birthday feast), Mark paints the setting in negative terms. In the only other reference to feasts in Mark we are told that the scribes sought the places of honor at feasts (12:39).

Herod invited three groups to his birthday feast: his great men (*megista-sin*, μεγιστᾶσιν, 6:21), his chiliarchs (chief officers, commanders over a thou-sand; *chiliarchois*, χιλιάρχοις, 6:21), and the "first men" of Galilee (*prōtois*, πρώτοις, 6:21). The setting contrasts dramatically with Jesus' meals with "tax collectors and sinners" (2:15-16), a multitude of common people (6:30-44), and apparently a crowd of Gentiles who had come a great distance (8:1-10).

Just as the exposition progresses through four narrative asides ("for"), the action builds through three participial clauses: "when an opportune day came" (6:21); "when his daughter Herodias entered" (6:22); "when she danced" (6:24). Joel Marcus catches the sense of this syntax: "The long periodic sentence in 6:21-22 builds up tension through a series of participles, a tension that is finally (and erotically!) released through the finite verb 'pleased' near its end."[39]

Two matters call for parenthetical comments: the identity of Herodias's daughter and the nature of her dance. Mark's text is so confusing that the scribes sought to clarify it. The Nestle-Aland 27th edition reads *tēs thygatros autou Hērōdiados* (τῆς θυγατρὸς αὐτοῦ Ἡρῳδιάδος), which the NRSV translates "his daughter Herodias." Matthew 14:6, perhaps the earliest interpreter of Mark, reads "the daughter of Herodias," and Josephus says that Salome was the daughter of Herodias by Herod Philip (*Ant.* 18.136). The majority reading is *tēs thygatros autēs tēs Hērōdiados* (τῆς θυγατρὸς αὐτῆς τῆς Ἡρῳδιάδος), "the daughter of Herodias herself." It appears, therefore, that Mark has misrep-resented the relationships, making the daughter Herod's own daughter and giving her the name Herodias.[40] Matthew corrects Mark, saying it was "the daughter of Herodias" who danced for Herod and his guests.

How old would Salome have been? Hoffeditz and Yates agree with Hoeh-ner, judging that she would have been twelve to fourteen.[41] Vincent Taylor

37. *Homilies on the Gospels* 2.23; cited by Thomas C. Oden and Christopher A. Hall, eds., *Mark* (ACCS.NT 2; Downers Grove, Ill.: InterVarsity Press, 1998), 85.

38. Cited by Schürer, *History of the Jewish People*, 1:347 n. 26.

39. Joel Marcus, *Mark 1–8* (AB 27; New York: Doubleday, 2000), 401.

40. Ibid., 396.

41. Hoffeditz and Yates, "*Femme Fatale* Redux," 216; Harold W. Hoehner, *Herod Anti-pas: A Contemporary of Jesus Christ* (Grand Rapids: Zondervan, 1972), 156.

calculates that she "is not likely … to have been more than about twenty years of age in A.D. 28–29," because she married Philip the Tetrach (who died in 34 C.E.) and later Aristobulous (Josephus, *Ant.* 18.136).[42] Mark says only that her dance "pleased" Herod. The verb "pleased" (*ēresen*, ἤρεσεν, 6:22) can have an innocent meaning (Acts 6:5; Rom 8:8; 15:1–3, etc.), but it is also used in contexts where it means to arouse sexual interest, which is suggested by the setting of a Herodian feast, the male audience, and the girl's dancing (Judg 14:3, 7; Esth 2:4, 9).[43]

The daughter's dance, whether it was erotic and lascivious or not, has tempted many interpreters. The Venerable Bede imagined "the lewd dancing of a girl" (*Homilies on the Gospels* 2.23), and Ambrose adds descriptive details:

> The daughter of the queen, sent for from within the private apartments, is brought forth to dance in the sight of all. What could she have learned from an adulteress but the loss of modesty? Is anything so conducive to lust as with unseemly movements to expose in nakedness those parts of the body which either nature has hidden or custom has veiled, to sport with looks, to turn the neck, to loosen the hair?[44]

Modern scholarship is divided on this issue. McVann describes it as "a shamelessly salacious dance" and "a sexually charged dance."[45] On the other hand, Hoehner quotes Kopp, describing the dance as "graceful," and Alice Bach argues that as a *korasion* (κοράσιον) the daughter (Salome?) would have been a young girl, "the virginal tool of her overbearing mother."[46] The dance is "innocent, a child charming an adult audience,"[47] but Hoffeditz and Yates respond, "the dance of Herodias' daughter at this birthday party suggests anything but innocence."[48]

René Girard, in a provocative essay on our passage, charts a way past the debate over the nature of the dance by focusing on the effect of the dance. Drawing on his work on mimetic desire, Girard interprets Salome as "a child-

42. Vincent Taylor, *The Gospel according to St. Mark* (London: Macmillan, 1952), 314.

43. R. Alan Culpepper, *Mark* (Smyth & Helwys Bible Commentaries; Macon, Ga.: Smyth & Helwys, 2007), 204.

44. *Concerning Virgins* 3.6.27, cited by Oden and Hall, *Mark*, 85.

45. Mark McVann, "The 'Passion' of John the Baptist and Jesus before Pilate: Mark's Warnings about Kings and Governors," *BTB* 38 (2008): 154.

46. See Clemens Kopp, *The Holy Places of the Gospels* (trans. R. Walls; New York: Herder & Herder, 1963), 139; Alice Bach, "Calling the Shots: Directing Salome's Dance of Death," *Semeia* 74 (1996): 109.

47. Bach, "Calling the Shots," 109.

48. Hoffeditz and Yates, "*Femme Fatale* Redux," 216.

victim of scandal," on one hand, and, on the other, says that by the end of the dance Herod and all his guests "are possessed by the desire of Salome."[49] As a result of the dance, "all desires converge upon one and the same object, the head on the platter, the head of John on Salome's platter."[50]

Herod's oath, the mechanism that will force him to execute John, is reported with carefully constructed emphasis. First, Herod says simply, "Ask me for whatever you wish, and I will give it" (6:22). Then, "he solemnly swore to her, 'Whatever you ask me, I will give you, even half of my kingdom'" (6:23). The oath is reminiscent of Artaxerxes' promise of half his kingdom to Esther (Esth 5:3, 6–7; 7:2–3), but whereas Esther asks for her life and the lives of her people (Esth 7:3), Herodias asks for the death of the prophet. The guest list for the birthday feast now takes on additional meaning. Because Herod had made his promise in front of his leading men, he was both morally and politically obligated to fulfill his promise. Otherwise, his leading men would have reason to doubt the validity of any promises he had made to them.

Although this story began very slowly, with the report of John's death in verses 14–16, the lengthy summary of the background in verses 17–20, and the delaying effect of the participles in verses 21–22, it begins to move quickly and decisively now:

> The king said to the girl…
> And he solemnly swore to her…
> She went out and said to her mother, "What should I ask for?"
> She replied, "The head of John the Baptizer."
> Immediately she rushed back to the king and requested, "I want you
> to give me at once the head of John the Baptist on a platter" (6:22–25).

Evil, like good in Mark, can move with haste. By asking her mother what she should ask for, Herodias's daughter gives Herodias the opportunity to fulfill her intent to have John killed. The request also shows that Herodias had not prompted her daughter before the dance. It was simply part of the "opportunity" of the moment. She asks not for half of Herod's kingdom but half of his prisoner: "the head of John the Baptizer." The daughter herself adds the macabre request, "on a platter," which further links the death of John to the banquet scene. Ironically, whereas Jesus will offer his disciples his body and blood (Mark 14:22–24), Herodias's daughter offers her mother John the Baptist's head.

---

49. Girard, "Scandal and the Dance," 316, 319.
50. Ibid., 317.

Mark underscores Herod's dilemma, the trap in which he is caught. He cannot deny the gruesome request because of his oath and the presence of his "great men." The rest of the story is a series of comings and goings. The king sends his officer to carry out Herodias's request. *Spekoulatōr* (σπεκουλάτωρ) is a Latin loanword used for soldiers who carry out executions and other covert actions.[51] The prison was presumably in the dungeon of the fortress where the banquet was held (Josephus [*Ant.* 18.119] reports that John was executed at Machaerus, Herod's stronghold northeast of the Dead Sea). The officer carries out the command in detail and brings John's head "on a platter." The banquet scene in Herod's court ends with Salome serving her mother this gruesome dish.[52] One final detail sets up a contrast with the noticeable absence of Jesus' disciples later: when John's disciples heard of his death, they came, took the body, and laid it in a tomb (6:29).

NARRATIVE FUNCTIONS AND THEMATIC CONNECTIONS

Having worked through the story of the beheading of John the Baptist and noted both its intertextual connections and the intricacies of the way the story is told, we may return to the question of its function in the Gospel. As we saw at the outset, interpreters have typically commented on the fact that it is an interlude in the narrative of Jesus' ministry that fills the time of the disciples' mission (6:7–13, 30–31). The explicit connections are made by Herod's response to the reports of what the disciples were doing (6:12–13, 14), the bracketing supplied by the verbs "they went out" in 6:13 and "the apostles gathered" in 6:30, and the more subtle contrast between the banquet scene in 6:21–28 and the report that the disciples "had no leisure even to eat" (6:31).

While set as an interlude, however, the story functions as an embedded narrative that sets key Markan themes in relief.

(1) *John's death foreshadows Jesus' death.* As is often observed, the death of John foreshadows Jesus' death. Guelich called it "a harbinger of Jesus' ultimate rejection,"[53] and Lane says, "The Gospel of Mark contains two 'passion narratives.'"[54] Hooker observes that "there are even similarities in the stories, since both John and Jesus are put to death by political rulers who recognize their goodness, but who are described as weakly giving in to pressure."[55] Some

---

51. Schürer, *History of the Jewish People*, 1:371.

52. Culpepper, *Mark*, 205.

53. Guelich, *Mark*, 328.

54. William L. Lane, *The Gospel according to Mark* (NICNT; Grand Rapids: Eerdmans, 1974), 215.

55. Hooker, *Mark*, 158–59.

of the same vocabulary appears in the two stories: "arrested" (6:17; 14:1, 44, 46, 49), "bound" (6:7; 15:1, 7), and "an opportune day" (6:21; 14:11). The presence of these terms in both accounts is incidental, however, with the last being the most suggestive. More important is the common motif of the persecution of the righteous one and the dynamics by which the righteous one is silenced. Both Jesus and John are arrested because of their preaching. The persecutors (Herodias, the Sanhedrin) want the death of the prophet without having the power to impose it on the political authorities (Herod, Pilate). In both stories there is also a third actor: "one who can be manipulated (Herodias's daughter, the crowd), [who] causes the person who does not want to kill to have someone else do the killing."[56]

2. *John's death foreshadows the persecution Jesus' disciples face.* The significance of John's death is heightened because it is part of a pattern (noted by Perrin) that Mark creates for the community of Jesus' followers.[57] The Gospel starts with John's appearance as the one who fulfilled the role of a forerunner (1:2–3). He came preaching, was arrested (1:14; 6:17), and was put to death. After John was arrested, Jesus came preaching (1:14–15), and the reader soon learns that he, too, will be put to death (8:31; 9:31; 10:32–34). The report of John's death comes at a strategic point in the narrative because it tempers the disciples' successes by advancing the pattern to the third step (death) just at the point that the disciples take their first step (preaching):[58]

John	Preaching (1:2–8)	Arrest (1:14; 6:17)	Death (6:20–29)
Jesus		Preaching (1:14–15)	
The disciples			Preaching (6:12–13, 30)

It should be no surprise, therefore, that the disciples, too, will be arrested and killed (13:9–11), and the intended readers can only expect that if they respond to Jesus' call to discipleship they also will be arrested and killed, as apparently was the case for some in the Markan community (see 4:17 and the parable of

---

56. Jean Delorme, "John the Baptist's Head—The Word Perverted: A Reading of a Narrative (Mark 6:14–29)," *Semeia* 81 (1998): 127.

57. Norman Perrin, *The New Testament: An Introduction* (New York: Harcourt Brace Jovanovich, 1974), 144.

58. Tolbert, *Sowing the Gospel*, 198.

the wicked tenants, 12:9). Mark therefore includes the account of John's death as a lesson to disciples that the mission to which they have been called will cost them everything. As Francis Moloney put it, "As followers of Jesus, the disciples are called to share in the destiny of Jesus, proleptically acted out in the martyrdom of John the Baptist."[59]

3. *Herod's banquet serves as the antithesis of Jesus' meals.* Eating and feasting often play a role in the stories of the *femme fatale,* either as signs of excess or means by which the tyrant is seduced to let down his guard or do something he had not intended to do. Mark adds to these functions subtle connections and contrasts with the Gospel narrative. Rhoads and Michie find commentary by contrast in the framing of the story of John's death: "sending disciples out with no food contrasts sharply with Herod's banquet."[60] When they return, Jesus leads them to a remote place because "they had no leisure even to eat" (6:31). Then, with five loaves and two fish, Jesus feeds the multitude of five thousand. Herod's great ones had leisure for a birthday celebration. Herod surrounded himself with courtiers, officers, and the leaders of Galilee (6:21). Jesus saw "a great crowd," had compassion on them because "they were like sheep without a shepherd" (6:34), and taught them "many things" (6:34). Both Herod and Jesus provide a meal for their followers, but the contrasts could hardly be greater. At the end of the meal the disciples collected twelve baskets of fragments (6:43). Herod's party ends with the serving of John's head on a platter. The platter underscores "a contrast bordering on the intolerable: a speaking man's head not only reduced to silence, but also to the status of food served at a table."[61]

4. *The serving of John's head on a platter anticipates the Last Supper.* The death of John the Baptist in a context connected with a meal scene sets up a striking resonance with Jesus' last meal with his disciples, at which he serves them his body and blood as signs of a new covenant (14:22–25). Herod's birthday banquet appears to have been a caricature of the meal of the new covenant.[62] Both involve the death of a prophet at the hands of a tyrant. Bach finds that the two meals are connected by the catchword *eukairos* (εὔχαιρος):

---

59. Francis J. Moloney, "Mark 6:6b–30: Mission, the Baptist, and Failure," *CBQ* 63 (2001): 660.

60. Rhoads and Michie, *Mark as Story,* 51.

61. Delorme, "John the Baptist's Head," 124.

62. Anderson, "Feminist Criticism," 132; Christine E. Joynes, "A Question of Identity: 'Who Do People Say that I Am?' Elijah, John the Baptist and Jesus in Mark's Gospel," in *Understanding, Studying, Reading: New Testament Essays in Honour of John Ashton* (ed. Christopher Rowland and Crispin H. T. Fletcher-Louis; JSNTSup 153; Sheffield: Sheffield Academic Press, 1998), 22; Focant, "La tête du prophète sur un plat," 351.

"The Markan text connects the two banquets of betrayal, the birthday celebration of King Herod and the seder which became the Last Supper of Jesus and his disciples, through the use of the word *eukairos* (εὔκαιρος): 'opportunity,' a term referring to a history-changing rent in the fabric of plain time."[63] The serving of John's head on a platter indicts the house of Herod and all who participate in the abuse of power and the miscarriage of justice. The serving of Jesus' body and blood draw all who eat and drink it into a new covenant of memory, participation in a "temple not made with hands" (14:58; 15:29), and hope for the kingdom of God (14:25).

5. *The characterization of Herod and his "kingdom" serves as the antithesis of Jesus' announcement of the kingdom of God.* Here we arrive at a connection between the story of John's death and the rest of the Gospel that has not been sufficiently appreciated: the conflict of kingdoms that it portrays. It is a tale of three kingdoms: God's, Satan's, and Herod's (and, by implication, Rome's). The kingdoms, their kings, and their "great ones" are diametrically opposed and set in irreconcilable conflict: "the Gospel, like some of the other literature of the period, envisioned two types of kingship: one, false and tyrannical; another, true and beneficial toward others."[64] John is the prophet and Jesus is the Messiah of God's kingdom; Herod and Rome, the vassals of Satan's power.

In *Mark as Story*, the authors highlight this conflict of kingdoms, commenting that, "[i]n Mark's gospel, the establishment of God's rule provides the larger background for the story."[65] John's beheading graphically illustrates the ultimate end of "the opposition and the blindness of the world."[66] Mark therefore takes broad swipes at the house of Herod:

> An ambitious and tyrannical but weak-willed ruler who married incestuously, unjustly imprisons a holy prophet, lusts after his own daughter … finally dispatches a henchman to kill the prophet in order to save face by keeping a shameful vow. It would be difficult to imagine a more scathing and contemptuous exposé of this, King Herod's latest display of scorn for genuine honor.… Mark wants us to understand, then, that the Herods *all*—husband, wife, and daughter—make up one despicable family.[67]

The great ones of earthly powers are tyrants (10:42), and Mark condemns the disciples for emulating them, but the Gospel sounds the note of hope that

---

63. Bach, "Calling the Shots," 111.
64. Smith, "Tyranny Exposed," 268 n. 35.
65. Rhoads and Michie, *Mark as Story*, 73.
66. Schweizer, *Mark*, 135.
67. McVann, "'Passion' of John the Baptist and Jesus," 154.

their power has been broken and will soon be overthrown.[68] Mark shows that the tyrants who exercise authority over others are themselves powerless. Herod, like Pilate, is forced to act against his will. Herodias forces Herod into a position in which he cannot lose face before his "great ones," but it is Herod's dependence on the patronage system that forces him to kill the prophet: "Mark presents a king trapped by the web of power over which he reigns."[69]

The graphic horror of John's death—the setting of excess, the dance of his daughter, the opportunity of Herod's rash promise, Herodias's malicious plotting, and the gruesome presentation of John's head on a platter—characterize the way of tyrannical power, but the end of their reign has come; God's kingdom is near at hand (1:15; 9:1; 14:25).[70] The tyrants who "lord it over" others (10:42) maintain power by taking life. The kingdom of God, in contrast, is brought near by the laying down of life: the Son of Man came "to give his life a ransom for many" (10:45). The Gospel comes, therefore, with an invitation to a meal.

CONCLUSION

The connections between Mark 6:17–29 and the rest of the Gospel advance some of the Gospel's major themes. They set in relief Jesus' death, the stark contrasts between the kingdom of God and the ways of earthly kings, the Herodian celebration and the meals Jesus provides, and the ever-present threat of persecution for Jesus' disciples. The change from the assumption that the Gospel is a compilation of discrete, unrelated units to the assumption that it is a coherent narrative has allowed interpreters to see these continuities more clearly. Perhaps narrative criticism has yet to take seriously the narrative's discontinuities, but it has exposed texture, richness, and depth that earlier interpreters missed.

---

68. Rhoads and Michie, *Mark as Story*, 117–18.

69. Alberto de Mingo Kaminouchi, *"But It Is Not So Among You": Echoes of Power in Mark 10:32–45* (JSNTSup 249; New York: T&T Clark, 2003), 186.

70. Kay Ehling, "Warum liess Herodes Antipas Johannes den Täufer verhaften? Oder: Wenn ein Prophet politisch gefährlich wird," *BN* 131 (2006): 63.

Good News about Jesus Christ, the Son of God

Morna D. Hooker

It is difficult today to think ourselves back to the time when Mark was *not* regarded as "story." Yet for almost two thousand years, it was neither thought of, nor listened to, as such. According to the earliest tradition, recorded by Papias around 140 C.E., the Evangelist had done no more than record what he remembered from the teaching of Peter: the content was reliable, but the order was not.[1] Then, for centuries, Mark was supposed to have abbreviated Matthew—though why he should have done so was not clear! Since almost all the material contained in Mark was reproduced in either Matthew or Luke or both, there was a natural tendency to regard Mark as less important than the other Gospels.

With the emergence of the theory of Markan priority in the nineteenth century, Mark came to be seen as an historian and biographer, and his ordering of events was now regarded—*pace* Papias—as reliable. In the ensuing quest for the historical Jesus, therefore, Mark—now regarded as the first Gospel—was seen as the primary source, and his narrative was regarded as an outline of the life of Jesus. In the early twentieth century, however, the rise of form criticism concentrated attention on the individual pericopes, which were likened to "pearls on a string," arranged in haphazard order, just as Papias had said—though the material itself was no longer regarded as reliable. Redaction criticism, the next major development, looked at the ways in which the Evangelists had *changed* the tradition, so was unhelpful in looking at the earliest Gospel, though attempts were made to distinguish Mark's style.[2] It was, however, the growing emphasis on literary-critical approaches that led scholars to consider

---

1. Papias, as recorded by Eusebius, *Hist. eccl.* 3.39.15. Similarly the *Anti-Marcionite Prologue* and Irenaeus, *Haer.* 3.1.2.
2. E.g., Ernest Best, *The Temptation and the Passion* (SNTSMS 2; Cambridge: Cambridge University Press, 1965; 2nd ed., 1990).

the Gospel as *narrative*, an insight set out definitively in the original edition of *Mark as Story*.[3]

One significant obstacle to thinking of the Gospel as "story" was the fact that it was normally heard as part of the liturgy, and so in snippets, rather than as a whole: the hearers' attention was thus concentrated on the individual pericopes. But while Mark's Gospel was certainly intended to be *heard* rather than read privately, the drama of the story is inevitably lost when it is divided up into short sections.[4] The fact that his Gospel was designed to be heard has affected Mark's manner of writing: repetitions and summaries remind listeners of what has already taken place and help them to understand where the story is going, while the breathless style—so often criticized by literary scholars—carries us along in its enthusiasm. As we listen, the tension rises: the short scenes in the early part of the story give way to a more connected narrative, and the Gospel comes to a climax with Jesus' crucifixion.

Whether by accident or design, the shape of the Gospel seems to fit Aristotle's description of a tragedy, though the final epilogue (16:1–8) means that the story is not, in fact, a tragedy, but—as the opening words declare—"good news."[5] A Greek tragedy would open with a "prologue" that provided essential information enabling the audience to understand the significance of the events they were about to see on the stage. Mark's opening verses (1:1–13) fulfill this function.[6] He begins by assuring us that what he is telling us is "good news." This phrase translates the Greek word *euangelion* (εὐαγγέλιον), which is normally translated "gospel." In the ancient world, the word was often used of the announcement of a special event, such as the birth or accession of a new emperor. Here the good news concerns Jesus the Messiah, "as it is written in the prophet Isaiah." If we turn to the later chapters of Isaiah, from which the quotation in Mark 1:3 comes, we find that the verb *euangelizomai* (εὐαγγελίζομαι, "to announce good news") occurs frequently. The good news announced there, and in Mark, is about God's salvation of his people.

---

3. David Rhoads and Donald Michie, *Mark as Story: An Introduction to the Narrative of a Gospel* (Philadelphia: Fortress, 1982). See also David Rhoads, Joanna Dewey, and Donald Michie, *Mark as Story: An Introduction to the Narrative of a Gospel* (2nd ed.; Minneapolis: Fortress, 1999).

4. See Bridget Gilfillian Upton, *Hearing Mark's Endings* (Leiden: Brill, 2006).

5. Aristotle, *Poet.* 10–12, 18; *Rhet.* 3.14.

6. Some commentators regard vv. 1–15 as the prologue, e.g., Leander E. Keck, "The Introduction to Mark's Gospel," *NTS* 12 (1966): 352–70. For arguments supporting vv. 1–13, see Morna D. Hooker, "The Beginning of the Gospel," in *The Future of Christology: Essays in Honor of Leander E. Keck* (ed. Abraham J. Malherbe and Wayne A. Meeks; Minneapolis: Fortress, 1993), 18–28. On the function of the opening verses, see Morna D. Hooker, *Beginnings: Keys That Open the Gospels* (London: SCM, 1997).

The subject of the good news he is about to relate is Jesus, the Messiah. To be sure, Mark's wording—"the good news of Jesus Christ"—is ambiguous and could mean simply that he is relating the good news *proclaimed by* Jesus, but though the story that follows will tell how Jesus announced good news, the way in which that story is told concentrates attention on the figure of Jesus himself. Jesus proclaims the kingdom of God, but Mark's concern is to proclaim Jesus. When Mark begins his book with the words "The beginning of the good news," therefore, we realize that there is a double entendre. The phrase could perhaps be a way of getting started and mean no more than the old introduction to lessons read in church worship, "Here beginneth...." But perhaps Mark means that the *whole* of his book, which recounts the ministry, death, and resurrection of Jesus, is the beginning of the good news. What he recounts is simply "the beginning of the good news" that is now being proclaimed by Jesus' followers. The abrupt ending of the Gospel in 16:8 suggests that the story continues in the lives and witness of Jesus' disciples.

JESUS, MESSIAH

Mark's opening words assure us that this Jesus is the Messiah—a fact that remains hidden from the characters in the story until Peter acknowledges him to be such at Caesarea Philippi (8:29). Peter's recognition of Jesus as Messiah has long been regarded as an important turning point in the narrative, and it corresponds to the crucial scene in a Greek tragedy identified by Aristotle as the moment when the course of the play changes. This scene is often a moment of recognition when the characters grasp something of the significance of what is taking place (e.g., the true identity of the central figures).[7] At this point in Mark's narrative, Jesus' true identity begins to dawn on those closest to him. Strangely, however, Jesus neither accepts nor rejects the title, and his response has led some to suggest that in fact he rejected it, but at his "trial" before Caiaphas he is said to have responded to the high priest's question, "Are you the Messiah, the Son of the blessed?" with a clear "I am" (14:62).[8] His claim is echoed by the chief priests, who taunt him at Golgotha with the words, "Let the Messiah, the king of Israel, come down from the cross" (15:32). These clear declarations of Jesus' identity at the beginning, at the turning point of the narrative, and at its climax, make it clear that Mark wants us to believe in Jesus as God's anointed one, the Messiah.

---

7. See above, n. 5. Aristotle describes the scenes between the prologue and this recognition scene as the "complication" and those that follow as the "dénouement."

8. On Jesus' supposed rejection of the title, see Theodore J. Weeden, *Mark: Traditions in Conflict* (Philadelphia: Fortress, 1971), 64ff.

It is the story of Jesus' crucifixion, however, that spells out what it *means* to be "the Messiah, the king of Israel," since Jesus is crucified, not in spite of his messiahship, but precisely *because* he is the Messiah. Pilate begins his investigation by asking Jesus, "Are you the king of the Jews?" (15:2), and although Jesus' reply is ambiguous, it appears to mean that Pilate is stating the truth, even though he does not understand it. When Pilate realizes that the accusations brought against Jesus are false, he offers to release "the king of the Jews" (15:9). Throughout these proceedings, he persists in referring to Jesus as "king of the Jews" (15:12). The soldiers mock Jesus as king, clothing him in purple and crowning him with thorns; they salute him—"Hail, king of the Jews"— kneel to him, and pay mock homage (15:16–20). The charge against him is that he is "the king of the Jews" (15:26), and the passers-by mock him as "the Messiah, the king of Israel" (15:32).

Jesus is revealed to us, the hearers of the Gospel, as Messiah at the beginning of the story, he is acknowledged to be Messiah by the disciples at its turning point, and he is proclaimed Messiah—a *suffering* Messiah—at its end. The word *Christos* (Χριστός) is also used three times between Caesarea Philippi and the trial, but not to *identify* Jesus. In 9:41 and 13:21, the reference is clearly to the future, after Jesus' messiahship has been openly proclaimed. In 12:35, Jesus is depicted as referring to himself obliquely as Messiah.[9] To the great majority of those taking part in the story, these references are unintelligible. To those in the know, however—those who have heard Mark's opening words—they are significant.

We may set out the way in which Mark uses the term *Christos* (Χριστός) in tabular form. The terms *prologue, complication, discovery,* and *dénouement* are those used by Aristotle. In Mark, however, the final scenes are more than the inevitable conclusion to the dénouement: they form a series of ironic recognition scenes. Here, in the climax to the story, Jesus' identity is openly revealed on the cross, even though no one fully comprehends.

CHRIST: A MARKAN SUMMARY

Prologue	**1:1–13**	**1:1, title**
Complication	1:14–8:21	(1:34, text dubious)
Discovery	**8:22–9:13**	**8:29, Caesarea Philippi**
Dénouement	9:14–13:37	9:41; 12:35; 13:21

---

9. In 1:34, where we are told that the demons recognized Jesus, some manuscripts read "they knew that he was the Messiah."

Climax	14:1–15:47	14:61, high priest's question
		15:32, mockery
		15 *passim*, Jesus crucified as king

As It Is Written

According to the opening line of Mark's Gospel as we have it today, Jesus is not only "Messiah" but "Son of God." There is, to be sure, some doubt about the authenticity of the words here, and so we shall for the moment postpone looking at their significance.[10] Before he begins the narrative, Mark sets out the information we need in order to understand why the story he is about to relate is "good news," and first of all he assures us that this good news is in accordance with what was written in the prophet Isaiah. After 1:1, we might expect a passage about the Messiah or the Son of God, but what we are given speaks rather about the coming of the Lord. In Mark, this "anchoring" of the story in scripture is unique. To be sure, there are many allusions to scripture and even quotations in what follows, but these are all found in the mouths of the characters in the story. It is only here that the author himself spells out the important fact that what is about to take place is the fulfillment of scripture. Mark's method contrasts with that of Matthew, who in his early chapters points out several times that what occurred in the birth and infancy of Jesus took place "in order to fulfill what had been spoken by the prophet."[11] For Mark, one such comment is sufficient: we are meant to hear his whole story in the light of what was said by the prophet.[12] The good news he is about to tell us is the fulfillment of God's promises, since it is "as it is written."

Mark begins, then, by assuring us that the story he is about to tell fulfills the promises written by the great prophet Isaiah. In fact, part of what follows comes from elsewhere, being an amalgam of Exod 23:20 and Mal 3:1; only verse 3 is from the book of Isaiah (Isa 40:3). How are we to explain this mistake? If Mark were a modern author, we might blame him for failing to check his source. But in his day, this was not so easy! The only way that Mark could have checked the passages would have been by working laboriously through scrolls, and one wonders whether he had access to them. He would almost

---

10. They are missing from the original version of א and Θ.

11. Matt 1:22–23; 2:5–6, 15, 17–18, 23; cf. 4:14–16.

12. Cf. Rikki E. Watts, *Isaiah's New Exodus in Mark* (WUNT 88; Tübingen: Mohr Siebeck, 1997).

certainly have been quoting from memory and not consulting any text. It may well be that he is quoting a "prooftext" that was already being used by other Christians, and wrongly assumed that the whole passage was from Isaiah. Or he may himself have been responsible for joining two such "prooftexts," only one of which was from Isaiah, together.[13] But had Mark been challenged and told that his reference was wrong, he might well have been unrepentant. For first-century Jews, Isaiah was the great prophet whose book contained the promises of God's coming salvation, and it was his words that were now being fulfilled! If Mark singled out Isaiah, this may well have been deliberate. Perhaps, therefore, we should classify this as a "deliberate mistake."

Interestingly, the passages quoted concentrate, not on the figure of Jesus, but on the messenger who is sent to prepare his way. The messenger's task is to announce the coming of the Lord in salvation and judgment. His only function is to prepare his way by urging men and women to be ready: he is simply "a voice, crying in the wilderness." So it is that the first figure to appear on the stage will be that of John, crying in the wilderness and proclaiming a baptism of repentance.

Although Mark's appeal to scripture in 1:2–3 is unique, there are interesting echoes of it throughout the narrative. First of all, we are reminded on various occasions of the importance of Isaiah's prophecies: Jesus is said to quote Isaiah (Isa 29:13) in 7:6–7 (where Isaiah is specifically mentioned), when he complains about the insincerity of the Pharisees' worship, and in 11:17 (quoting Isa 56:7), when he again protests about the failure of the religious authorities to worship God and the fact that they are preventing others from doing so. In a similar vein, though without specifically referring to scripture, he declares that the crowd's reaction to his teaching is a fulfillment of words taken from Isa 6:9–10 (Mark 4:12) and describes the Jewish leaders' failure to respond to his preaching in a parable that is clearly based on Isa 5:1–2 (Mark 12:1). There are further echoes of Isaiah in other passages, such as Mark 3:27 (Isa 49:24); 5:3 (Isa 65:4); 7:37 (Isa 35:5–6); 9:48 (Isa 66:24); 12:32 (Isa 45:21); 13:24–25 (Isa 13:10; 34:4); 13:31 (Isa 51:6).

It seems clear, then, that Mark does indeed see the story of Jesus as the fulfillment of the promises and warnings made through Isaiah. The messenger of God was sent to prepare the way of the Lord, who has now come to his people, bringing salvation to those who receive him and condemnation to those who do not.

---

13. While both Matthew and Luke quote Isa 40:3 when introducing John the Baptist's ministry (Matt 3:3; Luke 3:4–6), each of them uses the first half of the quotation (from Exodus and Malachi) elsewhere (Matt 11:10; Luke 7:27).

Throughout the story, too, there are quotations from other passages of scripture. In disputes between Jesus and the Jewish religious authorities, for example, appeal is made to Moses in 10:4 and 6–7 (regarding divorce), in 10:19–20 (regarding the greatest commandment), and in 12:19 and 26 (regarding resurrection). Jesus is hailed by the crowd on his entry into Jerusalem with words taken from Pss 118 and 148 (Mark 11:9–10), while he himself is said to have quoted Ps 118 in Mark 12:10–11 regarding his forthcoming rejection and vindication and Ps 110 in 12:36 regarding his messianic status. His only words on the cross are taken from Ps 22 (Mark 15:34).

These various quotations and allusions demonstrate the truth of Mark's opening assertion that the good news about Jesus is the fulfillment of scripture. There is another, more ominous way, however, in which the story demonstrates that this is true. In two other passages, Jesus is said to have appealed to scripture without any indication as to *what* scriptures might be in mind: in both cases, he is referring to his own destiny. The first of these occurs once again at the turning point of the Gospel, immediately after the transfiguration, where Jesus' true identity is revealed to three of the disciples. As they come down from the mountain, Jesus warns Peter, James, and John that they must say nothing about what they have seen and heard until the Son of Man has been raised from the dead (9:9), a saying that baffles the disciples, who ask about the promised coming of Elijah. Jesus then explains that Elijah has already come and that "they have done to him whatever they wished, as the scriptures say of him" (9:13). It is clear that the returning Elijah is here identified with John the Baptist, but the reference to the scriptures is puzzling, since, although Mal 4:5 promises that Elijah will be sent before the Day of the Lord, apparently identifying him with the "messenger" of 3:1, it says nothing about suffering. Possibly the reference is to what "they *wished*" to do to the first Elijah (1 Kgs 19:1–3). In the case of John, "they" have already carried out what they wished to do.

Linked with these words is Jesus' declaration that the scriptures say of the Son of Man that he must "endure great suffering and be treated with contempt" (9:12). By now, readers of the Gospel (and even the disciples) will have grasped that, when he speaks of the Son of Man, Jesus is referring to his own mission (see 2:10, 28; 8:31, 38). At the turning point in the narrative, therefore, we learn that this mission includes suffering and death (8:31; 9:12) and that this is foretold in scripture. Once again, there is no indication as to what scriptures are in mind.

The link with Elijah, who comes first and "puts everything in order" points us back to 1:2–3. The coming of the messenger sent to prepare the way was announced in scripture. In these opening verses of the Gospel there is no indication that John's mission will not be successful: the first hint of this comes in 1:14, which speaks of his "handing over" or arrest. Many refused to respond to Jesus himself, however, as the quotations from Isaiah in Mark 4:12 and 7:6–7 indicate. "The way of the Lord" that John was summoned to prepare proves to be the "way" that leads to Jerusalem and to death (9:33–34; 10:32, 52).[14] The "good news" about Jesus, Messiah, Son of God, will prove to be about his suffering, death, and resurrection, but all this nevertheless takes place according to scripture.

This insistence that what happens to the Son of Man takes place "as it is written" reappears in the passion narrative. In 14:21, "the Son of Man goes as it is written of him," while in 14:27 Jesus is said to have quoted Zech 13:7, which speaks of the shepherd being struck and the sheep scattered. When he is arrested in Gethsemane, Jesus declares, "let the scriptures be fulfilled" (14:49).

Although there are many references to scripture throughout Mark's Gospel—in particular to Isaiah—we see that this emphasis on the fulfillment of scripture in relation to Jesus' mission is especially marked in the prologue, at the turning point of the Gospel, and at its climax.

AS IT IS WRITTEN: A MARKAN SUMMARY

Prologue	**1:1–13**	**1:2–3, as it is written**
Complication	1:14–8:21	4:12, quote from Isaiah
		7:6–7, quote from Isaiah
		allusions to Isaiah in 3:27; 5:3; 7:37
Discovery	**8:22–9:13**	**9:12–13, as it is written of the Son of Man/Elijah**
Dénouement	9:14–13:37	11:17, quote from Isaiah
		12:1, parable (from Isaiah)
		allusions to Isaiah in 9:48; 12:32; 13:24–25, 31

---

14. The repetition of the phrase "in the way" in 9:33–34, which seems unnecessary, is perhaps meant to remind us that the road that Jesus is following leads to Jerusalem. If so, then Mark is subtly underlining the disciples' total misunderstanding of the situation. While accompanying Jesus on the way that leads to the cross, they argue about which of them is the greatest!

quotes from Law in 10:4, 6–7,
19–20 12:20, 26

quotes from Psalms in 11:9–
10; 12:10–11, 36

Climax	14:1–15:47	**14:21, as it is written of the Son of Man**
		14:27, for it is written (Zech 13:7)
		14:49, let scripture be fulfilled
		15:34–35, quote from Ps 22

John the Baptist

After being told that Mark is going to give us good news about Jesus, the Messiah, it is something of a surprise when the first person to appear on the stage is not Jesus himself but John. But of course the quotation in 1:2–3 has spoken of the one who is going to prepare the way for the Lord, and in John the Baptist we recognize Elijah, who is sent to announce the Day of the Lord (Mal 4:5–6). The arrival of John is a reminder of just how important his role is. John's mission is described in Mark 1:2–8. His baptism signifies the people's repentance, in preparation for forgiveness. He prepares the way for one who is far greater than he, whose baptism will be with Spirit rather than water. In 1:7–8, Mark sets out John's message. It contains three statements, each of which makes the same point: the one who follows him, and whose coming John announces, is far greater than he. Jesus' story will begin only after John has been "handed over" (1:14). John's role is that of the forerunner who heralds the coming of his successor.

As we have seen, John is referred to again, immediately after the transfiguration, now clearly identified with the returning Elijah, sent to prepare the way (9:11). Jesus tells his disciples that Elijah has already come and that "they" have done to him what they wished. To hearers of the Gospel, the meaning of Jesus' words is immediately clear, since in the section between the prologue and the recognition scene, Mark told at length the story of John's death (6:14–29). Arrested because his preaching was unpalatable to the authorities, he was put to death when Herodias found an opportunity to outwit her husband Herod. King Herod, knowing John to be a righteous and holy man, and therefore reluctant to execute him, nevertheless succumbed to pressure. The account ends with John's disciples taking his body and laying it in a tomb, and though there are rumors of John's resurrection (6:14–16), they are untrue. Elijah has indeed come: he has prepared the way of the Lord, "and they have done to him whatever they wished" (9:13).

To those of us who have heard the story of Jesus before, the significance of this account of John's death has ominous overtones. No wonder that we are reminded, in 9:12, that "Elijah's" fate is linked to that of the Son of Man. Just as John's baptism in water pointed forward to Jesus' baptism in Spirit,[15] so his death points forward to that of Jesus himself. Like John, Jesus—the Son of Man—will be "handed over" and put to death. Jesus' own story will in a sense mirror that of John, for when we come to the passion narrative we hear how the religious authorities, finding Jesus' teaching unpalatable, seized the opportunity to bring abut his death (14:1–2, 10–11). They, too, managed to outwit the political leader, Pilate, even though he believed Jesus to be innocent (15:1–15). Jesus' death is inevitable, and the story seems to end when Joseph of Arimathea lays Jesus' body in a tomb (15:42–47). This time, however, rumors of a resurrection are replaced by the scene at the empty tomb, where someone who appears to be a heavenly messenger assures us that Jesus has indeed been raised from the dead (16:6).

But what of John, alias Elijah? We look for him in the passion narrative in vain, but then realize that this is because his enemies have disposed of him. Yet his failure to appear is noted, when the crowd misunderstands Jesus' words from the cross and think that he is calling for Elijah to assist him (15:35–36). But how *could* Elijah come, when he, too, has been put to death? Jesus' forerunner has been silenced. Since "they" have done to him what they wanted, Jesus' own fate is sealed.

Mark clearly thinks of John as Jesus' forerunner, and we are reminded of this fact once again in the section between the recognition scene and the climax, when Jesus' challenges his enemies to say whether John's authority was human or divine (11:27–33). The answer they give—or fail to give—will determine the answer to the question they have posed him regarding his *own* authority. If John's authority came from God, so too does that of the one whose

---

15. Influenced by Luke, we are accustomed to thinking of this Spirit baptism as something that took place at Pentecost. Mark, however, does not relate this story, and it is likely that he regarded the ministry of Jesus, who received the Spirit at his own baptism, as a "baptism with Spirit." See Morna D. Hooker, "John's Baptism: A Prophetic Sign," in *The Holy Spirit and Christian Origins: Essays in Honor of James D. G. Dunn* (ed. Graham N. Stanton, Bruce W. Longenecker, and Stephen C. Barton; Grand Rapids: Eerdmans, 2004), 22–40.

coming John foretold. But if the religious authorities failed to recognize the source of John's authority, they will inevitably fail to recognize that of Jesus.

JOHN THE BAPTIST: A MARKAN SUMMARY

Prologue	1:1–13	**1:4–8, John: forerunner**
Complication	1:14–8:21	1:14, handed over
		6:14–29, John's death
Discovery	8:22–9:13	**9:11–12, John (= Elijah): forerunner in suffering**
Dénouement	9:14–13:37	11:27–33, authority
Climax	14:1–15:47	15:35–36, Elijah unable to help

JESUS, SON OF GOD

As we have noted, the words "Son of God" may be an addition in 1:1, but if so they clearly represent fairly Mark's own understanding, for as we shall see, the true meaning of the term "Christ" is found only when it is explained by that of "Son of God." The words occur again in 1:11, and this time there is no doubt at all about their authenticity. Here Jesus is addressed as "my beloved Son" by the heavenly voice at his baptism. According to 1:11, the heavenly voice speaks to Jesus alone, but the affirmation that he is Son of God is repeated at the transfiguration (9:7), which follows closely after Caesarea Philippi,[16] forming part of the "turning point" of the Gospel, and this time it is heard not only by Jesus but by three of his disciples. When we turn to the "trial" scene, at the end of the Gospel, the high priest's question seems to equate "Messiah" with "the Son of the Blessed" (14:61), and as with "Messiah," Jesus' clear acknowledgement of his identity as "Son" is echoed at the crucifixion, for when he dies, the Roman centurion declares, "Surely this man was [the] son of God" (15:39). Although a Roman centurion could hardly have used these words with the significance that Mark gave to them, they echo the words of the heavenly voice in 1:11 and 9:7, and as though to ensure that we see the connection, Mark links the centurion's confession with the statement that the temple curtain

---

16. Unusually, Mark links the two narratives with the phrase "six days later," ensuring that we see the link between the two narratives.

was torn in two, using the same verb that he used in 1:10 of the tearing apart of the heavens.[17] When the barrier between God and humankind is removed, the truth about Jesus is revealed.

Jesus' identity as Son of God is thus made plain at the beginning (in Mark's "prologue"), at the turning point (where Jesus' identity is first revealed to humans), and at the climax of his story (in the passion narrative). It seems as though, while it is natural for humans to consider the possibility that Jesus may be the Christ, God's anointed one (1:1; 8:27; 14:62; 15 *passim*), Mark is pushing us to recognize that the most profound understanding of what this means is conveyed by the words of the heavenly voice (1:11; 9:7), picked up in mockery in 14:61 and in astonishment in 15:39.

As with the term *Christos* (Χριστός), "Son of God" occurs in between these three significant passages, either in addressing or referring to Jesus. In 3:11 and 5:7, Jesus is addressed as "Son of God" by unclean spirits, and in 12:6 and 13:32 Jesus appears to be speaking of himself as "Son," though in neither case openly. Once again, however, these identifications are unheard or uncomprehended by the characters in the story, although they ring bells for those of us who are "in the know," since we have been privileged to witness the baptism and the transfiguration and to overhear the words spoken from heaven.

SON OF GOD: A MARKAN SUMMARY

Prologue	**1:1–13**	(1:1, text dubious)
		1:11, voice from heaven
Complication	1:14–8:21	3:11; 5:7, recognized by unclean spirits
Discovery	**8:22–9:13**	**9:7, voice from heaven**
Dénouement	9:14–13:37	12:6; 13:32, Jesus' self-reference
Climax	**14:1–15:47**	**14:61, high priest's question**
		15:39, centurion's "confession"

---

17. See Rhoads, Dewey, and Michie, *Mark as Story*, 48.

The Shape of Mark's Story

If we look at the shape of Mark's story, we find that there are certain themes that occur in the opening prologue, at the fulcrum of the narrative—the moment when some of his followers begin to understand who he is—and at its conclusion. These themes are Jesus' identity as Messiah; the fact that what takes place is "in accordance with scripture"; the witness of John, both in his proclamation of Jesus' coming and in his death; and Jesus' identity as Son of God. At these three points in the narrative, these facts about Jesus are revealed to a few of the characters in the story or to us, its hearers. There are also allusions to all these facts in the intervening narrative, though their significance here is hidden from the characters.

The good news is, as we are told in Mark's prologue, essentially about Jesus, the Messiah and Son of God, and is witnessed to by scripture and John the Baptist, who is himself fulfilling the role set out for him in scripture. What we might never have guessed from these opening verses is that the story would end with Jesus' rejection, suffering, death, and resurrection. True, when we hear the story for a second or third time, we notice possible hints of what is to come: Jesus, here baptized by John in Jordan, will later speak of a far more terrible "baptism" that he will have to undergo (10:38). Further, the fact that we are not told the outcome of Jesus' testing by Satan may hint that the battle is not finally over, even though the strong man has been bound and his property is being plundered (3:27). Certainly at Caesarea Philippi Peter is addressed as "Satan" and rebuked for tempting him, and in Gethsemane Jesus is said to be "troubled and distressed" (14:33) as he prays to be spared from drinking the cup prepared for him; he is surely being "tested" here, and he urges Peter to pray that *he* might be spared from being tested. But these hints in 1:1–13 are "echoes" of what is to come rather than clear indications of what lies ahead. In any case, we do not need to be told the *plot* of the story in the prologue; we simply need to be told who Jesus is so that we can understand the narrative that follows.

If we begin to read Mark's narrative at 1:14, we may well conclude that the story is about the kingdom of God. This, after all, is what Jesus proclaims, not himself. But the question of his identity continually intrudes. The unclean spirits recognize him as God's "Holy One" or "Son" (1:24, 34; 3:11; 5:7). In various ways, he is said to do what God alone can do: he forgives sins—and is accused of blasphemy (2:5–7); he stills a storm, and the disciples, astonished at his control over wind and waves, ask "Who is this?" (4:41)—unsurprisingly, since only God can exercise such power (Ps 89:8–9)! He claims to be working in the power of the Holy Spirit (3:29). He raises a dead child (5:35–43). In his home town, his neighbors acknowledge his wisdom and power but reject him (6:1–6). Elsewhere, however, he is acknowledged to be a prophet (6:14–16).

In a miracle reminiscent of one attributed to Elisha (2 Kgs 4:42–44), Jesus feeds a large crowd (6:30–44), though the emphasis placed on the numbers involved—a crowd of five thousand fed with five loaves and two fish—indicates a far greater miracle than that performed by Elisha, who is said to have fed one hundred men with twenty loaves. Mark's story suggests, too, that Jesus is seen as a second Moses; yet he is surely greater than Moses, since the exodus story tells us that it was *the Lord* who provided the manna, not Moses (Exod 16; cf. John 6:32). Moreover, there is food left over and to spare (6:43), whereas the manna could not be kept. Finally, although Moses walked *through* the sea, he certainly did not walk *on* it, which is what Jesus then does (6:47–52).[18] Again, this is something that God alone could do (Job 9:8). Jesus greets his disciples with words we normally translate as "It is I" but that also mean "I am." Does Mark understand Jesus to be using the divine name? A second feeding narrative (8:1–10) is followed by another boat trip, in which the disciples fail to understand Jesus' teaching and comment on the fact that they have no bread with them (8:14–21). But why should they be concerned about that when one who is greater than Moses and the prophets, and has twice supplied the crowds with food, is with them? They are blind and deaf to the truth, as were the crowds in 4:10–12, still unaware of who Jesus really is.

The recognition scene of 8:27–30 contrasts the idea we have already met in 6:14–16 that Jesus is John the Baptist, Elijah, or one of the prophets, with the truth: he is the Messiah. But like the blind man whose eyes are at first only partly restored (8:22–26), Peter can grasp only half the truth. He rejects the notion that Jesus must suffer, but Jesus continues by telling would-be disciples that they, too, must be prepared to share his sufferings (8:34–38). The truth half-grasped at Caesarea Philippi is confirmed by the story of the transfiguration, which Mark has firmly linked to it by the unusual use of the phrase "six days later" (9:2). Now Jesus is seen by Peter, James, and John conversing with Moses and Elijah, but is revealed as greater than they, since "This is my beloved Son." Again, however, they are told that Jesus' destiny is to suffer. Jesus sees messiahship and sonship as involving suffering, and this is because he sees his role as that of the Son of Man, given authority by God but rejected by others.[19] From now on, the narrative will show Jesus traveling to Jerusalem,

---

18. It was God, of course, who parted the waters of the Red Sea to enable the Israelites to pass through: Exod 14:21; Ps 77:19–20; Isa 43:16; 51:10.

19. There is enormous debate about the significance of the term "the Son of Man." Whatever Jesus himself may have meant by the term, however, Mark appears to have

followed by disciples who continually show that they do not understand why he is going there (9:30–37; 10:32–45).

As Jesus approaches Jerusalem, he heals another blind man, who hails him as "Son of David": even though he is blind, he already recognizes something of the truth. This time, the man's sight is immediately fully restored, and he follows Jesus "on the way" to Jerusalem; he is prepared to become a disciple of one who is heading for suffering and death. His healing signals the time of disclosure. Jesus then deliberately stages his entry into Jerusalem, riding into Jerusalem on the back of a donkey, an extraordinary action in view of the fact that all pilgrims *walked* into the city. This provocative action has to be seen as a claim to messiahship (cf. 1 Kgs 1:28–40). The cursing of the fig tree (11:12–14, 20) is best understood as a sign of Israel's imminent fate, since she, too, has failed to produce fruit when the Lord looked for it (see Jer 8:13; Hos 9:10, 16; Mic 7:1). The cleansing of the temple (11:11, 15–19) suggests the coming of the Lord to his temple foretold in Mal 3:1–4. Jesus condemns the commerce taking place in the temple, which is preventing people from worshiping God, and in the ensuing conversation with the religious authorities implicitly claims that his authority comes from God (11:27–33).

In his teaching, Jesus hints that he is God's Son (12:6) and greater than David (12:35–37), while privately to four disciples he again hints that he is Messiah (13:21) and Son (13:32), and he affirms that the Son of Man will come with great power and glory (13:26). Then, immediately before the passion story unfolds, a woman pours costly ointment over his head, a preparation, says Jesus, for his coming burial (14:3–9). But—anomalous as it may seem, since the action is performed by a woman—the fact that she pours the ointment *on his head* suggests that he is being anointed king.

And so we move into the passion narrative itself, where the truth about Jesus is found in the mouth of the high priest—a fact of great significance, even though he refuses to recognize the truth of his own words, since it was the high priest's task to anoint and proclaim Israel's king. The irony of a woman who anoints Jesus and a high priest who dismisses his own proclamation as blasphemy is then continued in the account of Jesus' condemnation and crucifixion as "the king of the Jews."

The story reaches its climax with the centurion's declaration that Jesus was "son of God." These are the last words spoken by a human in the Gospel,

---

understood it in terms of Dan 7:13 (see Mark 8:38; 13:26; 14:62). The Son of Man represents the faithful in Israel, presently suffering but promised vindication because of their obedience to God.

and they provide the moment of full revelation. With the death of Jesus, the temple curtain has been torn in two (15:38), and a Gentile has access to the presence of God. Jesus' executioner (no matter that he does not understand it) sees the truth.

Mark's story has an epilogue (16:1–8). We are told how the women who witnessed Jesus' death and burial come to the tomb and find it empty. They are told by a young man dressed in white that he has been raised, and they are commissioned to tell Jesus' disciples to follow him to Galilee. Terrified, they flee from the tomb and fail to tell anyone what they have seen and heard.[20]

The story ends, then, with total human failure. The religious authorities have failed to accept Jesus, Pontius Pilate has caved in to pressure, the crowds have melted away, the disciples have run away, Judas has betrayed him, Peter has denied him, and at the end even the women—hitherto faithful—have failed him. In spite of the centurion's confession, the story appears to be a tragedy. Yet Mark introduced it as "the beginning of good news," and now we realize that it is, indeed, only the beginning. The very fact that the story is now being told means that the women must have overcome their fear and that the disciples did indeed obey the command to go to Galilee. There they had to learn all over again what discipleship meant: taking up the cross and following Jesus. The message entrusted to the women is a message of forgiveness. The disciples—even Peter!—are being given a second chance.

But Mark's abrupt ending means that the final scene concerns not just the disciples but becomes an invitation to those who hear his story. "If you want to see the risen Christ," he seems to be saying, "You, too, must set out on a journey—set out on the way of discipleship, believing that he has indeed been raised. Go in spirit to Galilee, the place where men and women were challenged by the mighty acts and words of Jesus, and learn what discipleship means." The story Mark tells is only the beginning of a story that he invites his readers to continue for themselves, as they come to acknowledge Jesus as Messiah and Son of God and to preach the good news to the world (cf. Mark 13:10).

---

20. Neither of the endings that follow Mark 16:8 was written by Mark himself: the style and vocabulary of both are quite different from Mark's own. They seem to have been composed by early scribes who were dissatisfied with Mark's abrupt ending and who felt the need to add information about appearances of the risen Jesus.

"WHEREVER THE GOSPEL IS PREACHED": THE PARADOX OF SECRECY IN THE GOSPEL OF MARK

Kelly R. Iverson

The publication of *Mark as Story* in 1982 was a pioneering achievement.[1] The "book that broke the news" was the first monograph to adapt secular literary theory to the study of a Gospel narrative, launching a fresh and paradigmatic shift in Gospels research.[2] However, while many scholars were intrigued by the pursuit and eagerly adopted this new reading strategy, *Mark as Story* received a mixed response. To interpret the Gospel as a "story"— a "literary creation with an autonomous integrity"—was disconcerting for some within the guild.[3] In fact, as the discussion evolved, some insisted that the practice of narrative criticism ignored historical matters and was tantamount to "set[ting] sail on the shoreless sea of existential subjectivity."[4] Still others, beyond warning of the program's "reductive approach" and inherent "danger," demurred the perceived insignificance of *Mark as Story*, as well as narrative criticism in general. Not only was narrative criticism deemed methodologically suspect, but some argued it promoted a "pointless exercise" that "throw[s] no new light on the problems which have perplexed interpreters of

---

1. David Rhoads and Donald Michie, *Mark as Story: An Introduction to the Narrative of a Gospel* (Philadelphia: Fortress, 1982). See also David Rhoads, Joanna Dewey, and Donald Michie, *Mark as Story: An Introduction to the Narrative of a Gospel* (2nd ed.; Minneapolis: Fortress, 1999).

2. David Lee, *Luke's Stories of Jesus: Theological Reading of Gospel Narrative and the Legacy of Hans Frei* (JSNTSup 185; Sheffield: Sheffield Academic Press, 1999), 120.

3. Rhoads and Michie, *Mark as Story*, 3.

4. D. A. Carson, *The Gospel according to John* (Pillar New Testament Commentary; Grand Rapids: Eerdmans, 1991), 65. For other important narrative-critical discussions that followed in the wake of *Mark as Story*, see R. Alan Culpepper, *Anatomy of the Fourth Gospel: A Study in Literary Design* (Philadelphia: Fortress, 1983); Mark Allan Powell, *What Is Narrative Criticism?* (GBSNT; Minneapolis: Fortress, 1990).

Mark since 1901, when Wrede succeeded" in detailing the messianic secret in the Second Gospel.[5]

Though the first of these criticisms has been adequately addressed elsewhere, it is the latter assertion that is the focus of this study.[6] More specifically, the aim of this essay is to demonstrate that narrative criticism—in concert with performance criticism—is an indispensible tool for shedding light on the messianic secret. The hermeneutical trajectory it sets forth paves the way for a more complete understanding that pushes beyond the current discussion and fosters questions about the use of secrecy and the impact of Mark's narrative that have been widely overlooked. Attention to the literary features of the Gospel, in the context of a performance, suggests that Markan secrecy is an audience-elevating device that functions in service to a broader rhetorical agenda. While narrative criticism may not be able to unravel the history behind the secrecy theme, it nonetheless complements the traditional methods of interpretation and provides a richer understanding of the circumstances surrounding the use of Mark's Gospel.

Over a Century of Secrecy

Few would question that William Wrede is one of the more important contributors to Markan scholarship in the last century.[7] Though Wrede's work had far-reaching implications, his primary concern was to understand Mark's so-called "messianic secret": the perplexing depiction of a messianic Jesus who actively prohibits the revelation of his identity, often instructing others "to tell no one" (8:30). Wrede argued that the element of secrecy pervaded the whole of the Gospel and was evident in a number of diverse contexts, including the prohibitions addressed to demons (1:25, 34; 3:12), disciples (8:30; 9:2–9), and those who experienced healing or were witnesses of thaumaturgical events (1:43–45; 5:37–43; 7:33–36; 8:23–26), as well as Jesus' repeated attempt to maintain anonymity (7:24; 9:30) and his parabolic manner of speech (4:10–13, 33).[8] Against some of his contemporaries who interpreted these texts on an individual basis—as representative of Jesus' humility, lack of confidence,

---

5. Robert Morgan and John Barton, *Biblical Interpretation* (Oxford Bible Series; New York: Oxford University Press, 1988), 231–33.

6. For a response to some of the common criticisms, see David Rhoads, *Reading Mark: Engaging the Gospel* (Minneapolis: Fortress, 2004), 25–30.

7. William Wrede, *The Messianic Secret* (trans. J. C. G. Greig; Cambridge: Clarke, 1971); trans. of *Das Messiasgeheimnis in den Evangelien: Zugleich ein Beitrag zum Verständnis des Markusevangeliums* (Göttingen: Vandenhoeck & Ruprecht, 1901).

8. Wrede, *Messianic Secret*, 34–57. As a corollary to these five categories, Wrede also

or desire to guard against political misunderstanding—Wrede argued that the messianic secret is a unified theme and must be interpreted as a comprehensive whole.[9]

Though Wrede's description of the secrecy theme was problematic for some, it was his historical assessment that proved most controversial. Wrede argued that the secret did not begin with the historical Jesus but was a theological concept that originated in the early church and facilitated the blending of variant christological perspectives, the earliest of which is discernible in Acts 2:36, Rom 1:4, and Phil 2:6–11. According to Wrede, Jesus *became* the Messiah through the resurrection, and it was only due to the passage of time and theological reflection that his messianic status was retrojected back upon the pre-Easter Jesus. The "messianic secret" was thus a transitional doctrine that arose during a period when the early church proclaimed Jesus as the Messiah, but his earthly ministry was widely regarded as devoid of "sovereign dignity and power."[10] The secret alleviated the tension between these perspectives by suggesting that, although Jesus was the Messiah, he intentionally concealed his identity in order to anticipate the definitive revelation of his messiahship at the resurrection (cf. 9:9).[11] Contrary to what is often affirmed in the secondary literature, Wrede did not propose that the messianic secret originated with the Second Evangelist.[12] Wrede argued that such a "notion seems quite impossible," as the penetration and variability of the theme demonstrates that "material of this kind is not the work of an individual."[13] While Wrede did not hesitate to suggest that Mark influenced the presentation of the secret, he concluded that the Evangelist was working with traditional elements that were passed down through the community. As far as Wrede was concerned, "Mark *knew nothing of when Jesus was acknowledged* to be Messiah, and … in the historical sense he had absolutely no interest in this question."[14]

---

suggested that the disciples' incomprehension was an expression of the secrecy motif (231–36).

9. On the various interpretations of the secrecy theme in Mark, see ibid., 255–75.

10. Ibid., 216–17.

11. Ibid., 227–29.

12. For examples of this common misconception, see Lewis S. Hay, "Mark's Use of the Messianic Secret," *JAAR* 35 (1967): 16; Dwight N. Peterson, *The Origins of Mark: The Markan Community in Current Debate* (Biblical Interpretation Series 48; Leiden: Brill, 2000), 10–11; Joseph B. Tyson, "Blindness of the Disciples in Mark," *JBL* 80 (1961): 261; Ben Witherington, *The Gospel of Mark: A Socio-rhetorical Commentary* (Grand Rapids: Eerdmans, 2001), 40.

13. Wrede, *Messianic Secret*, 145.

14. Ibid., 115.

Not surprisingly, the response to Wrede was spirited, and the initial reaction was quite negative. Writing in 1907, William Sanday declared that, "so far as I know, Wrede's reconstruction of the Gospel history is accepted by no one," because his "strange hypothesis" is "not only very wrong but also distinctly wrong-headed."[15] In time, however, scholars such as Dibelius and Bultmann adopted a more favorable stance before the theory underwent a broad reappraisal beginning in the late 1960s. While the various contours of this discussion have been rehearsed elsewhere and need not detain us here, the importance of Wrede's work and its imprint upon the conversation can hardly be overemphasized.[16] As one scholar has observed, "whether strongly supported or vigorously opposed, Wrede has had more influence on the way in which the Gospel according to Mark has been interpreted than perhaps any other scholar."[17] Some sixty years after the publication of Wrede's study, Strecker noted that "the problem of the theory of the messianic secret in Mark's Gospel is still defined in exegetical research in the terms of William Wrede's epoch-making study."[18] Over a hundred years later, little has changed. Despite the passage of time, "William Wrede is still with us" and continues to exercise significant influence over scholarly discussions of Mark.[19] The questions that drove Wrede continue to resonate with and even dictate contemporary approaches to the messianic secret.[20] However, while questions of the

15. William Sanday, *The Life of Christ in Recent Research* (Oxford: Clarendon, 1907), 70, 75–76. T. W. Manson takes a similar perspective: "the farther we travel along the Wredestrasse, the clearer it becomes that it is the road to nowhere" ("The Life of Jesus: Some Tendencies in Present-Day Research," in *The Background of the New Testament and Its Eschatology* [ed. William David Davies and D. Daube; Cambridge: Cambridge University Press, 1956], 216). Ironically, it was one of Manson's students who responded to this critique. In a short review article, Norman Perrin suggested that "the Wredestrasse has become the Hauptstrasse" ("The Wredestrasse Becomes the Hauptstrasse: Reflections on the Reprinting of the Dodd Festschrift," *JR* 46 [1966]: 296–300).

16. See, for example, the helpful survey in Heikki Räisänen, *The 'Messianic Secret' in Mark* (Studies of the New Testament and Its World; Edinburgh: T&T Clark, 1990), 38–75.

17. Jack Dean Kingsbury, *The Christology of Mark's Gospel* (Philadelphia: Fortress, 1983), 1.

18. Georg Strecker, "The Theory of the Messianic Secret in Mark's Gospel," in *The Messianic Secret* (ed. Christopher Tuckett; Philadelphia: Fortress, 1983), 49.

19. David E. Aune, "The Problem of the Messianic Secret," *NovT* 11 (1969): 1.

20. See, for example, Michael F. Bird, *Are You the One Who Is to Come? The Historical Jesus and the Messianic Question* (Grand Rapids: Baker, 2009), 66–70; Craig S. Keener, *The Historical Jesus of the Gospels* (Grand Rapids: Eerdmans, 2009), 262–64; James R. Edwards, *The Gospel according to Mark* (Pillar New Testament Commentary; Grand Rapids: Eerdmans, 2002), 63–65.

historical Jesus and Christology deserve careful attention and offer a profitable avenue for inquiry, the conversation has stagnated in recent years due to
this uniformity of perspective.

Among the variety of reasons that *Mark as Story* is to be celebrated is
that narrative criticism has opened up new vistas for methodological investigation. Although historical criticism has traditionally focused on the world
behind the text (authorship, provenance, etc.), narrative criticism has drawn
attention to the entirety of the communication process—from sender to
receiver.[21] This concern for the world in front of the text, and the concomitant
experience of the message, poses one of the more exciting opportunities for
reflection, particularly as it relates to Markan secrecy. Although scholars have
readily postulated about the origins, continuity, and historical implications
of the secrecy theme, there has been little sustained discussion of the possible impact of this device. Before turning directly to the question of audience
experience, it is necessary to clear the way by addressing recent scholarship
that has challenged the unity of the theme.

A Secret or Secrets?

Since the effectiveness of a theme is dependent upon its coherency, it is important to consider whether Markan secrecy is an integrated concept. One of the
hallmarks of Wrede's thesis was that the messianic secret functioned as a collective whole, but the majority of scholars no longer regard this as a tenable
position.[22] Donahue and Harrington, for example, argue that "what are often
lumped together under the heading of 'messianic secret' are quite disparate
phenomena."[23] Luz is more specific but offers a similar assessment: "a look at
what is usually called the 'messianic secret' in Mark has shown that there are
really two phenomena: the messiainic secret, under the constraint of which
the demons and after Caesarea Philippi the disciples stand; and the miracle
secret which cannot be kept and shows that Jesus' miracles press onward into

---

21. Powell, *What Is Narrative Criticism*, 8–10. See also David Rhoads, "Narrative Criticism and the Gospel of Mark," *JAAR* 50 (1982): 422–24.

22. In one of the first reactions to Wrede, Albert Schweitzer noted that the inclusion
of the parable theory was "one of the weakest points of the entire construction" (*The Quest
of the Historical Jesus* [trans. J. R. Coates, W. Montgomery, Susan Cupitt, and John Bowden;
Minneapolis: Fortress, 2001], 346).

23. John R. Donahue and Daniel J. Harrington, *The Gospel of Mark* (SP 2; Collegeville,
Minn.: Liturgical Press, 2002), 28. See also William L. Lane, *The Gospel according to Mark:
The English Text with Introduction, Exposition, and Notes* (NICNT; Grand Rapids: Eerd-
mans, 1974), 198.

the public realm of proclamation."[24] Räisänen adopts a similar perspective but presses further, discerning four "loosely connected" themes: the commands to silence addressed to the demons and disciples, the secret healings, the parable theory, and the disciples' lack of understanding.[25] While delineating the number of strands remains a matter of debate, the broader question of a single, coherent theme has been sufficiently answered. The matter is so widely accepted that Dunn claims the issue is "beyond dispute."[26] As a result, contemporary discussions of the subject typically dissect the theme into numerous strata, often in an attempt to minimize the overall significance of Markan secrecy.

It should be noted that these perspectives offer a helpful corrective to Wrede's thesis. To assume, with Wrede, that the secrecy related texts convey a "*messianic* secret" appears to conflate certain episodes and minimize others. It is difficult, for example, to understand how the prohibitions associated with the miracles exemplify the *messianic* secret when the deeds of Jesus rarely lead to an accurate awareness of his identity.[27] Just the opposite seems to be the case. Although Jesus' hometown is cognizant of the "miracles performed by his hands," they remain convinced that he is nothing more than "the carpenter, the son of Mary, and the brother of James, Joses, Judas, and Simon" (6:1–3). Likewise, though Herod and others perceive that Jesus occupies a more exalted status, they do not identify him as *Messiah* but variously associate him with John (raised from the dead), Elijah, or one of the prophets (6:14–16; cf. 8:28). In terms of the narrative, the definitive revelation of Jesus' identity is not made through public displays of power but through the cross, at which point the first genuine confession of his messiahship is proffered (15:39).[28]

Despite these legitimate objections, it would be premature to conclude that the secret is not a unified theme, even though the above texts illustrate that the miracles do not necessarily lead to an understanding of Jesus' true identity. To draw this conclusion betrays a hermeneutical perspective that is driven by a concern for historical inquiry or by a text-centered approach that

---

24. Ulrich Luz, "The Secrecy Motif and the Marcan Christology," in Tuckett, *The Messianic Secret*, 86–87.

25. Räisänen, *Messianic Secret*, 242–43. According to Räisänen, only the first category may be classified as the messianic secret proper.

26. James D. G. Dunn, *Jesus Remembered* (Grand Rapids: Eerdmans, 2003), 626.

27. A notable exception occurs in 7:31–37, when the crowds begin to echo Isaianic language (Isa 35:5–6).

28. On the authenticity and genuineness of the centurion's confession, see Kelly R. Iverson, "A Centurion's 'Confession': A Performance-Critical Analysis of Mark 15:39," *JBL* (forthcoming).

brackets out the role of the audience. There may be no basis for arguing that the secret is *messianic* or that the Markan or historical Jesus invoked secrecy for a singular purpose, but this does not negate the potential for a uniformity of purpose on a different level. Although the role of the audience has often been disregarded, supposing that a "concern for the reader" is "a commercial blemish on the otherwise spotless face of art," it has become increasingly clear that the phenomenology of reading (or hearing) requires more than the exegesis of the actual text.[29] Wolfgang Iser, in an important article entitled "The Reading Process: A Phenomenolgical Approach," has shown that an appreciation of literature necessitates a consideration of the text as well as an understanding of how the text attempts to evoke and stimulate the audience.[30]

Of Iser's many insightful observations, the most relevant for the present discussion pertains to the reading experience. Iser repeatedly notes that interpretation is a "dynamic" process that is dictated by the interplay between author, text, and reader. Though understanding is shaped by the story's "component parts" and "various perspectives," the audience stands within and beyond the narrative world created by the writer and therefore makes connections between episodes that are seemingly unrelated in the narrative.[31] Indeed,

---

29. Wayne C. Booth, *The Rhetoric of Fiction* (Chicago: University of Chicago Press, 1983), 90. In narrative-critical discussions, the term "reader" typically refers to those who are the recipients of the story. However, given that only a small percentage of the population possessed the skills to "read," scholars have become increasingly aware of the oral milieu in which the Gospels were received and transmitted. The term *reader* is therefore somewhat anachronistic, as the Gospels were likely performed in an oral context. See Kelly R. Iverson, "Orality and the Gospels: A Survey of Recent Research," *CBR* 8.1 (2009): 71–106. More recently, scholars have begun to explore performance criticism as a means for understanding the delivery and interpretation of ancient texts. As with the rise of narrative criticism, David Rhoads and Joanna Dewey have been on the forefront of this movement. See Joanna Dewey, "Mark as Interwoven Tapestry: Forecasts and Echoes for a Listening Audience," *CBQ* 53 (1991): 221–36; idem, "Oral Methods of Structuring Narrative in Mark," *Int* 43 (1989): 32–44; David Rhoads, "Performance Criticism: An Emerging Methodology in Second Temple Studies—Part I," *BTB* 36 (2006): 118–33; idem, "Performance Criticism: An Emerging Methodology in Second Temple Studies—Part II," *BTB* 36 (2006): 164–84. Although there are differences between the two interpretive methods, both share a concern for the dynamics of storytelling. For an example of how oral performance affects one's conception of the narrator, see Philip Ruge-Jones, "Omnipresent, Not Omniscient: How Literary Interpretation Confuses the Storyteller's Narrating," in *Between Author and Audience in Mark: Narration, Characterization, Interpretation* (ed. Elizabeth Struthers Malbon; New Testament Monographs 23; Sheffield: Sheffield Phoenix, 2009), 29–43.

30. Wolfgang Iser, "The Reading Process: A Phenomenological Approach," *New Literary History* 3 (1972): 279–99.

31. Ibid., 280–82.

in the "imaginative game" between author and audience, these links are often intentionally obscured in order to stimulate audience participation. This rich interplay often results in "unforeseeable connections"[32] through which the elements of the story begin to take on "a far greater significance than [they] ... might have seemed to posses."[33] While the text guides the audience's understanding of the story and its "unwritten implications," the audience becomes a vital and active participant in the interpretive process—a process that may involve the formulation of "something that is unformulated in the text, and yet represents its 'intention.'"[34]

Iser's differentiation between that which is in the text and that which is formulated by the text is important, since commentators rarely consider the possibility that Markan secrecy includes subthemes that are not explicitly related *in the narrative*, yet function as coherent themes *beyond the narrative* (i.e., in terms of rhetorical impact). Though this statement might seem like a contradiction, it more accurately reflects the artistic and aesthetic potential of Mark's Gospel. At the exegetical level (the story), it is difficult, if not impossible, to account for the concealment of Jesus' actions, speech, and identity with a one-size-fits-all explanation; indeed, it might be argued that the narrative resists such an impulse.[35] Despite this exegetical uncertainty, ignoring the potential impact of Markan secrecy would be a significant oversight. The nuancing of the theme does not negate the sheer number of episodes betraying the secrecy theme nor the potential for an audience to assimilate "schematized views."[36] Even if Markan secrecy represents a broad and diverse conglomeration of texts at the exegetical level, it does not inexorably follow that an audience perceives these events as isolated, unrelated instances. Approach-

---

32. Ibid., 283.

33. Ibid.

34. Ibid., 281, 292.

35. The most recent attempt to posit a holistic explanation (from within the story) is by David F. Watson, *Honor among Christians: The Cultural Key to the Messianic Secret* (Minneapolis: Fortress, 2010). Watson argues that Markan secrecy must be understood in relation to the Mediterranean values of honor and shame. According to Watson, Mark utilizes secrecy in order to emphasize Jesus' reinterpretation of contemporary social conventions. Though a unique approach to the issue of secrecy, I am not convinced that the analysis accounts for the various occasions where Jesus manifests his power via public display. The natural byproduct of these episodes is the conception of honor that Watson argues is rejected by Mark. Watson attributes this conflicting portrayal to the nature of orally derived texts, but he fails to appreciate that the depiction is not congruent with a primary characteristic of such literature: the concept of "variation within the same" (Eric A. Havelock, *Preface to Plato* [Cambridge: Harvard University Press, 1963], 148).

36. Iser, "Reading Process," 280.

ing Mark's story from the audience's perspective, at issue is not the *messianic* secret per se but the element of *secrecy*, which cascades back and forth across the story like waves across a shore. The persistent and repetitive pattern within the narrative functions in service to the Evangelist's rhetorical strategy and potentially creates a distinct impression upon the audience's experience of the story. Moreover, the consistent element of secrecy, displayed in all of its manifold forms throughout the Gospel, is quite possibly the catalyst for the creation of "something that is unformulated in the text, and yet represents its 'intention.'"

That "intention" will be discussed in the next section; however, besides being a hermeneutical possibility, the unity of the theme can be demonstrated from a literary perspective. Though scholars quite often refer to the presence and/or absence of themes without methodological precision, William Freedman has outlined a helpful approach for the identification of thematic elements.[37] Freedman suggests that any literary motif (or theme) is based upon the notion of repetition, but the identification of a motif is typically not characterized by the verbatim reoccurrence of words and phrases. Rather, a motif is developed and enriched through a conceptual domain—or an "associational cluster"—that is reformulated in the narrative by the use of similar, though varied, elements.[38] The repetition of a motif is intentional and is a means by which the author communicates with the audience through the story. Ultimately, a motif is crafted for the sake of the audience and is intended to facilitate a cognitive, affective (emotional), or structural appreciation of the literary work.[39]

Freedman argues that the establishment of a literary motif is dependent upon two factors.[40] First, a motif requires conceptual frequency. Though

---

37. William Freedman, "The Literary Motif: A Definition and Evaluation," in *Essentials of the Theory of Fiction* (ed. Michael J. Hoffman and Patrick D. Murphy; Durham, N.C.: Duke University Press, 1996), 200–212. Freedman discusses a literary "motif" as opposed to a "theme." However, Freedman's work can be safely adapted to the present study with only minor qualification, given that Freedman himself defines a motif as "a recurrent *theme*" (206) and that narrative theorists often use the terms interchangeably. Some have argued that a "motif" refers to a pattern of verbal repetition that is concrete, as opposed to a "theme," which is abstract and conceptual. For instance, in Mark's Gospel one might refer to the bread motif (a specific image) as opposed to the theme of discipleship (a broad concept). On the similarities and differences between these literary devices, see H. Porter Abbott, *The Cambridge Introduction to Narrative* (Cambridge: Cambridge University Press, 2002), 95.

38. Freedman, "Literary Motif," 202.

39. Ibid., 203.

40. Ibid., 204–5.

Freedman correctly refrains from selecting an arbitrary, fixed number of times that an element must occur within the narrative, he affirms the centrality of thematic recurrence. At issue is the matter of purpose and the discernment between features derived from narratival coincidence and those intentionally marked by repeated appearance. Second, along with the necessary repetition of an element, Freedman also suggests that a motif exhibits the principle of avoidability. The more unlikely an element's appearance, the more likely a motif is deliberately at work in the narrative. This criteria is closely related to the first, since the question of frequency takes on greater significance if the context does not demand the appearance of the particular motif. For example, Freedman provides the illustration of a narrative whose principal subject is a milliner. Although the inclusion of hats may occur with noted repetition—thus satisfying the criteria of frequency—the contours of the narrative likely dictate these insertions and undermine the importance of the conceptual field. In this respect, the criteria of frequency and avoidability complement one another and aid the interpreter in detecting the presence of literary motifs/themes.

Returning to Mark's Gospel, the repeated focus on secrecy and concealment satisfy the criteria of frequency and avoidability that demarcate the presence and identification of literary themes. Though short in length, Mark's baptismal scene creates an aura of secrecy that permeates the story and launches the narrative in a unique trajectory. Perhaps most striking is that there is no indication that anyone *except Jesus* hears the heavenly voice that identifies him as "the beloved Son" (1:9–11). The subtle concealment of Jesus' identity is even more perceptible when viewed against the backdrop of Matthew's Gospel. In Mark, the heavenly voice declares that "*you* are my beloved Son" (1:11), while the Matthean voice states that "*this* is my beloved Son" (3:17). This shift from the second-person singular (Mark) to the near demonstrative (Matthew) might seem insignificant, but the rhetorical effect is pronounced. The Markan voice speaks directly to Jesus, as if engaged in private conversation, whereas the Matthean voice utters a public announcement to John and the crowds.

If the implicit secrecy in this text is uncertain, the repetition of the theme in the ensuing narratives alleviates the concern. The element of secrecy, first posed in the baptism, is thrust forward into Mark's story of Jesus. Not only is Jesus taken by the Spirit into the wilderness to be tested by Satan and later supported by angels (1:12–13)—all of which takes place in isolation—but upon his return Jesus himself begins to impose secretive elements upon his ministry. During his first encounter with a supplicant, Jesus commands an evil spirit to "be quiet" (1:24–25). Although Kee argues that the scene "has nothing to do with secrecy" and instead depicts a "struggle for dominance," his conclusion is problematic in view of the narrative arc set in motion through the baptism, temptation, and encounters that frame the exorcism.[41] Moreover, in the summary account that follows the scene (1:32–34), Jesus is described as performing "many" exorcisms and uniformly prohibiting the demons from speaking. Similar to 1:25, Jesus in essence commands the demons to "be quiet" (1:25), but not in an attempt to assert himself, as Kee suggests. Rather, Mark indicates that Jesus rebukes the demons "because they knew who he was" (1:34). Similar commands follow throughout the narrative and occur in individual episodes (1:40–44; 5:43; 7:36) and summary statements (3:11–12), further highlighting the discrete nature of at least some of Jesus' actions.

The element of secrecy is also accented in Jesus' interaction with the disciples. Of the numerous occasions where Jesus withdraws from the crowds to teach the disciples (7:17–23; 9:30–37; 10:32–34), the most revealing takes place in the region of Caesarea Philippi (8:27–30). Although Jesus has taught through word and deed, his identity remains largely an enigma among the (human) characters in the story, with no individual having yet perceived his true identity. Though Peter's conception of Jesus is deficient (8:31–33) and he, like the blind man, is in need of a second restorative touch (8:22–26), it is noteworthy that immediately after the confession Jesus commands the disciples "not to tell anyone about him" (8:30). At this stage in the story, the instruction both coincides with similar secrecy injunctions and the now discernible tendency in Jesus' ministry.

In addition to further establishing the frequency of the theme, the episode implicitly underscores patterns enacted at junctures throughout the narrative. The underlying assumption is that the disciples have been made privy to Jesus in a way that is unparalleled among the crowds. This perspective is further depicted in the ensuing episode, when Jesus selects Peter, James, and John— eliciting an additional element of secrecy—to go up the high mountain "by themselves" (9:2). Before descending, the disciples witness the appearance of Elijah, Moses, and the transfigured Jesus, which is accompanied by the voice from the cloud declaring, "this is my beloved Son" (9:7). While the statement is to be differentiated from the baptismal scene in that those alongside Jesus are cognizant of the heavenly voice, there is nevertheless a similarity in that both events are shrouded by secrecy. Though the disciples are participants in the transfiguration, they are ordered not to relate what they had seen until after the resurrection (9:9).

---

41. Howard Clark Kee, *Community of the New Age: Studies in Mark's Gospel* (Philadelphia: Westminster, 1977), 169.

That the disciples are the recipients of divine revelation and insiders to the teachings of Jesus is depicted in 8:27–30 and 9:2–9, but the seeds for this privilege lie in the disciples' calling to be "with him" (3:14–15) and are given verbal expression in 4:10–12. Following the teaching on the soils, Jesus provides insight concerning the use of parables: "The secret to the kingdom of God has been given to you; but to those on the outside, everything comes in parables" (4:11). Though it appears that this passage is related in some fashion to 8:27–30 and 9:2–9, Räisänen argues that the "idea found in these verses is not repeated elsewhere"[42] and that "there is no theory carried through in Mark's Gospel such as 4.11–12 might at first suggest."[43] Taken in isolation, these verses do present a rather jarring picture, particularly in view of the depiction of Jesus as one who enjoys the company of sinners (2:1–12; 3:15–17) and garners the attention of great crowds (2:1–12; 4:1–9; 6:53–56; 8:1–9). However, the scene does not present the interpretive problem that Räisänen supposes; rather, it accounts for and resonates with the various episodes that speak to the disciples' insider status. Though the disciples are certainly not the only insiders (see 7:24–30) and typically do not comprehend the revelation they are given (6:52; 8:14–21, 31–33; 9:30–32; 10:32–45), they are nonetheless recipients of instruction that is often excluded from others. This two-tiered distinction is enacted in various texts (4:33–34; often when Jesus teaches the disciples in a house [7:17–23; 9:28–29; 10:10–12] or elsewhere [13:1–37]) and emphasizes the disciples' unique calling, as well as underscoring the pattern of secrecy throughout Mark's narrative. It bears repeating that this does not imply that a single theological basis undergirds the episodes or that the element of secrecy is depicted for the same purpose *within* the story (i.e., in relation to the characterization of Jesus). Instead, these scenes portray the repetition of a similar phenomena that points to the presence of a literary theme.

A more exhaustive examination of the secrecy theme would provide additional support to this picture and draw further attention to the frequency of the theme in Mark's Gospel (e.g., 16:1–8). This brief sample indicates that secrecy is a key component in the dynamics of Mark's story and is featured prominently across the narrative. Moreover, the theme is situated in strategic contexts—for example, the baptism, temptation, Peter's confession, and the transfiguration—and evidences the flexibility and variation that Freedman suggests.

---

42. Heikki Räisänen, "The 'Messianic Secret' in Mark's Gospel," in Tuckett, *The Messianic Secret*, 133.

43. Räisänen, *Messianic Secret*, 243.

Considering the frequent reoccurrence in Mark, the question thus becomes whether the theme is avoidable. Upon initial reflection, this may seem like a rather daunting criterion to establish. How, after all, does one argue that a feature in the narrative is avoidable and can be omitted without disrupting the development of a particular episode? Ironically, many who have attempted to discount the coherency of the theme have unwittingly supplied the literary grounds for the opposite conclusion. In the judgment of these scholars, Mark has simultaneously juxtaposed secrecy and publicity, resulting in a dialect of contradiction that is not easily resolved, except by "violent and artificial manipulation."[44] If this is the case, then the inclusion of these traditions only complexifies and obscures the dynamics of the story, thus diminishing the overall effectiveness of the narrative. Though this conclusion is based upon hermeneutical presuppositions concerning the competency and role of the Evangelist, many who have attempted to undermine the unity of the theme have actually demonstrated its viability on literary grounds via Freedman's principle of avoidability.

Perhaps the most compelling and objective evidence for avoidability stems from an analysis of the secrecy theme across the Synoptic traditions. The earliest interpreters of the Second Gospel, Matthew and Luke, tell us a great deal about their perception of Mark's story and, considered together, tacitly affirm the avoidability of the theme. Their redaction suggests that neither Matthew nor Luke understood secrecy (as articulated by Mark) to be an unalterable feature of Mark's Gospel.

A brief survey of Markan secrecy as transmitted across the Synoptic Gospels illustrates this propensity. For example, Mark's initial exorcism scene establishes the element of secrecy in the public ministry of Jesus (1:21–28), but the episode is completely absent in Matthew's narrative. The summary account in Mark 1:32–34 is retained in Matt 8:16–17, but the First Evangelist omits Mark's silencing of the demons (Mark 1:34) and instead transforms the account into a fulfillment citation (Matt 8:17; cf. Matt 1:22–23; 2:15, 17–18, 23; 4:14–15; 12:17–18; 13:35; 21:4–5; 26:56; 27:9). While these episodes appear early in Mark's story, they are instructive and exhibit a repeated point of departure. Unlike Mark, where Jesus repeatedly commands demons to be quiet (1:25; 1:34; 3:12), the Matthean Jesus never prohibits the demons from speaking.[45]

---

44. Heikki Räisänen quoted in Udo Schnelle, *The History and Theology of the New Testament Writings* (Minneapolis: Fortress, 1998), 215. See also Étienne Trocmé and Pamela Gaughan, *The Formation of the Gospel according to Mark* (London: SPCK, 1975), 124 n. 1.

45. W. D. Davies and Dale C. Allison, *A Critical and Exegetical Commentary on the Gospel according to Saint Matthew* (3 vols.; ICC; Edinburgh: T&T Clark, 1988), 2:14.

The healing episodes display similar variation. For example, in the scene involving Jairus's daughter (Mark 5:21–24, 35–43), Matthew provides no indication that, along with the girl's parents, only Peter, James, and John were permitted to enter the room (9:18–26); neither does Matthew include the prohibition that Jesus "gave strict orders … that no one should know about this" (Mark 5:43). Furthermore, in the episode depicting the healing of the deaf mute (Mark 7:31–37), although the Markan Jesus commands the people "not to tell anyone" (7:36), Matthew only alludes to the story in a summary account that makes no reference to the element of secrecy (Matt 15:29–31).

In addition to the exorcism and healing stories, the Markan travel narratives also display significant redaction. When Jesus travels to the region of Tyre (Mark 7:24–30), which represents the farthest and presumably most isolated geographical setting in the narrative, the Evangelist indicates that Jesus entered a house and "wanted no one to know" (7:24). Luke, however, does not include this scene, and though Matthew does, it is not certain that Jesus actually ventures beyond the Jewish homeland (thus diminishing Mark's geographical secrecy). Furthermore, while many aspects of the Markan scene are repeated in Matthew, there is no suggestion that Jesus attempts to conceal his identity (Matt 15:21–28). Likewise, as Jesus begins to instruct the disciples concerning his passion, making his way through Galilee, the Markan narrator states that he "did not want anyone to know" (9:30). Though Matthew (17:22–23) and Luke (9:43–45) both retain this scene, neither Evangelist assumes the element of secrecy found in Mark.

This brief sketch is not intended to obscure the fact that aspects of the theme are carried across the Synoptic tradition. At times both Matthew and Luke preserve the commands to secrecy inscribed in Mark's story (Mark 1:26 || Luke 4:35; Mark 1:34 || Luke 4:41; Matt 13:10–11 || Mark 4:11–12 || Luke 8:9–10; Matt 16:20 || Mark 8:30 || Luke 9:21). However, despite the perceived value of Mark, evidenced by its use as a primary source (assuming Markan priority), it is not unusual to find that Matthew and Luke adopt portions of Mark (at times unconsciously) and ignore/redact other aspects of the tradition. What is more, both Matthew and Luke appear to exhibit different levels of understanding and appreciation for Mark's secrecy theme. According to Davies and Allison, who conclude along with Wrede that "the idea of the messianic secret no longer has the importance for Matthew that it has for Mark," the First Evangelist appears to have been a "little nonplussed" by Mark's use of the theme.[46] Luke, on the other hand, seems to have "retained and even sharpened the idea of the 'messianic secret' which is otherwise much more

---

46. Ibid.

prominent in Mark,"[47] modifying the theme by transforming it into a "passion secret."[48] Thus, while aspects of Markan secrecy have passed into Matthew and Luke, both Evangelists demonstrate a willingness to ignore, modify, and/ or adapt Markan material for their own theological purposes.

In terms of Freedman's criterion, this survey suggests that Markan secrecy, as reflected in these episodes, was often considered a redactable or "avoidable" feature of the narrative. Again, it is not disconcerting that Matthew and Luke include elements of Mark's secrecy theme, since a fidelity to the traditions is expected. More significant to the criterion of avoidability is the handling of the theme in what Freedman describes as the "particular uses" and "certain contexts."[49] When viewed from this perspective, a multitude of texts in a variety of contexts (e.g., exorcisms, healings, travel narratives) have been altered by either or both of the Evangelists. It seems that neither Matthew nor Luke considered the thematic instances, nor the particular Markan articulation of the theme, to be beyond modification. While Matthew and Luke adopted elements of the tradition, neither felt compelled or constrained to reproduce the theme with the frequency of occurrence or the same broad vision as Mark. In short, Matthew and Luke did not consider Mark's approach to the secrecy theme to be essential to the construction of what the Evangelists ostensibly believed was a faithful depiction of Jesus.

This section began by asking whether Markan secrecy represented a theme or themes. Though the conclusion runs counter to the trend in contemporary research, it is now possible to affirm that Markan secrecy is a coherent and unified feature of the narrative. While the *messianic* secret does not constitute a distinct theme, the element of *secrecy* pervades the narrative and evidences the frequency and avoidability indicative of a literary theme. Unfortunately,

---

47. Nils Alstrup Dahl, "The Purpose of Luke Acts," in *Jesus in the Memory of the Early Church* (ed. Nils Alstrup Dahl; Minneapolis: Augsburg, 1976), 89.

48. On Luke's passion secret and the comparison between Mark 8:30 and Luke 9:21 in particular, see Hans Conzelmann, *The Theology of St. Luke* (New York: Harper, 1961), 56. In addition, the transfiguration scene is particularly striking (Luke 9:28–36) and provides insight into Lukan redaction. Unlike the Markan Jesus, who prohibits the disciples from speaking about what they have seen until after the resurrection (Mark 9:9), Luke omits Jesus' command and suggests that the disciples' secrecy was a self-imposed injunction (Luke 9:36). With only one exception (4:35), this text reveals a broad editorial agenda. As James M. Dawsey points out, "the demand for secrecy never occurs on the lips of [the Lukan] Jesus" (*The Lukan Voice: Confusion and Irony in the Gospel of Luke* [Macon, Ga.: Mercer University Press, 1986], 90). Rather, such speech is uniformly placed in the commentary of the narrator, thus exposing a subtle but important interpretive distance from the Markan source.

49. Freedman, "Literary Motif," 204.

the conversation has all too often been framed in response to Wrede's *messianic* secret—a course that has unwittingly obscured a much broader theme that is discernible from a literary or performance perspective.

Secrecy as an Audience-Elevating Strategy

If Markan secrecy is a distinguishable theme, as seems to be the case, then what is its rhetorical function? Iser suggests that a thematic element "sinks into our memory"[50] and is evoked again and again in order to prompt "the awakening of responses within."[51] But how precisely is the repeated element of secrecy intended to evoke an audience, and what is the desired response?

Secrecy and Predestination

To date, Francis Watson is one of the few scholars to have explored the issue in detail. Watson argues that secrecy is a major concern of the Evangelist and is best understood in sociological terms.[52] Responding in part to those who suggest that Mark has stratified time according to salvation history (the era of secrecy surrounding Jesus' earthly ministry and the era of revelation following his death and resurrection), Watson instead argues that secrecy is closely aligned to a theology of predestination.[53] Watson suggests that the purpose of the theme is not to divide two epochs of history but to distinguish two groups of people: the disciples and the crowds.[54] Mark's concern for the theme is exemplified in the distinction between insiders and outsiders and is fully articulated in Mark 4:11–12 (cf. 4:34). According to Watson, the theological basis for this teaching is the doctrine of predestination, which functions as the theological framework on which Mark erects both the "parable secret" and the "teaching secret." It is through the various expressions of secrecy that Mark communicates a broader theological message concerning the revelation of God's saving will.

---

50. Iser, "Reading Process," 283.

51. Ibid., 280.

52. Francis Watson, "The Social Function of Mark's Secrecy Theme," *JSNT* 24 (1985): 46–69.

53. For those advocating the "history of revelation" interpretation, see Nils Alstrup Dahl, "The Purpose of Mark's Gospel," in Tuckett, *The Messianic Secret*, 29–34; Eduard Schweizer, "The Question of the Messianic Secret in Mark," in Tuckett, *The Messianic Secret*, 65–74; Strecker, "Theory of the Messianic Secret," 49–64.

54. Watson, "Social Function," 60.

Watson further suggests that the theme takes on additional meaning when situated within the context of the Markan community—a community plagued by the experience of persecution and suffering.[55] In the face of society's hostile reaction to the community, Mark utilizes a theology of predestination in order to encourage hope and reassurance among Markan disciples. In this respect, the secrecy theme has a social function, which Watson suggests is "to strengthen the barrier between the community and the world—a barrier which is in danger of being broken down."[56] In addition, besides fortifying the boundary between the community and the world, Mark's use of the theme provides validation for the community's "eliteness," as well as "an explanation for society's incomprehension and hostility."[57]

Watson's study is to be appreciated in that it attempts to break out of the Wredian shadow, as well as providing a seemingly pragmatic explanation for the secrecy theme. But while it is possible to imagine Mark's theological stance nurturing and inspiring a persecuted community, the persuasiveness of Watson's argument is limited by a number of factors, not the least of which is that his "social" analysis does not interact with any sociological research.[58] Most problematic, however, is the attempt to construct a comprehensive theory that accounts for the totality of the theme in relation to the teaching and activities of Jesus. If, as Watson argues, predestination is the basis for secrecy and "refers to the belief that God determines whether people are to be granted salvation or whether they are to be condemned," then it is extremely difficult to explain the thematic variations of the theme in Mark's Gospel.[59] Although Watson attempts to understand the theme in relation to miraculous healings, it is not at all clear how this reading fits within a theology of predestination. Why, for example, does Jesus prohibit the revelation of his miraculous works if their christological significance can only be comprehended by the elect? If God has already predetermined those who are to be saved and condemned, what purpose do the injunctions actually serve, since the transmittal of such information ostensibly has no bearing upon God's purposes? Even more specifically, why does Jesus communicate with the crowds, since they stand condemned?

---

55. Watson argues that the theme of suffering dominates the later half of Mark (8:31–33, 34–38; 10:32–34) and indicates that Mark is "therefore not motivated by historical interest but by the situation of the 'disciples' in his own day" (ibid., 61).

56. Ibid., 62.

57. Ibid.

58. The only attempt to interact with sociological data occurs in a single footnote, though this is mediated through a secondary, biblical source devoted to the particularities involving Petrine communities (see ibid., 69 n. 67).

59. Ibid., 68–69 n. 62.

Unfortunately, Watson's theory, rather than providing a coherent rationale for the secrecy injunctions, actually renders them perfunctory and superfluous to the narrative.

Equally as problematic is Watson's rigid bifurcation between the crowds and the disciples. He consistently argues that "the crowds who have gathered to hear him or to be healed by him are kept in ignorance" and that secrecy "differentiates[s] the disciples, to whom saving knowledge is given, from the crowds."[60] But this distinction does not account for the nuances of Mark's story nor the contextual features surrounding the parable of the soils. Watson assumes that the phrase "those who are outside" (4:11) is a circumlocution for the crowds, but this presumption is highly dubious, if not impossible to substantiate from the context. Considering what has just transpired in the preceding episode, those "who are outside" cannot refer to the crowds. Ironically, while Jesus is located in a home, those "outside" refer not to the crowds but to the family of Jesus (3:32) who believe that he is "out of his mind" (3:21).[61] Furthermore, instead of emphasizing the presence of the disciples with Jesus (whose place must be assumed), Mark twice notes the presence of the "crowd" (3:20, 22). Thus, those whom Watson assumes are "outsiders" are here depicted as "insiders" according to Mark's schematization. The differentiation is not between the crowds and the disciples but between those who do and do not do "the will of God" (3:35).[62] It therefore appears that Markan discipleship is more complex than Watson envisions and that he has attempted to provide a singular explanation for a complex locus of texts, when in fact a unified historical or theological rationale (in relation to Jesus' teaching) remains elusive.[63]

---

60. Ibid., 59–60.

61. Mary Ann Tolbert, *Sowing the Gospel: Mark's World in Literary-Historical Perspective* (Minneapolis: Fortress, 1989), 160.

62. Elizabeth Struthers Malbon argues that both the disciples and crowds are followers and that "discipleship is both open-ended and demanding; followership is neither exclusive nor easy" ("Disciples/Crowds/Whoever: Markan Characters and Readers," in *In the Company of Jesus: Characters in Mark's Gospel* [Louisville: Westminster John Knox, 2000], 96).

63. In addition, predestination does not account for the element of secrecy in relation to the distinction *among* the disciples. On three occasions Peter, James, and John are singled out from among the Twelve and given unique access to Jesus' activities and teaching: (1) the healing of Jairus's daughter (5:21–24, 35–43); (2) the transfiguration (9:1–13); and, (3) the eschatological discourse (13:1–37). The element of secrecy in these texts, as it relates to the differentiation among the disciples, is not explained by Watson. To take Watson's theory to its logical conclusion would be to suggest that the three are given a "saving knowledge" that supersedes and distinguishes them from among the other elect (who presumably have also received saving knowledge). The selection of some disciples

Watson further argues that Mark attempts to reify the "barrier" between the community and the world, since those outside were judged "unworthy" of the kingdom.[64] It may be true that the theme functions, in part, to circumscribe the identity of the community in relation to the nonbelieving world, but Watson's analysis overstates the case. In particular, the argument makes no attempt to address the concern for mission, an equally important and pervasive theme in Mark's Gospel. Though the Markan community was undergoing persecution and living in "opposition to society," it does not follow that the Gospel promotes a "sense of eliteness" in the face of pagan hostility.[65] On the contrary, modeled after Jesus' obedient suffering, Mark promotes a commitment to mission in spite of opposition. The centrality of mission is foundational to the narrative and is underscored by a brief selection of texts. The theme is detectable in the opening verses of the Gospel (1:2–3), which proleptically describe John's wilderness ministry and the coming of Jesus in terms of Mal 3:1 and Isa 40:3. Twice in these two verses, the "way" (1:2, 3) is depicted in relation to the mission of Jesus, inaugurating what scholars traditionally refer to as the "way" or "journey" motif. Though it may be argued that the motif undergirds the entire Gospel (see 2:23; 4:4, 15; 6:8; 8:3; 10:52; 11:8), the most concentrated use of the terminology is clustered around the midsection of the narrative (8:27–10:46; cf. 8:27; 9:33, 34; 10:17, 32, 46). On the "way" to Jerusalem, Jesus informs the disciples that he will be handed over for crucifixion and that through suffering and death God's purposes will be achieved for all humanity. The journey is not about self-aggrandizement but mission, a notion that is poignantly summarized in Mark's famous ransom saying (10:45): "the Son of Man did not come to be served but to serve and to give his life as a ransom for many" (10:45).

---

and the concomitant nonselection of others cannot be explained according to Watson's understanding of predestination and secrecy.

64. Watson, "Social Function," 62. It would appear that underlying Watson's thesis is an overemphasis upon and possible misunderstanding of the parable secret, which some suggest is not concerned with predestination but instead offers a "more limited goal when seen in its historical context" (Adela Yarbro Collins, *Mark: A Commentary* [Hermeneia; Minneapolis: Fortress, 2007], 249). Although Watson constructs his understanding of Markan secrecy by appealing to 4:11–12, there is no analysis of these debated verses. For a review of the issues surrounding this passage, as well as the interpretive options, see Craig A. Evans, *To See and Not Perceive: Isaiah 6.9–10 in Early Jewish and Christian Interpretation* (JSOTSup 64; Sheffield: Sheffield Academic Press, 1989); Klyne R. Snodgrass, *Stories with Intent: A Comprehensive Guide to the Parables of Jesus* (Grand Rapids: Eerdmans, 2008), 145–77.

65. Watson, "Social Function," 62.

That Mark is infused with a sense of mission is further indicated by the activities, teaching, and geographical movement of Jesus. In Mark's drama, Jesus displays a willingness to engage in missional work, even though it necessitates crossing traditional religious boundaries. Jesus repeatedly defies purity standards and demonstrates a compassion for the marginalized, including physical contact with the sick (1:29–31, 40–41; 7:31–37; 8:22–26), dining with tax collectors and sinners (2:15–17), and healing on the Sabbath (3:1–6). Though such actions draw the ire of the religious establishment (2:1–12, 15–17; 3:1–6, 20–30), the Markan Jesus presses onward to fulfill God's missional objective. Because he "did not come to call the righteous but sinners" (2:17), the Markan Jesus engages in activities often characterized by a disregard for social and religious tradition. Just as new wine demands new wineskins (2:19–22), so does Jesus transgress "all the boundaries" in the demonstration of his compassion for the disenfranchised.[66] This is perhaps no better illustrated than in the crossing of geopolitical borders that demarcate Jewish and Gentile space. Although Jesus has come first to satisfy the children of Israel (7:27), Mark describes various sea crossings (4:35–41; 6:45–51; 8:13–21) and land journeys (7:24, 27) that position Jesus beyond the Jewish homeland. The christological significance of these episodes cannot be underestimated and accentuates the universal implications of Mark's Gospel.[67] The unprecedented growth of the kingdom (4:30–32) is no doubt exhibited in Jesus' own ministry among the outcasts and rejected. And just as the disciples are sent out on mission, both in the narrative and presumably beyond (6:17–13, 30–32; 13:9–13), would-be disciples are commanded to follow the "way" of Jesus (8:33–38). Despite persecution and opposition, giving one's life for the sake of others is the heart of the gospel and the essence of Markan discipleship.

Watson's neglect of this theme is a major lacuna. While predestination and mission are not necessarily incompatible, he leaves little room for the interplay between these conceptual themes. The depiction of an isolated and elitest community does not harmonize with the sacrificial and missional exhortation of the narrative. Instead, this brief survey has shown that, "not only does mission have a firm place in Mark's Gospel, but it comes to the fore in precisely those texts and themes that are at the center of the Evangelist's

---

66. Donald H. Juel, *The Gospel of Mark* (Interpreting Biblical Texts; Nashville: Abingdon, 1999), 164.

67. On the theme of the Gentile mission in Mark, see Kelly R. Iverson, *Gentiles in the Gospel of Mark: Even the Dogs under the Table Eat the Children's Crumbs* (LNTS 339; London: T&T Clark, 2007).

concern."[68] The theme is so prominent that Senior and Stuhlmueller (following Pesch) describe Mark as a "Mission Book" due to the recurrent focus on the universality of the gospel. The discussion thus far has concentrated on establishing the presence of secrecy and the possible rationale for its occurrence, but the remainder of the essay will explore how a skilled performer might use secrecy to paradoxically advance a theology of mission.

DISCLOSURE AND MISSION

It may seem odd to suggest that, while secrecy is embedded within the narrative, there are no secrets for the audience of Mark's Gospel. Secrecy affects the way in which the story is experienced, but the truths of the gospel are concealed only from the characters in the narrative. As Dahl noted decades ago, "The so-called messianic secret ... is not a literary device intended to maintain suspense by keeping something hidden from the reader until he learns the solution of the enigma. The Christ-mystery is a secret only for those persons who appear in the book. The readers know the point of the story from the very beginning: it is the gospel of Jesus Christ."[69] Consequently, regardless of the audience's opinion of Jesus, they are made insiders to the mysteries of the Gospel, enjoying a perspective that is not shared by those within the story world. Rhetorically, this technique exposes the contrast between the perceptions of the characters and the audience. Sternberg refers to this as a "reader-elevating" strategy (or perhaps better, "audience-elevating") that capitalizes on the "discrepancies in awareness" enacted by the narrative design and places the audience in a semi-omniscient position over the story.[70] Thus while the characters in the story (usually) remain oblivious to the truths of Mark's Gospel, the secrets of the narrative are revealed to the audience.

The question that naturally follows is why Mark employs this audience-elevating strategy. Among those who have attempted to appreciate the rhetorical effect of this device, it is often suggested that Mark uses secrecy to

---

68. Donald Senior and Carroll Stuhlmueller, *The Biblical Foundations for Mission* (London: SCM, 1983), 229.

69. Dahl, "Purpose of Mark's Gospel," 29. *Contra* Dan O. Via, who argues that the audience is prone to the same confusion as the disciples (*The Revelation of God and/as Human Reception: In the New Testament* [Valley Forge, Pa.: Trinity Press International, 1997], 104–10). Though Via offers several insightful observations, he assumes that the audience's perspective is aligned with the disciples, when in fact it is more distinctly shaped by the narrator.

70. For a fuller discussion of "reader-elevating" techniques, as well as "character-elevating" and "evenhandedness," see Meir Sternberg, *The Poetics of Biblical Narrative* (Bloomington: Indiana University Press, 1985), 163–72.

enhance the tension in the story and to entice the audience further into the dramatic world of the narrative—a conclusion that resonates with many literary theorists who regard secrecy, mystery, and surprise as forms of suspense.[71] Others have argued that Mark uses secrecy "as a means of revelation to hearers/readers of the gospel" and to draw "attention to the real significance of the story."[72] But while secrecy may pique audience interest, it is questionable whether these descriptions pay due consideration to the religious make-up of Mark's Gospel. Further, although the theme raises awareness of certain features in the narrative, it is erroneous to assume that Markan secrecy is tethered to a single aspect of the storyline (the *real* significance). At the very least, it seems unlikely that the Evangelist utilized the theme merely to disseminate information or to generate audience interest.

At the heart of the use of secrecy is the interchange between the audience and performer. As Georges argues, "only by attempting to study storytelling events holistically can we begin to appreciate" that the dynamic between

---

71. Jerry Camery-Hoggatt has suggested that secrecy functions to actively involve the audience in the unfolding drama: "The [secret] insight the reader enjoys will naturally place him at an advantage over the characters of the story, and at virtually every point he will be called upon to pass judgment on them for their blindness or obtuseness" (*Irony in Mark's Gospel: Text and Subtext* [SNTSMS 72; Cambridge: Cambridge University Press, 1992], 93). Robert Fowler maintains that, although scholars have vigorously sought to unravel the messianic secret, little consensus has been achieved except to establish "just how captivating the weave of Mark's narrative fabric is" (*Let the Reader Understand: Reader-Response Criticism and the Gospel of Mark* [Minneapolis: Fortress, 1991], 175). For Fowler, "the act of unraveling and reknitting"—that is, the deliberately puzzlingly aspect of secrecy—is "*the thing*" or the ultimate purpose of Mark's rhetorical device (175, emphasis added). What is interesting is that, while these two scholars take slightly different approaches to the issue, both arrive at a similar conclusion. On the effect of secrecy in broader literary discussions, see John O'Toole, *The Process of Drama: Negotiating Art and Meaning* (London: Routledge, 1992), 163. Although O'Toole is primarily concerned with dramatic performance, his observations regarding secrecy are derived from literature.

72. Morna D. Hooker, *The Gospel according to Saint Mark* (BNTC; London: Black, 1991), 67–68. See also Hans Jürgen Ebeling, *Das Messiasgeheimnis und die Botschaft des Marcus-Evangelisten* (BZNW; Berlin: Töpelmann, 1939). William Telford adopts a similar perspective but suggests that Mark was a representative of Pauline Christianity and was attempting to expose the faulty Christology of the Jewish disciples (*The Theology of the Gospel of Mark* [Cambridge: Cambridge University Press, 1999], 53). In a slightly different but similar move, Elizabeth Struthers Malbon argues that the Markan Jesus uses secrecy in order to deflect attention away from himself and toward God ("The Christology of Mark's Gospel: Narrative Christology and the Markan Jesus," in *Who Do You Say That I Am? Essays on Christology* [ed. Mark Allan Powell and David R. Bauer; Louisville: Westminster John Knox, 1999], 37–44).

audience and performer is foundational to the process of interpretation.[73] Although the process of reading may evoke emotive responses, an enacted performance is something "palpably different ... [from] turning pages in a detached textual artifact."[74] Commenting on his first experience of a South Slavic oral epic, John Foley noted that it was "more vivid, more arresting, more demanding, more contingent. The audience played a much larger and more determinative role in the moment-to-moment reality of the evolving song than I had suspected."[75] This "unspoken agreement" between audience and performer represents an implicit contract, but it is a powerful force in performance. "If anything, its status as an understood, behind-the-scenes agreement only increase its word-power. Its rules ... [have] become part of the grammar of performance."[76] In light of the performative context in which the Gospels were enacted, the issue is how the revelation of perceived "secrets" impacts the audience. In order to better understand the aesthetic exchange that takes place between performer and audience, it is necessary "to unpack the dynamics" of this relationship by turning to the social sciences, particularly to what is referred to as the "disclosure-liking" relationship.[77]

In an important article entitled "Self-Disclosure and Liking: A Meta-analytic Review," Nancy Collins and Lynn Carol Miller discuss the social and psychological effects of revelatory disclosure.[78] Drawing from the wealth of research stemming from Jourard's groundbreaking study on the positive relationship between self-disclosure and liking, Collins and Miller adopt a comprehensive, meta-analytic approach that incorporates "all relevant studies available in published form."[79] Besides the sheer breadth of the project, the study's unique contribution is in the organization of the disclosure-liking relationships and the delineation of three disclosure-liking effects, which may be articulated as three separate, though related, questions: (1) Do individuals generally like people who disclose information to them, as compared to others

---

73. Quoted in Elizabeth Fine, *The Folklore Text: From Performance to Print* (Indianapolis: Indianapolis University Press, 1984), 46.

74. John Miles Foley, *How to Read an Oral Poem* (Chicago: University of Illinois Press, 2002), 84.

75. Ibid.

76. Ibid., 85.

77. Rhoads, *Reading Mark*, 37. Although narrative criticism is derived from literary theory, Rhoads suggests that narrative critics may profitably benefit from the social sciences.

78. Nancy L. Collins and Lynn Carol Miller, "Self-Disclosure and Liking: A Meta-analytic Review," *Psychological Bulletin* 116.3 (1994): 457–75.

79. Ibid., 460.

who do not? (2) Do individuals reveal more to people who they like? and (3) Do individuals show a stronger liking for those to whom they have disclosed?

Although the analysis of the data involves a number of variables (gender, relationship between individuals, etc.), Collins and Miller argue that "the meta-analyses revealed significant positive relations for all three disclosure-liking effects."[80] In general, as long as an act of disclosure does not violate normative, social expectations, "any information about oneself that a person verbally communicates to another person," including descriptive and/or evaluative information (i.e., beliefs), has a notable and defining impact upon the development of relationships.[81] The reason for this positive affiliation is that, "when people perceive that they have been personally selected for intimate discourse, they feel trusted and liked and are more apt to evaluate the discloser favorably."[82] In this respect, disclosure has a symbolic function in interpersonal relationships and communicates something beyond that which is transferred by the exchange of information: "disclosing to another communicates that we trust that person … [and] that we are interested in knowing them and having them know us."[83] The result is that disclosure unleashes a cycle of responses that build and nourish developing relationships. Typically, people like others who disclose to them, they themselves like those to whom they have disclosed, and those to whom information is revealed often reciprocate through mutual self-disclosure. What is more, the disclosure-liking effect is such a powerful phenomena that it is observable in interpersonal relationships and group contexts.[84]

In view of this research, it is profitable to consider Mark's use of the secrecy theme in relation to the disclosure-liking effect.[85] It bears repeating that there are no secrets for the audience of Mark's narrative, but the manner in which the story is told creates the impression that the performer is disclosing information that is not shared by all. This informational discrepancy is not derived from the exclusivity of the Markan community, as Watson surmised, but through the plotting of the narrative discourse. The performance of the

---

80. Ibid., 470.

81. Ibid., 458.

82. Ibid., 459.

83. Ibid., 471.

84. Susan T. Fiske, Daniel Todd Gilbert, and Gardner Lindzey, *Handbook of Social Psychology* (5th ed.; Hoboken, N.J.: Wiley, 2010), 870–71; Michael H. Kahn and Kjell E. Rudestam, "The Relationship between Liking and Perceived Self-Disclosure in Small Groups," *The Journal of Psychology* 78.1 (1971): 81–85.

85. A degree of prudence is always required when interpreting the ancient world through modern, social-scientific research. However, just because Mark was not familiar with the data does not mean the Evangelist was ignorant of the dynamics behind the theory.

Gospel creates an aura of secrecy, even though the community and its message are neither closed nor secretive.[86] Rather, the effectiveness of the technique—that is, the disclosure of information previously unknown—is dependent upon the historical situation of the first century and the yet-unfulfilled mission of the church. The repetitive use of secrecy establishes the audience as insiders to whom the revelation of Mark's story is disclosed and simultaneously fosters the positive rapport between performer and audience necessary for relational development. While the rhetorical device encourages the formation of community among those already established in the church, the impact of the technique is most pronounced among a different constituency. When viewed in relation to the importance of mission, Mark's narrative disclosures may be intended to complement a broader theological purpose. In particular, though Mark was likely written for Christians undergoing persecution, the concern for mission and the creative use of secrecy hint at another possibility. In line with the research of Collins and Miller, the manner in which the gospel is disclosed (i.e., through the use of secrecy) may provide subtle indication that Mark was also interested in the reception of the narrative by those not already committed to the faith. To state it another way, since the repeated telling of "secrets" has a diminishing effect among those who have already believed, the secrecy theme is most impactful among those who are not yet intimately familiar with Mark's story of Jesus.

This assertion is not to imply that Mark was written for the purpose of evangelizing unbelievers, but neither does it rule out the possibility that that objective was beyond the Evangelist's purview, as some would suggest.[87] Aune, for instance, has argued that the rapid expansion of the early church had a direct bearing upon the manner in which the Jesus story was depicted. Although the Gospels are written to reinforce and strengthen the faith of those who already believed that Jesus was the Messiah, the structure of the Mediterranean life (i.e., the inclusion of extended family, slaves, laborers, clients, etc.) necessarily meant that many household churches included some

---

86. Neyrey discusses the sociological function of secrecy in John but notes an element of "espionage" in Mark's Gospel (11:28–30; 12:13–15). This perspective, however, blurs the distinction between story and discourse and assumes that community practice mirrors the secrecy in the Gospel. Unfortunately, this approach addresses the function of secrecy but neglects the disclosure-liking theory. See Jerome H. Neyrey, *The Gospel of John in Cultural and Rhetorical Perspective* (Grand Rapids: Eerdmans, 2009), 252–81.

87. On the subject of mission and the scholarly neglect of the theme, see Elisabeth Schüssler Fiorenza, "Miracles, Mission, and Apologetics: An Introduction," in *Aspects of Religious Propaganda in Judaism and Early Christianity* (ed. Elisabeth Schüssler Fiorenza; Notre Dame, Ind.: University of Notre Dame Press, 1976), 1–26.

who were "outsiders" to the faith but "insiders" from a social perspective.[88] In this respect, the social location of the early church influenced the composition of the Gospels such that Aune describes them as a form of "Christian literary propaganda."[89] Furthermore, given that stories are not the most effective means to engage in theological debate, Tolbert has argued that Mark's selection of a narrative format is most readily explained as an attempt "to enlist the sympathy of an audience."[90] Having analyzed the rhetorical style of Mark in detail, she concludes that one of the Gospel's purposes is "to persuade its hearers to have faith in the gospel of Jesus Christ ... and to become themselves sowers of the good news of God's coming kingdom."[91] It appears that both from a social and rhetorical standpoint, Mark likely envisioned an audience that encompassed some who were already devoted to the faith, as well as "individuals interested in Christianity but not yet fully committed" and "who needed to be persuaded."[92]

This broad vision for the Gospel audience appears to have a firm basis in the text, for not only does the Evangelist note that the "gospel must first be preached to all the nations" (13:10)—essentially providing a mandate for the early church—but this same point is underscored in the subsequent episode when an anonymous woman anoints Jesus for burial with a costly vial of perfume (14:3–9). Though the disciples are incredulous at the women's apparent waste of resources, her actions are singled out for attention. Unlike the disciples, the Markan Jesus affirms the significance of the act, as well as the perpetuity of the memory surrounding the woman's provision: "Truly I say to you, wherever the gospel is proclaimed throughout the whole world, what

---

88. David E. Aune, *The New Testament in Its Literary Environment* (Philadelphia: Westminster, 1987), 60. Aune stops short of referring to the Gospels as missionary tractates, but he recognizes their broad rhetorical potential.

89. Aune argues that, while the Gospels are not missionary tractates, "the aggressive conversionist orientation of early Christians profoundly shaped their understanding of the mission and message of Jesus and imprinted itself indelibly on Gospel tradition" (ibid., 59).

90. Tolbert, *Sowing the Gospel*, 303–4.

91. Ibid., 302.

92. Ibid., 304. Tolbert goes on to state that "Mark's rhetorical goals are exhortation and proselytizing" (304). Adela Yarbro Collins makes a similar assumption about Mark's audience. See her "Mark and His Readers: The Son of God among Jews," *HTR* 92 (1999): 393–408. This perspective is confirmed by recent generic research, which has demonstrated that ancient biographies such as the Gospels were written "about friends, by friends, [and] for others" (Justin Marc Smith, "About Friends, by Friends, for Others: Author-Subject Relationships in Contemporary Greco-Roman Biographies," in *The Audience of the Gosepls: The Origin and Function of the Gospels in Early Christianity* [ed. Edward W. Klink III; LNTS 353; London: T&T Clark, 2009], 49–67).

she has done will be told in memory of her" (14:9). Like the eschatological discourse (13:10), the centrality of mission is restated ("throughout the whole world"), but here there is an explicit reference to the use of Mark as a tool to fulfill the missionary objective of the Evangelist. The "gospel" (14:9) that is to be proclaimed by the church appears to be a direct reference to the "gospel of Jesus Christ" (1:1), which Mark designates as the titular description of his own composition.[93] In other words, embedded within this laudatory statement concerning an anonymous woman's gracious display, Mark tips his hand at an anticipated function of the narrative.

Mark's concern for the mission of the church, indicated by the explicit statement that *his* story of Jesus would be used for these purposes, manifests itself in the rhetoric of the Gospel. Although there are many facets of the story that potentially contribute to this goal, the element of secrecy is perhaps the most unexpected feature to advance this objective. It seems, however, that Mark has carefully and deliberately narrated the story in order to place the audience in the enviable position of acquiring information that the characters in the story do not possess. While the numerous instances of concealment (e.g., Jesus' identity, miracles, teachings) cannot be explained according to a single theory within the narrative (i.e., Jesus' desire for rest or to avoid publicity), the element of secrecy nonetheless exists as a unified theme. By providing the audience with "insider" knowledge, Mark utilizes a rhetorical device to cultivate a favorable relationship between the audience and performer, since, as one scholar has noted, it is virtually impossible to "initiate, develop, or maintain a relationship without self-disclosure."[94]

It might be objected that, if this assertion were correct, it obscures Mark's ultimate concern, which is the reception of the gospel message, not the perception of the performer. However, while a distinction between the performer and message might be envisioned, those working in the field of rhetorical studies have shown that the perception of the speaker and the reception of the message are closely aligned. Ancient rhetoriticians such as Aristotle have long observed that the character (*ethos*) and perception of the speaker play an important role in the overall persuasiveness of an argument (Aristotle, *Rhet.* 1.2.1356), and more recent studies have only confirmed this assess-

---

93. Matthew clarifies this connection by redacting Mark 14:9 to read, "wherever *this* [i.e., Matthew's] gospel is preached" (Matt 26:13). Although likely not original, many Markan manuscripts (A C Θ Ψ f^1 et al.) follow Matthew's reading, reflecting the early perception that Mark's story of Jesus would be used for the preaching of the gospel.

94. Charles H. Tardy and Kathryn Dindia, "Self-Disclosure: Strategic Revelation of Information in Personal and Professional Relationships," in *The Handbook of Communication Skills* (ed. Owen Hargie; London: Routledge, 2006), 230.

ment. Scholars have shown that effective communicators often use "peripheral routes" to influence and persuade an audience.[95] Beyond the presentation and strength of an argument, audiences may also be influenced by indirect techniques, "such as whether the auditor considers the source to be credible … [and the] *liking for or attractiveness of the source.*"[96] In terms of the present study, this rhetorical assessment helps to explain the importance of the disclosure-liking relationship, and it is perhaps why some have argued that disclosure is an effective, goal-based strategy for obtaining desirable responses from others.[97]

When approached from this angle, Mark's secrecy theme is not simply a device that attracts the audience to the performer. Rather, the employment of the technique is an affective tool (see Freeman) that facilitates the very reception of Mark's message. As Elizabeth Fine observes, the rhetorical power of performance has the potential to change attitudes and alter events. Its capacity to function as a catalyst for change "lies in the epistemological nature of artistic verbal performance," which "embodies knowledge in an heightened self-conscious way that binds the audience and performer together in the creation and fulfillment of aesthetic form."[98] The rhetoric of the Gospel facilitates the construction of a relational bridge between the performer and audience, which ultimately impacts the audience's perception of the narrative. By revealing the "secrets" of the drama, the performer attempts to foster the mutual trust and admiration that are necessary for the reception of Mark's worldview. This, in essence, is the "paradox of secrecy." Through the measured disclosure of information, the gospel is proclaimed and received by those on the margins of the church.[99]

---

95. Richard E. Petty and John T. Cacioppo, *Communication and Persuasion: Central and Peripheral Routes to Attitude Change* (New York: Springer-Verlag, 1986).

96. William L. Benoit and Mary Jeanette Smythe, "Rhetorical Theory as Message Reception: A Cognitive Response Approach to Rhetorical Theory and Criticism," *Communication Studies* 54.1 (2003): 101, emphasis added.

97. Lynn Carol Miller and Stephen J. Read, "Why Am I Telling You This? Self-Disclosure in a Goal-Based Model of Personality," in *Self-Disclosure: Theory, Research, and Therapy* (ed. Valerian J. Derlega and John H. Berg; New York: Plenum, 1987), 35–58.

98. Fine, *Folklore Text*, 64.

99. Kingsbury comes closest to this position: "The purpose of this motif is to invite readers to appropriate for themselves that 'thinking' about Jesus which places them 'in alignment' with God's 'thinking' about Jesus" (*Christology of Mark's Gospel*, 155). While a helpful comment, Kingsbury does not provide an explanation for how this occurs, nor does he consider the more specific function of the theme in the context of mission.

Conclusion

Thanks in no small part to the work of Rhoads, Dewey, and Michie, the rise in narrative criticism has awakened scholars to fresh insights and alternative angles of vision. Despite these advancements, however, William Wrede continues to exert a controlling influence over the question of Markan secrecy. Although contemporary scholarship has effectively minimized the importance of the theme, its prominence and unity are rooted firmly in the text. Mark's use of secrecy has a powerful rhetorical effect and, when employed by a skilled narrator, is a strategic tool for developing and shaping the relationship between audience and performer. By subtly influencing the perception of the performer, the rhetoric of the Gospel encourages the audience to embrace the message communicated through Mark's story of Jesus. According to Iser, this is the "something that is unformulated in the text, and yet represents its 'intention.'"[100] Mark's narrative is only "the beginning of the gospel" (1:1), but the Evangelist has utilized a rhetorical device to ensure that it is not the end of the gospel story. Simply put, wherever the gospel is preached, the concealment of Jesus' activities *in the narrative* contributes to reception of Mark's message *by the audience.*

---

100. Iser, "Reading Process," 292. The upshot of this conclusion is that it fully accounts for the diverse contexts in which the theme appears without attempting to impose a unified theory of genesis. At the same time, this approach recognizes the broad use of the theme and its effect upon the audience.

FROM NARRATIVE TO PERFORMANCE: METHODOLOGICAL CONSIDERATIONS AND INTERPRETIVE MOVES

Holly E. Hearon

Since the publication of the second edition of *Mark As Story: An Introduction to the Narrative of a Gospel*, by David Rhoads, Joanna Dewey, and Donald Michie, there has been increasing interest in performance criticism. A growing number of scholars have argued that the writings of the New Testament are remnants of oral events.[1] Some of the texts represent transcripts of oral performances, while others were written or dictated for performance.[2] Recognition of the oral nature of the written text changes everything. It means that, as interpreters, we can no longer continue to focus exclusively on the words written on the page. We also need to discover what can be learned from seeing and hearing the text in performance.[3] According to Rhoads, this requires a shift in orientation "from private to public, from 'public readers' to perform-

---

1. E.g., Samuel Byrskog, *Story as History, History as Story: The Gospel Tradition in the Context of Ancient Oral History* (Leiden: Brill, 2002); Joanna Dewey, ed., *Orality and Textuality in Early Christian Literature, Semeia* 65 (1994); Holly E. Hearon and Philip Ruge-Jones, eds., *The Bible in Ancient and Modern Media: Story and Performance* (Eugene, Ore.: Cascade, 2009); Richard A. Horsley, *Hearing the Whole Story: The Politics of Plot in Mark's Gospel* (Louisville: Westminster John Knox, 2001); Werner Kelber, *The Oral and the Written Gospel: The Hermeneutics of Speaking and Writing in the Synoptic Tradition, Mark, Paul and Q* (Philadelphia: Fortress, 1983; repr., Bloomington: Indiana University Press, 1997); Whitney Shiner, *Proclaiming the Gospel: First-Century Performance of Mark* (Harrisburg, Pa.: Trinity Press International, 2003); Antoinette Wire, *Holy Lives, Holy Deaths: A Close Hearing of Early Jewish Storytellers* (Society of Biblical Literature Studies in Biblical Literature 1. Atlanta: Society of Biblical Literature, 2002).

2. David Rhoads, "What Is Performance Criticism?" in Hearon and Ruge-Jones, *The Bible in Ancient and Modern Media*, 83.

3. David Rhoads, "Performance Criticism: An Emerging Methodology in Biblical Studies" (paper presented at the Annual Meeting of the Society of Biblical Literature, New Orleans, 21 November 2009), 29.

ers, from silent readers to hearers/audience, from individual to communal, and from manuscript transmission to oral transmission."[4]

In this essay I explore the implications of this shift in orientation for the purposes of exegesis. Using Mark 5:21–43 as my focus text (the story of Jairus's daughter and the woman with the flow of blood),[5] I undertake a comparative analysis from the perspectives of both narrative criticism and performance criticism.[6] Specifically, I explore selected dimensions of the text that are lifted up in narrative criticism (setting, conflict, character, and narrator) and propose conceptual and methodological shifts that occur when engaging these same dimensions of the text through the lens of performance criticism.[7] My goal is to begin to describe ways in which performance criticism is distinguished from narrative criticism and to identify ways in which performance criticism can help interpreters gain increased access to the multiple meanings that can be drawn from the text.

Rhoads would invite us all, ideally, to become performers of biblical stories. Although I fall short of this goal, I will engage two performances of Mark 5 as a part of my analysis: *A Dramatic Presentation of the Gospel of Mark*, a video of a performance by David Rhoads recorded in 1992, and *The Beginning of the Good News*, a DVD of a performance by Philip Ruge-Jones recorded in 2009.[8] The performance by Ruge-Jones takes place before a live audience that can sometimes be seen and heard; the performance by Rhoads does not take place before a live audience. I have, in addition, had the opportunity to sit through a live performance of the Gospel of Mark by storyteller Tracy Radosevic at Christian Theological Seminary in 2009.[9]

---

4. Ibid., 6.

5. I will be working from the translation in David Rhoads, Joanna Dewey, and Donald Michie, *Mark as Story: An Introduction to the Narrative of a Gospel* (2nd ed.; Minneapolis: Fortress, 1999), 67. Rhoads, Dewey, and Michie do not include chapter and verse numbers because these create artificial divisions in the text. For this essay I will follow this convention when discussing the story of Jairus's daughter and the woman with the flow of blood. However, I will use chapter and verse numbers when citing other parts of the Gospel of Mark.

6. For Rhoads, performance criticism (broadly speaking) is analysis of the text in preparation for and inclusive of performance, with particular attention to the rhetorical impact of the storytelling event.

7. There are a variety of approaches to performance criticism in practice (see, e.g., the work of Whitney Shiner, Richard Swanson, and William Doane). In this paper, I will follow the example and work of David Rhoads.

8. Available at www.selectlearning.org.

9. These performances all involve single storytellers. Other kinds of performances could include formal readings of the Gospel, theatrical productions involving multiple

SETTING: NARRATIVE CRITICISM

In *Mark as Story*, Rhoads, Dewey, and Michie define "setting" as "the context within the story—the depiction of the cosmos, the social world of the story as well as the specific temporal and spatial contexts in which events take place."[10] It is tempting to think of "setting" as descriptive (i.e., markers that locate the events of the narrative in time and space) rather than imaginative, but this would not be wholly true. Because "setting" includes associations with Israel's history, it is created in consort with the mind, memory, and imagination of the reader.

The physical setting of the story in Mark 5:21–40 is the shore of the Sea of Galilee. Rhoads, Dewey, and Michie write that, within the narrative of the Gospel, "Galilee is the place where Jesus first brings God's rule and where its inbreaking is received enthusiastically."[11] This is reflected in the large crowd that gathers around Jesus as soon as he lands. The crowd itself is a significant part of the physical setting in the first half of the story and is mentioned five times, twice as pressing in on Jesus. In the second half of the story, the physical setting is focused on the house of the leader of the synagogue. This is a private setting, in contrast to the earlier public setting established by the crowds. The "privacy" of the setting is underscored by Jesus' driving out the mourners and allowing only chosen individuals to enter the house with him. Within the larger narrative of the Gospel, houses are also settings where Jesus heals (1:29; 5:38; 7:24) and teaches (2:15; 7:17; 9:33; 10:10). These interior spaces, then, function as revelatory space.

The setting of the story is also shaped by references to two social institutions within the narrative: a leader of the synagogue and physicians. The Gospel contains only one other reference to physicians (2:17), where it is stated that it is not the healthy who need a physician but those who are sick. In chapter 5, there is a certain irony that, despite having been under the care of many physicians, the woman with the flow of blood only got worse.[12] It may be that the story is playing off of a general negative impression of physicians held by many in the ancient Mediterranean world.[13] The story in chapter 5

---

actors, or musical settings of the Gospel. These would introduce additional dimensions to performance analysis.

10. Rhoads, Dewey, and Michie, *Mark as Story*, 6.

11. Ibid., 67.

12. On the nature of the "flow of blood," see Amy-Jill Levine, "Discharging Responsibility: Matthean Jesus, Biblical Law, and Hemorrhaging Woman," in *A Feminist Companion to Matthew* (ed. Amy-Jill Levine; Sheffield: Sheffield Academic Press, 2001), 70–87.

13. Joel Green, "Healing," *NIDB* 2:757.

contains the only reference to a leader of the synagogue in the Gospel; how-ever, synagogues are places where, earlier in the Gospel, Jesus has performed healings (1:21–29; 3:1–5). The appeal by the leader of the synagogue on behalf of his daughter, then, arises out of an expectation that has been established earlier in the narrative. Richard Horsley points out that the term *synagōgē* (συναγωγή) does not necessarily point to a building but, in this time period, to an assembly of the people. The *synagōgē* (συναγωγή) served a number of community functions, social and political as well as religious.[14] A leader of the synagogue would be viewed in relation to these functions and recognized as someone who served the well-being of the entire community.

Finally, because the narrative is set within the larger context of the story of Israel, the setting is shaped by echoes of and allusions to this story—what might be called the memorial setting. Horsley suggests that the number twelve is intended to evoke the twelve tribes of Israel. Thus the woman and the girl function metaphorically for Israel, representing how Israel has been continuously bled due to exploitation and has reached a state of near death, no longer able to generate new life. Trust in Jesus brings a reversal to this state.[15] Stories from the Hebrew Bible offer examples of those who both trust and fail to trust in God to bring healing. On the one hand, there is the story of Asa, who when he was afflicted with disease did not put his trust in God but sought the help of physicians and died (2 Chr 16:12–13). On the other is the story of the widow's son, whom Elijah raised from death (1 Kgs 17:17–24). This latter story draws a connection to the earlier reference to physicians in the Gospel of Mark through the widow's comment that Elijah has come to bring remem-brance of her past sin and consequently causes the death of her son. In Mark, Jesus follows his comment about physicians with the declaration that he has come not to call the righteous but sinners (2:17).

A narrative-critical analysis reveals a complex setting for the story in Mark 5. Setting is signaled not only by verbal cues within the story itself but by the ways in which these cues link the story to the Gospel as a whole and to the story of Israel. The key here is *verbal* cues. Narrative criticism focuses on the language of the text, its patterns, echoes, and resonances.

SETTING: PERFORMANCE CRITICISM

In a chapter on "Performing the Gospel of Mark," Rhoads observes that in performance-critical analysis the spatial dimension of setting takes on physi-

---

14. Horsley, *Hearing the Whole Story*, 39.
15. Ibid., 18–19, 106.

cal dimensions in two ways. First, the spatial setting must be blocked out in the performance space. For example, here is the shore of the Sea of Galilee, here is the crowd that marks the space "Jesus" in the first half of the story, and over there is the house of Jairus. By assigning particular areas of the performance space to certain places or kinds of events, the performer is able to direct the audience to build connections between events.[16] In this case, the house of Jairus, a leader of the synagogue, might be blocked out on the same space as synagogues, where healings have taken place earlier in the narrative, leading viewers to associate this space with healings.[17] The second way performance criticism signals spatial settings is through movement, gestures, and embodiment.[18] Jesus' movement from one side of the Sea of Galilee to the other is signaled as the performer moves from one part of the performance space to another. The texture of the landscape may be indicated by whether this movement is fast or slow, labored or energetic. Spatial dimensions are signaled as the performer responds to the setting. For example, Rhoads ducks his head as he enters the house of Jairus. While such movement might take place in the mind of the reader, it is visually articulated in performance. Thus, where a narrative-critical analysis depends on verbal cues (and resources such as a concordance) to make spatial connections, a performance-critical analysis establishes visual, as well as verbal, cues. These visual cues add a subtext to the verbal text, a kind of unspoken commentary that both describes and interprets.

Through the use of gestures, a performance-critical analysis also introduces an additional dimension to spatial setting that is not readily evident in narrative criticism: the physical presence of the characters as part of the spatial setting. A glance or a gesture signals that there is not just one person inhabiting the space but two or more. Ruge-Jones gestures with his hands to signal the crowd around Jesus each time the crowd is mentioned. This draws attention to the repetition of references to the crowd with a visual cue. It has an additional affect, however, in that it locates the crowd spatially in relation to the other characters in the story. This reveals that the crowd does not simply function as a group of bystanders but plays an active role in shaping how the audience literally sees the other characters in the story. Jairus approaches a

---

16. David Rhoads, *Reading Mark: Engaging the Gospel* (Minneapolis: Fortress, 2004), 180–81.

17. "Space" here can refer to either social space (synagogue as a "gathering of people") or physical space (synagogue as building). How it is understood will, in performance, be dependent on how the audience understands the term "synagogue" based on their own social, religious, and political experience.

18. Rhoads, *Reading Mark,* 189.

Jesus who is surrounded by a crowd. Jairus is not part of the crowd; he is able to gain Jesus' attention by falling at his feet. As Jesus departs with Jairus, the crowd follows. Rhoads introduces a beat between Jesus' departure with Jairus and the mention of the crowd, in this way separating the crowd from Jairus and establishing it as the setting that introduces the story of the woman. In contrast, Ruge-Jones places the beat after the mention of the crowd, making it clear that the crowd is following Jesus with Jairus in order to witness Jesus laying hands on Jairus's daughter and restoring her to life. A woman now appears. She approaches Jesus from behind by becoming a part of the crowd. She is not attempting to get Jesus' attention, as Jairus was. She wants to remain anonymous, and the crowd provides the cover that will allow her to approach Jesus without being witnessed. The presence of the crowd also tells us something about Jesus, who, despite their presence, knows that someone has drawn healing power from him, a moment that receives double comment when the disciples wonder how Jesus could know someone has touched him when a crowd is pressing in all around him. A performance-critical analysis, precisely because it adds a physical dimension to the text, calls attention to the physical proximity of characters in the story in a way that narrative criticism does not and invites reflection on how this physical proximity shapes our understanding of and response to the characters.[19]

Setting, in performance, refers not only to the setting of the story; it also includes the setting of the audience, both the physical setting in which the performance takes place (e.g., a church, a prison, a public square) and the social setting of the audience (e.g., social class or standing, gender, educational background). The physical setting of the audience both determines the performance space that can be used and creates an interpretive lens through which the performance is experienced. For example, Ruge-Jones performs in a church sanctuary where an altar, candles, and pulpit inhabit the performance space. These set the story in a liturgical context that frames the Gospel

---

19. In the story from Mark 5, the signaling of the physical proximity of the characters in the performance space has another affect. It underscores the movement from public to private space. In the first half of the story, characters are added to the story, one by one, creating an increasingly crowded performance space: to the crowd is added Jairus, then the woman, then the disciples. The presence of all these characters in one space at the same time creates a collision of needs: Jairus's daughter awaiting the restorative touch of Jesus and the woman whose touch causes Jesus to delay. The omnipresence of the crowd throughout this half of the story (indicated by repeated reference) keeps the space full and contributes to the sense of confusion and conflict. After the exchange between Jesus and the woman, characters begin to be dismissed from the scene, so that, in the end, only a few select witnesses enter the house and see Jesus restore the girl to life. All this is evident in a narrative analysis, but in performance it is experienced in a visceral way.

of Mark as a story that leads to faith. The effect is somewhat different when Rhoads performs Mark at a medium-security prison. Here the presence of guards and other security measures "interprets" the good news as that which empowers people to be free.[20] In this way, a dialectic is set up between performance and setting, each, in one way or another, interpreting the other. Although something similar happens in narrative criticism when the reader engages the text, the physical setting of performance elevates this to a more conscious level.

The presence of the audience in performance also presents a challenge to performance criticism—one not encountered in narrative criticism, or at least to a lesser degree. A narrative-critical analysis, because it is textually based, allows the reader to consult a variety of resources that explicate social customs and settings in the first-century world, as well as uncover allusions and echoes in the story. In performance, a challenge is presented. How does one perform allusions or echoes or draw attention to social customs and roles that are assumed by the text? A case in point is the reference in the story to the leader of the synagogue. What is a synagogue, and how do leaders function within them? An audience may project onto such a setting an anachronistic image that significantly alters the way they respond to the character Jairus. Or the reference to the number twelve: Horsley proposes that this is a politically charged reference, inviting the audience in antiquity to view the two female characters as metaphors for Israel. In a contemporary performance, the audience is more likely to form a completely different set of memorial associations that are rooted in their present social context.

While a narrative-critical analysis reveals a complex setting for the story in Mark 5, a performance-critical analysis reveals an even more complex setting, one that is the result of an ever-shifting performance context. It requires attention not only to verbal cues in the text but also to the shifting physical, social, and memorial cues embedded in different performance spaces and audiences. In performance criticism, setting is dialogical.

Conflict: Narrative Criticism

There are multiple levels of conflict in this story. Initially, the conflict in the story arises from the need for healing. This sets in motion a fairly straightforward miracle narrative in which Jairus approaches Jesus on behalf of his daughter with a request for healing. The need is heightened by Jairus's declaration that the girl is near death. An obstacle then arises. The obstacle is not

---

20. Rhoads, Dewey, and Michie, *Mark as Story,* 184.

the crowd, which in no way inhibits Jesus' progress toward the house of Jairus. Nor is the obstacle the woman who comes up behind Jesus and touches him in order that she might be restored. The obstacle arises when Jesus stops to ask who touched him. The subsequent dialogue between Jesus and the woman permits enough time to elapse for Jairus's daughter to die. Nonetheless, there is a temptation to blame the woman, who may be viewed as having snatched the healing that belonged to the child for herself. Has she drained Jesus' power to such a degree that there will be nothing left for the child?[21] Of course, had the woman not touched Jesus in the first place, there would have been no cause for the delay.

This sets in motion a second conflict. The conflict does not concern whether or not Jesus will restore Jairus's daughter. He is willing and able. The conflict surrounds whether Jairus and those with him have faith that Jesus can do this. This conflict is set in motion when people come from Jairus's house to announce that his daughter has died. They urge Jairus not to continue bothering Jesus. This represents a first obstacle to Jairus's faith. Jesus' responds by telling Jairus to have faith. When they arrive at the house, the mourners gathered jeer at Jesus when he asks why they are making such a commotion, saying that the child is only asleep. This represents a second obstacle that is an intensification of the first. Driving out the mourners (and their lack of faith), Jesus leads the parents and those with him in to where the child lies and resolves the conflict by restoring her to life.

This resolution has been anticipated by the earlier healing of the woman. In contrast to those surrounding Jairus, the woman demonstrates perfect confidence in Jesus. She believes that she need only touch the edge of his clothes and she will be healed, despite all the evidence to the contrary presented by her long, sorry encounters with physicians. This introduces an ironic twist into the story. The delay caused by the healing of the woman, which, at first glance, creates an obstacle leading to the death of Jairus's daughter, is shown in the end to have provided the model of faith that Jairus is encouraged to follow.

Conflict: Performance Criticism

In performance, the structure remains intact. The performer, however, gives shape to the structure and the conflict embedded in it through tone of voice and gesture, introducing what Rhoads calls a subtext: "the message that is

---

21. Richard Swanson reminds the interpreter that the word for power, *dunamis* (δύναμις), can refer to potency. Thus when Jesus feels power go out of himself, this could be understood as indicating that Jesus has become impotent (*Provoking the Gospel of Mark: A Storyteller's Commentary, Year B* [Cleveland: Pilgrim, 2005], 185).

conveyed by the 'way' a line is delivered."[22] The performances by Rhoads and Ruge-Jones illustrate how performance can articulate the conflict that drives the story in different ways without altering the structure itself.

In Rhoads's performance, the desperation of Jairus is emphasized by the script he employs and the tone of despair as he raises his hands in petition to Jesus: "my little daughter is about to die at any moment" (as opposed to "near death"). The narrator's voice states that Jesus went off with him, momentarily bringing resolution to Jairus's story. After a brief pause, Rhoads reintroduces the crowd and begins to narrate the story of the woman. The pause effectively separates the two stories, downplaying the tension that an audience might feel, being aware that Jairus's little daughter is "about to die at any moment" and hearing the description of the woman drone on. By keeping her visual focus on Jesus when she speaks the line "if I touch just his clothes, I'll be restored" and using a tone of voice filled with confidence, Rhoads emphasizes the woman's faith, which is affirmed when Jesus looks down at her and tells her that her faith has made her well. In Rhoads's performance, tension is introduced into the story when the people from Jairus's house enter the scene. This is signaled both verbally and visually: Jesus' words of assurance to the woman ("your faith has healed you") are followed by the narrator's words ("And while he was still talking, people came...") as the scene shifts to the role of "those who came." This invites the audience to view these two scenes side by side. Visually, Rhoads shows Jairus's people coming toward Jesus/the narrator as he faces the woman. They go past Jesus/the narrator to Jairus ("crossing" Jesus both literally and figuratively) and, looking Jairus directly in the eye, tell him that his daughter is dead and, placing an arm around him as if to lead him away, instruct him to not bother the teacher any longer. Jesus counters their message by also looking Jairus directly in the eye and using the imperative: "Don't be afraid; only have faith."

Rhoads has done two things here. First, he has placed the woman and Jairus on either side of himself visually. This placement has the effect of creating a literal "on the one hand, on the other" comparison. Second, his use of direct eye contact with Jairus, both when he assumes the character of the "people from Jairus's house" and when he assumes the character of Jesus, emphasizes the choice that is being placed before Jairus: to "give in" or to "have faith." When Jesus arrives at Jairus's house and confronts the mourners, he brushes them aside dismissively (signaled also by a picking up of the pace) so that the emphasis falls on the restoration of Jairus's daughter, which is signaled by a slowing of pace, through a use of gesture to act out the approach of

---

22. Rhoads, *Reading Mark*, 181.

Jesus and raising of the girl, and through tone of voice and facial expression relating the joy and wonder of her restoration.

Ruge-Jones's performance differs most dramatically from Rhoads at two points in the structure of the story. The first is the central section of the story where the narratives of the woman and Jairus overlap. Like Rhoads, Ruge-Jones shows the woman coming up behind Jesus, but at the moment she touches Jesus he adds a sudden intake of breath, signaling that something has happened. Where Rhoads has the woman looking at Jesus when she says, "If I just touch his clothes…," Ruge-Jones has her looking in the direction of the audience with her eyes almost closed. This indicates that we are hearing the woman's internal thought, a thought we are told she has been repeating to herself over and over again. When the woman reveals herself to Jesus, Ruge-Jones's Jesus bends down and takes her hand in both of his. He continues to hold on to her hands when, as the narrator, he reports that people came from the house of Jairus. This has the effect of placing all of the characters on the stage in the same moment (in contrast to Rhoads, where the scenes are more sequential). In Ruge-Jones's performance, the encounter between Jairus and the people who have come from his house takes place behind Jesus, who is shown still holding the hand of the woman. When Jesus overhears their comments, he continues to hold on to the hand of the woman but stretches out a hand to prevent Jairus's departure, then, turning his face toward Jairus, says, "Do not be afraid." Before continuing, he turns again toward the woman, pats her hand, and, pointing to her, says, "trust courageously," as he looks again at Jairus. Finally, before turning from the woman to go with Jairus, he kisses the woman's hand. Like Rhoads, Ruge-Jones presents the scene in a way that invites comparison between the two characters, but the gestures, tone of voice, and the timing of the lines make it clear that the woman establishes a model of faith for Jairus to follow. This has the effect of eliminating any suspicion that the encounter between Jesus and the woman has caused the death of the child by delaying Jesus' progress toward the house.

The second point at which Ruge-Jones differs from Rhoads most significantly in terms of conflict is when Jesus enters the house of Jairus. Ruge-Jones delivers the line "and they mocked him" as if it is an affront. Jesus, in response, drives them out of the house with raised arms. Whereas Rhoads's Jesus dismissively brushes off their lack of faith, Ruge-Jones's Jesus views their lack of faith as an obstacle to Jairus's ability to hold on to faith and consequently an obstacle that needs to be removed. Once the obstacle is removed, Jesus then takes the mother and father of the girl each by hand, one on either side, and leads them into the room where the girl lies. In this way, Jesus literally leads them to face what they fear (their sleeping daughter) and to find their faith affirmed through her restoration.

Both Rhoads and Ruge-Jones minimize the tension created by Jesus' delay, focusing instead on the need for faith. Rhoads's performance identifies the primary point of conflict as the moment when the people from Jairus's house tell him not to trouble the teacher any longer. He does this by having both the people from Jairus's house and Jesus each occupy the same physical space in front of Jairus and look him directly in the eye as they speak their lines. Ruge-Jones sets the conflict up differently. He contrasts the faith of the woman with the lack of faith on the part of those who would have Jairus drop his petition. This is reiterated in Ruge-Jones's performance when he has Jesus drive the mourners who have mocked Jesus out of the house. Both performances remain true to the structure of the story and the essential conflict (faith versus lack of faith), but their differing presentations articulate it differently. What the performances share in common is making the source of the conflict character-driven: the "theme" may be healing or faith, but it is worked out in performance by the interaction between and reactions of the characters.

Both narrative criticism and performance criticism draw attention to how the social location of the reader/audience can contribute to the interpretation and experience of the conflict in the story. In a narrative-critical analysis, however, this involves a private interaction between the reader and the text. In a performance-critical analysis, the interaction takes place in a public context. It may be manifested in the "energy" of the audience (signaled through posture, gestures, or facial expressions) or even articulated through jeers, shouts of approval, or applause.

CHARACTER: NARRATIVE CRITICISM

In a narrative-critical analysis, characters are described largely in terms of what they say and do, how they interact with others, and what others say about them. Characters show little inclination toward introspection. Rather, it is their outward actions and words that reflect what is in their minds or hearts.[23] Readers can also play a role here, adding dimensions to the characters as they interact with and respond to the characters in their imaginations.[24] This is particularly true at the point at which readers compare and contrast the characters in terms of their status, behaviors, and responses. While the text can invite comparisons and contrasts between characters, how these are drawn out will depend much on the mind and context of the reader.

23. Rhoads, Dewey, and Michie, *Mark as Story*, 99.
24. Ibid., 102.

The story in Mark 5 has multiple characters: the narrator, Jesus, the crowd, Jairus, the woman, the disciples, people from Jairus's house, the mourners, and the little girl. In New Testament terms, a cast of thousands. For the purposes of analysis, some of these characters can be eliminated. The girl, for example, plays no active role in the story. The crowd, as has been shown, functions primarily as part of the spatial setting. The disciples and the mourners each play a supporting role; that is, they function as a foil for the character of Jesus. The people from Jairus's house move the story along and help to underscore the conflict in the narrative. The primary characters, then, are Jesus, Jairus, and the woman.[25]

Of these three characters, Jesus speaks the most. This alone lends authority to his character. "Authority" is given to his character also in how he speaks: he issues three commands and asks two direct questions. While those around him (the disciples, mourners, Jairus) are shown to be confused or in a state of dismay or chaos, Jesus is shown by his words to be consistently in charge (e.g., "Daughter, your faith has restored you"; "Don't be afraid"; "Why are you making a commotion and sobbing?"). This is underscored by his actions and in what the narrator tells us about him. Jesus knows that power has gone out of him and persists in seeking out who touched him, despite the crowds. He overhears what others say, he chooses who will accompany him, he prevents other people from following and drives still others out, he heals the girl and orders the parents to give her something to eat, and he commands those present to tell no one what has happened. Jesus' actions and words also show him to be one who has power not only to heal but to restore those who are dead to life. Moreover, he is shown to be someone who does this willingly, whether of his own volition (when he follows Jairus) or because this healing power is simply a part of who he is (when the woman draws power from him). Through his willingness to heal is also shown compassion. Jesus does not rebuke the woman for snatching healing from him, and he consistently encourages Jairus to continue holding on to faith. He is a character motivated by the desire to bring restoration.

Although Jairus is present throughout the story, he plays an active role in the story only at the beginning, when he approaches Jesus. Here we learn that Jairus is one of the leaders of the synagogue. Richard Horsley emphasizes that this does not mean he is a ruler of the Jews; rather, he is a community leader of a local Galilean village assembly.[26] This locates Jairus as a member of the community and a leader within it. Since it is a village context, it does not locate

---

25. The role of the narrator will be considered in the next section.
26. Horsley, *Hearing the Whole Story*, 211.

him as a member of the ruling elite.[27] He does have a wife and a house, but whether the people who come from the house are other villagers or servants is not clear. Apart from this, we learn two things about Jairus in the course of the story: in particular, that he falls at Jesus' feet and that he pleads for Jesus to lay hands on his daughter that she may be restored to life. These words and actions demonstrate Jairus's belief that Jesus can do these things as one who has both power and authority.

Jairus continues to be present in the story, yet he is never again mentioned by name, nor does he initiate action. Instead, he is approached by others. Each time he is referred to in the role that describes how he is viewed by those approaching him. He is referred to as the synagogue leader when approached by people coming from his house, and at the end of the story he is described as the father of the little child when Jesus leads him into the room where the girl lies. It is Jairus's desire for this very thing (that Jesus should come to where his daughter lies) that has motivated him.

The greatest amount of descriptive space is given to the nameless woman. Like Jairus, the woman is identified first by her "social location." In particular, she is noted as having a flow of blood for twelve years, suffering under the care of physicians to no avail, and having spent all she had seeking a cure. Whether the woman began with a large sum of money or a little, it is all gone, and she is no better. Unlike Jairus's daughter, she apparently lacks a relative to intercede on her behalf. Thus her situation appears hopeless. Having heard about Jesus, the woman acts on her own behalf. She approaches Jesus from behind and in the crowd. This indicates that she does not want to be noticed or to draw attention to herself. Her words tell us of her utter confidence in Jesus' power to restore her to health, so that she has need only to touch his garment in order to be healed. The narrator reports that "immediately" she was healed and that she "knew in her body" that she has been healed. This language is picked up in the very next line when the narrator reports that "immediately, Jesus knew in himself" (i.e., his own body) that power had gone out from him. We are told that when the woman "realized what had happened to her," she fell before Jesus with fear and trembling and told him "the whole truth." Her action echoes that of Jairus. However, where Jairus falls before Jesus to plead for healing, the woman falls before Jesus to tell him of how she has been healed. There are gaps in the story at this point. What did the woman realize: that she had been healed? that she had been found out? Further, what is the source of her fear? All we learn is that Jesus affirms her faith and tells her to depart in peace. At this point she disappears from the story.

---

27. Ibid.

There are a number of ways in which the woman and Jairus stand in contrast to one another in the story. He has a name, she does not; he has a title, she does not; he has a family, she does not; he approaches Jesus directly, she approaches Jesus under the cover of the crowd; Jairus asks for restoration on behalf of his daughter, the woman claims restoration for herself; the woman is fearful because she has been found out, Jairus risks becoming fearful/losing faith in Jesus. It is only with respect to the latter that the two characters are brought into direct comparison with one another. Yet the woman seems to serve as an example rather than a rebuke, since Jairus never actually loses faith. He is only shown experiencing obstacles that could potentially cause him to lose faith.

Comparisons and contrasts are also invited between the woman and the young girl. Both are nameless; both are female; one has been afflicted for twelve years, while the other has reached the age of twelve years. Whether the woman's "flow of blood" is related to menstruation or not is not entirely clear.[28] The issue is that she is bleeding to death. In contrast, the young girl has died at the age when she would begin menstruation, bleeding that signals her capacity to bear life.[29] In this way the story points to restoration at more than one level—not only the restoration of the two women, but a restoration that stops the flow of blood leading to death and restores the flow of blood leading to new life.[30]

CHARACTER: PERFORMANCE CRITICISM

In performance criticism, characters also are described in terms of what they say and do, but with a difference. In performance, the characters are embodied. Their interior thoughts and emotions are expressed through posture, gesture, tone of voice, and facial expression, as well as the way they interact with other characters. Thus we see and hear more than is revealed in the words of the story. The embodiment of the characters in the performer points to another difference from narrative criticism. In a narrative-critical analysis, the characters are re-created in the mind of the reader. In this way, they are an extension of the reader. In performance, the characters are embodied by an "other," the performer. Although the audience may identify with the characters, their embodiment by the storyteller establishes a certain distance between the characters and the audience.

---

28. Levine, "Discharging Responsibility," 70–87.
29. Horsley, *Hearing the Whole Story*, 106, 211–22.
30. Ibid.

Rhoads and Ruge-Jones, although working from the same text, embody the characters differently.[31] This is most apparent in their presentation of Jesus. Rhoads's Jesus speaks with a commanding voice. There is an authority in his tone of voice that inspires confidence both in what he says and does and in his person. When he drives out the mourners from Jairus's house, it is with a dismissive gesture, like pushing away flies. This, too, lends authority to Jesus. In contrast, the three times Jesus engages another character directly (the woman, Jairus, the little girl), Rhoads's Jesus looks directly at them and speaks directly to them. This introduces a sense of intimacy to these encounters and gives the impression that Jesus is fully focused in the moment on the particular individual. The tone of voice used in each encounter underscores this impression. With Jairus, Jesus firmly commands, "Don't become afraid," and with the woman, Jesus speaks in reassuring tones to quell her fears. To the little girl, he adopts a softer tone that one would use when speaking to a young child. Above all, Rhoads's Jesus is a figure who is in control and in whom the characters can confidently place their trust.

Ruge-Jones's Jesus is less formidable. He interacts more with the other characters. The crowds are visibly present around him (signaled by hand gestures), he bends over to embrace the hand of the woman, kissing it in departing, and he takes the mother and father each by hand and leads them to where the child lies. This gives an entirely different feel to Jesus. The emphasis here is less on Jesus' power and authority and more on his empathy and compassion. This comes across also in his tone of voice. When Ruge-Jones's Jesus tells Jairus not to be afraid, his tone of voice sounds less of a command and more of an encouragement. The power of this Jesus arises from his presence with people, in contrast to Rhoads's Jesus, who is more nearly a presence in their midst.

There are smaller yet notable differences also in the ways they present Jairus. Rhoads's Jairus has an air of desperation when he falls at Jesus feet. Ruge-Jones's Jairus assumes a posture more akin to petition. What sets them apart particularly is how other characters respond to each Jairus. In Rhoads's performance, the people from Jairus's house look Jairus straight in the eye with their news of his daughter's death. When they tell him not to trouble the teacher any longer, Rhoads uses the voice of someone who is taking control in order to the let the one who has been devastated fall apart. In Ruge-Jones's performance, the people from Jairus's house look down, not daring to look Jarius in the eye when they share the devastating news. When they tell

---

31. Comments about the embodiment of the narrator will be taken up in the next section.

Jairus not to trouble the teacher any longer, Ruge-Jones pauses before saying "teacher," as if to suggest that they are skeptical of whether Jesus is worthy of this title. Each of these portrayals has an effect on how we experience Jairus. In Rhoads's performance, he seems to be portrayed as a leader, someone you look in the eye and whose dignity must be protected. In Ruge-Jones's performance, we experience Jairus more as a father who has suffered a devastating loss. This is underscored in the final scene of the narrative, when Jesus takes Jairus by hand to lead him to the little girl. This plays to the vulnerable side of Jairus, since he has become almost like a child who can be led. In Rhoads's performance we are hardly aware of his presence at this point. The focus is instead wholly on Jesus and the girl.

Differences occur also in their presentation of the woman. In Rhoads's performance, the woman is visible only for a short time, when she reaches out to touch Jesus' garment (keeping her eyes on Jesus all the time) and when Jesus speaks to her. Rhoads's focus is on the intensity of the encounter—in particular, the way in which the woman is drawn to Jesus and his acknowledgement of her. He gives little indication of her physical being. In contrast, Ruge-Jones portrays the woman with a distinct physical presence. She has a slightly stooped posture and continuously massages her abdomen, not grabbing at it in pain, but gently rubbing it as if this gesture has become an unconscious response to her body. By holding on to her hand as the character Jesus, Ruge-Jones keeps the woman physically present far longer than Rhoads. When Jesus points to her with his hand as a model of faith, then kisses her hand, she is elevated in the eyes of the audience from a woman who has been healed to a character we should aspire to be like.[32]

Performance takes the characters and pumps life into them. In the story, they perform actions and speak, whereas in performance they wear clothes, take on stature, adopt characteristic gestures, facial expressions, and poses, react to other characters, and express their words with feeling. They take on a life that does not exist in the written word. They spring from the mind and body of the performer and are burnished in response to an audience.

NARRATOR: NARRATIVE CRITICISM

The "narrator" refers to the voice in the text that tells the story. Although the narrator occasionally speaks directly to the reader through asides, the narrator represents a presence that, for the most part, remains anonymous and

---

32. Since I discuss ways in which the characters are compared in the section on "conflict," I have omitted exploration of that dimension here.

invisible. Thus the narrator has no expressed identity or social location and is not bound by time or space.[33] Rhoads, Dewey, and Michie note that "this effacing of the narrator's identity and presence enables the narrator to assume a position of authority in relation to the story recounted.... Because the reader experiences the story as the narrator tells it, the reader too has the sense of being invisibly present to witness these events of the story world."[34]

In the story from Mark 5, the narrator leads readers through the events of the story (e.g., "and when Jesus had crossed..." and "one of the synagogue leaders came..."). The narrator also describes the individual scenes in the story, making them visible to readers (e.g., "and a huge crowd was following him and pressing him"). In this way, the narrator controls what the reader sees. The narrator also controls what readers know by providing them with selected information about the characters (e.g. "there was a woman who had had a flow of blood over the course of twelve years...") or filling in "gaps" in the reader's general knowledge by, for example, translating unfamiliar phrases for the reader ("'Talitha koum' [ταλιθα κουμ], which is translated 'Little girl, I tell you, rise'"). This underscores the omniscience of the narrator and the dependence of the readers on the narrator for their encounter with the world of the story.

Because readers experience the story through the voice and eyes of the narrator, the readers' response to the characters and events in the story is also shaped by the narrator. The narrator cultivates sympathy for Jairus by letting readers hear the voice of Jairus "pleading urgently" for his daughter who is near death. In contrast, the narrator cultivates sympathy for the woman by placing the lengthy description of her condition in the voice of a reliable narrator. If the woman's own voice were used at this point, her words could be dismissed as "whining" or self-serving. When readers do hear the woman's voice, it expresses her confidence in the power of Jesus to restore her. This leads readers to view the woman positively, a view that receives confirmation when the readers hear the voice of Jesus praise the woman for her faith.

The order in which events are narrated also shapes the response of readers. After Jesus praises the woman for her faith, which has resulted in her healing, readers hear the people from Jairus's house tell him, "Your daughter has died." Whereas the voice of Jairus's pleading for his daughter has, earlier in the story, aroused sympathy, readers have now seen and heard things that have altered their perspective (i.e., the healing of the woman). When Jesus challenges the words spoken by the people from Jairus's house ("Don't become

---

33. Rhoads, Dewey, and Michie, *Mark as Story,* 40.
34. Ibid., 40–41.

afraid. Only have faith."), readers know to place their confidence in Jesus. This sets the readers at odds with the perspective of the characters in the story, who jeer at Jesus when he tells them the girl is not dead but sleeping. When the perspective of the readers is vindicated as Jesus restores the girl to life, the readers' confidence in both Jesus and the narrator is increased.

Narrative criticism draws attention to the significant role the narrator plays in shaping readers' experience of the story. Because the narrator is invisible, it is easy for readers to miss the several ways in which the narrator is controlling the narrative, not only through what is said, but the order in which it is said and by whom. However, there is also much that the narrator does not do and that falls to the reader. For example, the narrator does not ascribe tone of voice, although this may be suggested by adjectives. The narrator also leaves many gaps in the narrative that readers may fill in, such as the physical characteristics of characters or the nature of the crowd. Thus there is a kind of dialogue that takes place between narrator and reader that results in the cumulative effect of reading.

NARRATOR: PERFORMANCE CRITICISM

Viewed through the lens of performance criticism, the narrator takes on a radically different role. Far from being a disembodied voice existing outside of time and space, in performance, the narrator becomes a particular body located in both time and space, taking on characteristics associated with age, gender, physical size and agility, quality of voice, and facial expression. In addition, the narrator may be identified with a particular social location, as revealed by dress, hair style, gestures, expressions, and accent or speech patterns. In performance, the story is enacted in and through the body of this particular narrator/performer. As Rhoads asserts, the performer becomes the medium.[35]

The physical presence of the narrator in performance produces at least three significant changes in how the audience experiences the story.[36] First, the physical presence of the narrator calls attention to when the characters in a story are actually "on stage" and when they are present only in the narration. If one were to hand out scripts to the primary characters in this story, they would be stunned to discover how much of the time they spend sitting on the sidelines waiting to make an appearance. Although Jesus is mentioned

---

35. Rhoads, *Reading Mark,* 182–83; idem, "Performance Criticism," 12.

36. For a more thorough discussion of the role of the narrator, see Philip Ruge-Jones, "Omnipresent, Not Omniscient: How Literary Interpretation Confuses the Storyteller's Narrating," in *Between Author and Audience in Mark: Narration, Characterization, Interpretation* (ed. Elizabeth Struthers Malbon; Sheffield: Sheffield Phoenix, 2009), 29–43.

in the first line of the story ("when Jesus had crossed in the boat"), follows Jairus after his plea for help, and is touched by the woman, he does not actually appear as a fully embodied character until he realizes power has gone out of him and turns around to discover who has touched him. This is the first time we hear his voice. In every other instance he exists only in the descriptive voice and body of the performer. Indeed, the two cannot be neatly separated. Rhoads, in his performance, tends to give the greatest presence to the narrator. Characters become visible only when they have lines to speak. It is, in this respect, the narrator's story. In contrast, Ruge-Jones gives far more presence to the characters through the way his narrator embodies the characters. Thus, when the narrator is describing characters, Ruge-Jones tends to take on the characteristics of the character in his body, thus blurring the line between narrator and character. This brings the audience into a closer relationship with the characters than in Rhoads's performance. In both cases, however, the audience experiences a far more conscious relationship with the narrator than a reader does.

This points to a second impact that results from the presence of a real-time narrator/performer: much of the interpretive process shifts from the reader to the performer. Gaps that are filled by the reader in narrative criticism are filled in instead by the performer. This is illustrated in the two performances examined here by the use of tone of voice. In the Ruge-Jones performance, the narrator's description of the woman is delivered in an empathetic voice that emphasizes the extent of her suffering. In the Rhoads's performance, an edge of disgust is added when speaking about the abuse she has suffered at the hands of physicians, which focuses attention on the inadequacy of the ancient medical profession. It also seems intended to appeal to similar experiences that the audience may have had with physicians. Both Rhoads and Ruge-Jones play the line spoken by the disciples ("You see the crowd pressing in around you and yet you ask 'Who touched me?'") as a laugh line by representing the disciples as "clueless." A reader might project a different tone of voice onto these lines, producing a different effect. Each of these moves is an interpretive move—one that is performed by the reader in narrative criticism but by the performer in performance criticism.

This, in turn, points to a third shift that is produced by the physical presence of the narrator. The narrator, now fully visible to the audience, must gain the trust of the audience. It is not, says Rhoads, a given.[37] Ruge-Jones describes this shift as a move from an omniscient narrator to one who is "an obser-

---

37. Rhoads, "Performance Criticism," 13.

vant, well-informed and trustworthy describer of the events she recounts."[38] Yet how is this trust to be earned? It is earned in part by the quality of the performance. Is the performer able to create an imaginative space in which the audience is willing to participate? (Rhoads invites the audience into a first-century context by wearing a robe and performing on a bare stage. Ruge-Jones performs in street clothes in a contemporary church sanctuary.) Does the performer represent the characters in a manner that the audience finds credible? Is the conflict presented in a way that is believable? In performance, the narrator is forced to engage the audience and to shape the performance to the particular audience in order to gain the audience's trust.[39] As Rhoads observes, this makes every performance unpredictable.[40]

There are, in addition, other factors involved that are closely tied to the physical presence and social location of the performer. Both Rhoads and Ruge-Jones, for example, are male. The woman, then, is filtered through a male presence in performance that may or may not be viewed as credible, depending on how the audience perceives the presentation. Both are also European-American and middle-class, as evidenced in their speech patterns and accents, as well as mannerisms and dress. Rhoads ponders to what degree his social location creates an obstacle for presenting the marginalized, peasant communities that are represented in the story world of Mark's Gospel.[41]

Both narrative criticism and performance criticism draw attention to the significant role the narrator plays in shaping the reader's experience of the story. However, interpretive moves that belong to the reader in narrative criticism are shown to be the prerogative of the performer when viewed through the lens of performance criticism, and they are filtered through the social location and physical presence of the performer (e.g., filling in of gaps through tone of voice, gestures, or facial expressions). Nonetheless, there is a dialogue between audience and performer that is not unlike the dialogue between nar-

---

38. Using a personal example, he describes how, when his son talks about a day at school, he describes not only the events of the day but what others thought or how they reacted. The source of his insight into their interior thoughts is revealed in the way he mimics their actions and facial expressions. He perceives these interior thoughts not because he is omniscient but because he is observant. His narration also involves reflection on past events, which contribute additional insights (Ruge-Jones, "Omnipresent, Not Omniscient," 38).

39. A distinction needs to be drawn here between a live audience and an implied audience. Rhoads's performance is before an implied audience; that is, no audience is physically present. Although it is a performance, it is similar to the situation envisioned by a written text because the audience Rhoads engages is in his imagination.

40. Rhoads, *Reading Mark*, 184.

41. Ibid., 182.

rator and reader. Yet this relationship is far more fluid because both performer and audience have active roles in the dialogue, whereas in narrative criticism the active role belongs to the reader.

FROM NARRATIVE TO PERFORMANCE CRITICISM

A narrative-critical analysis forms, in many respects, the basis for a performance-critical analysis of the text. Most important, it offers a first step in unpacking setting, conflict, character, and narrator. However, where a narrative-critical analysis focuses on a written text, a performance-critical analysis takes that same text and turns it into a hologram. By translating the story world into a physical setting located in time and space, performance criticism introduces an entirely new set of questions and concerns that the interpreter must address. Among these are the following:

- ► How would you block out the spatial setting of the story world in a performance space? What movements and gestures are needed to help the audience visualize the setting?

- ► What is the physical setting in which the storytelling performance will occur? What values and beliefs are reflected in this space? In what ways does the story provide commentary on the space? How does the space provide commentary on the story?

- ► In what ways do characters function as part of the physical setting? Who is present at any one point in the story? How is each character's presence signaled (e.g., through gesture, a glance, a line spoken, pauses)?

- ► How does the physical proximity of characters in the performance space contribute to our understanding of the relationship between the characters? How does it shape our response to the characters?

- ► How can tone of voice, gestures, posture, and facial expressions be used to draw attention to conflict in the story? How does the physical placement of characters in the performance space, and their movement relative to one another, draw attention to or introduce conflict in the story?

- ► Where are there "points of decision" in the story? How are these points enacted through gesture, tone of voice, pace, placement, and the interaction of the characters?

- ▶ Who are the characters in the story, and how are they embodied?

- ▶ How do the different characters relate to one another? How might this relationship be expressed physically?

- ▶ What is the narrator's age, gender, physical condition, and social location?

- ▶ To what degree and in what ways does the narrator interact with the audience?

- ▶ Who is the audience? What social customs, roles, and settings does the audience share with the story? What anachronistic perceptions might an audience project onto the story?

- ▶ As the narrator, how do you gain the trust of the audience?

- ▶ In what ways do you want the audience to be moved?

- ▶ To what degree do you play to the audience? At what point does playing to the audience compromise the values or beliefs that you are trying to communicate through performance?

These questions not only uncover new and unexplored dimensions of the story world; they also point to two distinctive contributions that performance criticism makes to the interpretive task. First, it reveals the degree to which the stories of the New Testament are character driven. This is revealed not only in what the characters say and do but in how they interact both verbally and spatially with one another and with the space they inhabit. It also pulls back the curtain to reveal that the narrator is not a disembodied voice that exists outside of time and space but an individual whose beliefs and values shape the world being set before the audience. Located in time and space, the narrator becomes an "other" whom the audience sees, engages, and evaluates. The second contribution is related. Because a performance-critical analysis presents the interaction between characters in time and space, it challenges us to engage the ethical issues that emerge in time and space not as abstract ideas but as issues that directly impact the lives of people in real time. There are no hypothetical situations in performance. Further, a performance-critical analysis forces the interpreter to engage an audience. In this way it presses us to see the ethical issues posed by the story in relationship to communities of people, not just individuals. It moves us out of isolation into relationship. We do not necessarily need to become performers to enjoy these benefits, but we do at least need to engage the questions that performance criticism sets before us.

In the Boat with Jesus: Imagining Ourselves in Mark's Story

Robert M. Fowler

It is a delight to contribute to a celebration of almost thirty years of *Mark as Story: An Introduction to the Narrative of a Gospel.*[1] When I pondered what I might contribute to the celebration, I thought of an exercise in collaborative interpretation of the Gospel of Mark that I often conduct in a college classroom. All students of Mark's Gospel are familiar with the three sea stories carefully positioned in Mark 4:35–41, 6:45–52, and 8:14–21. The first two of the three stories might be called "miracle stories," and in a classroom setting they can raise all of the predictable interpretive challenges associated with making sense of ancient miracle stories in the postmodern, high-tech world of the twenty-first century. For a number of years, I have invited students to join me in a thought experiment in which we pretend to be a Steven Spielberg or George Lucas-type filmmaker, with abundant imagination and unlimited special-effects budget with which to create films of the three sea stories. Contemporary students have little experience interpreting two-thousand-year-old miracle stories, and they certainly step into the classroom with little acquaintance with literary theory, but they have plenty of experience in watching and making sense of movies and television. However, even though they have encountered the grammar, syntax, and rhetoric of film their whole lives, they usually have little conscious awareness of how films are constructed in order to affect their audiences. Even so, again and again in our classroom discussions, students are easily able to exercise their imaginations to propose countless ingenious ways to film Mark's three sea stories. Invariably, we decide together that the filmmaker's camera must, sooner or later, place the audience

---

1. David Rhoads and Donald Michie, *Mark as Story: An Introduction to the Narrative of a Gospel* (Philadelphia: Fortress, 1982); David Rhoads, Joanna Dewey, and Donald Michie, *Mark as Story: An Introduction to the Narrative of a Gospel* (2nd ed.; Minneapolis: Fortress, 1999).

members "in the boat with Jesus." Concerns about the ostensible miraculousness of these stories fade from our minds as we imagine ourselves, perhaps quite surprisingly, in the thick of the action on the silver screen. Thinking together about how Mark's story might work as a film also helps us to understand better how Mark works as oral performance or written story. Thinking across the various media possibilities for telling, hearing, or seeing Mark's story helps us to appreciate with sharper awareness its overflow of narrative potential.

When I agreed to write this essay, immediately I reread *Mark as Story*, to refresh my memory of its contents. I was not at all surprised to rediscover what a thorough, solid survey of the basic features of Mark's story this book is. After all these years, *Mark as Story* holds up very well. One would still be hard pressed to find a better introduction to the narrative features of Mark's Gospel for beginning and intermediate students of the Gospel.

One thing I was surprised to rediscover in *Mark as Story* was all the references to film. All these years I have conducted my Spielberg/Lucas thought experiment in countless classrooms, and I had forgotten the frequency with which *Mark as Story* invokes exactly this kind of exercise of cinematic imagination. Indeed, as I read, I found eleven passages in which the terms "film," "camera," or "lens" are explicitly invoked. Several of these passages are extensive, and together they almost comprise an introductory essay on the similarities and differences between cinematic and other forms of storytelling:

> We have also been influenced by postmodern approaches, including various feminist, deconstructionist, and cultural interpretations. We have learned that every reading is a reading through a particular **lens**. (xi)[2]

> As a coherent narrative, Mark's Gospel presents us with a "story world," a world that engages and grips us, a world such as we experience when we get "lost" in reading a novel or watching a **film**.
>
> As a way to grasp the notion of a story world, recall the experience of seeing a **film**: The images and sounds on the screen draw us into another world, a world with its own imaginative past and future and its own universe of values. For a time, it seems as if we are no longer sitting in a movie theater or our own living room but are immersed in a different time and place, sharing the thoughts and emotions of the characters, undergoing the events they experience. In a sense, then, this story world has a life of its own, independent of the actual history on which the **film** might be based.

---

2. Page references are to Rhoads, Dewey, and Michie, *Mark as Story*. I use boldface to highlight film-related terms.

Clearly, we as viewers are engaging with a **film** through the filter of our own experiences, making our sense of this world as it unfolds before us. Nevertheless, depending on the power of the **film** and its relation to our lives, we may come away from the experience with a deeper understanding of life or a new sense of purpose or a renewed capacity for courage and creativity. We have entered another world, and it has changed us. Reading stories has the same power as seeing **films**, and in reading we participate even more fully, because as readers we ourselves visualize the world suggested by the words we read.

Thus, when we approach Mark as a work that creates a story world, we see that the statements in Mark's narrative refer to the people, places, and events *as portrayed in the story*. Just as a **film** may be a version of historical events, so also Mark is a version of historical events. Although Jesus, Herod, and the high priests were real people, they are, in Mark, nonetheless characters portrayed in a story. The desert, the synagogue, and Jerusalem are settings as depicted in the story world. The exorcisms, the journeys, the trial, and the execution are events depicted in the story world. It is this story world that readers enter. It is this story world that is the subject of our study. *Thus, unless otherwise identified as helpful background information from the general culture of the first century, all subsequent references to people, places, and events refer only to the story world inside Mark's narrative.* (4–5, italics original)

[Some] narrators are "third-person" narrators, unidentified voices who are in the narrative but external to the story, that is, a voice telling the story but not one of the characters in the story being told. The reader is not usually aware of such a third-person narrator any more than one is aware of a **movie camera** while watching a **film**, because the focus is not on the narrator but on the story. (39)

Such a situation creates tension and suspense, leading the reader to wonder: How will the authorities respond when they find out that Jesus acts as God's choice for the anointed one? Will the disciples ever figure out who Jesus is? And what will happen when they do? Hearing Mark's story for the first time is like watching a Hitchcock **film** in which the viewer is aware of a threatening situation at the opening of the **film**, then nervously watches the unsuspecting characters in the story become aware of the situation for themselves. (42–43)

The style of the Markan narrator is simple and direct, using ordinary language to tell this amazing story.... The narrator's style is also terse, using few words to suggest images and evoke pictures.... The style keeps the narration moving along, with occasional overviews, like long-distance shots in a **film**. Instead of "telling" about the story in generalities and abstractions, the narrator "shows" the events by a straightforward recounting of actions and dialogue. (46)

In this pattern of repetition ["sandwiched episodes"], two similar episodes are placed in juxtaposition with each other. One episode is "sandwiched" (as an interruption) between the beginning and ending of another episode. In **film**, a scene will change in the middle of the action, leaving the viewer in suspense, while the **camera** cuts to another scene. The **camera** will return to resolve the action begun in the initial scene, thus creating a frame around the middle story.... Such sandwiching of episodes occurs frequently in Mark's story. (51)

[S]ettings provide a world for the narration. Settings also present readers with a world to consider in their imagination. As with **film**, a spoken or written story draws readers into another time and place, into the possibilities and limitations of another way of viewing the world. Readers may emerge from the experience with some new ways of seeing their own world and a different sense of belonging in the world. (72)

Character analysis is really what we do all the time when we make judgments about people we meet or characters we encounter in a story or a **film**. In our study, we are only making explicit what tends to happen unconsciously as we size up other people and make decisions about them. We have simply tried to clarify some ways we look at characters before turning to the analysis of the characters themselves. (103)

You may have read a novel that kept you on pins and needles. To ask about the rhetoric of that story is to ask: How did the story do that to you? You may respond to a **film** with a softened heart toward people you had formerly condemned or with a sense of personal courage you did not know you had. To ask about the rhetoric of that **film** is to ask: How did the **film** lead you to react like that? Here we are asking about the rhetoric of Mark: What are the effects of Mark's story on the reader? How does the story work to create that effect? (137)

For those of us so used to stories with a resolution, it is tempting to dull the shock of this ending [of Mark's story] by adding in what we know from other Gospels or the history of the Christian movement. But imagine reading a story or seeing a **film** in which virtually everything is left up in the air, unresolved at the end. Mark's story is such a story: It is not resolved. It cries out for a resolution, cries out for the hope that someone will proclaim the good news. And who is left at the end of the story to do this? Not Jesus. Not the disciples. Not the women who fled the grave. Only the readers are left to complete the story! (143)

One way to help us to avoid reading our own selves into a story is to be aware of our limited and relative perspective. We cannot help bringing presuppositions to our reading experience. First, we bring the ideas and assumptions of our culture and society.... Second, we read from a particular social place within a culture, in terms of gender, race, social class, and so on. Third, we each come with personal experiences, as well as with our particular beliefs and ethical commitments. All these shape the way we read—how we see a story through the **lens** of our experience. (148)

I cannot remember when, where, or how I started to conduct my cinematic thought experiment in my classes, but I must surely have been inspired once upon a time by reading passages such as these in *Mark as Story*. However, the more I sort through the closet of memory, the less certain I am that this was actually so. Upon reflection, I can recall a number of experiences and influences through the years that might also have encouraged me in this classroom exercise. I will describe briefly some of these possible influences, before turning to the main task of this essay, a summary of some of the insights into the sea stories in Mark that have emerged from years of classroom conversation.

1. *Narratology.* For many years I applied to the Gospel of Mark a version of literary criticism known as "reader-response criticism."[3] Along with many other biblical scholars in the 1970s and 1980s who were promoting new literary approaches to the Bible, I found the work of "narratologists" (scholars who study how narrative works) to be of immense value. In particular, many of us were reading, among others, the work of Gérard Genette and Seymour Chatman.[4] In retrospect, I was always intrigued especially by Chatman's work, in part because he always took care to compare and contrast the workings of narrative in different media, especially film. I can no longer recall how much of Chatman's reflections of cinematic storytelling seeped into my own comprehension of how Mark's Gospel operates as story.

---

3. Robert M. Fowler, *Loaves and Fishes: The Function of the Feeding Stories in the Gospel of Mark* (SBLDS 54; Atlanta: Scholars Press, 1981); idem, *Let the Reader Understand: Reader-Response Criticism and the Gospel of Mark* (Minneapolis: Fortress, 1991; repr., Philadelphia: Trinity Press International, 2001); idem, "Reader-Response Criticism: Figuring Mark's Reader," in *Mark and Method: New Approaches in Biblical Studies* (2nd ed.; ed. Janice Capel Anderson and Stephen D. Moore; Minneapolis: Fortress, 2008), 59–93.

4. Gérard Genette, *Narrative Discourse: An Essay in Method* (trans. Jonathan Culler; Ithaca, N.Y.: Cornell University Press, 1979); Seymour Chatman, *Story and Discourse: Narrative Structure in Fiction and Film* (Ithaca, N.Y.: Cornell University Press, 1978); idem, *Coming to Terms: The Rhetoric of Narrative in Fiction and Film* (Ithaca, N.Y.: Cornell University Press, 1990).

2. Biblical scholars engaged in film criticism. I should make clear that I do not regard myself as an expert in film—I am a mere amateur—however, many of my colleagues in biblical studies are genuine experts in the interdisciplinary study of Bible and film. I think especially of the work of George Aichele, Adele Reinhartz, Bernard Brandon Scott, Jeff Staley, Barnes Tatum, William Telford, and Richard Walsh.[5] I have no doubt learned more than I realize from these individuals over many years.

3. Academic seminars in professional organizations. For many years I was an active participant in the Bible in Ancient and Modern Media Section of the Society of Biblical Literature, including a number of years serving as co-chair of BAMM with my colleague, Art Dewey. Since its origin in 1983, BAMM has provided an important (and often, in the early days, the only) venue in which the entire sweep of the media history of the Bible could be explored within the SBL, from ancient oral cultures to the emerging electronic age.[6] Sessions on Bible and film are now common within SBL, but back in the early days of BAMM, ours were often the only such sessions included in the schedule of the SBL Annual Meeting. Most, if not all, of the biblical scholars involved in film studies that I have named in this essay have made valuable presentations in those BAMM sessions on the Bible and film.

The study of Bible and film has even found an occasional foothold in the rather more traditional and international Studiorum Novi Testamenti Societas. From 2003 through 2008, I was co-chair, along with Birger Olsson and Werner Kelber, of an SNTS seminar on "The Bible in History and Culture." Here, too, our scope was wide-ranging, and over the course of five years we

---

5. George Aichele and Richard Walsh, eds., *Screening Scripture: Intertextual Connections Between Scripture and Film* (Harrisburg, Pa.: Trinity Press International, 2002); Adele Reinhartz, *Scripture on the Silver Screen* (Louisville: Westminster John Knox, 2003); idem, *Jesus of Hollywood* (Oxford: Oxford University Press, 2007); Bernard Brandon Scott, *Hollywood Dreams and Biblical Stories* (Minneapolis: Fortress, 1994); Jeffrey L. Staley and Richard Walsh, *Jesus, the Gospels, and Cinematic Imagination: A Handbook to Jesus on DVD* (Louisville: Westminster John Knox, 2007); W. Barnes Tatum, *Jesus at the Movies: A Guide to the First Hundred Years* (rev. ed.; Santa Rosa, Calif.: Polebridge, 2004); Eric S. Christianson, Peter Francis, and William R. Telford, eds., *Cinéma Divinité: Religion, Theology and the Bible in Film* (London: SCM, 2005); Richard G. Walsh, *Reading the Gospels in the Dark: Portrayals of Jesus in Film* (Harrisburg, Pa.: Trinity Press International, 2003).

6. For a variety of retrospective insights into the history of BAMM, including my own cursory sketch of the media history of the Bible, see Holly Hearon and Phil Ruge-Jones, eds., *The Bible in Ancient and Modern Media: Essays in Honor of Thomas Boomershine* (Eugene, Ore.: Wipf & Stock, 2009). My own essay in that volume is entitled "Why Everything We Know about the Bible Is Wrong: Lessons from the Media History of the Bible," 3–18.

managed to devote several sessions to the reception of the New Testament in film.

4. *Film production projects.* My interests in the narrative features of the Gospels and the media history of the Bible led to two invitations to participate as a scholar-consultant in projects where portions of the Bible were actually turned into film. One of these was the "New Media Project" of the American Bible Society.[7] From the late 1980s to the late 1990s, the New Media Project produced six videos of Gospel stories, as well as CD-ROMs and an extensive website. Ambitious in its vision and scope, ABS brought together biblical scholars, translators, artists, musicians, filmmakers, and many others in a collaborative, pioneering effort to "transmediate" the Bible "from one medium to another."[8] In spite of the many successes of the effort, regrettably, the American Bible Society decided to end the project in the late 1990s, and few traces of the project and its creations remain on the ABS website.

After my involvement in the ABS project ended, I had another brief fling with Bible movie-making. This was with the Visual Bible International, Inc. Here again I joined a team of biblical scholar-consultants, but this time with a commercial company that had undertaken a somewhat grandiose scheme to film whole books of the Bible. They were just finishing their first film, *The Gospel of John*, when I came on board, and my wife and I attended the premiere of the John film at the Toronto Film Festival in September 2003. I had been recruited to join the scholarly advisory team because I was reputed to be an expert on the Gospel of Mark, which was to be their next film project. This project also, like the ABS New Media Project, was intended to be a collaborative effort, involving scholar-consultants along with the rest of the creative team, from beginning to end. This project also ended suddenly and sadly. On Ash Wednesday of 2004, Mel Gibson's film, *The Passion of the Christ,* was released, and any excitement that had been generated for *The Gospel of John* was quickly drowned by the tsunami of popular acclaim for Gibson's film. That, combined with massive debts accumulated by VBI, followed later by charges of fraud

---

7. For an account of this work, see Paul A. Soukup, "Transforming the Sacred: The American Bible Society New Media Translation Project," *Journal of Media and Religion* 3.2 (2004): 101–18.

8. Several collections of essays were produced by the scholars involved in the ABS New Media Project, including: Paul A. Soukup and Robert Hodgson, eds., *From One Medium to Another: Communicating the Bible through Multimedia* (Kansas City: Sheed & Ward, 1997); idem, *Fidelity and Translation: Communicating the Bible in New Media* (Franklin, Wis.: Sheed & Ward; New York: American Bible Society, 1999); Robert M. Fowler, Edith Blumhofer, and Fernando Segovia, eds., *New Paradigms in Bible Study: The Bible in the Third Millennium* (London: T&T Clark, 2004).

against the producers, led to the bankruptcy and demise of VBI. The Mark film project to which I had hoped to contribute never materialized.

To summarize thus far, I must reiterate that I make no pretense of being an expert on film in general or on the Bible and film in particular. But as I reflect back over the past thirty years or so, it certainly appears that I have rubbed elbows with many scholars who do have such expertise, and I have managed to stumble my way into situations where serious, talented people worked hard to imagine how ancient biblical texts might be transformed into the new media of our day, including the medium of film. It is little wonder that at this point I cannot begin to reconstruct what might have led me to start my classroom exercise about filming the Markan sea stories. The inspiration for it might have come from any number of sources mentioned above, including *Mark as Story*. One thing is for certain: if anyone wishes to pursue the study of Bible and film, or to launch a Bible and film production company, there is an abundance of material, both in print and in film, available to guide the way, as well as a number of savvy individuals who have a great deal of experience in a host of relevant creative fields.

Now, at last, we turn to the main event of this essay, a report on my class-room thought experiment in which my students and I brainstorm about how we might film the three sea stories in Mark 4:35–41, 6:45–52, and 8:14–21. With each story I will quote the text first, using the New Revised Standard Version, then describe briefly how the classroom conversation often proceeds.

> Mark 4:35–36 On that day, when evening had come, he said to them, "Let us go across to the other side." And leaving the crowd behind, they took him with them in the boat, just as he was …

To make sense of these verses, we need to look backward to what has preceded in Mark 4. Jesus has been sitting in a boat, on the Sea of Galilee, teaching a crowd gathered on the shore, ever since Mark 4:1. "Just as he was" is a reminder to the audience of Mark's story that Jesus is already in the boat, on the lake, as the sea story in 4:35–41 gets under way. "On that day, when evening had come" also makes clear that verses 35–41 continue the episode begun in 4:1–34. This already presents a serious challenge to anyone attempt-ing to film the three sea stories. However much biblical scholars or preachers have been inclined to examine each episode in Mark (or in any of the Gospels) as distinct, independent "pericopes," the reality is that Mark as storyteller has often gone out of his way to connect one episode with another, sometimes in close proximity to each other, but sometimes leaping over many chapters to make connections. Anyone attempting to film the three sea stories *only* faces a dilemma, because it would be difficult at many points to film the three sea stories without also filming the other, surrounding episodes that are in fact intertwined with them.

In our filmmaking thought experiment, the question I pose most often to my students is, "How would you position the camera to film this moment?" Clearly many options would be available to allow the movie audience to see Jesus sitting in the boat,[9] presumably very near the shoreline, at first teaching the crowd, but then at last pulling away from the shore, in order to proceed "to the other side." One camera shot could adopt the perspective of the crowd on the shore, watching the boat pull away as it moves farther out on the lake. Another shot could be from the perspective of Jesus and the disciples in the boat, watching the crowd and shoreline recede into the distance. Still another shot could be from the side, allowing the audience to watch a growing gap between the crowd on the shore and the boat on the water.

Seldom do we have opportunity in class to discuss adequately settings, costumes, casting, music, and the like, but on occasion I can sneak in some consideration of these. For example, regarding setting, having seen the Sea of Galilee (or Lake Kinneret) in person, I happen to know it is a small fresh-water lake, nowhere near the size of Lake Erie, one of the Great Lakes shared by the United States and Canada. Lake Erie is quite familiar to all of my students in northeast Ohio. When one stands on the shore of Lake Erie at Cleveland, Ohio, one cannot see the opposite shore, which is Ontario, Canada, roughly 50 miles away. By contrast, the Sea of Galilee is only 13 miles long from north to south, and only 8 miles wide from east to west, and it is surrounded by hills, so there is no place to stand on its shores where one would not see the opposite shore. I confess to students that if I see a Jesus film and its lakeshore scenes do not show hills on the horizon, then I cease to think about the story that is being presented to me, and I instead begin to wonder where on earth the scene was shot: on the Mediterranean somewhere? the Atlantic? Surely not Lake Erie? As filmmakers, will we strive for verisimilitude in our choice of a setting to represent the Lake Kinneret shoreline, or will we settle for any shoreline anywhere in the world? Computer-generated graphics would allow us, I suppose, to create whatever horizon we might want our audience to see. Certainly computer-generated special effects might come in handy once the action gets lively out in the middle of the lake.

Also, seldom do I have the time to raise the question about what actors we would want to cast for our film, but it is at least fun to ask at this point how many actors we are going to put in the boat. Presumably Jesus is in the

---

9. Jesus is sitting in the boat in Mark 4:1, so I assume he is still sitting in 4:36. But that is an assumption.

boat with his "disciples" (*mathētai*, μαθηταί), because they were mentioned explicitly off and on through 4:1–34, especially in verse 34. But are all twelve of them in the boat with Jesus in 4:35–41? Mark does not say, so it is entirely up to the filmmaker to make the crucial decision. Here is an example of something that can be left unstated in an oral or written story, and thus left totally up to the imagination of the audience member, but in the cinematic retelling of the story one must decide precisely how many people are going to be in the boat. Are we to imagine thirteen men together in one small fishing boat? Once again, is verisimilitude desirable?

In the mid-1980s, a drought lowered the water level of Lake Kinneret, resulting in a remarkable archaeological discovery of a two-thousand-year-old fishing boat.[10] With great ingenuity, the boat was rescued and preserved. As best the experts can tell, it is indeed approximately two thousand years old, and thus it dates roughly to the days of Jesus. There is no way to tell, of course, whether Jesus and friends were ever in the boat, but it seems reasonable to guess that the Gospels refer to boats very much like this one. At 26.5 feet long, 7.5 feet wide, and 4.5 deep, it is conceivable that thirteen men could have been accommodated in the boat, but that seems like a very tight squeeze to this landlubber, especially if the weather was threatening. Again, it would be the filmmaker's prerogative whether to aim for historical verisimilitude or not in the choice of the boat. Filmmakers have to make myriad decisions about what their audiences will see and hear in the movie theater, decisions that oral or literary storytellers can leave entirely up to the imaginations of their hearers.

Back to the question of the camera, we also cannot help but ask a few questions about lighting for the camera. After all, the first two of the three sea stories explicitly take place at night ("when evening had come"; "when evening came"; "the fourth watch of the night" [King James Version]), so it must be dark, especially if the weather is understood to be windy. (Does that also imply stormy? cloudy?) I remind students that countless television and movie scenes purport to show incidents in the darkness of night, yet lighting solutions are always available. Enough light from some source must be provided to allow the camera to show the audience what is going on!

Mark 4:36 … Other boats were with him.

This is a throwaway line in Mark: nothing has been said before about these other boats, and nothing is said about them afterward, so I throw up my

---

10. Shelley Wachsmann, "The Galilee Boat—2,000-Year-Old Hull Recovered Intact," *BAR* 14.5 (1988): 18–33.

hands and ask, "What are you going to do with these other boats? Since Mark himself does nothing with them, shall we just eliminate from the script?" That certainly seems a reasonable choice. But if you do want to include them, how would you handle them? Do you want to have them floating along with the Jesus boat, as Jesus and crew float away from the shore? Would you have them still accompanying the Jesus boat out in the middle of the lake, once the storm is raging? Filmmaker's choice.[11]

> Mark 4:37 A great windstorm arose, and the waves beat into the boat, so that the boat was already being swamped.

At last the filmmaker's imagination is invited to throw off all shackles; here almost anything goes. We would surely want a camera shot from within the boat, showing the waves beating into it, but there is no end to the possibilities for how we might shoot the boat from the outside looking in, seeing it tossed up and down in the waves. An unlimited special-effects budget would be especially useful in creating computer-generated images of the windstorm in the middle of the lake, in the middle of the night. If the boat is being swamped, that must mean it is in danger of sinking. On a lake, in the dark, in a fierce windstorm, with waves pounding into the boat, all lives are in peril.

> Mark 4:38 But he was in the stern, asleep on the cushion; and they woke him up and said to him, "Teacher, do you not care that we are perishing?"

Mark has given us a script that allows us wide latitude to choose camera angles up until this moment, but it is easy to secure agreement from my collaborators that in verse 38 we definitely need the camera in the boat, so we can have a close-up shot of Jesus asleep in the stern. Even as the boat is in danger of sinking, even as all on board are threatened with drowning ("we are perishing"), Jesus is sleeping through it all! I ask, "Shall we have the waves splashing over Jesus' slumbering body? How about water inside the boat lapping into his mouth or his ears?" At the risk of dominating the discussion momentarily, I always insist that we must not only show Jesus sleeping; we must also have him snoring![12]

---

11. Both Matthew and Luke choose to omit Mark's reference to other boats in their artistic retelling of Mark's story (Matt 8:23–27; Luke 8:22–25), so it is clear that they decided to throw away Mark's throwaway line.

12. In discussing this passage, Adela Yarbro Collins observes that in the Greek Septuagint version of the Jonah story, unlike the Hebrew Masoretic Text, Jonah is said not only to have been sleeping below decks, in the hold of the ship, but was also snoring! (Jonah

It is also good fun to ask my student filmmakers what they would like to do with the cushion on which Jesus slumbers. Since we are usually using a Gospel synopsis in my classes, it is easy to point out that Matthew and Luke both choose to throw the cushion overboard, omitting it from their revisions of Mark's story (Matt 8:23–23; Luke 8:22–25). Did Matthew and Luke merely find the cushion to be irrelevant and therefore expendable, or was there something offensive about the idea of Jesus not only sleeping but sleeping comfortably on some sort of cushion, while hardy fishermen were panic-stricken? This is neither the first nor the last time in filming Mark's sea stories where comprehending what Mark is doing goes hand in hand with comprehending what the other Gospel writers are doing in their own versions of the same story—more interpretive complications for budding filmmakers.

> Mark 4:39 He woke up and rebuked the wind, and said to the sea, "Peace! Be still!" Then the wind ceased, and there was a dead calm.

Obviously, the filmmaker, perhaps in collaboration with the special-effects expert, would have countless possibilities for how to put before the audience's eyes the "miracle" of calming wind and wave. I am more interested, however, in the mundane question of the manner in which Jesus awakes. Mark does not give us many clues in his script. Does Jesus spring spritely to his feet and into action, or does he rise slowly, groggily, perhaps stretching and yawning before addressing wind and wave? I am pretty sure his "rebuke" should be sharp and loud, because I assume that the storm is noisy (another perennial question for the filmmaker: what sound effects should the audience hear?), and the word for "rebuke" in Greek (epitimaō, ἐπιτιμάω) is the same word commonly used in exorcism stories,[13] which I take to be fairly boisterous episodes.

> Mark 4:40–41 He said to them, "Why are you afraid? Have you still no faith?" And they were filled with great awe and said to one another, "Who then is this, that even the wind and the sea obey him?"

I have long loved the unanswered, "rhetorical" questions in Mark. Long ago I sat down to work carefully through Mark, attempting to identify every

---

1:5; Adela Yarbro Collins, *Mark: A Commentary* [Hermeneia; Minneapolis: Fortress, 2007], 260). I cannot remember whether I knew this once upon a time and incorporated that feature into my own personal visualization of Mark 4:38 or whether I accidentally stumbled upon the idea on my own. Regardless, I would insist on snoring in our film of Mark 4:35–41, to demonstrate to the audience how imperturbable Jesus is.

13. See especially Mark 1:25; 3:12; 9:25; a surprising double "exorcism" might also be implied by the use of *epitimaō* (ἐπιτιμάω) in Mark 8:30, 32, 33.

question in the story. The best count I could come up with was approximately 116 questions, many of them posed within the story without any explicit answer provided.[14] In most instances, however, it is not too difficult to draw illuminating inferences from even unanswered questions. At this point I like to jump back to verse 38 and ask my students what the disciples' unanswered question there reveals about what they are thinking. "If the disciples ask, 'Do you not care?' then what must they be thinking about Jesus?" "That he doesn't care," is the usual reply. Exactly so.

Then we move on to the unanswered questions in verses 40–41. From 4:40 it is not too difficult to elicit the inference that, one, Jesus thinks the disciples are afraid and that, two, he thinks they lack faith (or trust, courage, or confidence).[15] At this point I make a confession to my students: I find it very easy, personally, to identify with the disciples' terror, as well as with their bewilderment over Jesus' apparent lack of concern. (How can anyone sleep through a raging storm in a small boat, as the boat is about to go down?) I find the disciples' terror and their frustration with Jesus entirely believable and reasonable; I can imagine myself behaving in exactly the same manner.[16]

At the end of the episode, the biggest question of all is the final unanswered question: "Who then is this, that even the wind and the sea obey him?"

---

14. Fowler, *Let the Reader Understand*, 126 and *passim*. Identifying the precise number of questions in the text of Mark is impossible, because of the nature of Mark's Greek. For one thing, Mark likes to use double questions (see Mark 4:40) or single questions with multiple parts (see Mark 4:41), which makes enumerating the questions a challenge. Also, in Greek, as in other languages, the wording of a declarative sentence can often also work as the wording of a question and vice versa. If only we could hear Mark's tone of voice, so we could determine whether he was intending certain utterances to be statements or questions (198).

15. If there is time, this is an opportune moment to discuss how, for Mark, fear and faith are opposites. Most of my students first arrive in my classroom assuming from their Christian upbringing that faith (*pistis*, πίστις) is synonymous with belief, the opposite of which would be doubt. But if the absence of faith is fear, as seems to be the case for Mark, then faith is better understood as trust, courage, or confidence (see also Mark 5:36; cf. 6:50).

16. I can imagine the disciples screaming something like this to Jesus: "How can you sleep through this? Why don't you wake up and die with us?" I doubt that they are waking Jesus in order to have him save them, because I doubt that they think he can! Since no words like these are given to us in Mark's script, however, I am a little reluctant to insert them into my hypothetical film script, even though I think they would be a defensible interpretation of the disciples' frame of mind. Also, if time permits in class, I have two anecdotes from my youth that I can share about being in small boats, once on a lake and once on a river, in the pitch-blackness of night. In neither case was there a storm, which was just as well, since I was already scared to death.

Working backward from the question to the thinking that must have led to it, it is not too difficult to surmise that the disciples do not understand who Jesus is! And this comes at the end of chapter 4 of Mark's Gospel, approximately one-quarter of the way through the Gospel. The disciples have been called by Jesus to accompany him in all that he does, and they have witnessed his exorcisms, healings, and authoritative teaching, yet they do not know who he is? Apparently so. However, three-quarters of the Gospel remains to be told by the storyteller and experienced by the audience, so maybe we will have a chance to watch the disciples grow in understanding.

Bringing this part of our exercise to a close, I usually gain easy agreement from my collaborators that the camera had better be inside the boat most of time, at least once we are past 4:37. In short, in most of Mark's first sea story, the movie camera has got to put us, the audience, in the boat together with Jesus and the disciples. Speaking only for myself, I find it quite easy to identify with the disciples in this episode. Everything they say and do I find quite understandable and defensible in the situation portrayed by the storyteller, at least up to their final unanswered question. But I am willing to give them the benefit of the doubt on the "Who is this?" question, since I know that so much of Mark's story lies yet ahead. I may think that I have begun to understand Mark's Jesus fairly well by the time we reach 4:41, but if the disciples need more time to figure things out, surely we can allow them that courtesy, can't we?

> Mark 6:45–46 Immediately he made his disciples get into the boat and go on ahead to the other side, to Bethsaida, while he dismissed the crowd. After saying farewell to them, he went up on the mountain to pray.

Here we begin the second sea story, and just as with the first, we open with an allusion backward to the preceding episode in Mark, in this case the feeding of the five thousand (Mark 6:30–44). (Once more, our new sea story is explicitly linked by the storyteller to other, surrounding episodes. Once more, does it make sense to attempt to film this episode without also filming these other episodes?) In the feeding story, Jesus had fed a remarkably large crowd of "five thousand men,"[17] and now he dismisses the crowd, while simultaneously sending the disciples out onto the lake in the boat, while he remains alone on the shore, even climbing a mountain. This is a very busy scene for a filmmaker,

---

17. Oddly enough, it is indeed "men" or "males" (*andres*, ἄνδρες). Luke and John keep the "men" in their versions of the story, but they soften Mark's precise head count to an approximate ("about") five thousand. Matthew heightens the magnitude of the miracle by adding "women and children" to the "men" (Luke 9:14; John 6:10; Matt 14:21).

with countless possibilities and challenges for choosing settings and deciding upon the movements of the actors. But one thing is certain: whereas in the prior sea story Jesus and the disciples were in the boat together from beginning to end, in the second sea story we begin the episode with Jesus on the shore and the disciples in the boat, out on the lake. This multiplies greatly the possibilities for how to orchestrate the action that follows.

> Mark 6:47–48 When evening came, the boat was out on the sea, and he was alone on the land. When he saw that they were straining at the oars against an adverse wind …

First of all, it is evening once again, so this is another sea story that needs to play out in the dark. Once again, the filmmaker faces decisions about lighting, camera angles, and special effects, in order to allow the audience to "see in the dark." Possibilities for lighting and camera positions are endless in order to show the audience the boat out on the lake—never mind that at night no one can see far! Similarly, it is up to the filmmaker's imagination to decide how to allow the audience to experience Jesus "alone on the land." No other character in the story is with him on the land, yet through the magic of the movie camera, we are there, too.

With verse 48, cinematic options are necessarily narrowed when the camera must make the audience see specifically what Jesus saw. This is crucial: we see along with Jesus, as it were, that the disciples are "straining at the oars against an adverse wind." Once again, as in the earlier sea story, the wind is blowing, the going is rough, and the boaters are presumably in danger. We see this all from Jesus' perspective, not from the disciples' perspective. The camera might be positioned alongside of Jesus on the shore, or it might be positioned behind him (my favorite suggestion), peeking over his shoulder to let us experience the exact same angle of vision that he has with which to see the struggling boaters.

> Mark 6:48 … he came towards them early in the morning, walking on the sea.

Here is perhaps the greatest cinematic challenge of all in this thought experiment: how to film Jesus walking on the water. Before tackling that, however, let us be clear about the time of night: "early in the morning" is literally the "fourth watch of the night," which most scholars agree is from 3:00 AM to 6:00 AM.[18] Thus, it is in the dead of night, with near zero visibility, presumably. On a clear, still, moonlit night, I suppose one might see a little way

---

18. Yarbro Collins, *Mark*, 333.

across a lake, but once again, in my world windy nights are often also cloudy nights, so the persnickety interpreter might well wonder how anyone could see anything at all under such circumstances. Here we must suspend our disbelief and allow the storyteller to tell his story the way it suits him. Even so, it presents a technical challenge to a filmmaker: how to film a night scene so that the audience can see perfectly well what is going on. With the right lighting techniques, computer-generated special effects, or film-editing techniques, this technical problem in filmmaking is easily solved.

Now we come to the walking on the water itself. When I ask students where they would place the camera to film this, often they want to jump immediately into the boat with the disciples and have the camera show the audience what the disciples see from the boat: Jesus walking toward us, across the water. I resist this suggestion and urge patience. Putting the camera in the boat might be the right move to make in verses 49–50, but I suggest that it is premature here in verse 48. Let us consider other possibilities, I suggest, before putting the camera in the boat and allowing the audience to see what the disciples see.

So disallowing a camera in the boat, for now, what are the other options? The options are virtually unlimited, as a few minutes of thought quickly reveal. As Jesus begins his walk across the water, toward the boat, the camera could be placed anywhere between the shore and the boat. Students dream up intriguing solutions, such as camera shots taken from jet skis or helicopters! Again, with an unlimited special-effects budget, almost anything is possible. But sooner or later, either the students or I will suggest that Jesus' walk on the water begins from the shore, so surely we must have at least a few seconds showing Jesus step off of the land and onto the water. (More suspension of disbelief: people do not walk on Lake Erie, at Cleveland Harbor, but in the world of Mark's story someone unquestionably does walk on water, so all reservations and misgivings about the possibility or impossibility of water-walking must be set aside, for the purposes of filming this scene. Thus does a biblical scholar avoid a lot of arguments in the classroom about whether "miracles" are possible or not!) Just as we might have placed a camera behind Jesus, looking out onto the lake, while he was still on the shore, I will always insist to students that a camera has to be placed on or near the body of the actor playing Jesus, as he steps out onto the lake. The storyteller makes it emphatically clear in his story that Jesus is walking on the water, and somehow the camera has got to make that a tangible experience for the audience. In other words, thanks to the magic of the movie camera, we get to join Jesus in his walk across the water![19]

---

19. There is no way to prove this, but I suspect that Matthew had this same insight

Mark 6:48 … He intended to pass them by.

How does one film intention, which most of us probably take to be an interior and therefore invisible state of mind? There are ways to attempt to achieve this: have Jesus trudge resolutely past the boat, not even glancing at it, perhaps with a stern look on his face and his eyes fixed on the distant horizon? Students invariably ask, "*Why* does he want to pass them by?" I have to confess to them that I do not have a great answer, and I tell them that this is the kind of interpretive puzzle into which scholars love to sink their teeth. I offer the possibility that the "passing by" of Jesus in Mark 6:48 is reminiscent of theophanies in the Hebrew Bible, where God "passes by" Moses or Elijah, granting them a glimpse of divine glory.[20] Perhaps Jesus thinks that putting on a display of his (divine?) power ought to be enough to encourage and therefore rescue the struggling boaters. Perhaps he thinks that such a display ought to suffice to remind the disciples of the positive outcome of the earlier incident on the lake. But Mark does not explain Jesus' intention. Once more, a sideways glance at other Gospels is instructive: Matthew drops this statement from his revision of Mark, and it is also missing from the water-walking story in John's Gospel (Matt 14:22–34; John 6:16–21).[21] In their Gospel scripts, these two storytellers omit any mention of intention, and we might decide to do the same in our Mark film.

One thing is clear: regardless of *why* he is doing it, we know without question *that* he is doing it. It is *Jesus* who intends to pass them by. We do not understand fully what he is thinking, but we are allowed into his mind to at least a degree, just as we also experience vicariously what his body is doing as it walks on the water. Through the magic of the camera, both our bodies and our minds are invited to imagine what Jesus is experiencing.

Mark 6:49–50 But when they saw him walking on the sea, they thought it was a ghost and cried out; for they all saw him and were terrified …

I probably spoke too hastily above, when I said that filming the water-walking is the greatest cinematic challenge in this episode. Mark 6:49–50 is

---

when he inserted the verses about Peter walking on the water with Jesus in his revision of the Markan story (Matt 14:22–23). Peter walks with Jesus on the water in Matthew just as the audience walks with Jesus on the water in Mark.

20. Yarbro Collins, *Mark*, 334.

21. As is well-known to Gospel scholars, Luke's Gospel does not contain the walking on the water, because it falls within Luke's "Great Omission," the apparent deletion of Mark 6:45–8:26 from Luke's revision of Mark's story.

surely a greater challenge still, because it is essentially impossible to film! From Mark 6:45 up until now, the focus of the story has been upon the actions, perceptions, and intentions of Jesus: *he* made his disciples get into the boat; *he* dismissed the crowd; *he* said farewell to the crowd; *he* climbed the mountain; *he* was alone on the land; *he* saw that the boaters were struggling against the wind; *he* came walking toward them on the water; *he* intended to pass them by; and, finally, they saw *him*. Whether we are experiencing an oral, written, or cinematic presentation of Mark's story, the story makes it unmistakably clear to the audience that it is *Jesus* who is doing all of these things and it is *Jesus* whom the disciples see. At the same time, however, the story also makes clear to the audience that the disciples do not grasp that it is Jesus who is walking on the water. Instead, they think it is a ghost. So how would we film this moment? Certainly, the camera must be placed in the boat at last, because finally we are being given the disciples' perceptual point of view. The camera must allow us to see what the disciples see, but at the same time we cannot join them in their misperception of what it is they are seeing. We in the film audience know too much already: we know without any doubt whatsoever that it is *Jesus* walking on the water, not a ghost. So how *do* we film this? I am not sure that there is a good solution, but that does not prevent my collaborators and me from trying. Some suggest that the figure on the lake should be a gauzy white blob, thereby trying to represent visually the disciples' misperception. [22] But playing devil's advocate, I counter that idea with the suggestion that the figure walking on the water ought to be shown with crystal clarity, because, after all, we know it is Jesus, don't we? It is certainly a challenge to put something on the silver screen that is simultaneously crystal clear to the audience but hopelessly incomprehensible to the characters in the film. An ambiguity that may work just fine in an oral or written story may be virtually impossible to put on film.

---

22. For a fascinating discussion of ancient beliefs about ghosts in connection with this episode, see Jason Robert Combs, "A Ghost on the Water? Understanding an Absurdity in Mark 6:49–50," *JBL* 127 (2008): 345–58: "contrary to some depictions in modern media, in antiquity it was believed that ghosts did not glow; therefore, a minute amount of light was required for them to be seen. Rather than luminescent, ghosts are described as being as pale as death or as black as ash, having the image of their mortal body either in life or often at the time of their gruesome death" (351–52). As interesting as it is to consider ancient views on ghosts, in filming this episode for a twenty-first-century audience we should probably give primary consideration to what a contemporary audience would think a ghost should look like. (Hence, glowing?) As always, the filmmaker may have to choose between, on the one hand, striving for fidelity to the ancient perspectives of the original storyteller and, on the other hand, creating a cinematic version of the story that can be understood by a contemporary audience. It would do little good to film a ghost so that an ancient person would recognize it as such but a contemporary person would not.

Turning to the disciples' terror in verse 50, a rich vein for conversation in my classroom exercise is the consideration of the many ways in which the first sea story is echoed in the second. For example, the first sea story ends with the disciples' haunting question: "Who then is this, that even the wind and the sea obey him?" In the second sea story, Jesus once again displays his mastery over wind and wave, and once again the disciples do not comprehend. But whereas in the first sea story I am willing to confess to my students that I find it easy to identify with the fear of the disciples, in the second I find it impossible to join the disciples in their terror at the sighting of the apparition that approaches them. The camera may put me in the boat along with the disciples, offering me their perceptual point of view, but I know from the steady drum beat of masculine pronouns in Mark 6:45–52 that it is *Jesus* who approaches on the water. Moreover, I also recall Jesus' mastery over wind and wave back in Mark 4:35–41. Even if we decided to film the "ghost" (*phantasma, φάντασμα*) in verse 49 as gauzy white blob, that would not fool me for one second. I would still know that this is *Jesus* who approaches, and I would be confident that all will be well for the struggling boaters. Jesus saved their lives (saving, so to speak, the audience as well) once before on the lake, and I suspect that he is about to do so again.

> Mark 6:50–51 … But immediately he spoke to them and said, "Take heart, it is I; do not be afraid." Then he got into the boat with them and the wind ceased.…

Here the rescue at sea is accomplished, just as the audience must surely have anticipated. Once again, echoing the earlier episode, Jesus speaks to the disciples' fear, bidding them to take courage (*tharseō, θαρσέω*). The average student in my classroom will think little of the "it is I" comment, so I have to decide whether I want to provide some historical and literary background at this point. The Greek here (*egō eimi, ἐγώ εἰμι*) is in fact often a potent formula of divine self-revelation, regularly used by Greek-speaking gods and goddesses in the ancient world to reveal their majestic glory to their devotees. Once the Hebrew scriptures were translated into Greek, the God of Israel at times also reveals himself by using the *egō eimi* formula.[23] This observation lends support to the inference back in verse 48 that Jesus is performing some sort of theophany.

The struggle of the boaters does not actually end until Jesus enters the boat in verse 51. It is at that moment that the storyteller explicitly states that the wind ceases, thus ending the problem originally observed by Jesus (and

---

23. Yarbro Collins, *Mark*, 334–35.

the audience) from the shore, back in verse 48. Apparently, when Jesus is in the boat (with us), all will be well, no matter how severe the threat is from wind or wave.

> Mark 6:51–52 ... And they were utterly astounded, for they did not understand about the loaves, but their hearts were hardened.

Surprisingly, even with the calming of the wind we are not through dealing with the fear and incomprehension on the part of the disciples. First, we are told that the disciples were "utterly astounded."[24] This should not be too hard to film. Whatever directorial instructions for displaying fear and amazement we have previously made to the actors playing the disciples should work again here. But then verse 52 becomes a huge challenge to film, because it is a psychological "inside view" into the disciples' minds.[25] Inside views are easy to offer or to receive in oral or written storytelling; they are much harder to handle in cinematic storytelling, unless the filmmaker chooses to record a narrator's voiceover or decides to let us "overhear" what people are thinking, as they are thinking it. But since the disciples say nothing at this point, it is not even clear that they themselves are conscious of what they are thinking, nor is it likely that they grasp the aspects of what it is that they do not understand! It is entirely thanks to the storyteller that the audience of Mark's story is made to know that the disciples do not comprehend (the loaves!), because their hearts were hardened (in modern parlance, their "minds were closed"). Strangely, the storyteller links their lack of insight and amazement in the water-walking episode to a different episode, the feeding of the multitude that preceded the water walking. Nothing explicit was said in the feeding incident about the disciples not understanding it—we had to wait until 6:52 to be told that, and then it is verbalized only by the storyteller, not by the disciples themselves. Apparently, in the mind of the storyteller, we will not understand the sea story unless we understand what happened previously in the feeding story, and neither will we understand the feeding story until we have encountered all of the sea story. As we have seen before, to film 6:45–52 thoughtfully we should anguish over the question of whether we actually need to film other episodes as well, in order that this episode might make sense. To put it another way, Mark 6:52 wields two episodes together almost as one. What appears to the eyes of a modern scholar to be two episodes may, in the mind of the ancient

---

24. The Greek is redundant (or "pleonastic," in scholarly jargon) in order to emphasize the severity of the disciples' bewilderment. Yarbro Collins (*Mark*, 317) translates the phrase thus: "they were very, exceedingly amazed within themselves."

25. Fowler, *Let the Reader Understand*, 97, 123–24.

storyteller, have just been one. It is we who fail to see the extent to which Mark has connected his episodes, and it is we who have created our own interpretive problem by attempting too often to disconnect them!

> Mark 8:14 Now the disciples had forgotten to bring any bread; and they had only one loaf with them in the boat.

Here begins the third sea story in Mark, the third and final time in Mark that Jesus and the disciples (and therefore the audience) are together in a boat. Unlike the two prior sea stories, however, this one does not hinge upon danger at night from wind and wave. Rather, the supposed problem this time is the disciples' lack of bread ("only one loaf"), which echoes two previous episodes in Mark in which the disciples had only a few loaves of bread on hand. The first of these episodes was the feeding of the five thousand in Mark 6:30–44 (see esp. 6:38), and the second was yet another feeding story, the feeding of the four thousand in Mark 8:1–10 (see esp. 8:5). Mark's third in-the-boat-with-Jesus story is thus also his third disciples-fret-about-lack-of bread story.[26] We have already raised the question about whether the first feeding story needs to be filmed, in order to make the second sea story understandable to the audience. Now we need to ask if the second feeding story also needs to be filmed, so that the third sea story will make sense!

By plunging us immediately into the question of the bread, the storyteller bypasses all of the preliminary considerations about who is on the shore and who is in the boat that we encountered in the earlier sea stories. Again, this time there is no storm on the lake. The only storm, we might say, takes place entirely inside the boat, in the form of a fierce confrontation that erupts between Jesus and the disciples.[27] Since every bit of this episode transpires, not as action but as dialogue within the boat, that is where the camera will need to be positioned, throughout the scene.

> Mark 8:15–17 And he cautioned them, saying, "Watch out—beware of the yeast of the Pharisees and the yeast of Herod." They said to one another, "It is because we have no bread." And becoming aware of it, Jesus said to them, "Why are you talking about having no bread?"

The disciples fret about having little bread on hand, and Jesus seems to follow suit by talking about "yeast" or "leaven," with which bread may be made.

---

26. I have been thinking about the interplay of all of these episodes for many years; see Fowler, *Loaves and Fishes*.

27. Ibid., 145.

That may be all we need to know about "yeast" in order to film this scene, but it would greatly enrich the audience's experience if the audience knew that leaven is a symbol of moral corruption throughout the Bible.[28] Thus, "yeast" or, better, "leaven" is probably intended by the storyteller to be an image of sharp negativity.

Regardless of what the audience may know about ancient attitudes toward leaven, clearly the Pharisees and Herod are sharply negative characters in Mark's story. The audience has known since Mark 3:6 that the Pharisees and Herodians are conspiring to kill Jesus, so do we now need to film Mark 3:1–6 also, in order that the third sea story might make sense to the audience? Is the leaven of the Pharisees and the leaven of Herod an allusion to the ongoing threat against Jesus' life in Mark's story?

That "leaven" in verse 15 is not literal language, but instead a metaphor, is not difficult to discern. For one thing, nowhere in Mark's story are the Pharisees or the Herodian faction ever shown busily baking bread. Presumably, therefore, their bread-baking practices are not the real issue at hand. Furthermore, when the disciples do take literally Jesus' leaven language ("it is because we have no bread"), Jesus directly challenges them ("Why are you talking about having no bread?"). Without question, therefore, the storyteller has put us in the realm of metaphor and not literal language. This is a crucial insight to have at the beginning of the episode, as a frustrated Jesus is about to hurl a series of devastating metaphors, one after another, at our companions in the boat.

> Mark 8:17–18 … Do you still not perceive or understand? Are your hearts hardened? Do you have eyes, and fail to see? Do you have ears, and fail to hear?

Reminiscent of the multiple unanswered questions in the first sea story, we have here also one unanswered question after another. And just as we gained experience earlier in working backward from unanswered questions to the thoughts that must have given rise to them, so also here it is not too difficult to draw inferences from Jesus' questions. Do the disciples not perceive or understand? They may be able to perceive at the basic level of biological sense perception, but if the question is really whether they understand or not, then the answer can only be no. The audience member may remember the storyteller's comment back in Mark 6:52, where it was stated explicitly that the disciples did not understand the walking on the water because they did not

---

28. Bernard Brandon Scott, *Re-imagine the World: An Introduction to the Parables of Jesus* (Santa Rosa, Calif.: Polebridge, 2001), 24–27.

understand the feeding of the five thousand. Are the disciples' hearts hard-ened? Again, in Mark 6:52 the storyteller told us emphatically that this was so, using exactly the same language. Do they have eyes, but do not really "see" and ears but do not really "hear"? Without doubt, it is as if the disciples in Mark's story are habitually "blind" and "deaf." Consistently, Mark has portrayed for us their total lack of comprehension of anything that has happened to them in the company of Jesus.

The two metaphors of blindness and deafness are especially interesting because Jesus is portrayed in Mark's story healing one deaf mute (7:31–37) and two blind men (8:22–26; 10:46–52). The episode of the healing of the deaf mute occurs just a little bit before the third sea story in Mark, and the first healing of a blind man comes immediately after the third sea story. While the deafness in Mark 7:31–37 and the blindness in 8:22–26 appear to be literal, in the world of Mark's story, the use of deafness and blindness as metaphors in the storyteller's language in 8:14–21 makes me wonder whether the storyteller is opening the door just a little, inviting his audience members to think meta-phorically even when a story's language at first appears to be literal.[29]

If time allows, a rich conversation may take place in the classroom about the use of metaphor and other nonliteral language by this storyteller and other biblical authors. This is a conversation that needs far more class time than we ever have available. One of my persistent challenges as a teacher is how to get literal-minded students to awaken to the importance and richness of nonliteral (figurative, symbolic, poetic) language. I am convinced that, if we are able to step through the storyteller's magical portal leading us to the land of metaphor, wonderful new worlds may open before us. My challenge is to persuade students to join me in stepping through that portal.

> Mark 8:18–20 "And do you not remember? When I broke the five loaves for the five thousand, how many baskets full of broken pieces did you collect?" They said to him, "Twelve." "And the seven for the four thousand, how many baskets full of broken pieces did you collect?" And they said to him, "Seven."

---

29. Mark has also signaled that "seeing" and "hearing" may be taken metaphorically back in Mark 4:12, where Isa 6:9–10 is quoted: "for those outside, everything comes in parables; in order that 'they may indeed look, but not perceive, and may indeed listen, but not understand; so that they may not turn again and be forgiven.'" Mark 4:12 is a difficult verse to interpret, because in it Jesus seems to be talking about "outsiders," and we may still regard the disciples as "insiders" at this point in the story. But when we arrive at Mark 8:18, there can be little doubt that the disciples have shown themselves to be "blind" and "deaf." These "insiders" have turned out to be "outsiders" after all.

Jesus' questions continue, and now he focuses on the two feeding stories. Once again, to make sense of the third sea story, apparently we also need to comprehend the two feeding incidents. Once again, we have to consider the possibility that filming the three sea stories will not make sense to the audience unless we also film the two feeding stories.

Even though it is well established that the disciples do not understand Jesus, have hardened hearts, and neither "see" nor "hear" what Jesus has done, apparently they can count to twelve! They recall that, after the feeding of the five thousand, twelve baskets full of leftovers were collected, and seven baskets of leftovers after the feeding of the four thousand. As we sit in the boat with them, it is interesting for us to hear them say this, because they made no such comment in the feeding incidents themselves. In fact, one of the most extraordinary features of the two feeding stories in Mark is that no one in the stories—neither Jesus, nor the disciples, nor the crowds—makes any comment about how astonishing the feedings were. Now, later, in the boat with Jesus for one last time, we learn at last that the disciples were at least able to count the baskets full of leftovers in both incidents. But even though they could count to twelve, apparently they could not put two and two together to conclude that anything out of the ordinary had happened! Yes, they can count to twelve, but Jesus' questions lead us to infer that he suspects that they really do not understand at all; their hearts are hardened; they are both "blind" and "deaf." The disciples twice provided loaves and fishes out of their own supplies, twice distributed them to the crowd, and twice collected the leftovers—and the best they can do is to count to twelve?

Mark 8:21 Then he said to them, "Do you not yet understand?"

With this anticlimactic verse, our third sea story and our filmmaking experiment end. Is there any doubt about the implied answer to Jesus' final question? That is easy to answer. However, the more thoughtful students will ask, "*What* were they supposed to understand but did not?" That is not so easy to answer.

One of the dangers of highlighting the three sea stories in Mark, two of which are "miracle" stories, is that one runs the risk of implying to one's film audience that, to understand Jesus correctly, one simply needs to grasp that he possessed miracle-working power. I think it is rather clear in Mark that the disciples largely do not comprehend Jesus' "deeds of power" (*dunameis*, δυνάμεις), but I think it is also clear that deeds of power are not the totality of what Jesus is about in Mark's Gospel. Indeed, it is widely recognized that, when we arrive at the second half of Mark's Gospel, the wonder-worker of the first half of the story gives way to the suffering Son of Man who renounces power and authority and who advocates being least of all, even slave of all. If we insist on understanding Jesus as miracle worker par excellence, based largely on Mark 1–8, we run the risk of losing the self-sacrificing servant of all, based largely on Mark 8–16. In short, when students ask me what it was that the disciples did not understand in 8:21, I tell them honestly that I am not entirely sure. I do not think it is possible for us to understand fully what the disciples do not understand.[30] From our three boat trips with them and Jesus, we have surely come to understand a lot, and at times in those stories we definitely understand more than the disciples, but here at Mark 8:21 we might be wise to consider that we still have a lot to learn about Jesus, as do the disciples.

To summarize, I find this exercise to be a valuable way to lure students into thinking seriously about how stories work as stories. Few of my students have any experience in reading and interpreting ancient texts, but they have abundant experience in viewing television and movies, so their experience with more familiar forms of storytelling can be enlisted to help them to begin to make sense of less familiar forms of storytelling. Whether we are encountering ancient religious texts or contemporary secular films, the mental discipline of critical examination of storytelling needs to be encouraged and taught—it does not come naturally to anyone. Also, thinking together collaboratively about how we might put a portion of Mark's story on film is a valuable way to promote reflection on the differences in storytelling possibilities between various media. In an ever-increasing multimedia world, we all need to develop skills in "transmediation," the ability to translate "from one medium to another."

Finally, one exegetical lesson about Mark's story that can be learned from this exercise is the extent to which these three episodes are connected, not only with each other, but also with the other episodes in Mark's story that are interspersed amongst the three sea stories. For example, can we legitimately film the first sea story without also filming Jesus teaching from the boat in Mark 4:1–34? The linkages between the three sea stories and the two feeding stories are also strong and clear: Does it make sense to film the sea stories apart from the feeding stories? What about the linkage between the Pharisees and Herodians in 8:14 and 3:6? Or the possibility that the metaphorical "blindness" and "deafness" of the disciples in 8:14–21 is meant to be linked in the mind of the audience members with other, surrounding episodes ostensibly involving literal blindness or deafness? The list could go on and on. In

---

30. Fowler, *Let the Reader Understand*, 146. What it is exactly that the disciples ought to understand about Jesus in Mark 8:14–21 (and often elsewhere in the Gospel) often lies behind a veil of opacity (209–20).

light of these connections and echoes within Mark's story, it is interesting to observe how some scholars persist in attempting to identify and isolate two parallel pre-Markan cycles of miracle stories that they think lie behind Mark 4–8.[31] This effort attempts to disconnect not only one sea story from another but also one feeding story from another, and maybe one healing story from another, and so on, typically breaking these matched pairs of stories apart and putting them into separate cycles of stories that Mark supposedly inherited from his predecessors. Such an effort effectively severs the ties that bind together many of the episodes in Mark 4–8. Why any of us persist in ignoring or negating Mark's narrative skill in explicitly linking one episode to another baffles me. What Mark the storyteller has joined together, let no filmmaker or biblical scholar put asunder!

---

31. For example, Yarbro Collins (*Mark*, 91 and *passim*) embraces without discussion the hypothesis advanced by Paul Achtemeier that Mark incorporated two already-existing, parallel cycles of miracle stories into his composition of Mark 4–8. See Paul J. Achtemeier, "Toward the Isolation of Pre-Markan Miracle Catenae," *JBL* 89 (1970): 265–91; idem, "The Origin and Function of the Pre-Markan Miracle Catenae," *JBL* 91 (1972): 198–221. Actually, a number of such reconstructions of supposed pre-Markan cycles of miracle stories have been proposed for many years. Besides Achtemeier's hypothesis, there are also the reconstructions proposed by Luke H. Jenkins, Vincent Taylor, Leander Keck, Rudolf Pesch, and Heinz-Wolfgang Kuhn. Once upon a time I examined all of these proposals and found them all to be problematic (Fowler, *Loaves and Fishes*, 5–31). In general, the matched pairs or triplets of episodes in Mark should be credited to the storyteller Mark, and not to hypothetical pre-Markan storytellers.

Reflections

David Rhoads, Joanna Dewey, and Donald Michie

We express our gratitude for the leadership of Chris Skinner and Kelly Iverson in generating this volume, inviting the contributors to participate, and bringing it to publication. Writing essays and editing books are no mean feats, so we are grateful for the time, thoughtfulness, and creativity that have gone into this volume. We are fortunate to have been among the many voices in the movement that began to analyze the Gospels as narrative. Like most of the authors who have contributed here, we believe narrative criticism has been one of those paradigm shifts in biblical studies that opened up new avenues of creativity and exploration and that contributed to further streams of change. It is a privilege to have our efforts in this movement honored by many of the very colleagues with whom we were together on that journey. This book is about narrative criticism. It honors all the contributors for their efforts to bring forth something new and to celebrate it decades from its inception.

We offer our reflections in three parts. The first part involves anecdotal reflections on the ways we came to contribute to the narrative-critical movement in terms of the evolution of the first and second editions of *Mark as Story*. In the second part, we express appreciation for the essays in this book in terms of the strengths and limitations of the discipline of narrative criticism in its diverse expressions. In the third section, we share some of our current ideas about narrative criticism as it relates to the interpretation of the Gospel of Mark.

Part 1: Retrospect

First Edition

Dave: The occasions that led to *Mark as Story* happened rather by chance in the mid-1970s. Every student at Carthage College had to take a required New Testament introduction course. Every semester, I taught two sections of about forty students each. Most students took it only because it was required; they were not enamored with learning the New Testament. I loved teaching and was experimenting with new possibilities to engage the students. I was somewhat bored with the redaction-critical approach to the Gospels, which had been in favor during the years of my training. Students could be shown how scholars used redaction criticism, but it was not easy for them to do it, and there was almost no payoff for their lives or for a deeper understanding either of first-century society or our own culture. I wanted the students to be able to do things on their own, and I wanted it to be meaningful.

I had met Don Michie in the English department. We met frequently over lunch for a number of conversations. I was fascinated by interdisciplinary scholarship and teaching. He is a master teacher, and I was learning a lot from these discussions. When I shared with him my frustrations about teaching the Gospels, Mark in particular, Don suggested to me that I teach it as a short story. I was intrigued and responded, "So would you be willing to come to my class and show us how to read Mark as you would read a short story?"

Don: Initially, I did not think the Bible would lend itself particularly well to a literary analysis. I had been trained in formalism, and my proficiency was the interpretation of a story or novel or play as a closed universe. However, when I started work on the Gospel of Mark the night before the class, I was amazed. I was fascinated by the unity and coherence of Mark, seeing patterns and motifs and connections in the text, how the characters of Jesus and the disciples were gradually revealed through what they say, what they do, and what the author and other characters say about them, positively and negatively. I told Dave that I stayed up all night reading and interpreting the text. I could not put it down. I kept saying to myself, "This man is a genius." Based on all my work with Mark through the years, I consider Mark to be perhaps the most tightly written story I have ever read.

I began the class by pointing out how the story started in the midst of things with no preliminaries, how Jesus seemed to have a plan but often had to improvise and adapt when the crowds or the authorities or people without faith thwarted his efforts to bring the power of God to them. I described specifically some traits of Jesus' character, such as being "crotchety" with the disciples. I also explained how Jesus throughout was limited and contingent in his actions and especially in relation to his death. Jesus was human. He could not choose not to die. All of these insights helped me to demonstrate the suspense in the story and to point out some of the twists and turns in the plot.

Dave: When Don appeared for my class, I had no idea what to expect. When he proceeded to share his insights with us, I was stunned by his approach. I was bowled over by what he said and how he looked at Mark.

We may take these things for granted now, but at that time I had never heard anyone talk about Mark or any Gospel this way. I had a thousand questions.

Don and I started having many conversations about narrative. I had so much to unlearn from my training and so much new to learn in narrative studies. I had to make the shift from fragmentation to unity, from the historical world to the narrative world, from the author putting a text together to the audience experiencing it as a story, and much more. Don and I had opportunities to team-teach together in contemporary literature, making use of narrative analysis of plot and characters and settings. I began to change my teaching patterns to involve exercises that compared the characters and plots of the four Gospels rather than using the Synoptic parallels. Pretty soon, we hatched the idea of writing a book for our students that would enable them to see how the Gospels work as stories. So we began writing.

On my first sabbatical at the end of the 1970s, I spent most of my time in the bowels of Duke University library trying to get up to speed on secular literary criticism. As a result of this research, I presented a paper in the final year of the SBL Markan Seminar on "Narrative Criticism and the Gospel of Mark," which basically outlined the approach that would become the book. What we were moving toward was a comprehensive approach for interpreting Mark as a narrative and for understanding the narrative as a whole.

Don: In writing the book, several goals governed our thinking. First, we wanted the book to be brief enough and adequately accessible to first-year college students, the students we expected most to be reading the book. Second, rather than argue for the legitimacy of the approach, we wanted to show people what this approach was like and what its payoffs in understanding might be. Third, we wanted to make it transparent so that people who read it would say, "Why, of course, that makes perfect sense." Finally, we wrote with the idea that scholars in biblical and literary fields would be reading over our shoulders and the shoulders of their students. To make the broadest reach to biblical scholars, it made sense to provide a book they might use in their teaching. Then they would be inclined to read it!

At the same time, in addition to the innovative nature of the approach itself, we took some other risks. For example, Dave made a new translation that reflected the literary patterns of Mark's narrative. This was pretty much a word-for-word translation, because we were both eager to demonstrate the many levels of interconnections in Mark's Greek that were not apparent in other translations. Further, we were eager to choose words that were fresh and that had not been overlaid with later theology used in religious contexts. In addition, we produced a translation with no chapters and verses, because we wanted to set it out like a short story with paragraphs that reflected the dialogue and the plot developments and with no breaks between sections or subtitles of episodes. In addition, this meant that we would not use chapter and verse references in the analysis of the Gospel throughout the book. People did not have information to look something up. There was no index of passages. People would have to search through the Gospel to find the reference. We decided that this is exactly how short stories are analyzed in literature. So why not here? In all of it, we had great delight and excitement that we were putting things together in a way that had not been done before.

Another anecdote to add to this process: I was concerned about what scholars in secular literary criticism might think about someone in literary studies writing a narrative analysis of a book of the Bible. My advisor Stan Henning at the University of Wisconsin in Madison, a formidable literary scholar in his own right, would be the acid test for me. Hesitantly, I shared a rough copy of the text with him and awaited his response. His response to me was remarkable. "This is a good little book. In fact, it's a book I wish I had written myself." His reaction was a significant affirmation for the two of us. About that time, literary critics were already beginning to take an active interest in writing about biblical narrative, critics such as Robert Alter and, later, Meir Sternberg and Frank Kermode.

Dave: several other factors contributed to our work. First of all, many parallel developments were taking place in the Society of Biblical Literature. In the SBL Markan Seminar, the work of Norman Perrin and Werner Kelber had been leading the seminar in the direction of treating the Gospel of Mark as a narrative. Many there began writing papers, publishing articles, and working on books that dealt with some aspect of the literary qualities of Mark and other Gospels: Tom Boomershine, Bob Tannehill, Alan Culpepper, Joanna Dewey, Norman Petersen, Mary Ann Tolbert, Robert Fowler, among others. Conversations and feedback came from many friends: Joanna, Tom, Alan, Bob, Mary Ann, and Vernon Robbins. Several dissertations were written on different features of Mark's story. Don and I benefited from all these developments.

Another factor fed into our work. In the late 1970s, I heard about Alec McGown, a British actor who was performing the King James Version of the Gospel of Mark in major theaters in the U.K. and the U.S. to rave reviews. I believed that I, too, could memorize and perform Mark and that I would have the advantage of performing a literary translation Don and I had been working on for the book. I figured there would be no better way to demonstrate to our students that Mark was a story, and a very good one, than to give them the experience of hearing the entire Gospel as a performance. Since that time, I have performed Mark over three hundred times for various audiences. It would be hard to overestimate how much my memorizing and performing of Mark has affected my grasp of Mark's Gospel as a story. Clearly, performance showed me precisely how deep and profound are the integrity and power of Mark's story.

Don and I were both astounded—and pleased—at the popularity of the book. I learned that many of my colleagues were using the book in their classes. Many Ph.D. students said they were using the book in their work. However, as Chris Skinner noted, there was resistance among some scholars to the idea that one could read the Gospels as one would read Shakespeare's plays, as one scholar put it. Many scholars had and still have legitimate critiques and caveats about our work and about narrative criticism in general. Nevertheless, our colleagues who were doing work in this area welcomed it as supportive of their own endeavors, and over the next decade, because of the appearance of many works by other scholars, both on Mark and on the other Gospels, the movement became and has remained a standard approach in biblical studies.

Second Edition

Dave: Through the first decade, the book continued in print, sold mostly for classes in college and seminary. By the mid-1990s, I was beginning to feel somewhat self-conscious about the book. A lot of work had been done on Mark since that time. Some of my own ideas about the Gospel of Mark and about narrative analysis had changed and become more refined. So I wondered about doing a new edition. I was then teaching at the Lutheran School of Theology at Chicago, and I was eager to revise *Mark as Story* to be current for seminary students. So I began work on a second edition. At this point, however, Don had become Dean of the College at Carthage, and his wife Mary Alyce had a very serious illness. There was no way he was going to be able to participate in this round.

Asking Joanna to join me as co-author of the second edition was an easy decision that grew quite naturally out of our relationship. I knew that Joanna—as a feminist, a Markan scholar, and a literary critic—would bring many insights to a new edition that I did not have to offer. Joanna and I had been good friends since the days of the Markan Seminar in the 1970s. We had a tradition of lengthy meals together at SBL meetings and had made a covenant to read and react to drafts of each other's articles, papers, and manuscripts. I had already solicited her help in developing a draft of the second edition, and I was overjoyed when she agreed to become co-author.

Joanna: It was also natural for me to join formally with David for the second edition. I was already spending hours on the manuscript, and I knew that our overall approaches to Mark were similar. Working with Dave is always a pleasure. Everything was up for grabs in the second edition. We basically revised everything. We scoured all the new secondary literature for insights. We made all new analyses of each aspect of Mark's story. To work through the material together, Dave visited me in Cambridge and I visited him in Racine. We did *New York Times* Sunday crossword puzzles for breaks. We had numerous and lengthy phone conferences, and, of course, we used email. By the time we were done, it would have been hard for either one of us to determine to whom any one of the points or paragraphs belonged. It was truly a joint effort.

We had different points of view as we went along and agreed that if we could not work them through we would just say, "One of us thinks this, and the other thinks that." Dave was more insistent on letting the text transform us; as a feminist, I was rather more resistant to the text—I wanted the reader to judge the text as well. In this regard, our approaches complemented each other well. Our major point of contention was over the meaning and status of the death of Jesus. I wanted to avoid any hint of exalting suffering. Yes, suffering happens as the result of persecution and must be endured; however, it is not a value in itself. Dave agreed wholeheartedly but was still not sure that was what Mark was saying. After many conversations about various Markan passages, we came to an understanding of Jesus' execution that we both could live with. The key for us was this: when Mark says, "he came ... to serve and to give his life a ransom for many," we came to understand that the life he gave referred to "his whole life" in service, as the Markan two-step repetition ("serve," "give his life") would suggest.

Dave: In the second edition, we lost some of the brevity and simplicity of the first edition. We hoped that the changes would make it worthwhile and not discourage use in the classroom. We changed the literary framework of the first edition, expanded the methodological sections of each chapter, deepened the analysis of all of it with greater detail and insight, added material on the implied rhetorical impact, added an appendix on ethical reading, and included student exercises for narrative interpretation that we had been using in our classes. It was good to be able to do all of this together. We had so much fun!

All three of us are pleased at the positive response and ongoing use of the book. At the beginning of our careers, it seemed sometimes as though we were groping in the dark. It would have been inconceivable thirty years ago for Don and me to imagine that our book would contribute to a movement of narrative criticism in such a way as to be honored three decades later. Now here we are, celebrating with so many others who have all contributed to this effort to bring narrative criticism into the mainstream of biblical scholarship and who in this volume offer new insights to the discipline.

PART 2: REFLECTIONS ON THE ESSAYS

In this section we reflect on the essays in this volume by identifying what we consider to be their significance in the broad movement of narrative criticism, looking at both the possibilities and the limitations inherent in narrative criticism. All three of us have read and reread the essays and discussed them with each other. Our reflections represent our common point of view.

STUDIES OF THE GOSPEL AS A WHOLE

There is no question now that comprehensive analyses of a whole Gospel as a narrative are not only feasible but also extremely fruitful in bringing new insights into the Gospels. It is gratifying to be part of this larger movement that has, as Stephen Moore notes, gone "from the margins to the mainstream of the discipline." The essays in this volume illustrate some of the incredible diversity of narrative approaches. In the opening chapter, Chris Skinner has traced the rise of narrative criticism and the various directions it has taken and how "it set in motion a process that helped to spawn" other movements. In addition, two other essays in this volume give a broad overview of narrative-critical work. Mark Powell surveys much of the development of narrative criticism, seeing it as a reading strategy used in various ways by different scholars. Elizabeth Struthers Malbon also surveys developments, focusing primarily on characterization.

STUDIES OF KEY FEATURES OF THE NARRATIVE

One of the significant contributions of narrative critics has been to produce articles and full-length studies on specific aspects of a Gospel narrative. Four articles in this volume add to this richness. Malbon's essay shows the ongoing fecundity of narrative criticism in unpacking the dynamics of characters in Mark's Gospel. She presents her own new narrative-critical understanding that the implied author is not identical with the narrator; rather, the implied author presents both the view of the narrator, who focuses on Jesus, and the view of Jesus, who consistently points away from himself to God. One of the striking things about her survey is the insight that each character needs to be analyzed in relation to other characters in the narrative world as a whole.

Malbon's survey shows how scholars have focused on different characters as significant—the disciples, the authorities, God—depending on how each scholar views the story as a whole. Also, scholars view the characters in different ways. Does Mark portray Jesus as divine? What is the fate of the disciples in the future of the story world? Such issues elicit diverse interpretations and attest to the polyvalence of Mark's story. This diverse treatment of characters moves easily from a focus on character to a focus on plot.

Francis Moloney identifies plot analysis as an extremely challenging task, especially in light of the richness and complexity of Mark's narrative texture. Many scholars have proposed diverse plot outlines of the narrative structure of this Gospel as the best way to get at the meaning and impact of Mark's story. However, the complexity of patterns in Mark's Gospel is so marked that Joanna has used the image of an "interwoven tapestry" to depict the interrelated and overlapping narrative structures of Mark's Gospel. Yet each proposal is of value in serving to illuminate different dimensions of the story. For example, drawing from his narrative commentary, Moloney has traced "the unfolding of a unified plot" by identifying a structure based on characters' responses to Jesus and by showing how the plot progressively takes readers from one place to another. Plot is also the approach taken by Morna Hooker in following structures of Aristotelian tragedy evident in the course of Mark's story, pointing out elements of the drama introduced to the reader in the opening of Mark, and tracing them through the Gospel from prologue to complication to recognition to dénouement and finally to climax.

Kelly Iverson offers a different approach by focusing not on character or plot but on a literary motif or theme, in this case "secrecy." Iverson points out that traditionally the "messianic secret" has been treated in isolation from the dynamics of the larger narrative and from the implied audience. Narrative criticism enables him to broaden the study so as to see the element of the "messianic" and the dynamics of "secrecy" within the larger orbit of the dynamics of "concealment" and "disclosure," of "sight" and "blindness" throughout Mark's whole narrative and to shift the focus to the readers/audience in front of the text. Based on this approach, he suggests that the dynamics of secrecy and disclosure serve the functions of reader enhancement, clarifying perspective, engendering commitment, and fostering mission. We see how narrative criticism of the whole story can shed new light on a thematic feature of Mark that has been dealt with differently in traditional scholarship. This essay raises for us the issue of whether and in what ways one can "isolate" a theme for analysis.

CLOSE NARRATIVE ANALYSIS OF EPISODES

The interrelatedness of so many parts of the story brings us to close narrative analysis of individual episodes as part of the whole. An interplay takes place here between the episode and the whole narrative such that the larger narrative illuminates the episode and in turn the episode contributes to an understanding of the overall narrative. Some scholars in secular studies use one key episode or one revealing quotation in a story or a novel as an aperture through which to view and interpret the entire narrative. In turn, the entire narrative becomes grist for illuminating the meaning of the episode or quotation in question. The point is expressed well by Don Michie's comment, noted above, that Mark is a "tightly written narrative."

The essays in this volume by Alan Culpepper, Morna Hooker, and Robert Fowler illustrate this. Culpepper demonstrates the ways in which the episode of the death of John the Baptist was not just dropped willy-nilly in this place in the text from an independent life in pre-Markan tradition. Rather, as Culpepper shows, Mark has carefully composed (or recomposed) the episode as an integral expression of at least five important themes in this Gospel. In turn, these themes serve the larger narrative goal of contrasting two kingdoms. If Culpepper were to cover all the types of Markan interconnections of this one episode with other related aspects of Mark's narrative, he could have written a book. We would add a structural parallel, namely, the common narrative dynamics between this episode and the story of Pilate responding to the crowd's appeal (stirred up by the high priests) to have Jesus executed. Likewise, Hooker sees the prologue as a segment of the story that introduces key themes, which are then developed throughout the story.

The point is given an exclamation mark by Robert Fowler's essay on the three boat scenes in Mark. Previous studies had seen the first two similar scenes as signs of sloppy repetition of one oral tradition or as the conflation of different sources. Using the device of imagining how one might film the episodes, Fowler shows how the scenes build on each other and on other episodes in the narrative. Similarly, Dave's experience of performing these three scenes in the context of the whole narrative elicits from audiences a clear recollection of previous episodes, develops the theme of the disciples' incomprehension, and elicits quite a bit of appropriate humor. Fowler concludes: "Why any of us persist in ignoring Mark's narrative skill in explicitly linking one episode to another baffles me. What Mark the storyteller has put together let no … biblical scholar put asunder!"

Nonetheless, these essays also raise the issue: do we overstate the coherence of the narrative? Are we at times forcing the narrative into a unified whole and ignoring narrative contradictions and inconsistencies? The danger of narrative criticism is that, when you look for coherence, you will sometimes find it where it does not exist. It is hoped that seeking coherence will help us to see examples of inconsistencies more clearly. To be sure, Mark does present a number of conundra. Culpepper's concluding comment states it well: "Perhaps narrative criticism has yet to take seriously the narrative's discontinuities, but it has exposed texture, richness, and depth that earlier interpreters missed." It may also be time to turn more seriously to a study of the discontinuities.

THE NARRATIVE WORLD AND HISTORICAL CONTEXT

The question of coherence relates not only to the tightness of the text but also to the holistic experience of the narrative world. The story evokes the imagination of the audience to experience this narrative world with its settings, characters, movement in time, its past and future, and its view of the world. The story is experienced as a "closed universe" with a life of its own, as Don has described it. However, the narrative is not closed to the reader or hearer. In fact, the teller of any story takes for granted knowledge and understanding that can be assumed of those who will read/hear the story. For their part, the hearers will fill the gaps to make sense of the story world.

Fowler's analysis highlights such gaps. In imagining filming the boat scenes, it becomes clear how many decisions the filmmaker would need to make that are not spelled out in the narrative. What is the boat like? How many disciples are in the boat? What are storms like in that place? And so on. In any case, no narrative exhausts the description of things, given the gaps and fissures and leaps and inconsistencies common to all narrative, features of narrative that are more commonly characteristic of ancient narratives than of the typical modern novel. In some cases, there will be gaps not really relevant to understanding the story. In other cases, filling the gaps appropriately is critical to understanding. There are limits to our ability to construct how implied hearers were to have imagined the story, and, of course, real hearers/readers will fill gaps in differently.

This is where it is critical for narrative criticism to affirm the narrative as a historical artifact of the first century. Unfortunately, narrative criticism has sometimes tended to "dissociate" the narrative from an historical context. But to analyze the narrative world of the story is not to detach it from history, any more than studying the world created by a Shakespearean play is to detach it from sixteenth-century history, and should be interpreted as such. The Markan narrative is to be studied as a first-century narrative composed and heard in a particular historical, political, and cultural context of the first century. Moloney calls for attention "to the historical and cultural context that produced the text." In our narrative research, we should expect to make use of historical criticism, cultural practices, religious traditions, archaeology, and other disciplines as means to imagine the narrative world in the different ways first-century hearers may have imagined it.

The different ways in which scholars imagine the world within the story and the context of the first-century audiences is the basis for many of the diverse interpretations of the Gospels. However powerful narrative criticism is for unpacking the dynamics of the Gospel, narrative criticism cannot answer all the questions, because we do not possess all the extrinsic information that the composer and the audiences shared and because narrative is by nature polyvalent. Narrative criticism can distinguish between readings that the text may suggest as well as readings that resist or ignore the text's signals, but it cannot (and should not) isolate one correct reading. In this regard, narrative criticism lends itself to multiple and creative interpretations.

THE TURN TO THE READER

As noted above, the focus in narrative criticism shifts quite naturally from the story world to a focus on the reader—on the hearers or audience "in front of the text" rather than on the history behind the text. The hearer is not sitting there thinking, "Now that line was pre-Markan oral tradition, and those last words were what Mark added." No, the reader/hearer is caught up in the movement of the story, waiting to learn what will happen next. The reader takes the story as a whole. So how does that experience happen, and what impact does the story have on the audience? These questions lead to reader-response criticism. The shift to the reader is apparent in the move from the first to the second edition of *Mark as Story*. While we were not aware of it at the time, both Powell and Malbon noted the shift, and we now see it in retrospect. We all were intrigued by Malbon's "redaction-critical" work on the changes we made in the chapters on characters in the second edition.

The world in front of the text is quite complex. Shifting focus to the front of the text opened things to a wide range of implied and real readers, implied hearers and real audiences. Powell refers to text-oriented reader-response criticism—the effort to determine the implied impact that the text's designs would have on ideal readers/hearers—as "reader-oriented narrative criticism." We dealt above with how we use history to understand better the readers'/hearers' experience of the story world of the Gospel. Now we are asking how we can use the text to (re)construct history, that is, how we can infer the nature and location of actual readers/hearers for which the narrative was intended. We believe that efforts to move from the narrative world to the actual first-century world, from the implied reader/audience to actual first-century audiences, are difficult to make and, at least in part, necessarily speculative.

Tom Boomershine raises this question most directly in his essay. He analyzes the internal audiences of Mark's Gospel, exploring the dynamics of audience identification that take place in performance as a clue to the intended implied audience. Boomershine is helpful in focusing our attention on the phenomenon of identification and its importance for understanding a narrative. He makes a direct connection between the internal audiences of the narrative and the original implied audiences, and he concludes that Mark's implied audiences were non-Christian Jews (with the possibility of some Gentiles among the audience), partly because the majority of characters in the story were Jews and partly because the temporal movement of the performer-audience dynamics leads from nonbelief to a commitment to follow Jesus.

Again, we see the limitations and uncertainties of narrative criticism. There may be more than one conclusion that could be drawn from the performative dynamics Boomershine discusses. For example, we need not assume that the actual audiences were Jewish because the characters are Jewish. Nevertheless, this is new territory, and we applaud Boomershine's critical inroad, especially since his conclusion has powerful implications for countering notions of anti-Judaism often associated with the Gospels.

NARRATIVE IN PERFORMANCE

The essays by Boomershine and Holly Hearon bring narrative criticism into explicit relationship with performance criticism. Boomershine shows clearly the bases for the now widely accepted notion that Mark's Gospel was composed for oral performance to communal audiences in a predominantly oral culture. Hearon calls for "conceptual and methodological shifts" to the dynamics of narrative criticism to address this new context. She demonstrates ways to rethink settings, characters, and events. Both Boomershine and Hearon also emphasize how performance creates an intimacy with the audience in relation to the characters in the narrative world, how it restores the affective dimensions to the story, and how it makes the story a "visceral" experience.

In a sense, narrative criticism moved quite organically into performance analysis. In fact, many of the early proponents of performance criticism are people who know narrative criticism and who have done performances of the narratives they have studied—Boomershine, Rhoads, Dewey, Ruge-Jones, Whitney Shiner, among others—although, as Hearon makes clear, one does not need to be a performer to engage in this kind of oral analysis.

Performance criticism, or perhaps when applying it to a narrative we should say "performance-oriented narrative criticism," intensifies and expands the realm of imagination integral to narrative criticism. In order to put the narrative in the context of performance, one needs to imagine very concretely a performance context, with an actual performer to proclaim the narrative, an actual audience to experience it, a cultural and historical context in which to understand it, and maybe also all the noise involved! As Hearon puts it, there are "no hypothetical situations in performance." This makes concrete how essential is the need to root Mark's Gospel in a historical context. Both Boomershine and Hearon go further. They indicate that the text not only has cultural and historical codes and a performance scenario to imagine, but also there are in the text what we might call *stage directions* for the performer—

such as "the demon screamed" or "Jesus laid hands on him"—in terms of the performer's use of voice, facial expressions, gesture, and movement, as well as implied dynamics for the interaction between performer and audience.

The performer inevitably inserts another layer of interpretation between the story and the hearers. An audience hearing a story cannot easily separate the story from the particular interpretation of the performer. The performer embodies the story. That *is* the story. Hearon's analysis of the differences between Rhoads's performance and that of Phil Ruge-Jones exemplifies how every performance is different and every performance is an interpretation. Malbon noted that her students, watching Rhoads's and Ruge-Jones's performances, did not want the performer to do the interpretive work for them; they wanted to reserve that for themselves. Yet virtually all people in antiquity experienced the story only in embodied particularity. The dynamics of performance complicate notions of the narrative audience and provide opportunities for narrative critics to deepen our grasp of the story and its rhetoric and to expand its many possibilities of interpretation.

HERMENEUTICS AND ETHICS

Like *Mark as Story*, most of the essays in this volume deal with the narrative basically as a given. Two essays explicitly raise hermeneutical and ethical issues. Mark Powell explores the different uses of narrative analysis as a reading strategy serving different hermeneutical aims of various scholars. Some scholars want to make inferences about the "historical intentions of the work's actual author," others attribute normative value to the text itself, while others are interested in "discerning and understanding disparate and polyvalent responses," including resistant responses. Powell makes clear that narrative criticism in all its guises is not an objective value-neutral enterprise; interpretations are affected by the cultural and theological presuppositions of the modern scholar—even as the scholar seeks to construct possible ancient hearer-responses.

We need to read with each other to discern the range of faithful interpretations in order to appreciate the "polyvalence of perimeters," as Powell calls it. We also need to read together to see the dangers in the text and in our interpretations. Narrative criticism must pair with ideological criticism to discern whose interests are being served and whose interests are suppressed as well as who is visible and who is marginalized by the narrative and by its interpretations. We must be resisting readers of texts and interpretations. In this way, we may find liberating ways to promote the text and liberating ways to resist and oppose it. Like others of the dominant culture, the three of us unwittingly take for granted so many rights and privileges that most people do not enjoy. We are often blindsided by the unintended impacts of our scholarship in relation to people from other social locations.

This is the great benefit of Stephen Moore's essay, where he turns his critique of narrative criticism to the issue of our reliance on modern understandings of the integrated human being in contrast to animals and thus makes us aware of the negative impact of our work on other creatures, in this case evident especially in our treatment of characters and our understanding of the Markan cosmos. Scholars have made some progress in seeing how scholarship might create harm to women or the poor or the oppressed; however, anthropocentrism in our relationship with nature is an area that we are only beginning to address in biblical studies. We need to ask new "posthumanist" questions. Do "subaltern" creatures have a voice? Can we biblical scholars hear the "cry of the earth" in the Bible? Can we speak for the suppressed voice of the sparrow represented in the text? Like our interpretations, our methods are never neutral. They bless some and curse others. We clearly need to widen our circle of awareness in studying the Bible.

CONCLUDING REMARKS

The contemporary recovery of biblical narrative, powerful in its own right, has indeed been a fruitful and meaningful pursuit, both for us personally and for the academy. It has also been salutary for our teaching. The exercises at the end of the second edition of *Mark as Story* reflect some of the narrative approaches the three of us have taken in our teaching. We have also had opportunities to see how the narrative approach to the Bible has been meaningful in religious settings with people of faith. Novelist Reynolds Price (who wrote the preface to the first edition) has observed that "next to food and shelter, story is essential for human life." We thrive on stories, hearing them and telling them, and living them; story is constitutive of what it means to be human. Being in dialogue with biblical stories of depth and power in many settings—academy, classroom, faith communities, and in our personal relationships—has enhanced our lives and our work considerably.

PART 3: TRAJECTORIES

Many authors would relish the opportunity to update their books a decade after publication. But since there will be no third edition of *Mark as Story*, we are indeed grateful to have this chance to add a few of our recent insights and shifts in thinking. Since 1999, studies in the Gospel of Mark have offered an explosion of fresh interpretations of the story world and have placed Mark in dynamic interaction with its historical context. Furthermore, many new movements in biblical studies have had their impact on narrative criticism and on Mark. There have also been advances in contemporary secular literary studies as well as in contemporary studies in ancient narrative, particularly the work done on Hebrew and Greek narrative. We have been influenced in our own thinking by all these developments.

Like some other contributors to this volume, Dave and Joanna have been very involved in the burgeoning field of performance criticism and orality. In writing the second edition of *Mark as Story*, we discussed with each other whether to shift to a more oral, performance-related approach and decided against it, considering that most students and scholars are readers and that there was—and still is—a real need for a narrative introduction for readers.

At the same time, the new studies in ancient orality/aurality and performance criticism have convinced us to rethink the medium in which we analyze the narrative of Mark. The assumption that the Gospel of Mark was a narrative created by an author in the act of writing and that it was read silently and individually by ancient people in manuscript form is clearly anachronistic. Such an approach treats ancient literature as if it flourished in modern print culture, when in fact the Gospel arose in an oral/aural culture in which it is likely that 95 percent or more of the people were functionally nonliterate. Virtually everyone would have *heard* an oral performance as their only experience of Mark's story—a performer performing the whole story from memory to a communal audience. Performers would not have memorized the story verbatim; hence each performance would be somewhat different, adapted to the performer's style, the makeup and response of the audience, and the circumstances. The change in medium results in a paradigm shift, and it affects everything: the performer would evoke the world of the story; the narrator would always be an embodied presence; all characters would be acted out by the performer; and the delivery would involve pitch, tone, volume, pace, gestures, physical movement, and facial expressions. A level of interpretation that we have traditionally attributed to the imagination of an implied reader would have been embodied by the performer and presented whole to the audience.

In one sense, none of this changes the fact that the Gospel of Mark is a narrative and that much of what scholars have learned by treating Mark with a print mentality is by no means lost. In fact, experiencing Mark as a narrative composition with characters, plot, setting, and so on is precisely what happens in performance. In another sense, however, it changes things significantly by immersing Mark in in orality/aurality. Furthermore, the shift to performance requires interpreters to situate Mark in a specific performance event. Just as performance criticism has led us to imagine an actual embodied narrator, so we are also led to imagine an actual communal audience with a certain makeup in a specific time and place.

Although we think Mark's story was performed before audiences with many different makeups, in the scenario that follows we are imagining one example of an early presentation of Mark. We imagine a peasant performer, probably not literate but nevertheless a master storyteller, telling this story of Jesus in its entirety in the marketplace of a village or in the context of a meal of Jesus' followers, perhaps in or near Galilee or in southern Syria, to a pre-dominantly peasant audience of Jews and Gentiles, some of whom are follow-ers of Jesus, shortly after the Roman Judean War of 66 to 70 C.E. The narrative does not yet present itself as a "Christian" Gospel distinct from Judaism. It is a story rooted in Judaism, addressing both Jews and Gentiles. We think that this concrete performance scenario involves three key aspects of its context: the Roman Empire, Jewish and general Mediterranean cultural values and practices, and the Roman Judean War of 66 to 70 C.E. These three aspects of the Markan context have impacted our interpretation of the Gospel. We begin with our new emphasis on the cosmic forces in the story and then move to the relevance for interpretation of the three aspects of the context we have noted.

REIGN OF GOD OVER ALL CREATION

We now give greater emphasis to the way in which Mark depicts the reign of God moving toward a universal realm throughout creation. As such, we are putting more stress on the cosmic conflict in the story world. In the discussion of plot in the second edition, we began with "The Rule of God Initiates the Conflicts," then followed with three levels of conflict: conflicts with nonhu-man forces, conflicts with both Roman and Judean authorities, and conflicts with the disciples. We now see the cosmic conflict between God and Satan as the foundational conflict to all other conflicts. The conflict with demons and other nonhuman forces are part of this cosmic conflict. In the second level, this cosmic conflict gets acted out among humans on earth as the conflict with the Roman and Judean authorities. As such, the struggle between God's rule inaugurated by Jesus, on the one hand, and the powers-that-be who reject God's rule, on the other hand, takes a more prominent role. On the third level is the conflict with disciples, the struggle of those who try to follow the way of God in this age, a struggle with which audiences will identify.

As a result of this emphasis on the cosmic conflict, we would also shift the interpretive center of gravity from the end of the story to the beginning of the story. With various nuances, most scholars have accepted the view that Mark is a "passion narrative with an extended introduction." This view places the death of Jesus as the key watershed event. By contrast, we focus on the cosmic shift that occurs at the opening of the story with the arrival of the reign of God (also to be translated "kingdom" or "rule" or "empire" or "realm"). The arrival of this reign of God—the heavens opening, the defeat of Satan in the desert, and its announcement by Jesus—is the key watershed event. What we have in Mark, then, may be described as "the arrival of the reign of God with an extended dénouement." The performative arrival of the rule of God inaugurates a new world characterized by exorcism of demons, healing, restoration to wholeness, an abundance of food, among other things. All the events in the story that follow the announcement play themselves out as manifestations of the establishment of the reign of God and its consequences for the characters and for the future in the story world.

This shift to the beginning of the narrative does not diminish the power and climactic force of the death of Jesus. Nevertheless, the shift does serve to give much greater weight to the opening of the narrative, and it does place the narrative firmly in the cosmic framework of God's activity in establishing God's reign over all of life. In making this shift, we now give greater significance throughout the story to the cosmic forces that drive the plot. The arrival of the rule of God changes the realities of space, as the heavens are opened and there is unlimited and universal access to divine power for good, wherever agents of God's reign may go. The arrival of God's rule changes the realities of time, both opportune time that is "ripe" as well as eschatological time in which the rule of God is already present and moving toward imminent fulfillment. As the focus of the story moves to interactions between Jesus and the authorities and Jesus and the disciples, the audience of a performance of Mark will not forget the forces that lie behind the entire story and what is being played out: the arrival of God's rule on earth.

Now when we take the next step mandated by performance criticism and imagine a concrete audience, we lift up three related aspects of the context that reflect the shifts we have made: (1) the political empire of Rome and its Judean agents in Israel; (2) the cultural context of core values as expressed by the authorities (and the disciples) in the narrative world; and (3) the specific historical context of the aftermath of the Roman Judean War of 66 to 70 C.E. These three aspects of the Markan context have shaped our thinking about the rhetorical dynamics of the way this story related to audiences in the context of the realities in which it was experienced. When these three things are taken into account, Mark may be seen as a much more radical Gospel—radical in the deepest sense of the word—than we have tended to see it.

COUNTERIMPERIAL

First, when we take into account the imperial context of a Markan performance, our shift to a focus on the cosmic dimensions God's reign magnifies the contrast between the reign of God and the reign of Rome. Consider these contrasts *within* the story world of Mark's Gospel. Rome works from the center out; God's empire begins at the margins, in the wilderness, initiating a new sociopolitical order. Rome works from the top down; God's empire starts from the bottom up, a peasant movement spreading like invasive mustard plants. Rome secures the strongest of its people and exploits the weak; God's empire restores the weakest and most vulnerable. Rome possesses the land and the people much like a demon possesses a human being; God's empire liberates people from dominating demonic forces. The Judean authorities collaborating with Rome's empire in Israel establish boundaries of purity that exclude and marginalize; in God's empire, agents cross boundaries to restore the unclean to wholeness. The Judean collaborators of the Roman Empire in Israel use laws to control and marginalize; in God's empire, laws are interpreted or discarded in order to bring life to people. Agents of the Roman Empire lord over people and exert authority over them; agents of God's empire serve and bring good news. Agents of the Roman Empire accumulate wealth ("acquire the whole world"), seek greatness, and acquire power to protect and aggrandize themselves; agents of God's empire are to relinquish wealth to the poor, be least so others may be elevated, and use power to serve. The Roman Empire inflicts cruel and shameful death; the agents of God's empire are called to be faithful to God's empire despite humiliation and persecution. A performance imagined in the actual context of Roman power makes clear that the story offers a counterworld, and the performer seeks to draw audiences into this new world.

Countercultural

Second, when we take into account the cultural context in which Mark's Gospel would have been first performed, we see that the Markan Jesus challenges core cultural values and practices as they are portrayed *within* the story world. The reign of God reverses the direction of purity so that, instead of withdrawing for fear of defilement, its agents are to spread holiness and wholeness through the Holy Spirit. And, instead of fear of external contact with food and people and places considered to be unclean, followers are now to guard against internal uncleanness in their hearts resulting in actions harmful to others. The reign of God breaks the patronage cycle: Jesus does not seek followers who are beholden to him; instead of seeking honor for healing, Jesus tells suppliants to be quiet and go home. The rule of God subverts the core value of wealth: instead of wealth seen as a blessing, people are to relinquish their wealth to the poor. Kinship is reordered: instead of families ordered by patriarchy, the metaphorical kinship relations of the realm of God are structured so that no one serves as father and all are to function as servants to each other. The core value of honor is redefined: instead of seeking honor in the eyes of others as a mark of goodness, people are to choose to be least rather than engage in competition for honor. The core definition of power is reconfigured: instead of using authority to one's advantage, people are to limit their power or use it to be servants to others. Even the visceral human drive for survival is challenged: instead of securing life at the expense of others, people are to risk their lives to bring the life-giving words and actions of God's reign to others. In experiencing a performance, the audience could not escape the challenge to certain values and taken-for-granted ways of life in so far as they were evident in their cultural context.

RESPONSE TO THE WAR

Third, when we look at the concrete historical circumstance in which the Gospel of Mark was composed, we see how much this Gospel works against the grain of the immediate historic events that attend the story: the Roman-Judean War of 66–70 C.E., a war in which Israel revolted against the Roman Empire, and the armies of the empire invaded Israel and crushed the nation. The war involved a widespread peasant rebellion within Israel, both against the empire and against the prevailing Judean leadership under the Romans—leading to a four-year war that ended in the destruction of the city of Jerusalem and the burning and dismantling of the massive temple that served as the center of Judaism. If, as we have suggested, the Gospel of Mark was composed in the immediate aftermath of this war, and if it was performed in or around Israel/Palestine at that time, then this war becomes the most compelling historical context in which to interpret Mark's Gospel.

Scholars regularly see Mark as a response to the fact of the war, but rarely do they see the Gospel responding to the specific course, motives, causes, and dynamics of that war. For example, imagine hearers of Mark living in villages devastated by Roman armies, with vivid memories of lost loved ones, dashed hopes, and the sounds of war still ringing in their ears. Now imagine how much the announcement of "good news," the declaration of an "anointed one" who was "Son of God," the preparation of the "way" of the "Lord," the announcement of the arrival of "the empire of God," and the call for fealty to this new empire—imagine how all of this may have echoed and yet contrasted with the entrance of the Roman armies into Palestine from the north with their trumpets and shouts and clash of arms. As he moved south, the Roman general Vespasian waged a scorched-earth campaign of domination and destruction of cities and villages throughout Galilee and the surrounding regions. Imagine an audience of Mark shortly after the Roman Judean War, recalling the war in vivid memory, hearing Mark's story of Jesus as virtually a counter-campaign. Indeed, the Markan Gospel does portray Jesus waging

a campaign in Galilee also, but a campaign against Satan and other manifestations of evil as a means to bring restoration and healing—driving out
demons where the Romans had acted like demons, restoring wholeness where
the Romans had maimed, bringing life where the Romans had brought death,
providing bread where the Romans had burned the fields of grain, and calming storms on the lake that Romans had turned blood-red.

The Gospel of Mark presents an ironic and countercultural empire—a
grass-roots movement that involved "fishing" and "sowing seeds" of words
and deeds and trusting God for the harvest. As the narrative progresses, the
journey to Jerusalem continues to provide a contrast to Roman conquest.
Along that journey, Jesus teaches that disciples are not to lord over anyone "as
the Gentile nations do" but to be servants and slaves to the needs of others.
The subsequent entrance to Jerusalem shows that the Markan Jesus is no con-
queror who will usher in a Davidic kingdom, as the crowds hope, but a royal
figure who comes in peace on a donkey. In Jerusalem, more contrasts occur:
Jesus clears the temple of "brigands"; he predicts the downfall of the temple
and offers prayer and faith as an alternative; he warns against false prophets;
the insurrectionist Barabbas is chosen over Jesus; an innocent Jesus is executed with two revolutionaries; and God splits apart the curtain of the sanctuary and leaves the temple to its destruction. Hearers of this story would
clearly experience these and many other sayings and events of the narrative
in light of the cataclysmic war that was so recently in their midst.

In rejecting Jesus as a Davidic warrior-messiah, the rule of God in Mark
stands as a stark contrast not only to the Roman Empire and the rulers within
Israel, but also to the hopes and actions of the revolutionary peasants. Jesus'
instruction to his followers to be servants and slaves must have been bitter
to hear in the situation where so many of those who were not killed in the
war were forced into slavery by the Romans. In the narrative, the crucifixion
of Jesus reveals the crushing power of the Roman Empire, supported by the
Judean leadership. It also reveals Jesus' commitment to the reign of God as
an absolute commitment not to use force over others. Again, the call of the
Markan Jesus to take up the cross and the depiction of the crucifixion must
have recalled for hearers the horror of the massive crucifixions that came at
the end of the war. And here is Jesus telling them to *choose* to take up the
cross, not as an act of revolution but as a commitment to live for the reign
of God even if it means dying for it. In Mark, Jesus resists the call to replace
one empire of domination with another; rather, he seeks the end of imperial
domination as such. In the Gospel, Jesus is most explicitly contrasted with
the revolutionaries when the crowds choose Barabbas, who had committed
murder in the insurrection. Despite being executed with two revolutionary
brigands, Jesus was, in the view of Mark, the true "king of the Judeans."

The Markan Jesus was a political figure. No doubt about it. He lived in the service of the empire of God. But it was not politics as usual. He chose twelve peasants as core disciples to be agents to spread liberation and healing in the villages of Galilee. He considered human need to be the legal imperative for applying the law. He did not seek wealth and status and power. He did not aggrandize himself in any way. He confronted oppression without himself becoming an oppressor. He acted for the good of the society and trusted God for the rest. As such, the Markan Gospel presents a radical reorientation of politics.

RETHINKING MARK

The challenge for the three of us is to reconsider narrator, settings, plot, characters, and rhetorical force in a particular performative event in that particular context—that empire, that culture, and that war. To do so combines the narrative and the context in a symbiotic way. Some have argued that such a countercultural treatment of Mark founders on the fact that the Markan Gospel expects the world to end within the generation. Because the Gospel expects such an imminent end, the argument goes, action or agency is gutted, and therefore people are simply to stay put and hold out to the end. On the contrary, we are convinced that the entire narrative is oriented to overcoming quietism and to generating agency—an agency that dislodges disciples from their secure worlds of community and place and sends them out to act on behalf of God's reign in the face of resistance, rejection, even death.

In the Gospel of Mark, fear is the opposite of faith or trust in God's rule. It is the major obstacle to embracing the rule of God and its values. Fear is what leads people to save their lives rather than lose them. Fear is what leads the authorities to secure their position at whatever cost to others. Fear is the paralyzing emotion that stops even the most determined followers of Jesus from living their commitments. The Gospel of Mark takes fear very seriously. It seeks nothing less than to break the juggernaut of the powerful protective interest people have for themselves and their own groups, so that they can embrace the paradox: "whoever will lose/risk their life for me and the good news will save it." The whole narrative urges hearers to get to a point at the end of the story when they are led to say: "Even if the authorities are determined to destroy us, even if the disciples flee in terror, even if the women flee in awe and fear from the empty grave, we will be faithful." In Mark, this is what it means to follow Jesus, not so much to believe something about him as to be like him, to act like him.

Hence, the entire Gospel of Mark moves audiences toward mission, the mission to bring liberation, healing, forgiveness, wholeness, food, and much more to as many communities and individuals as possible and with a commitment to resist oppression—their own as well as that of others. In this narrative, the expectation of an imminent end does not stifle agency. Quite the opposite. The assurance that God will usher in this kingdom, fully and soon, provides the springboard for the capacity to take whatever risks might come—"for the good news must first be proclaimed to all the Gentile nations."

The Gospel of Mark seeks to present a new world to its hearers. In a sense, the Gospel is apocalyptic in its hearing. To embrace this narrative represents the end of one way of being in the world and the onset of another way, already in the lived experience of the hearers. As such, the experience of the story is an experience of enculturation into a new world, a new cosmos, a reordering of creation, a new grasp of power, a new set of relationships, a new ethos of values, and a new release from self-orientation to orientation for others—new wine for new wineskins. The performance event attempts resocialization at the primary level, designed not only to change individuals but, more importantly, to generate new communal relationships and new societies, a new creation—the realm of the rule of God. What is the world like when God reigns and people are open to it and loyal to it? That is what the Gospel of Mark is all about. And what is it like for people to enter this realm of God when the rest of the world has not yet changed and the rule of God has not come fully? That is what the Gospel is about.

We do not mean to cover over difficult aspects of Mark's Gospel. Readers and listeners in the twenty-first century will be troubled by many aspects of the ancient story of Mark: the world is flat and filled with demons; paralysis may be caused by sin; everything is possible if one only has faith; people will be healed if they touch the master's garment; Jesus may be turned into another dominating authority figure; women do not play major and active roles in the narrative; the narrative comes dangerously close to suggesting that martyrdom is redemptive; people will be judged and thrown into Gehenna to be destroyed; God will in the end forcibly put Christ's enemies down under his feet; the expected apocalyptic end never came. We could go on. We have to be honest about these problems, honest about what they say about Mark, and honest about the dangers they may have presented to audiences then and the dangers they may present to readers of today.

At the same time, we believe today's readers need also to hear the radical, and we mean radical, call to a personal lifestyle, a communal formation, and a societal order that enthrones service to those in need above the securing of wealth, status, and power. We need to hear that living such a life may well risk resistance and rejection as much today as it did in the first century. And we need to know that life lived in service to God's realm as Mark portrays it can also bring deep meaning and profound joy, now just as it did then.

BIBLIOGRAPHY

Abbott, H. Porter. *The Cambridge Introduction to Narrative*. Cambridge: Cambridge University Press, 2002.

Abrams, M. H. *A Glossary of Literary Terms*. 5th ed. New York: Holt, Rinehart, & Winston, 1985.

Achtemeier, Paul J. "The Origin and Function of the Pre-Markan Miracle Catenae." *JBL* 91 (1972): 198–221.

———. "Toward the Isolation of Pre-Markan Miracle Catenae." *JBL* 89 (1970): 265–91.

Adam, A.K.M. *What Is Postmodern Biblical Criticism?* GBS. Minneapolis: Fortress, 1995.

Ahuja, Neel. "Postcolonial Critique in a Multispecies World." *PMLA* 124 (2009): 556–63.

Aichele, George, and Richard Walsh, eds. *Screening Scripture: Intertextual Connections Between Scripture and Film*. Harrisburg, Pa.: Trinity Press International, 2002.

Alter, Robert. *The Art of Biblical Narrative*. New York: Basic, 1981.

Anderson, Janice Capel. "Feminist Criticism: The Dancing Daughter." Pages 103–34 in *Mark and Method: New Approaches in Biblical Studies*. Edited by Janice Capel Anderson and Stephen D. Moore. Minneapolis: Fortress, 1992.

Aristotle. *Poetics*. Edited and translated by Stephen Halliwell. LCL 199. Cambridge: Harvard University Press, 1995.

Armstrong, Nancy. *Desire and Domestic Fiction: A Political History of the Novel*. Oxford: Oxford University Press, 1987.

———. *How Novels Think: The Limits of Individualism from 1719 to 1900*. New York: Columbia University Press, 2005.

Aune, David E. *The New Testament in Its Literary Environment*. Philadelphia: Westminster, 1987.

———. "The Problem of the Messianic Secret." *NovT* 11 (1969): 1–31.

Bach, Alice. "Calling the Shots: Directing Salome's Dance of Death." *Semeia* 74 (1996): 103–26.

Bakhtin, Mikhail. *The Dialogic Imagination: Four Essays*. Edited by Michael Holquist. Translated by Caryl Emerson and Michael Holquist. Austin: University of Texas Press, 1981.

Bar-Efrat, Shimon. "Some Observations on the Analysis of Structure in Biblical Narrative." *VT* 30 (1980): 154–73.

Bauckham, Richard. "For Whom Were Gospels Written?" Pages 9–48 in *The Gospels for All Christians: Rethinking the Gospel Audiences.* Edited by Richard Bauckham. Grand Rapids: Eerdmans, 1997.

———. "Jesus and the Wild Animals (Mark 1:13): A Christological Image for an Ecological Age." Pages 3–21 in *Jesus of Nazareth: Lord and Christ. Essays on the Historical Jesus and New Testament Christology.* Edited by Joel B. Green and Max Turner. Grand Rapids: Eerdmans, 1994.

Becker-Leckrone, Megan. "Salome: The Fetishization of a Textual Corpus." *New Literary History* 26 (1995): 239–60.

Benoit, William L., and Mary Jeanette Smythe. "Rhetorical Theory as Message Reception: A Cognitive Response Approach to Rhetorical Theory and Criticism." *Communication Studies* 54 (2003): 96–114.

Berlin, Adele. *Poetics and Interpretation of Biblical Narrative.* Bible and Literature Series. Sheffield: Almond, 1983.

———. "Point of View in Biblical Narrative." Pages 71–113 in *A Sense of Text: The Art of Language in the Study of Biblical Literature.* Edited by Stephen A. Geller. Winona Lake, Ind.: Eisenbrauns, 1983.

Berman, S. "Revolution in Literary Criticism." *Princeton Alumni Weekly* (1984): 10.

Best, Ernest. *Mark: The Gospel as Story.* Edinburgh: T&T Clark, 1983.

———. "Mark's Readers: A Profile." Pages 839–58 in vol. 2 of *The Four Gospels 1992: Festschrift Frans Neirynck.* Edited by Frans van Segbroeck, Christopher M. Tuckett, Gilbert van Belle, and Jozef Verheyden. 2 vols. BETL 100. Leuven: Leuven University Press, 1992.

———. *The Temptation and the Passion.* 2nd ed. SNTSMS 2. Cambridge: Cambridge University Press, 1990.

Bieler, Ludwig. *Theios Aner: Das Bild des "Göttlichen Menschen" in Spätantike und Frühchristentum.* Vienna: Hofels, 1935.

Bird, Michael F. *Are You the One Who Is to Come? The Historical Jesus and the Messianic Question.* Grand Rapids: Baker, 2009.

Black, C. Clifton. *The Disciples according to Mark: Markan Redaction in Current Debate.* JSNTSup 27. Sheffield: Sheffield Academic Press, 1989.

———. *Mark: Images of an Apostolic Interpreter.* Studies on Personalities of the New Testament. Minneapolis: Fortress, 2001.

Boehrer, Bruce. "Animal Studies and the Deconstruction of Character." *PMLA* 124 (2009): 542–47.

Boomershine, Thomas. "Mark 16:8 and the Apostolic Commission." *JBL* 100 (1981): 234–39.

———. "Mark the Storyteller: A Rhetorical-Critical Investigation of Mark's Passion and Resurrection Narrative." Ph.D. diss., Union Theological Seminary (New York), 1974.

———. "The Medium and Message of John: Audience Address and Audience Identity in the Fourth Gospel." Forthcoming in *The Fourth Gospel in First-Century Media Culture.* Edited by Anthony Le Donne and Tom Thatcher. London: T&T Clark, 2011.

Booth, Wayne C. *The Rhetoric of Fiction.* 2nd ed. Chicago: University of Chicago Press, 1983.

Boring, M. Eugene. *Mark: A Commentary*. NTL. Louisville: Westminster John Knox, 2006.

Bornkamm, Gunther, Gerhard Barth, and Heinz Joachim Held, eds. *Tradition and Interpretation in Matthew*. Philadelphia: Westminster, 1963.

Braidotti, Rosi. "Animals, Anomalies, and Inorganic Others." *PMLA* 124 (2009): 526–32.

Braund, D. C. "Berenice in Rome." *Historia* 33 (1984): 120–23.

Brower, Kent. Review of David Rhoads and Donald Michie. *Mark as Story: An Introduction to the Narrative of a Gospel. CBQ* 45 (1983): 701–2.

Byrskog, Samuel. *Story as History, History as Story: The Gospel Tradition in the Context of Ancient Oral History*. Leiden: Brill, 2002.

Bucher-Gillmayr, Susanne. "'…und brachte seinen Kopf auf einem Teller…': Das Schicksal des Johannes, Mk 6,14–29." *Protokolle zur Bibel* 4 (1995): 103–16.

Bultmann, Rudolf. *History of the Synoptic Tradition*. Translated by John Marsh. Oxford: Basil Blackwell, 1968.

Burnett, Fred W. "Characterization and the Reader Construction of Characters in the Gospels." *Semeia* 63 (1993): 1–28.

Bussmann, W. *Synoptische Studien*. 3 vols. Halle: Buchhandlung des Waisenhauses, 1925–1931.

Byrne, Brendan. *A Costly Freedom: A Theological Reading of Mark's Gospel*. Collegeville, Minn.: Liturgical Press, 2008.

Camery-Hoggatt, Jerry. *Irony in Mark's Gospel: Text and Subtext*. SNTSMS 72. Cambridge: Cambridge University Press, 1992.

Carson, D. A. *The Gospel according to John*. Pillar New Testament Commentary. Grand Rapids: Eerdmans, 1991.

Carter, Warren. *Matthew: Storyteller, Interpreter, Evangelist*. Peabody, Mass.: Hendrickson, 1996.

Chatman, Seymour. *Coming to Terms: The Rhetoric of Narrative in Fiction and Film*. Ithaca, N.Y.: Cornell University Press, 1990.

———. *Story and Discourse: Narrative Structure in Film and Literature*. Ithaca, N.Y.: Cornell University Press, 1978.

Christianson, Eric S., Peter Francis, and William R. Telford, eds. *Cinéma Divinité: Religion, Theology and the Bible in Film*. London: SCM, 2005.

Collins, John J. *Daniel: A Commentary on the Book of Daniel*. Hermeneia. Minneapolis: Fortress, 1993.

Collins, Nancy L., and Lynn Carol Miller. "Self-Disclosure and Liking: A Meta-Analytic Review." *Psychological Bulletin* 116.3 (1994): 457–75.

Combs, Jason Robert. "A Ghost on the Water? Understanding an Absurdity in Mark 6:49–50." *JBL* 127.2 (2008): 345–58.

Conzelmann, Hans. *The Theology of St. Luke*. Translated by Geoffrey Buswell. New York: Harper & Row, 1961.

Cranfield, C. E. B. *The Gospel according to St. Mark*. Cambridge Greek Testament Commentary. Cambridge: Cambridge University Press, 1959.

Culpepper, R. Alan. *Anatomy of the Fourth Gospel: A Study in Literary Design*. Philadelphia: Fortress, 1983.

———. *Mark*. Smyth & Helwys Bible Commentaries. Macon: Smyth & Helwys, 2007.

———. Vingt ans d'analyse narrative des Évangiles: Nouvelles perspectives et problèmes en suspens." Pages 73–93 in *La Bible en récits*. Edited by Daniel Marguerat. Geneva: Labor et Fides, 2003.

Dahl, Nils Alstrup. "The Purpose of Luke Acts." Pages 87–98 in *Jesus in the Memory of the Early Church*. Edited by Nils Alstrup Dahl. Minneapolis: Augsburg, 1976.

———. "The Purpose of Mark's Gospel." Pages 29–34 in *The Messianic Secret*. Edited by Christopher Tuckett. Philadelphia: Fortress, 1983.

Danove, Paul L. *The Rhetoric of Characterization of God, Jesus, and Jesus' Disciples in the Gospel of Mark*. JSNTSup 290. London: T&T Clark, 2005.

Darr, John A. *Herod the Fox: Audience Criticism and Lukan Characterization*. Sheffield: Sheffield Academic Press, 1998.

———. *On Character Building: The Reader and the Rhetoric of Characterization in Luke-Acts*. Louisville: Westminster John Knox, 1992.

Davies, W. D., and Dale C. Allison. *A Critical and Exegetical Commentary on the Gospel according to Saint Matthew*. 3 vols. ICC. Edinburgh: T&T Clark, 1988.

Dawsey, James M. *The Lukan Voice: Confusion and Irony in the Gospel of Luke*. Macon, Ga.: Mercer University Press, 1986.

DeKoven, Marianne. "Guest Column: Why Animals Now?" *PMLA* 124 (2009): 361–69.

Delorme, Jean. "John the Baptist's Head—The Word Perverted: A Reading of a Narrative (Mark 6:14–29)." *Semeia* 81 (1998): 115–29.

Derrida, Jacques. *The Animal That Therefore I Am*. Edited by Marie-Louise Mallet. Translated by David Wills. New York: Fordham University Press, 2008.

———. "The Animal That Therefore I Am (More to Follow)." Translated by David Wills. *Critical Inquiry* 28 (2002): 369–418.

———. *The Beast and the Sovereign*. Vol. 1. Translated by Geoffrey Bennington. Seminars of Jacques Derrida 1. Chicago: University of Chicago Press, 2009.

Descartes, René. *A Discourse on the Method*. Translated by Ian Maclean. Oxford World's Classics. Oxford: Oxford University Press, 2006.

———. *Philosophical Essays and Correspondence*. Translated and edited by Roger Ariew. Indianapolis: Hackett, 2000.

Dewey, Joanna. *Disciples of the Way: Mark on Discipleship*. Cincinnati: Women's Division, The United Methodist Church, 1976.

———. "The Gospel of Mark." Pages 470–509 in *Searching the Scriptures: A Feminist Commentary*. Volume 2 of *Searching the Scriptures*. Edited by Elisabeth Schüssler Fiorenza. New York: Crossroad, 1997.

———. "The Gospel of Mark as Oral-Aural Event: Implications for Interpretation." Pages 145–63 in *The New Literary Criticism and the New Testament*. Edited by Edgar V. McKnight and Elizabeth Struthers Malbon. Sheffield: Sheffield Academic Press, 1994.

———. "Mark as Aural Narrative: Structures as Clues to Understanding." *STRev* 36 (1992): 45–56.

———. "Mark as Interwoven Tapestry: Forecasts and Echoes for a Listening Audience." *CBQ* 53 (1991): 221–36.

———. *Markan Public Debate: Literary Technique, Concentric Structure and Theology in Mark 2–3:6.* SBLDS 48. Missoula, Mont.: Scholars Press, 1980.

———. "Oral Methods of Structuring Narrative in Mark." *Int* 43 (1989): 32–44.

———. "Point of View and the Disciples in Mark." *SBLSP* 21 (1982): 97–106.

———. "The Survival of Mark's Gospel: A Good Story?" *JBL* 123 (2004): 495–507.

Dewey, Joanna, ed. *Semeia 65: Orality and Textuality in Early Christian Literature.* Atlanta: Scholars Press, 1994.

Donahue, John R., and Daniel J. Harrington. *The Gospel of Mark.* Sacra Pagina 2. Collegeville, Minn.: Liturgical Press, 2002.

Doody, Margaret Anne. *The True Story of the Novel.* New Brunswick, N.J.: Rutgers University Press, 1996.

Doty, William G. Review of David Rhoads and Donald Michie, *Mark as Story: An Introduction to the Narrative of a Gospel. Int* 37 (1983): 301–4.

Dowd, Sharyn, and Elizabeth Struthers Malbon. "The Significance of Jesus' Death in Mark: Narrative Context and Authorial Audience." *JBL* 125 (2006): 271–97.

Driggers, Ira Brent. *Following God through Mark: Theological Tension in the Second Gospel.* Louisville: Westminster John Knox, 2007.

Dunn, James D. G. *Jesus Remembered.* Grand Rapids: Eerdmans, 2003.

Duran, Nicole. "Having Men for Dinner: Deadly Banquets and Biblical Women." *BTB* 35 (2005): 117–24.

———. *Having Men for Dinner: Deadly Banquets and Biblical Women.* Cleveland: Pilgrim, 2006.

Dyer, Keith D. "When Is the End Not the End? The Fate of Earth in Biblical Eschatology (Mark 13)." Pages 44–56 in *The Earth Story in the New Testament.* Edited by Norman C. Habel and Vicky Balabanski. The Earth Bible 5. Cleveland: Pilgrim, 2002.

Ebeling, Hans Jürgen. *Das Messiasgeheimnis und die Botschaft des Marcus-Evangelisten.* BZNW 19. Berlin: Töpelmann, 1939.

Edwards, James R. *The Gospel according to Mark.* Pillar New Testament Commentary. Grand Rapids: Eerdmans, 2002.

Edwards, Richard A. *Matthew's Narrative Portrait of Disciples: How the Text-Connoted Reader is Informed.* Harrisburg, Pa.: Trinity Press International, 1997.

———. *Matthew's Story of Jesus.* Philadelphia: Fortress, 1985.

Ehling, Kay. "Warum liess Herodes Antipas Johannes den Täufer verhaften? Oder: Wenn ein Prophet politisch gefährlich wird." *BN* 131 (2006): 63–64.

Elliot, Scott S. *Reconfiguring Mark's Jesus: Narrative Criticism after Poststructuralism.* Sheffield: Sheffield Phoenix, 2011.

———. "'The Son of Man Goes as It Is Written of Him': The Figuration of Jesus in the Gospel of Mark." Ph.D. diss., Drew University, 2009.

Evans, Craig A. *To See and Not Perceive: Isaiah 6.9–10 in Early Jewish and Christian Interpretation.* JSOTSup 64. Sheffield: Sheffield Academic Press, 1989.

Fetterly, Judith. *The Resisting Reader: A Feminist Approach to American Literature.* Bloomington: Indiana University Press, 1978.

Fishbane, Michael. *Text and Texture: Close Readings of Selected Biblical Texts.* New York: Schocken, 1979.

Fiske, Susan T., Daniel Todd Gilbert, and Gardner Lindzey, eds. *Handbook of Social Psychology*. 5th ed. Hoboken, N.J.: Wiley, 2010.

Focant, Camille. "La tête du prophète sur un plat, ou, L'anti-repas d'alliance (Mc 6.14–29)." *NTS* 47 (2001): 334–53.

Fokkelman, J. P. *Reading Biblical Narrative: An Introductory Guide*. Louisville: Westminster John Knox, 1991.

Forster, E. M. *Aspects of the Novel*. London: Arnold, 1927.

Fowler, Robert M. *Let the Reader Understand: Reader-Response Criticism and the Gospel of Mark*. Minneapolis: Fortress, 1991.

———. *Loaves and Fishes: The Function of the Feeding Stories in the Gospel of Mark*. SBLDS 54. Atlanta: Scholars Press, 1981.

———. "Reader-Response Criticism: Figuring Mark's Reader." Pages 50–93 in *Mark and Method: New Approaches in Biblical Studies*. Edited by Janice Capel Anderson and Stephen D. Moore. 2nd ed. Minneapolis: Fortress, 2008.

———. "Why Everything We Know about the Bible is Wrong: Lessons from the Media History of the Bible." Pages 3–18 in *The Bible in Ancient and Modern Media: Essays in Honor of Thomas Boomershine*. Edited by Holly Hearon and Phil Ruge-Jones. Eugene, Ore.: Wipf & Stock, 2009.

Fowler, Robert M., Edith Blumhofer, and Fernando Segovia, eds. *New Paradigms in Bible Study: The Bible in the Third Millennium*. London: T&T Clark, 2004.

Freedman, William. "The Literary Motif: A Definition and Evaluation." Pages 200–212 in *Essentials of the Theory of Fiction*. Edited by Michael J. Hoffman and Patrick D. Murphy. Durham, N.C.: Duke University Press, 1996.

Frei, Hans. *The Eclipse of Biblical Narrative*. New Haven: Yale University Press, 1974.

Gamble, Harry Y. *Books and Readers in the Early Church: A History of Early Christian Texts*. New Haven: Yale University Press, 1995.

———. "Literacy and Book Culture." Pages 644–48 in *Dictionary of New Testament Background*. Edited by Craig A. Evans and Stanley E. Porter. Downers Grove, Ill.: InterVarsity Press, 2000.

Genette, Gérard. *Narrative Discourse: An Essay in Method*. Translated by Jane E. Lewin. Ithaca, N.Y.: Cornell University Press, 1980.

Gilhus, Ingvild Saelid. *Animals, Gods and Humans: Changing Attitudes to Animals in Greek, Roman and Early Christian Ideas*. New York: Routledge, 2006.

Girard, René. "Scandal and the Dance: Salome in the Gospel of Mark." *New Literary History* 15 (1984): 311–24.

Glancy, Jennifer A. "Unveiling Masculinity: The Construction of Gender in Mark 6:17–29." *BibInt* 2 (1994): 34–50.

Grant, Robert M. *Early Christians and Animals*. New York: Routledge, 1999.

Green, Joel. "Healing." *NIDB* 2:757.

Guelich, Robert A. *Mark 1–8:26*. WBC 34A. Dallas: Word, 1989.

Hadas, Moses. *Ancilla to Classical Reading*. New York: Columbia University Press, 1954.

Hanson, James S. *The Endangered Promises: Conflict in Mark*. SBLDS 171. Atlanta: Society of Biblical Literature, 2000.

Haraway, Donna. *The Companion Species Manifesto: Dogs, People, and Significant Otherness*. Chicago: Prickly Paradigm, 2003.

———. *Primate Visions: Gender, Race, and Nature in the World of Modern Science.* New York: Routledge, 1990.

———. *When Species Meet.* Posthumanities. Minneapolis: University of Minnesota Press, 2007.

Harris, William. *Ancient Literacy.* Cambridge: Harvard University Press, 1989.

Harrison, Paul V. "Competing Accounts of the Baptist's Demise: Josephus versus the Gospels." *Faith and Mission* 24 (2007): 26–42.

Hay, Lewis S. "Mark's Use of the Messianic Secret." *JAAR* 35 (1967): 16–27.

Hearon, Holly E., and Philip Ruge-Jones, eds., *The Bible in Ancient and Modern Media: Story and Performance.* Eugene, Ore.: Wipf & Stock, 2009.

Heil, John Paul. *The Gospel of Mark as Model for Action: A Reader-Response Commentary.* New York: Paulist, 1992.

Henderson, Suzanne Watts. *Christology and Discipleship in the Gospel of Mark.* SNTSMS 135. Cambridge: Cambridge University Press, 2006.

Hoehner, Harold W. *Herod Antipas: A Contemporary of Jesus Christ.* Grand Rapids: Zondervan, 1972.

Hoffeditz, David M., and Gary E. Yates. "*Femme Fatale* Redux: Intertextual Connection to the Elijah/Jezebel Narratives in Mark 6:14–29." *BBR* 15 (2005): 199–221.

Hooker, Morna D. "The Beginning of the Gospel." Pages 18–28 in *The Future of Christology: Essays in Honor of Leander E. Keck.* Edited by Abraham J. Malherbe and Wayne A. Meeks. Minneapolis: Fortress, 1993.

———. *Beginnings: Keys That Open the Gospels.* London: SCM, 1997.

———. *The Gospel according to Saint Mark.* BNTC. London: A. & C. Black, 1991.

———. "John's Baptism: A Prophetic Sign." Pages 22–40 in *The Holy Spirit and Christian Origins: Essays in Honor of James D. G. Dunn.* Edited by Graham N. Stanton, Bruce W. Longenecker, and Stephen C. Barton. Grand Rapids: Eerdmans, 2004.

Horsley, Richard. *Hearing the Whole Story: The Politics of Plot in Mark's Gospel.* Louisville: Westminster John Knox, 2001.

Howell, David B. *Matthew's Inclusive Story: A Study in the Narrative Rhetoric of the First Gospel.* JSNTSup 42. Sheffield: JSOT Press, 1990.

Hunter, Adrian. *The Cambridge Introduction to the Short Story in English.* Cambridge: Cambridge University Press, 2007.

Iser, Wolfgang. *The Act of Reading: A Theory of Aesthetic Response.* Baltimore: Johns Hopkins University Press, 1978.

———. *The Implied Reader: Patterns of Communication in Prose Fiction from Bunyan to Beckett.* Baltimore: Johns Hopkins University Press, 1978.

———. "The Reading Process: A Phenomenological Approach." *New Literary History* 3.2 (1972): 279–99.

Iverson, Kelly R. "A Centurion's 'Confession': A Performance-Critical Analysis of Mark 15:39." *JBL* (forthcoming).

———. "A Further Word on Final Γάρ." *CBQ* 68 (2006): 79–94.

———. *Gentiles in the Gospel of Mark: "Even the Dogs under the Table Eat the Children's Crumbs."* LNTS 339. London: T&T Clark, 2007.

———. "Orality and the Gospels: A Survey of Recent Research." *CBR* 8.1 (2009): 71–106.

Joynes, Christine E. "A Question of Identity: 'Who Do People Say That I Am?' Elijah, John the Baptist and Jesus in Mark's Gospel." Pages 15–29 in *Understanding, Studying, Reading: New Testament Essays in Honour of John Ashton*. Edited by Christopher Rowland and Crispin H. T. Fletcher-Louis. JSNTSup 153. Sheffield: Sheffield Academic Press, 1998.

Juel, Donald H. *The Gospel of Mark*. Interpreting Biblical Texts. Nashville: Abingdon, 1999.

Kahn, Michael H., and Kjell E. Rudestam. "The Relationship between Liking and Perceived Self-Disclosure in Small Groups." *The Journal of Psychology* 78.1 (1971): 81–85.

Kaminouchi, Alberto de Mingo. *"But It Is Not So Among You": Echoes of Power in Mark 10:32–45*. JSNTSup 249. New York: T&T Clark, 2003.

Kealy, Sean P. *Mark's Gospel: A History of Its Interpretation*. New York: Paulist, 1982.

Keck, Leander E. "The Introduction to Mark's Gospel." *NTS* 12 (1966): 352–70.

Kee, Howard Clark. *Community of the New Age: Studies in Mark's Gospel*. Philadelphia: Westminster, 1977.

Keener, Craig S. *The Historical Jesus of the Gospels*. Grand Rapids: Eerdmans, 2009.

Kelber, Werner H. *The Kingdom in Mark: A New Place and a New Time*. Philadelphia: Fortress, 1974.

———. *Mark's Story of Jesus*. Philadelphia: Fortress, 1979.

———. *The Oral and the Written Gospel: Hermeneutics of Speaking and Writing in the Synoptic Tradition, Mark, Paul and Q*. Philadelphia: Fortress, 1983. Repr., Bloomington: Indiana University Press, 1997.

Kingsbury, Jack Dean. *The Christology of Mark's Gospel*. Philadelphia: Fortress, 1983.

———. *Conflict in Mark: Jesus, Authorities, Disciples*. Minneapolis: Fortress, 1989.

Kopp, Clemens. *The Holy Places of the Gospels*. Translated by R. Walls. New York: Herder & Herder, 1963.

Kort, Wesley. *Modern Fiction and Human Time: A Study in Narrative and Belief*. Gainesville: University of Florida Press, 1986.

———. *Moral Fiber: Character and Belief in Recent American Fiction*. Philadelphia: Fortress, 1982.

———. *Narrative Elements and Religious Meaning*. Philadelphia: Fortress, 1975.

———. *Shriven Selves: Religious Problems in Recent American Fiction*. Philadelphia: Fortress, 1972.

———. *Story, Text, and Scripture: Literary Interests in Biblical Narrative*. University Park: Pennsylvania State University Press, 1988.

Kraemer, Ross S. "Implicating Herodias and Her Daughter in the Death of John the Baptist: A (Christian) Theological Strategy?" *JBL* 125 (2006): 321–49.

Kuhn, Thomas. *The Structure of Scientific Revolutions*. Chicago: University of Chicago Press, 1962.

Kurz, William S. *Reading Luke-Acts: Dynamics of Biblical Narrative*. Louisville: Westminster John Knox, 1993.

Lane, William L. *The Gospel according to Mark: The English Text with Introduction, Exposition, and Notes*. NICNT. Grand Rapids: Eerdmans, 1974.

Lee, David. *Luke's Stories of Jesus: Theological Reading of Gospel Narrative and the Legacy of Hans Frei*. JSNTSup 185. Sheffield: Sheffield Academic Press, 1999.

Lee, Margaret Ellen, and Bernard Brandon Scott. *Sound Mapping the New Testament*. Salem, Ore.: Polebridge, 2009.

Levine, Amy-Jill. "Discharging Responsibility: Matthean Jesus, Biblical Law, and Hemorrhaging Woman." Pages 70–87 in *A Feminist Companion to Matthew*. Edited by Amy-Jill Levine. Sheffield: Sheffield Academic Press, 2001.

Licht, Jacob. *Storytelling in the Bible*. Jerusalem: Magnes, 1978.

Loader, William. "Good News—for the Earth? Reflections on Mark 1.1–15." Pages 28–43 in *The Earth Story in the New Testament*. Edited by Norman C. Habel and Vicky Balabanski. The Earth Bible 5. Cleveland: Pilgrim, 2002.

Lohmeyer, Ernst. *Das Evangelium des Markus*. KEK. Göttingen: Vandenhoeck & Ruprecht, 1953.

Luz, Ulrich. "The Secrecy Motif and the Marcan Christology." Pages 75–96 in *The Messianic Secret*. Edited by Christopher Tuckett. Philadelphia: Fortress, 1983.

Malbon, Elizabeth Struthers. "The Christology of Mark's Gospel: Narrative Christology and the Markan Jesus." Pages 33–48 in *Who Do You Say That I Am? Essays on Christology*. Edited by Mark Allan Powell and David R. Bauer. Louisville: Westminster John Knox, 1999.

———. "Disciples/Crowds/Whoever: Markan Characters and Readers." Pages 70–99 in *In the Company of Jesus: Characters in Mark's Gospel*. Louisville: Westminster John Knox, 2000.

———. "Echoes and Foreshadowings in Mark 4–8: Reading and ReReading." *JBL* 112 (1993): 211–30.

———. *In the Company of Jesus: Characters in Mark's Gospel*. Louisville: Westminster John Knox, 2000.

———. *Mark's Jesus: Characterization as Narrative Christology*. Waco, Tex.: Baylor University Press, 2009.

———. "Narrative Criticism: How Does the Story Mean?" Pages 29–58 in *Mark and Method: New Approaches in Biblical Studies*. Edited by Janice Capel Anderson and Stephen D. Moore. 2nd ed. Minneapolis: Fortress, 2008.

———. Review of M. Eugene Boring, *Mark: A Commentary*. *Int* 62 (2008): 440–42.

Malbon, Elizabeth Struthers, and Adele Berlin, eds. *Semeia 63: Characterization in Biblical Literature*. Atlanta: Society of Biblical Literature, 1993.

Manson, T. W. "The Life of Jesus: Some Tendencies in Present-Day Research." Pages 211–21 in *The Background of the New Testament and Its Eschatology*. Edited by William David Davies and D. Daube. Cambridge: Cambridge University Press, 1956.

Marcus, Joel. "The Jewish War and the *Sitz im Leben* of Mark." *JBL* 111 (1992): 441–62.

———. *Mark 1–8*. AB 27. New York: Doubleday, 2000.

———. *Mark 8–16*. AB 27A. New Haven: Yale University Press, 2009.

Marguerat, Daniel, and Yvan Bourquin. *How to Read Bible Stories: An Introduction to Narrative Criticism*. Translated by John Bowden. London: SCM, 1999.

Marxsen, Willi. *Der Evangelist Markus: Studien zur Redaktionsgeschichte des Evangeliums*. Gottingen: Vandenhoeck & Ruprecht, 1959.

———. *Mark the Evangelist: Studies on the Redaction History of the Gospel.* Translated by James Boyce et al. Nashville: Abingdon, 1969.

McEvenue, Sean E. *The Narrative Style of the Priestly Writer.* AnBib 50. Rome: Pontifical Biblical Institute, 1971.

McKeon, Michael. "Introduction." Pages xiii–xviii in *Theory of the Novel: A Historical Approach.* Edited by Michael McKeon. Baltimore: Johns Hopkins University Press, 2000.

———. *The Origins of the English Novel, 1600–1740.* Baltimore: Johns Hopkins University Press, 1987.

McKnight, Edgar V. *Postmodern Use of the Bible: The Emergence of Reader-Oriented Criticism.* Nashville: Abingdon, 1988.

McVann, Mark. "The 'Passion' of John the Baptist and Jesus before Pilate: Mark's Warnings about Kings and Governors." *BTB* 38 (2008): 152–57.

Merenlahti, Petri. "Characters in the Making: Individuality and Ideology in the Gospels." Pages 49–72 in *Characterization in the Gospels: Reconceiving Narrative Criticism.* Edited by David Rhoads and Kari Syreeni. JSNTSup 184. Sheffield: Sheffield Academic Press, 1999.

———. *Poetics for the Gospels? Rethinking Narrative Criticism.* Edinburgh: T&T Clark, 2002.

Merenlahti, Petri, and Raimo Hakola. "Reconceiving Narrative Criticism." Pages 13–48 in *Characterization in the Gospels: Reconceiving Narrative Criticism.* Edited by David Rhoads and Kari Syreeni. JSNTSup 184. Sheffield: Sheffield Academic Press, 1999.

Miller, Lynn Carol, and Stephen J. Read. "Why Am I Telling You This? Self-Disclosure in a Goal-Based Model of Personality." Pages 35–58 in *Self-Disclosure: Theory, Research, and Therapy.* Edited by Valerian J. Derlega and John H. Berg. New York: Plenum, 1987.

Miller, Susan. "The Descent of Darkness over the Land: Listening to the Voice of Earth in Mark 15:33." Pages 123–30 in *Exploring Ecological Hermeneutics.* Edited by Norman C. Habel and Peter Trudinger. SBLSymS 46. Atlanta: Society of Biblical Literature, 2008.

———. *Women in Mark's Gospel.* JSNTSup 266. London: T&T Clark, 2004.

Miscall, Peter D. *The Workings of Old Testament Narrative.* Philadelphia: Fortress, 1983.

Moloney, Francis J. "The Centrality of the Cross: Literary and Theological Reflections on Mark 15:20b-25." *Pacifica* 21 (2008): 245–56.

———. *The Gospel of Mark.* Peabody, Mass.: Hendrickson, 2002.

———. "Literary Strategies in the Markan Passion Narrative (Mark 14,1–15,47)." *SNTSU* 28 (2003): 5–25.

———. *The Living Voice of the Gospels.* Peabody, Mass.: Hendrickson, 2007.

———. "Mark 6:6b-30: Mission, the Baptist, and Failure." *CBQ* 63 (2001): 647–63.

Moore, Stephen D. *Empire and Apocalypse: Postcolonialism and the New Testament.* The Bible in the Modern World 12. Sheffield: Sheffield Phoenix, 2006.

———. *Literary Criticism and the Gospels: The Theoretical Challenge.* New Haven: Yale University Press, 1989.

———. *Poststructuralism and the New Testament: Derrida and Foucault at the Foot of the Cross*. Minneapolis: Fortress, 1994.

———. "The SS Officer at the Foot of the Cross: A Tragedy in Three Acts." Pages 44–61 in *Between Author and Audience in Mark: Narration, Characterization, Interpretation*. Edited by Elizabeth Struthers Malbon. New Testament Monographs 23. Sheffield: Sheffield Phoenix, 2009.

Moore, Stephen, and Janice Capel Anderson, eds. *Mark and Method: New Approaches in Biblical Studies*. 2nd ed. Minneapolis: Fortress, 2008.

Moore, Stephen D., and Fernando F. Segovia, eds. *Postcolonial Biblical Criticism: Interdisciplinary Intersections*. Bible and Postcolonialism. London: T&T Clark, 2005.

Moore, Steven. *The Novel: An Alternative History. Beginnings to 1600*. New York: Continuum, 2010.

Morgan, Robert, and John Barton. *Biblical interpretation*. Oxford Bible Series. New York: Oxford University Press, 1988.

Morrison, Gregg S. "The Turning Point in the Gospel of Mark: A Study in Markan Christology." Ph.D. diss., The Catholic University of America, 2008.

Myers, Ched. *Binding the Strong Man: A Political Reading of Mark's Story of Jesus*. Maryknoll, N.Y.: Orbis, 1986.

Oden, Thomas C., and Christopher A. Hall, eds. *Mark*. ACCS.NT 2. Downers Grove, Ill.: InterVarsity Press, 2005.

Omanson, Roger L. *A Textual Guide to the Greek New Testament*. Stuttgart: Deutsche Bibelgesellschaft, 2006.

O'Toole, John. *The Process of Drama: Negotiating Art and Meaning*. London: Routledge, 1992.

Painter, John. *Mark's Gospel: Worlds in Conflict*. London: Routledge, 1997.

Parsons, Mikeal C. "Re-membering John the Baptist." Pages 96–106 in *Redeeming Men: Religion and Masculinities*. Edited by Stephen B. Boyd, W. Merle Longwood, and Mark W. Muesse. Louisville: Westminster John Knox, 1996.

Parunak, H. van Dyke. "Some Axioms for Literary Architecture." *Semitics* 8 (1982): 1–16.

———. "Transitional Techniques in the Bible." *JBL* 102 (1983): 525–48.

Perrin, Norman. *The New Testament: An Introduction*. New York: Harcourt Brace Jovanovich, 1974.

Perrin, Norman. "The Wredestrasse Becomes the Hauptstrasse: Reflections on the Reprinting of the Dodd Festschrift." *JR* 46 (1966): 296–300.

Petersen, Norman. *Literary Criticism for New Testament Critics*. GBS. Philadelphia: Fortress, 1978.

———. "Point of View in Mark's Narrative." *Semeia* 12 (1978): 97–121.

Peterson, Dwight N. *The Origins of Mark: The Markan Community in Current Debate*. Biblical Interpretation Series 48. Leiden: Brill, 2000.

Petty, Richard E., and John T. Cacioppo. *Communication and Persuasion: Central and Peripheral Routes to Attitude Change*. New York: Springer-Verlag, 1986.

Powell, Mark Allan. "Authorial Intent and Historical Reporting: Putting Spong's Literalization Thesis to the Test." *JSHJ* 1 (2003): 225–49.

———. *What Is Narrative Criticism?* GBS. Minneapolis: Fortress, 1990.

Praeder, Susan Marie. Review of David Rhoads and Donald Michie, *Mark as Story: An Introduction to the Narrative of a Gospel. JBL* 103 (1984): 483–84.

Rabinowitz, Peter J. *Before Reading: Narrative Conventions and the Politics of Interpretation.* Ithaca, N.Y.: Cornell University Press, 1987.

Räisänen, Heikki. *The 'Messianic Secret' in Mark.* Studies of the New Testament and Its World. Edinburgh: T&T Clark, 1990.

———. "The 'Messianic Secret' in Mark's Gospel." Pages 132–40 in *The Messianic Secret.* Edited by Christopher Tuckett. Philadelphia: Fortress, 1983.

Reinhartz, Adele. *Jesus of Hollywood.* Oxford: Oxford University Press, 2007.

———. *Scripture on the Silver Screen.* Louisville: Westminster John Knox, 2003.

Resseguie, James L. *Narrative Criticism of the New Testament: An Introduction.* Grand Rapids: Baker, 2005.

Rhoads, David. *From Every People and Nation: The Book of Revelation in Intercultural Perspective.* Minneapolis: Fortress, 2005.

———. *Israel in Revolution: 6–74 C.E. A Political History Based on the Writings of Josephus.* Philadelphia: Fortress, 1976.

———. "Narrative Criticism and the Gospel of Mark." *JAAR* 50 (1982): 411–34.

———. "Performance Criticism: An Emerging Methodology in Biblical Studies." Paper presented at the Annual Meeting of the Society of Biblical Literature. New Orleans, 21 November 2009.

———. "Performance Criticism: An Emerging Methodology in Second Temple Studies—Part I." *BTB* 36 (2006): 118–33.

———. "Performance Criticism: An Emerging Methodology in Second Temple Studies—Part II." *BTB* 36 (2006): 164–84.

———. *Reading Mark: Engaging the Gospel.* Minneapolis: Fortress, 2004.

———. "Reading the New Testament in an Environmental Age." *CurTM* 24 (1997): 259–66.

———. "What Is Performance Criticism?" Pages 83–100 in *The Bible in Ancient and Modern Media.* Edited by Holly E. Hearon and Philip Ruge-Jones. Biblical Performance Criticism. Eugene, Ore.: Cascade, 2009.

———. "Who Will Speak for the Sparrow? Eco-Justice Criticism of the New Testament." Pages 64–86 in *Literary Encounters with the Reign of God.* Edited by Sharon H. Ringe and H. C. Paul Kim. New York: T&T Clark, 2004.

Rhoads, David, and Donald Michie. *Mark as Story: An Introduction to the Narrative of a Gospel.* Philadelphia: Fortress, 1982.

Rhoads, David, Joanna Dewey, and Donald Michie. *Mark as Story: An Introduction to the Narrative of a Gospel.* 2nd ed. Minneapolis: Fortress, 1999.

Rimmon-Kenan, Shlomith. *Narrative Fiction: Contemporary Poetics.* New Accents. London: Methuen, 1983.

Robbins, Vernon K. *Jesus the Teacher: A Socio-rhetorical Interpretation of Mark.* Philadelphia: Fortress, 1984.

Ruge-Jones, Philip. "Omnipresent, Not Omniscient: How Literary Interpretation Confuses the Storyteller's Narrating." Pages 29–43 in *Between Author and Audience in Mark: Narration, Characterization, Interpretation.* Edited by Elizabeth Struthers Malbon. New Testament Monographs. Sheffield: Sheffield Phoenix, 2009.

Sanday, William. *The Life of Christ in Recent Research.* Oxford: Clarendon, 1907.

Schearing, Linda S. "Queen." *ABD* 5:583–85.

Schnelle, Udo. *The History and Theology of the New Testament Writings.* Minneapolis: Fortress, 1998.

Schürer, Emil. *The History of the Jewish People in the Age of Jesus Christ.* Revised and edited by Geza Vermes. 3 vols. Edinburgh: T&T Clark, 1973.

Schüssler Fiorenza, Elisabeth. "Miracles, Mission, and Apologetics: An Introduction." Pages 1–26 in *Aspects of Religious Propaganda in Judaism and Early Christianity.* Edited by Elisabeth Schüssler Fiorenza. Notre Dame, Ind.: University of Notre Dame Press, 1976.

Schweitzer, Albert. *The Quest of the Historical Jesus.* Translated by J. R. Coates, W. Montgomery, Susan Cupitt, and John Bowden. Minneapolis: Fortress, 2001.

Schweizer, Eduard. *The Good News according to Mark.* Atlanta: John Knox, 1970.

———. "Mark's Theological Achievement." Pages 42–63 in *The Interpretation of Mark.* Edited by William Telford. Investigations in Religion and Theology 7. Philadelphia: Fortress, 1985.

———. "The Question of the Messianic Secret in Mark." Pages 65–74 in *The Messianic Secret.* Edited by Christopher Tuckett. Philadelphia: Fortress, 1983.

Scofield, Martin. *The Cambridge Introduction to the American Short Story.* Cambridge: Cambridge University Press, 2006.

Scott, Bernard Brandon. *Hollywood Dreams and Biblical Stories.* Minneapolis: Fortress, 1994.

———. *Re-imagine the World: An Introduction to the Parables of Jesus.* Santa Rosa, Calif.: Polebridge, 2001.

Searle, Leroy. "New Criticism." Pages 691–98 in *The Johns Hopkins Guide to Literary Theory.* Edited by Michael Groden, Martin Kreiswirth, and Imre Szeman. 2nd ed. Baltimore: Johns Hopkins University Press, 2005.

Segovia, Fernando F., and Mary Ann Tolbert, eds. *Social Location and Biblical Interpretation in Global Perspective.* Vol. 2 of *Reading from This Place.* Minneapolis: Fortress, 1995.

———. *Social Location and Biblical Interpretation in the United States.* Vol. 1 of *Reading from This Place.* Minneapolis: Fortress, 1995.

Senior, Donald, and Carroll Stuhlmueller. *The Biblical Foundations for Mission.* London: SCM, 1983.

Shannon, Laurie. "The Eight Animals in Shakespeare; or, Before the Human." *PMLA* 124 (2009): 476.

Shepherd, Tom. "The Narrative Function of Markan Intercalation." *NTS* 41 (1995): 522–40.

Shiner, Whitney. *Proclaiming the Gospel: First-Century Performance of Mark.* Harrisburg, Pa.: Trinity Press International, 2003.

Skinner, Christopher W. "'Whom He Also Named Apostles': A Textual Problem in Mark 3:14." *BibSac* 161 (2004): 322–29.

Smith, Abraham. "Tyranny Exposed: Mark's Typological Characterization of Herod Antipas (Mark 6:14–29)." *BibInt* 14 (2006): 259–93.

Smith, Justin Marc. "About Friends, By Friends, For Others: Author-Subject Relationships in Contemporary Greco-Roman Biographies." Pages 49–67 in *The Audience of the Gosepls: The Origin and Function of the Gospels in Early Christianity*. Edited by Edward W. Klink III. LNTS 353. London: T&T Clark, 2009.

Snodgrass, Klyne R. *Stories with Intent: A Comprehensive Guide to the Parables of Jesus*. Grand Rapids: Eerdmans, 2008.

Soukup, Paul A. "Transforming the Sacred: The American Bible Society New Media Translation Project." *Journal of Media and Religion* 3.2 (2004): 101–18.

Soukup, Paul A., and Robert Hodgson, eds. *Fidelity and Translation: Communicating the Bible in New Media*. Franklin, Wis.: Sheed & Ward; New York: American Bible Society, 1999.

———. *From One Medium to Another: Communicating the Bible through Multimedia*. Kansas City: Sheed & Ward, 1997.

Spittler, Janet E. *Animals in the Apocryphal Acts of the Apostles: The Wild Kingdom of Early Christian Literature*. WUNT 2/247. Tübingen: Mohr Siebeck, 2008.

Staley, Jeffrey L., and Richard Walsh, eds. *Jesus, the Gospels, and Cinematic Imagination: A Handbook to Jesus on DVD*. Louisville: Westminster John Knox, 2007.

Stanton, Graham N. *A Gospel for a New People: Studies in Matthew*. Edinburgh: T&T Clark, 1992.

Sternberg, Meir. *The Poetics of Biblical Narrative: Ideological Literature and the Drama of Reading*. Indiana Literary Biblical Series. Bloomington, Ind.: Indiana University Press, 1985.

Strecker, Georg. "The Theory of the Messianic Secret in Mark's Gospel." Pages 49–64 in *The Messianic Secret*. Edited by Christopher Tuckett. Philadelphia: Fortress, 1983.

Stibbe, Mark W. G. *John as Storyteller: Narrative Criticism and the Fourth Gospel*. Cambridge: Cambridge University Press, 1992.

Sugirtharajah, R. G. *Postcolonial Criticism and Biblical Interpretation*. Oxford: Oxford University Press, 2002.

Swanson, Richard. *Provoking the Gospel of Mark: A Storyteller's Commentary, Year B*. Cleveland: Pilgrim, 2005.

Talmon, Shemaryahu. "The Presentation of Synchroneity and Simultaneity in Biblical Narrative." Pages 9–26 in *Scripta Hierosolymitana*. Edited by Joseph Heinemann and Shnuel Werses. Jerusalem: Magnes, 1978.

Tannehill, Robert C. "The Disciples in Mark: The Function of a Narrative Role." *JR* 57 (1977): 386–405.

———. "The Gospel of Mark as Narrative Christology." *Semeia* 16 (1980): 57–95.

———. *The Narrative Unity of Luke-Acts: A Literary Interpretation*. 2 vols. Minneapolis: Fortress: 1986.

Tardy, Charles H., and Kathryn Dindia. "Self-Disclosure: Strategic Revelation of Information in Personal and Professional Relationships." Pages 229–66 in *The Handbook of Communication Skills*. Edited by Owen Hargie. London: Routledge, 2006.

Tatum, W. Barnes. *Jesus at the Movies: A Guide to the First Hundred Years*. Revised ed. Santa Rosa, Calif.: Polebridge, 2004.

Taylor, Vincent. *The Gospel according to St. Mark*. London: Macmillan, 1952.

Telford, Willaim R. *The Theology of the Gospel of Mark*. Cambridge: Cambridge University Press, 1999.

Tyson, Joseph B. "Blindness of the Disciples in Mark." *JBL* 80 (1961): 261–8.

Tolbert, Mary Ann. *Sowing the Gospel: Mark's World in Literary-Historical Perspective*. Minneapolis: Fortress, 1989.

Tolmie, D. F. *Narratology and Biblical Narratives: A Practical Guide*. San Francisco: International Scholars Publications, 1999.

Upton, Bridget Gilfillian. *Hearing Mark's Endings*. Leiden: Brill, 2006.

Via, Dan Otto. *The Revelation of God and/as Human Reception: In the New Testament*. Valley Forge, Pa.: Trinity Press International, 1997.

Wainwright, Elaine. "Healing Ointment/Healing Bodies: Gift and Identification in an Ecofeminist Reading of Mark 14:3–9." Pages 131–40 in *Exploring Ecological Hermeneutics*. Edited by Norman C. Habel and Peter Trudinger. SBLSymS 46. Atlanta: Society of Biblical Literature, 2008.

Walsh, Richard G. *Reading the Gospels in the Dark: Portrayals of Jesus in Film*. Harrisburg, Pa.: Trinity Press International, 2003.

Wachsmann, Shelley. "The Galilee Boat—2,000-Year-Old Hull Recovered Intact." *BAR* 14.5 (1988): 18–33.

Watson, Francis. "The Social Function of Mark's Secrecy Theme." *JSNT* 24 (1985): 46–69.

Watt, Ian. *The Rise of the Novel: Studies in Defoe, Richardson and Fielding*. London: Chatto & Windus, 1957.

Watts, Rikki E. *Isaiah's New Exodus in Mark*. WUNT 88. Tübingen: Mohr-Siebeck, 1997.

Weeden, Theodore J. *Mark: Traditions in Conflict*. Philadelphia: Fortress, 1971.

———. "The Heresy That Necessitated Mark's Gospel." *ZNW* 59 (1968): 145–58.

Wellek, Rene, and Austin Warren. *Theory of Literature*. New York: Harcourt, Brace, 1942.

Wimsatt, William K. "The Intentional Fallacy." Pages 3–20 in *The Verbal Icon: Studies in the Meaning of Poetry*. Lexington: University Press of Kentucky, 1954.

Wire, Antoinette. *Holy Lives, Holy Deaths: A Close Hearing of Early Jewish Storytellers*. SBLSBL 1. Atlanta: Society of Biblical Literature, 2002.

Witherington, Ben. *The Gospel of Mark: A Socio-rhetorical Commentary*. Grand Rapids: Eerdmans, 2001.

Wolfe, Cary. "Human, All Too Human: 'Animal Studies' and the Humanities." *PMLA* 124 (2009): 564–75.

———. *What Is Posthumanism?* Posthumanities. Minneapolis: University of Minnesota Press, 2009.

Wrede, William. *Das Messiasgeheimnis in den Evangelien: Zugleich ein Beitrag zum Verständnis des Markusevangeliums*. Göttingen: Vandenhoeck & Ruprecht, 1901.

———. *The Messianic Secret*. Translated by J. C. G. Greig. Cambridge: James Clarke, 1971.

Yarbro Collins, Adela. *Mark: A Commentary*. Hermeneia. Minneapolis: Fortress, 2007.

———. "Mark and His Readers: The Son of God among Jews." *HTR* 92 (1999): 393–408.

Contributors

Thomas E. Boomershine (Ph.D., Union Theological Seminary, New York) is Professor of New Testament (1979–2000) and Professor of Christianity and Communications (2004–2006) Emeritus at United Theological Seminary, Dayton, Ohio. He was also Vice-President of Lumicon Digital Communications and Dean of the Lumicon Institute in Dallas from 2000 to 2004 and Professor of Biblical Studies at New York Theological Seminary in Manhattan (1972–1979). Tom founded the Network of Biblical Storytellers in 1977 and has led biblical storytelling workshops around the world. Tom served as Chief Consultant for Multimedia Translations for the American Bible Society (1989–1993) and was an Executive Producer for the award-winning ABS video/multimedia program "Out of the Tombs." He has published *Story Journey: An Invitation to the Gospel as Storytelling* (Abingdon, 1988) and a range of articles on the Gospels as story.

Alan Culpepper (Ph.D., Duke University) is the founding dean of the McAfee School of Theology at Mercer University. Prior to coming to Mercer, Alan taught New Testament at Southern Baptist Theological seminary in Louisville, Kentucky (1974–1991) and at Baylor University in Waco, Texas (1991–1995). His writings reflect a sustained interest in the Gospels, especially the Gospel of John: *The Johannine School* (Scholars Press, 1975), *Anatomy of the Fourth Gospel* (Fortress, 1983), *John the Son of Zebedee: The Life of a Legend* (1994), "The Gospel of Luke," in *NIB* 9 (Abingdon, 1996), *The Gospel and Letter of John* (Abingdon, 1998), and *The Gospel of Mark* (Smyth & Helwys Bible Commentary, 2007).

Joanna Dewey is a graduate of the University of California-Berkeley (M.A.), the Church Divinity School of the Pacific (M.Div.), and the Graduate Theological Union (Ph.D.). She is the Harvey H. Guthrie Jr. Professor Emerita of Biblical Studies at the Episcopal Divinity School, where she taught for many years and was Academic Dean. Prior to that she taught at the Graduate Seminary, Phillips University, and at Oklahoma State University, both in Oklahoma. In addition to *Mark as Story* (Fortress, 1999), she is the author of *Markan Public Debate: Literary Technique, Concentric Structure and Theology in Mark 2:1–3:6* (Scholars Press, 1981) and numerous articles. A collection of her articles on Mark and Orality is forthcoming from Wipf & Stock.

Robert M. Fowler is Professor of Religion and Chairperson of the Department of Religion at Baldwin-Wallace College, Berea, Ohio, where he has taught for thirty years. He earned his Ph.D. from the Divinity School of the University of Chicago. He is perhaps best known for his literary-critical studies on the Gospel of Mark: *Loaves and Fishes: The Function of the Feeding Stories in the Gospel of Mark* (Scholars Press, 1981) and *Let the Reader Understand: Reader-Response Criticism and the Gospel of Mark* (Fortress, 1991; Trinity Press International, 2001). As a member of "The Bible and Culture Collective," he also collaborated in the writing of *The Postmodern Bible* (Yale University Press, 1997).

Holly Hearon received her Ph.D. from the Graduate Theological Union (Berkeley, Calif.) under the direction of Antoinette Clark Wire. She is currently the Virginia and T. J. Liggett Professor of Christian Traditions at Christian Theological Seminary (Indianapolis). She has written extensively on the relationship between written and spoken word in the ancient world, with a particular emphasis on storytelling. Among her publications are *The Mary Magdalene Tradition: Witness and Counter-witness in Early Christian Communities* (Michael Glazer, 2004) and essays in *The Bible in Ancient and Modern Media* (ed. with Philip Ruge-Jones; Wipf & Stock, 2009), *Jesus, the Voice and the Text* (ed. Tom Thatcher; Baylor University Press, 2008), and *Performing the Gospel: Orality, Memory, and Mark* (ed. Richard Horsley, Jonathan Draper, and John Miles Foley; Fortress, 2006).

Morna Hooker is Lady Margaret's Professor of Divinity Emerita in the University of Cambridge and a Life Fellow of Robinson College. Her first research work was undertaken at the University of Bristol (*Jesus and the Servant*, SPCK, 1959), and her Ph.D. (*The Son of Man in Mark*, SPCK, 1967) was awarded by the University of Manchester. She holds a D.D. from the University of Cambridge. Her books include *The Message of Mark* (Epworth, 1983), *A Commentary on the Gospel according to Mark* (Black, 1991), *The Signs of a Prophet* (Trinity Press International, 1997), *Beginnings* (Trinity Press International, 1997), and *Endings* (SCM, 2003). She has also written extensively on St. Paul. For many years she was co-editor of *The Journal of Theological Studies*, and she is currently editor of Black's New Testament Commentary.

Kelly R. Iverson received his Ph.D. from The Catholic University of America (Washington, D.C.) and is a Lecturer in New Testament at St. Mary's College, the University of Saint Andrews, in Scotland. His research interests include Jesus and the Gospels (particularly Mark and Matthew), ancient media, performance criticism, and the Catholic Epistles. He is the author of numerous articles, as well as *Gentiles in the Gospel of Mark: "Even the Dogs under the Table Eat the Children's Crumbs"* (T&T Clark, 2007). In addition to the present volume, he is co-editor (with Christopher Skinner) of a forthcoming book on unity and diversity in the New Testament (Society of Biblical Literature, 2012).

Elizabeth Struthers Malbon (Ph.D., Florida State University), Professor in the Department of Religion and Culture at Virginia Polytechnic Institute and State University (Virginia Tech), is author of five books: *Mark's Jesus: Characterization as Narrative* Christology (Baylor University Press, 2009), *Hearing Mark: A Listener's Guide* (Trinity Press International, 2002), *In the Company of Jesus: Characters in Mark's Gospel* (Westminster John Knox, 2000), *Narrative Space and Mythic Meaning in Mark* (Harper & Row, 1986; Sheffield Academic Press, 1991), and *The Iconography of the Sarcophagus of Junius Bassus* (Princeton University Press, 1990). She has also edited or co-edited four volumes, most recently *Between Author and Audience in Mark: Narration, Characterization, Interpretation* (Sheffield Phoenix, 2009), and her articles have appeared in *JBL, CBQ, Semeia, NTS, NovT, BibInt, BTB, JAAR, JR*, and elsewhere.

Donald M. Michie is a graduate of The University of Wisconsin-Madison (Ph.D.). His dissertation was on the anonymous *The True Chronicle History of King Leir*, a bland early version of Shakespeare's *King Lear*. Don has taught at Carthage since 1965, and during that time he was Dean of the College for ten years. He is now Professor Emeritus of English. Don is one of the authors of *Mark as Story* and currently lives in Kenosha, Wisconsin.

Francis J. Moloney is currently the Provincial Superior of the Salesians of Don Bosco in Australia and the Pacific (New Zealand, Fiji and Samoa) and an emeritus Professor at The Catholic University of America and Australian Catholic University. He completed his D.Phil. at the University of Oxford and his dissertation, "The Johannine Son of Man," was first published in 1976 (2nd ed. 2007). Among his many published works are a commentary on the Gospel of John (Sacra Pagina, 1998) and a commentary on the Gospel of Mark (Hendrickson, 2002), which won the Academy of Parish Clergy's 2003 award for the best reference book of the year. Among his recent works are *The Living Voice of the Gospels* (Hendrickson, 2007), *The Gospel of John: Text and Con-*

text (Brill, 2005), and *Mark: Storyteller, Interpreter, Evangelist* (Hendrickson, 2004).

Stephen D. Moore (Ph.D., University of Dublin, Trinity College) is Professor of New Testament at the Theological School, Drew University in Madison, New Jersey. He has authored many books, most recently *The Bible in Theory: Critical and Postcritical Essays* (Society of Biblical Literature, 2010) and (with Yvonne Sherwood) *The Invention of the Biblical Scholar: A Critical Manifesto* (Fortress, 2011). He has also edited many essay collections, most recently (with Tom Thatcher) *Anatomies of Narrative Criticism: The Past, Present, and Futures of the Fourth Gospel as Literature* (Society of Biblical Literature, 2008) and (with Mayra Rivera) *Planetary Loves: Spivak, Postcoloniality, and Theology* (Fordham University Press, 2010).

Mark Allan Powell received his Ph.D. in New Testament from Union Theological Seminary in Virginia in 1988 and he is currently Professor of New Testament at Trinity Lutheran Seminary. He is editor of the *HarperCollins Bible Dictionary* (2011) and author of more than twenty-five books on the Bible and religion, including the textbook *Introducing the New Testament* (Baker, 2009). His works on literary criticism and the Gospels include *What Is Narrative Criticism?* (Fortress, 1990) and *Chasing the Eastern Star: Adventures in Biblical Reader Response Criticism* (Westminster John Knox, 2001).

David Rhoads is a graduate of Oxford University (M.A.) and Duke University (Ph.D.). He taught at Carthage College for fifteen years. He is now emeritus Professor of New Testament at the Lutheran School of Theology at Chicago, where he taught for twenty-two years. In addition to *Mark as Story* (Fortress, 1982, 1999), he is author of *Israel in Revolution: 6–74 C.E.* (Fortress, 1976), *The Challenge of Diversity: The Witness of Paul and the Gospels* (Fortress, 1996), and *Reading Mark, Engaging the Gospel* (Fortress, 2004) and editor of *From Every People and Nation: The Book of Revelation in Intercultural Perspective* and *Earth and Word: Classic Sermons on Saving the Planet* (Fortress, 2005). His current work focuses on performance criticism, which can be seen at a website he directs: www.biblicalperformancecriticism.org.

Christopher W. Skinner (Ph.D., The Catholic University of America) is Assistant Professor of Religion at Mount Olive College in North Carolina. His research interests include narrative criticism, the canonical Gospels, the Gospel of Thomas, the historical Jesus, and the crossroads of biblical literacy and popular media. In addition to dozens of articles and book reviews, he has authored two books, *John and Thomas: Gospels in Conflict? Johannine Charac-*

terization and the Thomas Question (Wipf & Stock, 2009) and *What Are They Saying about the Gospel of Thomas?* (Paulist, 2011). He is also currently editing a volume on characters and characterization in the Gospel of John (T&T Clark, 2012).

Author Index

Abbott, H. Porter, 189
Abrams, M. H., 20, 73, 101
Achtemeier, Paul J., 147, 258
Adam, A. K. M., 8
Ahuja, Neel, 93
Aichele, George, 238
Allison, Dale C., 193, 194
Alter, Robert, 4, 264
Anderson, Janice Capel, 8, 35, 39, 45, 46, 58, 93, 152, 161, 237
Ariew, Roger, 80
Armstrong, Nancy, 74
Aune, David E., 184, 206
Bach, Alice, 152, 157, 162
Bakhtin, Mikhail, 75
Balabanski, Vicky, 90
Bar-Efrat, Shimon, 4
Barth, Gerard, 3
Barton, John, 182
Barton, Stephen C., 174
Bauckham, Richard, 89, 118
Bauer, David R., 202
Becker-Leckrone, Megan, 152
Bennington, Geoffrey, 81
Benoit, William L., 208
Berg, John H., 208
Berlin, Adele, 4, 7, 67
Berman, S., 27
Best, Ernest, 8, 30, 117, 165
Bieler, Ludwig, 5
Bird, Michael F., 184
Black, C. Clifton, 3, 96, 101

Blumhofer, Edith, 239
Boehrer, Bruce, 81, 82, 86
Boomershine, Thomas, 6, 13, 20, 46, 112, 122, 135, 264, 271, 272
Booth, Wayne, 20, 37, 115, 187
Boring, M. Eugene, 63
Bornkamm, Gunther, 3
Bourquin, Yvan, 59
Bowden, John, 59, 185
Boyd, Stephen B., 153
Braidotti, Rosi, 92
Braund, D. C., 152
Brower, Kent, 4
Bultmann, Rudolf, 114
Burnett, Fred W., 77
Buswell, Geoffrey, 2
Byrne, Brendan,101
Byrskog, Samuel, 211
Cacioppo, John T., 208
Camery-Hoggatt, Jerry, 31, 202
Carson, D. A., 181
Carter, Warren, 30
Chatman, Seymour, 10, 20, 21, 45, 65, 66, 67, 95, 115, 237
Christianson, Eric S., 238
Coates, J. R., 185
Collins, John J., 88
Collins, Nancy L., 203, 204
Combs, Jason Robert, 250
Conzelmann, Hans, 2, 195
Cranfield, C. E. B., 147, 148
Culler, Jonathan, 237

CPSIA information can be obtained at www.ICGtesting.com
234258LV00001B/212/P